W9-CRH-864

the essence of

England, Scotland Wales & Ireland

A Historic Journey through Britain & Ireland

Printed in the United Kingdom for 2001

Front Cover ....Stourhead, Wiltshire (Courtesy of the National Trust)
Above Photo.............................Waddesdon Manor, near Aylesbury, Buckinghamshire
Published by...The Heritage Handbook Company
Production Director...Simon Waite
Advertisement Director...Patrick Jennings
Typesetting..Type Technique 020 7636 7736
Colour Repro...Blaze Creative 020 7 253 0099
Photography...Graham Waite Photo Library

Heritage Handbook Company Ltd
Compass House, 30-36 East Street,,
Bromley, Kent, BR1 1QU
Published in November 2000 for the year 2001
Distributed in the USA, Canada and U.K.
The publisher extends his warmest and sincerest thanks
to the The National Trust, The British Tourist Authority
Cormac Power, Mary Anne Waite, Graham Waite, Billy Waite,
Tom Francis, Stuart Riches, and all those whom by appearing within these
pages have supported this publication so magnificently.

1

Top: Forde Abbey, Somerset
Middle: Royal Pavilion, Sussex
Bottom: Burghley House, Lincs

STUART CRYSTAL
FACTORY SHOP & VISITOR CENTRE

- Open 7 days a week all year round
- 2nd Quality crystal available at up to 40% off normal 1st Quality prices
- Large range of 1st Quality crystal
- Selection of Waterford crystal
- Engraving service
- Large gift shop area featuring ceramics and cutlery
- Refreshments and free parking – coaches welcome

STUART CRYSTAL Redhouse Glassworks, Stourbridge, West Midlands, DY8 4AA Tel: 01384 828 282

stuart
CRYSTAL

Top: Norwich, Norfolk
Middle: Roman Baths Museum, Bath
Bottom: Warwick Castle, Warwicks

2001

Top: West Coast of Ireland
(Courtesy of Graham Waite)
Middle: Stranglough, N. Ireland
(Courtesy of N.Ireland Nat' Trust)
Bottom: Jersey, Channel Islands

Continued on Page 8

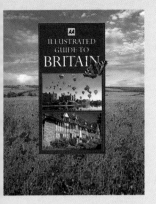

A rich heritage of reading at the *lowest* of prices

PostScript offers an extensive range of quality books on history, heritage, Britain, architecture, and much more at reduced prices. Order today from this special selection or phone **020 8767 7421** for your free catalogue.

Illustrated Guide to Britain
A lavishly illustrated touring guide in the best AA tradition, with road maps, practical information for tourists and geographical and historical background information on over 500 of Britain's most interesting destinations.
AA Illus 300x228mm
[16679]
Originally £25.00
Now £9.99

Historic Houses of the National Trust
Adrian Tinniswood
A detailed and highly illustrated account of 30 of the most interesting NT properties, plus a gazetteer of all of the Trust's houses.
National Trust Illus
[16373]
Originally £25.00
Now £8.99

Uppark Restored
Christopher Powell; John Martin Robinson
Built in 1690, for over 200 years Uppark remained unaltered until destroyed by fire in 1987. This account follows the National Trust's five-year programme of restoration of both house and contents.
National Trust Illus 246x211mm Originally £19.99
[16376]
Now £7.99

Timpson's Book of Curious Days
A Year of English Oddities
John Timpson
An enticing collection of the eccentric miscellanies that make up the English calendar year.
Jarrold Illus
[14080]
Originally £17.95
Now £8.99

A Companion to the English Parish Church
Stephen Friar This illustrated alphabetical guide covers all aspects of the English parish church, such as architecture, furniture, monuments and the role in the community.
Bramley Illus
[13090]
Originally £25.99
Now £9.99

William Morris: *by himself*
Ed. Gillian Naylor In this beautifully presented book, Naylor has brought together selections from William Morris's published writings and letters, arranged to provide a personal statement of his life and work. Over 200 colour photographs.
Little, Brown Illus 309x240mm
[16925]
Originally £50.00
Now £19.99

Lucinda Lambton's A to Z of Britain
Lucinda Lambton With an unerring instinct for the weird and wonderful cracks and crannies of English buildings, Lambton continues her quest for architectural eccentricities.
HarperCollins PB Illus 211x208mm
[14872]
Originally £12.99
Now £5.99

Images: *Artist's Views of Places in the Care of the National Trust*
Oliver Garnett A presentation of 116 artists' views of places in the National Trust's care, with complementary texts by visitors past and present.
National Trust Illus 213x236mm Originally £14.99
[16374]
Now £6.99

Wainwright in Scotland
A Wainwright; Derry Brabbs This gloriously illustrated book, written to accompany the major BBC television series draws on almost half a century of appreciation and knowledge of the Scottish landscape.
Michael Joseph Illus
[15266]
Originally £16.99
Now £7.99

POSTSCRIPT
BOOKS BY MAIL

Top: Duff House, Banff, Aberdeenshire
Middle: Cawdor Castle, Nairn, Inverness-shire
Bottom: Portmerion, Gwynedd

Heritage Britain

| HOTELS INNS & B & B | PLACES TO VISIT | MUSEUM & GALLERIES | ANCESTRY & FAMILY TREES | ANTIQUES & CURIOS | ARTS CRAFTS & FAIRS | MILLEN-NIUM BRITAIN | BOOKS & TOURS |

Welcome to Heritage Britain, a brand new website with more than 2000 years of history and culture. Whatever your interest in Britain, we aim to help you find out more within these pages.

Visit the definitive heritage site and discover the history behind Britain and Ireland's long and colourful past.

Stay in a splendid country house hotel or a medieval inn and savour the delights of the British countryside or a historic British town.

Travel back in time by visiting the myriad of historic houses, castles and gardens or museums and galleries that adorn this Sceptred Isle

Scour the local shops or fairs for arts and crafts, antiques, collectables, curios or objets d'art.

You can even contact a genealogist to help you trace your family tree.

Heritage Britain - the essential website for domestic travellers and overseas visitors to Britain and Ireland.

www.heritagebritain.com
mail@heritagebritain.com

NEXT

heritagebritain.com
Compass House
30-36 East Street
Bromley, Kent
BR1 1QU
Tel: 020 8290 6633
Fax: 020 8290 6622
mail@heritagebritain.com

My word, that year went by in a flash but as usual there are many events to look forward to or places to visit in 2001 - other than the marvellously successful Millennium Dome.

In a tiny pocket of Cornwall, overlooking St Austell Bay, Cornwall, a wonderful construction is being created. Eden Project, due to open in the spring of 2001, has been described as the eighth wonder of the world! Space technology meets the lost world in this giant 5o metre crater. It's purpose is to create a living theatre of plants and people - a global garden that was ready for planting in the summer 2000 - in an area the size of 35 football pitches.There are two gigantic geodesic conservatories - the largest in he world which have been made from over 800 huge steel hexagaons with no internal support. They are a remarkable feat of engineering. The Eden Project's mission is to promote the understanding and practice the responsible management of the vital relationship between plants, people and resources, leading towards a sustainable future for all. You'll have to wait a little longer before you can experience the sights and smells of the rainforest within the 'Biomes' but it will most certainly be worth it! Eden Project. Bodelva, St Austell, Cornwall PL24 2SG. Tel: 01726 811911 Fax: 01726 811912 Website: www.edenproject.com

Above: Humid Tropics Biomic (Architects' model) - Eden Project, St Austell, Cornwall
Below: Sunflowers at Eden Project's Watering Lane Nursery

**Skerries Mills and Ardgillan Castle
Courtesy of Dublin Tourism**

In recent years Dublin has been one of the most popular European destinations for long weekend breaks or a starting point for a tour of the Emerald Isle. There are, however, many historic attractions that are certainly worth a detour. Ardgillan Castle, Malahide Castle and the Talbot Botanic Gardens, the Guinness Hopstore, Dublin's Viking Adventure, The James Joyce Museum and Shaw's Birthplace are just a few. Then there is Skerries Mills, an industrial heritage centre and town park comprising a watermill, 5 - sail windmill and a 4 - sail windmill with associated mill-races, mill pond and wetlands. The history of the mills can be traced to the early 16th century and a bakery was established on the site by 1840. All three mills were restored to working order by FAS and Fingal County Council and are open to visitors throughout the year. Skerries Mills demonstrates to visitors an efficient and clean use of water and wind power and a rare survival of 17th, 18th and 19th century industrial history. Self guided and guided tours of the mills are available to tourists and facilities also include an exhibition area, tea rooms and a craft shop. For further information please contact Skerries Mills, Skerries, Co Dublin Tel: (00353) 1 849 5208   or Dublin Tourism Centre, Suffolk Street, Dublin 2 Tel: (00353) 1 605 7755 Fax: (00353) 1 605 7757 Email: marketing@dublintourism.Ie

HELP US SAVE YOUR HERITAGE

There are more than 20,000 parish churches in England and Wales - many built by our forefathers over 500 years ago and passed down to us by succeeding generations. We, in turn, hold them in trust for those who will follow.

Many of our finest churches are situated in small country villages which cannot always afford to maintain them. The Historic Churches Preservation Trust, a non-denominational registered charity, depending entirely on voluntary support, exists to help preserve these churches for the future.

**Please write or phone,
to learn how you could help
preserve our priceless heritage.**

HISTORIC CHURCHES PRESERVATION TRUST

Reg. Charity 207402

FREEPOST, Fulham Palace, Room 110, London SW6 6BR. Tel: 020 7736 3054

PUBLISHER'S NOTES

It's no secret that Warwickshire is the home of many of England's historic attractions - Shakespeare's Birthplace, Anne Hathaway's Cottage, Warwick Castle, Coughton Court and Arbury Hall to mention just a few. But, more recently, Rugby has given birth to a new art gallery and museum where one can share the excitement of archaeologists uncovering of Tripontium. Pottery used nearly 2,000 years ago by Roman settlers can be seen together with the spectacular finds from the Tripontium site which have kept Archaeologists busy for the past four decades. The social history gallery relates the history behind the industrial past, the impact of war and the changing pattern of life over the past two centuries. The art gallery can boast a collection of over 140 paintings, prints and drawings from the 20th century including works by Spencer, Freud, Lowry, Hepworth and Sunderland - artists of international renown.
For opening times contact:
Rugby Art Gallery and Museum, Little Elborow Street, Rugby, Warwicks.
Tel: 01788 533201. Fax: 01788 533204.
Email: rugbyartgallery&museum@rugby.gov.uk

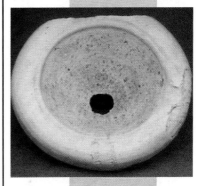

2,000 year old pottery can be seen at The Rugby Art Gallery and Museum

If you're looking for a small organised tour to take in the historic sights and beauty spots then Tailor Made Tours could be perfect for you requirements. They specialise in small group travel for the independent minded who don't wish to waste their time getting lost or obeying a stop watch. Using comfortable vehicles, you can visit famous sights or explore the delightful country lanes and beauty spots which are inaccessible to tour coaches. You can chose between excellent inns, manor houses, castles, auberge and pensione. They offer ten different tours or tailor make them to demand whether it be Great Britian, Ireland, France, Spain, Italy or Switzerland.
For further contact Tailor Made Tours
Tel: 020 8892 6852 or email: tmt@ndirect.co.uk

The independent traveller can explore Britain's dramatic castles, beautiful stately homes and gardens and medieval manor houses with The Great British Heritage Pass. Visitors pay only once and can then enjoy free entry to almost 600 of Britain's finest historic properties with the exception of the Tower of London which is half price. This unique pass is a superb opportunity to visit a wide variety of properties including Stonehenge, Blenheim Palace, Windsor Castle, Shakespeare's Birthplace and many more. There are three types of pass. The Seven Day Pass which is £35 (US$54, Can$78) or the 15 day and One Month option which are £46 (US$75, Can$110) and £60 (US$102, Can$145) respectively. Further information about the pass can be obtained from The British Tourist Authority on 0208 846 9000 or can be found on their website - www.visitbritain.com.

Above: Stained glass by Baillie Scott prior to restoration at Blackwell, Windermere.

Below: Tiles by William De Morgan at Blackwell, Windermere

In July 2001 a new arts and crafts attraction will be opening at Blackwell - The Artistic House. Opening it's doors for the first time, this superb example of an Arts and Crafts Movement house sits in an elevated position overlooking Lake Windermere. Visitors will delight at the fine examples of decorative arts, Lakeland birds and local wild flowers can be seen in the original stained glass windows, wrought iron work and oak panelling The summer exhibition will include pottery by the Kenyan born artist, Magdalene Odundo and in the autumn there will be a major exhibition of work by the most respected contemporary craftspeople of Japan. Blackwell is managed by the Lake District Art Gallery and Museum Trust which manages Abbot Hall in Kendal (also worth a visit!) and has been funded with the assistance of The Heritage Lottery Fund together with donations from charitable trusts and individuals. Blackwell, Bowness on Windermere, Cumbria. Tel: 01539 722464. Abbot Hall Art Gallery, Kendal, Cumbria. Tel: 015394 722464

Museum Replicas Limited UK

Historically Accurate

Battle-Ready Swords,

Daggers,

Axes &

Helmets

Plus Shields, Jewelry,

Sculpture,

Period Clothing,

Books & More

Paisley Brocade Dress-Available in **wine** or **green**. Please specify **S, M, L** or **XL**. Dry clean only. #8-146...£80.00

Crusader Surcoat-Available in white w/**red** cross only. Please specify **S/M** or **L/XL**. #8-108...£32.00

Museum Replicas Limited UK®
85 High Street • Dept. E11p
Godstone, Surrey, RH9 8DT • England
Rush me your free catalogue

Name _____

Address _____

_____

_____

_____ Postcode _____

email _____

HAVE YOU RESEARCHED YOUR FAMILY TREE?

Next year there will be more people than ever before trying to trace their ancestral heritage either under their own steam or with the help of the many companies specialising in Ancestry and Genealogical Research.

Sometimes the discoveries are quite astounding. You may find that you're a distant relative to Bob Marley, Oscar Wilde or Ghengis Khan. You may even be astonished to discover that your long departed Auntie was Oliver Reed's great grand father's niece..... and drinking partner.

Whatever the outcome, tracing your roots can become the most exciting and surprising journey that you have ever embarked upon.

Ancestors & Family Trees
at
www.heritagebritain.com

You will also find a myriad of Hotels, Pubs, & Inns, Historic Houses, Castles, & Gardens, Museums & Art Galleries, Arts & Crafts, Antiques, Collectables & Curios, Books & Tours. Please pay us a visit!

THE ROYAL OAK FOUNDATION
285 West Broadway, Suite 400 New York, NY 10013-2299
www.royal-oak.org

JOIN

The Royal Oak Foundation, the US membership affiliate of the National Trust. Royal Oak is an American charity which actively supports the Trust's mission and promotes cultural exchanges through scholarships and internships. Whether you travel by rail or car, or simply remain at home in your armchair, explore and experience the United Kingdom through Royal Oak membership.

RECEIVE

Free admission to
National Trust properties!

VISIT

240 of Britain's most splendid houses, castles, abbeys, gardens and historic ruins. And be welcomed as an honoured guest!

CALL

For further information or to join by phone using Mastercard or Visa: 212-966-6565, 1-800-913-6565; x205. Email: membership@royal-oak.org Visit our Website for all these details and more! www.royal-oak.org

ANNUAL MEMBERSHIPS

Individual Member $50

- One card for FREE admission to all National Trust properties and sites open to the public in England, Wales & Northern Ireland, as well as to those properties of the National Trust for Scotland.

- Free subscription to the National Trust magazine, published three times a year, and quarterly Royal Oak Newsletter.

- Receipt of the annual National Trust Handbook of properties and sites open to the public in England, Wales & Northern Ireland.

- Advance notice and free or reduced price admission to lectures, symposia, art exhibitions, events and tours in both the US and the UK.

- Opportunity to purchase distinctive merchandise from The Royal Oak Newsletter.

Family Membership $75

All benefits of Individual Membership plus:
- Separate, non-transferable cards for up to four additional persons living at the same address.

HOW TO USE THIS GUIDE

BARTON MANOR HOTEL
32 Church Street, Dorking, Surrey, RH4 1DW
Telephone: 01330 214242 Fax: 01330 224141
36 Rooms (all en suite), 2 Four Posters.
AA III, RAC III, ETB MMMM
Grade 1 listed Georgian building – the former home of the world-famous egotist! – within easy reach of the historic attractions of South East England.

RS ♈ (⊘ ✆ ⎕ ⬛ ▯ P ⵞ V GF ⬍ 🄢 SP ⊘ ⅃ ↦ ⬐ ❀ 🏛 🏠
SPECIAL **1** **2** **3** **4** B

KEY TO SYMBOLS					
ROOM SERVICE	1	RS	RESTAURANT	10	ⵞ
MINI BAR	2	♈	SPECIAL DIETS CATERED FOR	11	V
NIGHT PORTER	3	(	GROUND FLOOR ROOMS	12	GF
NO SMOKING ROOMS	4	⊘	LIFT	13	⬍
DIRECT DIAL TELEPHONES	5	✆	INDOOR SWIMMING POOL	14	🄢
TELEVISION IN ALL ROOMS	6	⎕	OUTDOOR SWIMMING POOL	15	SP
SATELLITE TV	7	⬛	TENNIS COURT	16	⊘
TEA/COFFEE MAKING	8	▯	GOLF COURSES NEARBY	17	⅃
PARKING	9	P	FITNESS CENTRE	18	↦
			FISHING	19	⬐

GARDEN OVER ½ ACRES	20	❀	
BUILDING OF HISTORIC INTEREST	21	🏛	
HISTORIC ATTRACTION NEARBY	22	🏠	
SPECIAL OFF-SEASON BREAKS	23	SPECIAL	
CREDIT CARDS EXCEPTED	24		
AMEX		**1**	
BARCLAYCARD/VISA		**2**	
ACCESS/EUROCARD/MASTERCARD		**3**	
DINERS		**4**	

Most also have a box with either an A, B, C or D displayed. This is a price band and is based on a price for DOUBLE ROOM BED + BREAKFAST (price per room not per person).

> A. £150+
> B. £100–£149
> C. £50–£99
> D. £00–£49

It should be stressed that all prices and details should be checked before booking. In many cases you may find that special rates are available for short breaks.

NEW DIALLING CODES AS FROM 22ND APRIL 2000

ON 22ND APRIL 2000, SIX AREAS CHANGED THEIR DIALLING CODES AND LOCAL NUMBER RANGES:

CARDIFF (01222) xxx xxx
BECOMES (029) 20xx xxxx

COVENTRY(01203) xxx xxx
BECOMES (024) 76xx xxxx

LONDON (0171) xxx xxxx
BECOMES (020) 7xxx xxxx

LONDON (0181) xxx xxxx
BECOMES (020) 8xxx xxxx

PORTSMOUTH(01705) xxx xxx
BECOMES (023) 92xx xxxx

SOUTHAMPTON(01703) xxx xxx
BECOMES (023) 80xx xxxx

*BELFAST (01232) xx xxxx
BECOMES (028) 90xx xxxx

* Belfast is used purely as an example (028) will be the code for the whole of Northern Ireland.

NEW HARMONISED QUALITY RATINGS FOR HOTEL AND GUEST HOUSE ACCOMMODATION

Harmonised quality standards for hotels and guest accommodation in England were introduced last year to meet consumer demand and to raise standards in service and accommodation.

Research has shown that visitors are confused by the variety of different accommodation schemes currently being operated. They see the various Tourist Boards and Motoring organisations operating different schemes using different criteria and different ratings and would like a common standard.

With that in mind, the new Harmonsied Quality Standards were developed and are now being used by the English Tourist Board throughout England and by the AA and RAC (motoring organisations) throughout Britain and Ireland to ensure consistency. The rating achieved by any establishment will be the same regardless of which organisation awarded the rating. The new Quality Standards also reflect what the visitor considers to be important, based on consumer research.

A more comprehensive report can be obtained from the English Tourist Council, AA and RAC guides all of whom feature serviced accommodation ratings against the new Quality Standards.

Unfortunately, at the time of going to press, the new ratings for all the establishments in this handbook were not available to us. For that reason some will show the new star awards and others will have the old crown or key ratings. I am sure that any establishment within these pages will be happy to inform you of their new rating upon request. Better still ask them to send you one of their brochures which will show all their ratings and commendations for service, comfort and cuisine.

* The above details were supplied by The English Tourist Council

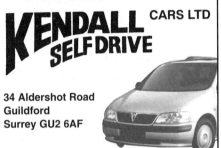

If you require a list of Tourist
Information Centres. Please
contact one of the following:

English Tourist Council
Tel: 020 8846 9000

Scottish Tourist Board
Tel: 0131 332 2433

Welsh Tourist Board
Tel: 02920 499909

Northern Ireland Tourist Board
Tel: 02890 23 1221

Irish Tourist Board
00353 1 602 4000

For the benefit of the roaming tourist, England has been divided into the following regions each of which consists of several counties - apart from London of course.

GREATER LONDON
London and it's suburbs
THE SOUTH EAST
Kent, Surrey & Sussex
CENTRAL SOUTHERN
Berkshire, Buckinghamshire, Hampshire, Isle of Wight, Oxfordshire
THE WEST COUNTRY
Bristol, Somerset, Wiltshire, Dorset, Devon & Cornwall
THE HEART OF ENGLAND
Gloucestershire, Herefordshire, Worcestershire, Warwickshire, Derbyshire, Leicestershire, Shropshire, Warwickshire, West Midlands, West Oxfordshire, Northamptonshire & Staffordshire
EAST OF ENGLAND
Bedfordshire, Cambridgeshire, Essex, Hertfordshire, Lincolnshire, Norfolk & Suffolk
NORTH COUNTRY
Cheshire, Cleveland, Cumbria, Durham, East Yorkshire, Greater Manchester, Lancashire, Merseyside,Northumberland, Tyne & Wear, Yorkshire - North, South, East & West

TOURIST BOARD RATINGS

At the point of going to press some of the advertisers had not been advised of their new tourist board ratings which are now commended in stars rather than crowns.

Therefore some of the establishments will be showing their new ratings in stars whilst others will be showing the old crown ratings.

All the hotels should now know their ratings and will be happy to let you know upon request.

The same applies to the various symbols for Bed and Breakfast, Guest House and Self Catering accommodation

For a detailed account of all ratings please contact

British Tourist Authority
Thames Tower
Blacks Road
Hammersmith
London, W6 9EL
TEL: 020 8846 9000

ENGLAND

Chatsworth, Bakewell, Derbyshire

" WHEN one is tired of London, one is tired of life." - Dr Samuel Pepys words are as true today as they ever were and for those visiting the 'Capital of Cool' (and millions do) will find bustling streets and a vibrancy unmatched anywhere in the world. With architecture that spans one thousand years, the city can offer just about something for everyone.

Perhaps two of the best known symbols of the city are Tower Bridge and the Tower of London. The latter, dating from the time of William the Conqueror has been palace, fortress and prison, but is now best known for housing the stunning Crown Jewels, recently re-located here in a state-of-the-art display. Videos explain their importance in history and how they are now used. Tower Bridge (a mere upstart at 103years old) was built specially to blend with the austere stone of its near neighbour. The fascinating engine rooms have recently been opened to the public and are fine examples of the triumphs of Victorian engineering. The views down the River Thames from the bridge's walkways are some of the most spectacular of the Capital.

Pageantry lives on in the city. Ceremonies like the Changing of the Guard have existed for hundreds of years and provide a marvellous free

Sheffield Park , East Sussex

The King's Staircase, Hampton Court Palace, London/Surrey

arts, seek out the Victoria & Albert Museum in South Kensington, where there is a wealth of jewellery, silver and crafts on display - and a stunning glass gallery.

Perhaps surprisingly, London holds two of the most visited gardens in the country. Hampton Court Palace has opened a remarkable formal garden, faithfully recreated as it was in the 1700s. Meanwhile, the Royal Botanic Gardens at Kew have some of the rarest flowers in the world - and beautiful displays of plants year-round.

London has long been known as a world centre of entertainment. It boasts five resident symphony orchestras and over 100 theatres. The famous musicals of the West End are joined by numerous thrillers, plays and new works. The London music and club scene are renowned throughout the world and currently are heralded as the most fashionable anywhere with venues such as the Ministry of Sound and the Blue Note. Visitors to London can dine out in style. London is one of the world's top three gastronomic cities, offering a choice of over 50 different cuisine's in over 5000 restaurants. Last, but certainly not least, this great capital is a shopping mecca. From historic shopping areas such as Jermyn Street to all the most modern designer stores, Oxford Street, Knightsbridge and Covent Garden, it has something for everyone.

spectacle for visitors. The ceremony takes place outside Buckingham Palace at 11.30am daily during the summer (every other day for the rest of the year). The State Rooms of the Palace itself are open through August and September each year, displaying magnificent works of art, tapestries and furniture belonging to the Royal Collection.

London is, of course, an art lover's paradise - head to Millbank for the Tate Gallery's national collection of British paintings, including some fabulous Turners. Lovers of Impressionism will want to head to the Courtauld Gallery in Somerset House, whose collection of works of art spans six centuries and includes priceless Manets and Van Goghs. For wonderful collections of decorative

Heritage and history is everywhere in London - even in the shops. One of the most historic shopping areas is Jermyn Street, off Piccadilly. For 300 years, Jermyn Street has been the pinnacle of London shopping - this is where the English aristocracy shops, for standards of craftsmanship and quality such as this are now rarely found. Delightful little shops sell hand-made shirts (minimum order, a half dozen), traditional headgear (deerstalkers and panamas) and gentlemen's sports attire. Cross Piccadilly and headup through the Georgian architecture of Burlington Arcade, which is cared for by its own private police force, the Beadles. Maybe pick up a small souvenir among the tiny trinket and cashmere shops to take home along with the memories of one of the most fascinating cities in the world.

SOUTH EAST ENGLAND consists of the four counties of Kent, East and West Sussex and Surrey with over two hundred and seventy miles of coastline, plenty of open spaces, attractive countryside and evidence of our historic past round every corner, there's something for everyone to enjoy.

The South East is also Britain's gateway region, the first glimpse of the country for visitors from overseas, with Gatwick Airport and the ports of Dover and Folkestone and the Channel Tunnel, providing routes into the region. Heathrow Airport and the ports of Portsmouth and Southampton are just on the doorstep and with so many cruise ships starting

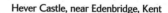

Hever Castle, near Edenbridge, Kent

Above: Painshill Par, Surrey
Below: The Yellow Room, Goodwood House, Sussex

or finishing their northern European tours at the new cruise terminals in Dover, the South East is an ideal place to spend a couple of post-or pre-cruise days experiencing 'the real England'.

For visitors enjoying history and heritage, there's a real feast of interesting, cultural places to visit – famous castles such as Dover Castle overlooking the English Channel, Leeds Castle, sometimes known as 'the loveliest castle in the world', the childhood home of Anne Bolelyn – Hever Castle – tucked away in the heart of the Kent countryside and Bodiam Castle, built to withstand the invasion that never came, is a typical

Scotney Castle, nr Lamberhurst, Kent - Courtesy of The National Trust

example of a splendid medieval moated English castle.

Many religious buildings offer much to interest the secular visitor. Historic Canterbury, mother church of the Church of England and site of the murder of Thomas A Becket, Rochester, the second oldest cathedral in England, Chichester which combines Norman architecture with the work of 20th century artists such as John Piper and Marc Chagall within Chichesterand Guildford Cathedral, consecrated in 1961 and refreshingly light with clean design lines.

Conveniently situated on London's doorstep, South East England has been chosen by many of the rich and famous as their adopted home. Sir Winston Churchill and his family lived at Chartwell, Kent from 1922 until his death. The house and grounds are now in the care of the National Trust and open to visitors. The National Trust also has the care of the former home of author, Rudyard Kipling, 'Batemans' in Sussex. Dickens readers will enjoy visits to Broadstairs where 'Bleak House' (now a museum) was his holiday home and to Rochester, the scene of many of his novels. Festivals dedicated to Dickens and his time are held every year in both these towns.

Shopping is an important feature of any vacation and South East England can offer a whole range. Antique hunters will enjoy Petworth, Tenterden, the Brighton Lanes and Westerham. There are many speciality shops in Arundel, Tunbridge Wells and the cobbled streets of Rye. There are also factory outlets in Dover and shortly at Ashford.

For entertainment, pre-London run's with allstar casts can be seen at Brighton's Theatre Royal and the

Chichester Festival Theatre. There is of course Glyndebourne Festival Opera and many of the larger venues play host to major pop and orchestral concerts, opera and ballet. Famously Leeds Castle stages two open air orchestral concerts each summer and this type of event has increasingly become a part of the South East England summer season with similar concerts at other historic house and garden venues.

The region, though, is definitely not all hustle and bustle – there are wide open spaces and hundreds. of footpaths and scenic viewpoints for the walker and cyclist to appreciate. The North and South Downs in particular provide not too demanding, but rewarding walking. Long-distance footpaths run along the top of these hills and provide spectacular walking countryside, picnic areas or just places for a gentle stroll. The North Downs begin at the famous White Cliffs of Dover and stretch west passing through many well known view points such as the Devil's Punchbowl, and Box Hill – made famous in Jane Austen's 'Emma'.

The South Downs start near Eastbourne at the famous Beachy Head cliff, and include the Seven Sisters, continuing westwards offering excellent views of the South coast along the way, including Chichester Harbour and the Isle of Wight.

Country pubs abound on the quieter

The Royal Pavilion, Brighton, Sussex

roads and in the many old-world attractive villages – sometimes they are situated alongside a river or village green where boating activity or a game of cricket can be watched while enjoying the local ale and good pub food for which England is renowned. In the summer months there may be Morris dancing for entertainment and in some pubs traditional games such as skittles, dominoes or shove ha'penny are still played.

Hundreds of interesting events take place in South East England throughout the year. Sporting venues

Corfe Castle, Dorset - Courtesy of Purbeck District Council

such as the world-famous Brands Hatch motor-racing circuit, Hickstead Showjumping Course and Wentworth Golf Course provide a variety of spectator sports and often attract visitors from all over the world. At Goodwood there is horse racing – Glorious Goodwood week is in July - motor sports with the Goodwood Festival of Speed in June and Revival weekend in September. The Arundel Corpus Christi Carpet of Flowers in June sees the nave of the cathedral turned into a carpet of colour. Re-enactments of important moments in English history – usually battles or sieges – are staged at many castles by English Heritage, with dedicated participants painstakingly re-creating every last detail of life of the period, even down to the food served!

The beautiful SOUTH OF ENGLAND takes in the counties of Hampshire (and the Isle of Wight), Dorset, Berkshire, Buckinghamshire and most of Oxfordshire - naturally there is much to both see and do. From Maritime Heritage to Bronze Age settlements, people have travelled this land for centuries and left and indelible mark that is still apparent today.

The area is just a short distance from London with good road and rail links. Central Southern England is an ideal destination. History truly comes to life in this magical area. The story begins about 5,000 years ago at Stonehenge, when the huge stones were hauled into place on the edge of Salisbury Plain. You can also visit the Rollright Stones near Chipping Norton, a Neolithic Bronze Age site dating back over 3,000 years. Take time out to enjoy a stay in one of the region's fascinating cities and towns such as, Winchester, Salisbury, Windsor, Portsmouth, Southampton or Oxford. Explore the places that have shaped England's heritage, take in the atmosphere and enjoy some time shopping in lovely surroundings. Top class and varied entertainment and cuisine are also on offer.

The South Coast of England provides endless opportunities for the visitor. Traditional seaside resorts such as Bournemouth, Weymouth or Poole offer safe bathing, clean beaches and fun-packed activities for all ages. Take the ferry to the Isle of Wight and explore both the coast and inland of one of Britain's outstanding offshore islands. Other areas are blessed with ideal conditions for a range of watersports and plenty to do in the evening - theatres, cabarets, clubs and restaurants. Spectacular scenery abounds with high cliffs, quiet coves and coastal paths and walks. Just inland from the coast is the timeless beauty of the New Forest, 250 sq. km of forest and heathland in the heart of Hampshire, planted by William the Conqueror.

You will find peace, tranquillity and enjoyment in the countryside of rural Southern England. Discover some of

Sherborne Castle, Sherborne, Dorser

Top: Bristol Cathedral
Courtesy of Bristol Tourism

Bottom: Abbey & York Street Arch, Bath
Courtesy of Bath Tourism

the best walks in England, through forest and woodland or over hills and farmland. Explore the many magnificent gardens and follow rivers that meander through the region. You can be sure of a warm and friendly welcome in the region's country pubs and inns, many of which serve excellent home cooked food and real ale.

The charm of Central Southern England with history, heritage, coast and countryside creates a picture of variety to attract any visitor.

The counties of Cornwall, Devon, Dorset, Somerset and Wiltshire. This is ENGLAND'S WEST COUNTRY, the great south-western peninsula stretching out into the Atlantic ocean.

The popularity of the region owes much to its geography and landscape. The coastline alone offers such variety and such choice for the holidaymaker.

If imposing scenery and bracing cliff walks are for you, then make for North Cornwall. There are the traditional seaside resorts of Torquay,

Weston-super-Mare, Minehead and Weymouth. And around the coast you can seek out the little ports and villages where visitors rub shoulders with the working fishermen.

Inland are the two magnificent National Parks of Dartmoor and Exmoor. At the heart of Devon lies Dartmoor, 365 square miles of great natural beauty and rugged grandeur, where you can sense the history and legend and discover a real peace and quiet. From the sparkling streams of the outskirts to the starker granite tors of the "high moor", new pleasures unfold. Exmoor is a place where "time runs slowly". The wild heather moorland and deep wooded valleys are the home of red deer and the legendary Doones of R. D. Blackmore's famous novel. It is a place for relaxation, for walking perhaps or resting in one of Exmoor's sleepy villages.

Bristol, the largest city in the West Country, is steeped in history. You can stroll down cobbled King Street, famous for its Theatre Royal, Almshouses, and Llandoger Trow. The city docks area is of great interest, providing a home for the SS Great Britain, Brunel's famous iron ship, the Industrial Museum and the Watershed shopping centre.

A few miles up the River Avon is Britain's oldest and most famous spa, the city of Bath. Bath's two thousand year history started with its popularity as a resort for the Romans, with a second great era in the eighteenth century which gave us the superb Georgian architecture of the Assembly Rooms, Royal Crescent, the Circus, Lansdown Crescent, The Holburne Museum, Claverton Manor and others.

Cornwall, too, has its urban attractions; there is the historic county town, Bodmin, the cathedral city of Truro, and Launceston, once the ancient capital of Cornwall. In Devon you can visit Exeter, its 2000 years of history represented by its Roman

Henrietta Laura Pulteney by Angelica Kauffman
The Holburne Collection, Holburne Museum, Bath

Longleat, Warminster, Wiltshire

walls, underground passages, the fine cathedral and the oldest Guildhall in the kingdom. Plymouth is a happy blend of holiday resort, tourist centre, historic and modern city; the famous Hoe has its associations with Drake and the Barbican with the Pilgrim Fathers.

The county town of Dorset is Dorchester, founded by the Romans and later to become the fictional "Casterbridge" of Thomas Hardy's novels, and Judge Jeffreys lodged in High West Street during his Bloody Assize. While in Somerset visit the city of Wells which is dominated by the great cathedral, with its magnificent west front; and do not miss Vicars' Close, one of the oldest medieval streets in Europe, and the moated Bishop's Palace. Also dominated by its cathedral, whose 404ft spire stands supreme, is Salisbury, in Wiltshire;

and all around, set back from the extensive close, there are many outstanding historic buildings.

Every county of the West Country has a wealth of 'Stately Homes', an apt destination for these impressive buildings in their landscaped parks. However, the oldest of these buildings were originally built for other than domestic reasons, and the present stately structures are the results of the restorations and developments of a later age of greater peace and wealth. The military origins of Powderham Castle and Dunster Castle are reflected in their names, and Buckland Abbey and Forde Abbey were originally Cistercian monasteries. The purpose built stately home is largely a creation of the last 400 years, and demonstrates the works of our greatest architects, not only in brick and stone, but also in landscaping – the settings of great houses like Wilton, Longleat, Bowood and Montacute are often as important as the building itself.

The first great era of castle building started with the Norman Conquest and in the West Country many of the castles were built by the conquerors themselves in an effort to control the native population. Some towns and villages are to this day dominated by these Norman structures. Launceston, especially when approached from the north, is an impressive sight and at Totnes the Elizabethan shops and houses contrast with the Norman castle. With a coastline of 650 miles, the West Country is to this day strongly influenced by the sea, and this is reflected in the other main era of castle building, as witnessed by the river-mouth castle at Dartmouth

England is a nation of garden lovers and the mild climate, which makes the West Country so popular with tourists, offers a long growing season. In fact, some gardens, like those at Abbotsbury and Tresco, specialise in sub-tropical plants. Spring is the best time of all for visiting the gardens of the West. Few sights can compare with the flowering of the

Blenheim Palace, Woodstock, Oxfordshire

rhododendrons and azaleas across the lake at Stourhead. At gardens like Killerton, where hardwood trees are numerous, the warm tones of autumn create another riot of colour to reward the late visitor.

The variety of museums is almost endless. Most counties, cities and towns cherish the treasures of their heritage in local museums, many of which highlight local specialities like Bristol glass, Honiton lace, Bridport rope or Cornish mining, and maritime collections are outstanding in the West Country.

THE HEART OF ENGLAND - This is the land of Shakespeare and Robin Hood, a region steeped in history and heritage, which offers an unrivalled variety of countryside, towns, villages and places of interest to visit.

From the gently undulating hills of the Cotswolds to the dramatic vistas of the Derbyshire Peak district - from the black and white villages of The Marches to the honey-toned villages of Leicestershire - from the classic spa and market towns of Worcestershire to cosmopolitan cities like Birmingham and Nottingham - you'll find all this and more just waiting to be discovered.

Ancient customs like well dressing sit alongside major arts festivals offering the best in music and drama Local craftsmen demonstrate their skills and sell their wares, while local delicacies like Melton Mowbray pork pies and Stilton cheese will tempt your tastebuds - and internationally renowned names like Wedgwood, Spode, Royal Doulton and Royal Crown Derby provide a feast of beauty, with plenty of bargains to be found in a host of factory shops.

From castles to caves, galleries to gardens, historic houses to heritage centres - the list is endless, the choice is yours when you choose the Heart of England.

Get away from it all amid the rolling hills and hidden valleys of The Cotswolds, the largest area of outstanding natural beauty in the country, in a landscape known for its charm the world over. Explore Shakespeare's Country, from the home of the Bard in Stratford-upon-Avon to historic Warwick, Regency Royal Leamington Spa and the city of Coventry; or enjoy the tranquil scenery of The Marches of Herefordshire and Shropshire, the beautiful Borderlands of England and Wales, and discover the secrets of its turbulent past among the ruins of a wealth of ancient fortifications and castles.

Shop for bargains in The Potteries of Stoke-on-Trent, where you'll find world-famous names like Minton, Spode, Doulton and Wedgwood, before heading for the gardens, canals and rugged beauty of The Staffordshire Moorlands. Enjoy the invigorating air of The Malvern Hills and English countryside at its best in the surrounding Severn Vale; take your pick from over 50 attractions in The Black Country, with its diverse industrial heritage; enjoy a feast of entertainment in Birmingham, one of Europe's most exciting, energetic and sophisticated cities; or re-live the legend of Robin Hood in Nottinghamshire.

Make the most of the great outdoors in The Peak District and Derbyshire; discover why Northamptonshire, with its abundance of parish churches and historic homes, is known as the county of 'spires and squires'; enjoy life in the slow lane aboard a traditional barge or in the peaceful forests and country parks of Leicestershire; or explore the mellow stone villages of Rutland, England's smallest county.

Famed as the lace capital of the world, Nottingham too offers a wealth of opportunities for shopping dining out and entertainment; and there's sport galore on the menu too, with football, test-match cricket and the Olympic-standard National Water Sports Centre to name just a few.

The cosmopolitan city of Leicester is filled with surprises - from its historic Roman core to the excellent shops, cathedral and multi-cultural events, it's also a city of culture and entertainment, a tradition reflected in the huge range of high quality festivals throughout the county.

Gloucester's Cathedral is among England's finest and its restored Victorian docks now house museums, cafes, shops and a vast antique centre; Coventry is famous for the legend of Lady Godiva and its old and new Cathedrals' while in Derby, you'll find snatches of the past hidden between and behind the shops and offices of a modern city.

Throughout the Heart of England you'll find a wealth of local customs. Some, like the ancient art of well

Chatsworth House, Bakewell, Derbyshire

dressing, have been celebrated for hundreds of years and provide a unique insight into the region's rural heritage; others are of more modern origin but provide just as much enjoyment for young and old.

Believed to originate in pagan times, well dressing was first revived in the early 17th century and has now become a cornerstone of village life. Every year, dedicated villagers make their masterpieces from petals, mosses, lichen, leaves and bark, to decorate the wells as a way of giving thanks for the precious gift of water.

In Leicestershire, the annual 'Bottle Kicking and Hare Pie Scrambling' contest is a game with few rules and the source of much boisterous entertainment for locals and visitors alike; the village of Wetton in Staffordshire is home to the annual World Toe-Wrestling Championships; and throughout the region you'll find a host of battle re-enactments and jousting tournaments which bring the past to life before your eyes. With so much to see and do, you'll need time to fortify the inner man! Help yourself to a slice of the Heart of England - throughout the region you'll find the best of home-grown, delicious foods. Try Herefordshire beef, arguably the best in the world or Evesham asparagus from the Garden of England. For the perfect Ploughman's Lunch, try creamy Stilton, known throughout the world as the 'King of English cheeses',

Burghley House, Stamford, Lincolnshire

Athelhampton, Dorchester, Dorset

Double Gloucester or Buxton Blue; and don't forget Worcester sauce, added spice for those Cotswolds pork sausages or Melton Mowbray pork pies.

Indulge you sweet tooth with a slice of Bakewell Pudding, made from a secret recipe arrived at over a century ago by a fortuitous accident; then quench your thirst with Herefordshire cider, Belvoir fruit cordials or a pint of the local brew, like Baz's Bonce Blower, one of the strongest ales in the country from the tiny brewery in Somerby, guaranteed to satisfy even the strongest thirst!

Follow the literary trail across the Heart of England. In historic Stratford-upon-Avon, home of William Shakespeare, five beautifully preserved Tudor properties administered by the Shakespeare Birthplace Trust between them tell the story of five generations of the same family. The modest terraced house in Nottinghamshire where D H Lawrence was born is now a museum providing an insight into both the author's early life in Victorian times; while in the rather grander home of Lord Byron at Newstead Abbey, the poet's manuscripts and possessions are displayed in fine buildings set in lovely gardens.

Memories of darker days are evoked by the might of Warwick Castle, where you can experience medieval life in 'Kingmaker - a preparation for battle', a series of dramatic scenes set in 1471.

Re-live the sights and sounds of the Battle of Bosworth Field, where Richard III lost his crown and his life to the future Henry VII in 1485; trace

ENGLAND

the story of the Pilgrim Fathers from the north Nottinghamshire villages of Babworth and Scrooby; then experience the sights and sounds of 12th century England at the Shrewsbury Quest; or visit Hereford's fine Cathedral, hosting the famous 13th century Mappa Mundi.

From the birthplace of Elgar to the site of Mary Queen of Scots' execution; from Roman remains and Norman castles to the momentous times of the Industrial Revolution, told at the World Heritage Site of Ironbridge - the Heart of England has been at the very centre of events which shaped the country's history.

Throughout the Heart of England, you'll find a host of historic houses, castle and halls, whose grand design and antique treasures are matched only by the splendour of their gardens and grounds.

Home of the Dukes of Rutland since Henry VIII's time, Belvoir Castle is a must for art lovers, with its collection of works by Rubens, Poussin, Reynolds and Holbein; while medieval Warwick Castle, the finest in England, boasts splendid State Rooms, the chilling Ghost Tower and gruesome Torture Chamber.

Blenheim Palace, home of the Duke of Marlborough and birthplace of Sir Winston Churchill, must be high on every visitor's list of ' essential places to see' - as must Chatsworth, Derbyshire's 'Palace of the Peak', with its magnificent collections of paintings, sculpture, silver and porcelain.
From Sulgrave Manor, once owned by the Washington family whose

descendant became the first President of the Untied States, to Stokesay Castle, its solid walls and crenellated battlements set in a charming cottage-style garden formed by the tranquil Welsh border; from Calke Abbey, 'the house that time forgot', with its rare Caricature Room, cluttered Victorian drawing room and natural history collections, to Moseley Old Hall, where Charles II hid from Roundhead troops in the secret room - you'll find a feast of history and heritage in the great houses and castles of the Heart of England.

And a further feast awaits you amid the peaceful parklands and glorious gardens. From the first snowdrops heralding the approach of spring to a riot of roses at the height of summer - from the stately and formal to the individually enthusiastic and colourful - from the internationally renowned to the little known gems - the gardens of The Heart of England unfold in a rich tapestry which blooms from spring to fall.

Meet the gardeners and share their techniques and secrets or just admire their eye-catching displays - primroses or primulas, daffodils or dahlias, lavender or lilies, sweet peas or spring bulbs, the choice is yours and the list is endless.

Warwick Castle, Warwickshire

Knebworth House, Hertfordshire

Take your pick - from the terraced rose gardens of Derbyshire's Haddon Hall, the perfect example of a medieval manor house, to the magical Biddulph Grange Garden in Staffordshire, its themed gardens representing China, Egypt, the Scottish glens, Italy and America - from Hawkstone Park in Shropshire, its combination of hidden pathways, concealed grottos, secret tunnels and follies enjoyed by visitors for more than 200 years, to the old English garden of Coton Manor, with its hedges and herbaceous border, lakes and lawns set in the Northamptonshire countryside - just a few of the delights waiting to be explored.

EAST OF ENGLAND is a relatively undiscovered region covering Bedfordshire, Cambridgeshire, Essex, Norfolk and Suffolk, Hertfordshire, and Lincolnshire.

Visit historic cities and towns where you'll find cathedrals, castles, riverside gardens, bustling shopping centres, museums and lively bars and restaurants, such as Cambridge with the magnificent King's College Chapel and punting along the banks of the River Cam, and East of England's capital, Norwich, a fine and beautiful city with its Norman castle and cathedral. Lincoln too, is dominated by a magnificent Castle and cathedral and it is easy to see why the city was once one of the most important settlements in the Kingdom. England's oldest recorded town is Colchester, where over 2000 years of history comes alive. While Peterborough to the north of the region is a new city with a heart of history, dominated by its cathedral.

Ipswich is Suffolk's county town with its medieval churches, pargetted buildings and the lovely Christ-church Mansion. For maritime heritage head to King's Lynn where medieval streets lead to quays, merchants houses and the famous custom house. Bedford, set on the river Great Ouse, dates back to before Saxon times and has attractive water meadows and gardens. Nearby is Luton, with its popular shopping centre, and extensive areas of parkland. Other notable towns of the region are the ancient market town of Bury St. Edmunds with its abbey ruins, Ely with its magnificent cathedral, Saffron

Walden which has revolved around its market for many generations, Woburn, a beautifully preserved Georgian town, and Newmarket, the horseracing capital of the world.

The green rolling countryside hides picturesque and beautiful villages, where time has stood still. The rolling wolds of Lincolnshire typify this timeless charm of the region and while the county is large it is under-populated and therefore largely unspoilt. Explore narrow streets and cobbled lanes to find pastel washed and timber-framed buildings, thatched and flint cottages, and soaring church towers. Sample the local brew or enjoy a traditional afternoon tea.

The coastline ranges from the busy resorts of Great Yarmouth, Hunstanton, Lowestoft, Skegness, Clacton and Southend-on-Sea with their long sandy beaches and family fun, to quieter more sedate resorts such as Cromer, Sheringham and Aldeburgh. Much of the remaining coastline is of outstanding natural beauty combining saltmarshes, windswept sand-dunes and lonely beaches, weatherboarded houses, windmills and fishing villages full of old world charm.

The region offers four distinctive areas, The Lincolnshire Wolds, The Norfolk Broads with its reed-fringed waterways, explore them abroad a cruiser for hire. The Cambrideshire Fens with its wide open skies and unforgettable sunsets. Or the Dunstable Downs where gliders fly high above these chalk downs of outstanding natural beauty.

Places to visit range from castles and gardens to stately homes, museums, theme and wildlife parks. For the more

Hatfield House, Hertfordshire

active, enjoy cycling, golf, sailing and walking, or for the lazy, cruise the canals and take to the skies in a hot air balloon. Or visit one of the East of England's events, from airshows and agricultural shows to musical concerts and special customs such as Cheese Rolling!

On the cultural trail Tennyson country lies to the North and is much the same terrain that the nature loving Poet Laureate so enjoyed. The landscape that inspired Constable to paint so vividly still lies on the Suffolk and Essex border and again remains virtually unchanged.

This region was once the Kingdom of the Iceni, a war like tribe with Boadicca (Boadiccea) as Queen. Evidence of the Romans is everywhere with St Albans in Hertfordshire the primary centre and Colchester the site of a great Roman city.

The North Country - Immortalised by artists, poets and writers, Cumbria – the Lake District attracts many visitors to return year after year and enjoy magnificent scenery which provides a backcloth to a wealth of attractions and events.

This unique area offers fascinating places to visit, from historic houses and castles steeped in legend, to delightful country gardens and craft workshops. The visitor can enjoy leisurely cruises on a lake steamer or take a ride through the countryside by steam-powered trains. Traditional events such as sheep dog trials, colourful country fairs and sports add to the abundance of ideas for special interest tours.

Cumbria is the perfect venue for anybody looking to experience the challenge of the great outdoors whether it is a leisurely stroll, horse

Japanese Garden, Tatton Park, Knutsford, Cheshire

riding or even rock climbing and canoeing, there is something for every level of ability.

Cumbria, of course, is famous for its floral gems, the spring daffodils for instance were immortalised by the poet William Wordsworth. Cumbria's summer flower shows continue this legacy and are a must for those wishing to see the floral beauty of the area. The Holker Garden Festival at Cark-in- Cartmel at the beginning of June is the largest of the garden events. Those with a wider interest in the countryside will not be disappointed with the variety of agricultural events from the small shepherds' meets such as Buttermere or Borrowdale to the larger county shows.

Throughout the summer there are many traditional events including the Ambleside and Grasmere sports where fell running, hound trailing and Cumberland and Westmorland Wrestling can be seen. The wrestling contests began with the Norsemen and were once widespread across the country but are now limited to Cumbria.

For the less active there are simply views to be absorbed or the chance to visit some of Cumbria's specialist shops.

Carlisle combines an enviable cultural and historical heritage with a wealth of modern attractions and facilities. The pedestrianised city centre offers some of the most comprehensive shopping in the region as well as entertainment with theatres, concert venues, bowling, golfing, clubs, pubs and cinemas and a vast array of establishments to wine and dine,

55

many with a continental theme. From its turbulent past, through Roman domination and Scottish occupation, Carlisle has grown into a peaceful English city, full of charm and character.

Carlisle is the ideal base to discover two thousand years of turbulent Border history, including Hadrian's Wall, now a World Heritage Site. Tullie House Museum & Art Gallery, where history is brought dramatically to life, has interactive displays, exhibits of Hadrian's Wall and the Border Reivers

The countryside around the city is rich with the fortifications which betray the turbulent past of the times of the Border Reivers. The dispute between England and Scotland over the border lands led to a long period of lawlessness. The history of the time left its mark on both the land and the language. Their theft of cattle and the killing brought the term "bereaved" into common usage.

A more peaceful corner of Cumbria is the Eden Valley – an area of rolling green landscapes contrasting with the open moors of the North Pennines alongside. The Eden Valley is blessed with a wonderful array of quiet villages and a wealth of culture and history. Attractions include Lowther Leisure & Wildlife Park, the unusual and entertaining Eden Ostrich World and the outstanding gardens at Acorn Bank and the historic houses of Hutton-in-the- Forest and Dalemain. The heart of Cumbria is the Lake District1 an area of outstanding beauty which inspired the Lake Poets including Wordsworth and has continued to inspire many artists and writers since.

The literary trail starts at Wordsworth's birth place in Cockermouth but also includes Dove Cottage and the Wordsworth Museum, in Grasmere where he wrote most of his best poetry. His other home nearby, at Rydal Mount1 is also open to the public. Events held during the year at Grasmere include the Wordsworth Winter School in February and the Summer Conference in August.

Coniston Water was the lake which inspired Arthur Ransome to write Swallows and Amazons and had also been the home of the Victorian writer and critic John Ruskin whose home, Brantwood is open to the public. Nine days of fun in and around the lake and village are held each year at the end of May at the Coniston Water Festival.

There are sixteen major lakes in Cumbria radiating from a central area and each with their own charm and character. One of the best ways to see the district is from the lakes themselves with cruises available on several of the larger lakes.

There are many delightful market towns in Cumbria – not least Keswick – the jewel of the northern lakes. In

Fountains Abbey, Yorkshire - A National Trust Property

early December the Market Place is turned back to Victorian days for the annual Victorian Fayre with a host of traditional entertainments and market stalls.

The town, in the shadow of the 934m high Skiddaw, offers a range of attractions including the Cars of the Stars Motor Museum – home to world famous film cars including the Batmobile, Chitty Chitty Bang Bang and cars from the Bond films.

The contrasts of Cumbria are best seen in the west where the Lakeland fells drop down to a long and varied coastline. There are many undiscovered and quiet corners from Ennerdale and Eskdale to the sandstone cliffs of St Bees Head, part of a designated Heritage Coast and home to England's only Black Guillemot colony.

Whitehaven is a lovely Georgian town currently undergoing its renaissance thanks to National Lottery money. The award winning Beacon heritage centre, situated on the harbour tells the history of the port once one of the largest in the country.

The unusual is a feature of the west coast where the world Gurning championships take place in September at the Egremont Crab Fair. The winner is the person capable of

57

pulling the strangest face while wearing a horse collar.

In November the world's biggest liar competition is held at the Wasdale Inn. Will Ritson was a former inn keeper who gained a reputation for his tall stories. Anybody is eligible to enter except for politicians on the grounds that they lie professionally!
The southern coast of Cumbria – the Lake District Peninsulas – were recent winners of the English Holiday Destination of the Year largely due to its spectacular scenery and the mildest climate in the North.

This newly revealed destination is quickly becoming a favoured option for many travellers. Grange-Over-Sands is an Edwardian seaside resort with a traffic free promenade. The Queen's official guide still leads walks across the treacherous quick sands of Morecambe Bay to Grange on a route which once linked the county to Lancashire and the south.

Ulverston has many claims to fame – birthplace of Quakerism, pole vaulting, Hartley's Beer and home to the world's only Laurel and Hardy Museum. Visitors can meet a world champion town crier on market days (every Thursday/Saturday) or gaze at glass blowing at Heron Glass or Cumbria Crystal where crystal is made exclusively by hand.

History and mystery abound in Barrow-in-Furness and Furness Abbey, one of the wealthiest Cistercian monasteries, is steeped in both.

YORKSHIRE - A county of outstanding scenic variations, an historic past and a wealth of attractions.

Scenic splendour and rural charm, ancient properties, historic towns, magnificent stately homes and cosmopolitan cities abound in a region served by an excellent communications network. This makes Yorkshire a favourite with both day visitors and those looking for a longer break.

Value for money is a local tradition and our famous warm Yorkshire welcome is assured in cities, towns and villages alike in all types of accommodation. It really is no wonder so many visitors return year after year always finding something new to discover.

For many people, the scenic grandeur of the Yorkshire Dales National Park – nearly 700 square miles of unspoilt countryside, rivers, caves, castles and unforgettable views – is a major attraction. This is the landscape made famous worldwide in the books, films and TV programmes featuring Dales Vet – James Herriot. The surgery where the author, Alf Wight, actually practiced was in the market town of Thirsk which lies midway between the Yorkshire Dales and North York Moors and a new visitor attraction –

The World of James Herriot – is due to open in the former surgery in Easter 1999.

The purple, heather clad vistas of the North York Moors National Park are another favourite – not only with holiday makers – the Moors area has become a favourite with TV and movie makers in more recent times. Who is not familiar with 'Heartbeat', filmed mainly in the Moors village of Goathland? The Norh Yorkshire Moors Railway and the fishing port of Whitby also appear regularly. The Moors are dotted with sleepy villages and hamlets waiting to be discovered, however, driving these minor roads with their steep gradients is not for the faint hearted. Perhaps one of the best ways to enjoy this magnificent scenery is using the local bus networks with pick-ups throughout the Moors area.

Neariy 2,000 years of history are on display for you in the magnificent City of York – the Jewel in Yorkshire's Crown. Built on the confluence of two rivers making the city easy to defend from the onslaught of invaders, the Romans made Eboracum (York) their northern capital. Roman remains can be seen throughout the city, including the undercroft in York Minster. The Viking invasion of York in the 9th Century saw the City renamed Jorvik and this period can be seen in vivid detail at the Jorvik Viking Centre in York's Copperate Centre. For defence, the City was encircled by a wall in Roman times, however, the City Walls in view today are mainly medieval. Overseeing all of this historical splendour is the magnificent York Minster, badly damaged by fire In 1984 but now restored to its former glory.

Cosmopolitan is perhaps not the first word which springs to mind to describe a Yorkshire City, but Leeds is just that. Don't take our word for it, Leeds was chosen as the city to house the arms and armour of the Tower of London in the magnificent Royal Armouries Museum with its tower of Steel. Harvey Nichols selected Leeds as the base for their only store outside London and it's easy to see why – with the Corn Exchange and the Victoria Quarter, as well as Granary Wharf, Leeds really Is becoming a shoppers' paradise.

Yorkshire boasts over 120 miles of coastline, much of which is designated 'Heritage Coastline', is as diverse as the region itself. From soaring clifftop scenery in the North, to vast expanses of beach in our southern resorts. England's first seaside resort can be found in Yorkshire – Scarborough rose to stardom in the Victorian era when it became fashionable to partake of the foul smelling (and tasting) waters. To the North of Scarborough lies the historic whaling port of Whitby where Captain James Cook sailed from on his voyage to discover Australia. The haunting ruins of Whitby Abbey, now maintained by English Heritage,

Castle Howard, York

provided the inspiration for Bram Stoker's 'Dracula'.

West Yorkshire's Pennine Countryside provided much inspiration for perhaps Yorkshire's most famous literary family – the Brontes. The parsonage in Haworth was where Branwell and his sisters Arine, Emily and Charlotte spent most of their lives. This is now a museum dedicated to the history of the Bronte family and a popular visitor attraction with both overseas and UK visitors.

Pennine Yorkshire is also another popular walking area in this region and one of the country's most taxing long distance footpaths, The Pennine Way, wends its way through this rugged, yet beautiful countryside.

Yorkshire is a haven for sports enthusiasts, the region is home to three premier football clubs at Sheffield Wednesday and Leeds United and 1999 sees Headingley hosting four of the ICC Cricket World Cup matches. Yorkshire is also home to eight of the country's racecourses, including Doncaster – home of the St Leger, and York which has been voted many times as England's top racecourse.

During a visit to Yorkshire, visitors will be spoilt for choice in the wide range of local cuisine available. From Wensleydale cheese (the only cheese according to a certain Wallace) to sumptuous Bamsley Chops. From mouthwatering afternoon teas at Betty's to, perhaps our most famous dish, fish and chips – the world's most famous fish and chip shop, Harry Ramsden's, can be found at Gulseley, near Leeds.

A memento of your time In Yorkshlre Is a must and there are many locally made craft products for you to choose from. Whltby Jet became fashlonable after Queen Victorla was so taken by it and still remains a popular seml-preclous stone to this day. Sheffield was once provider of most of the country's cutlery and Is still regarded as home to some of the best crafted In the country. For those with a sweet tooth, try Harrogate toffee or Pontefract Cakes or, for something a little more permanent, Yorkshlre Is home to an array of craft shops. One thing Is for sure, whatever you are looking for, there will be something to suit every taste.

Much of Northumbria is part of the National Park, a bracken-strewn place of untouched splendour where more sheep than people gaze on its panoramic views of the far-reaching Cheviot Hills. At its heart is Kielder Water, a vast man-made lake. From here the River Tyne leads towards Newcastle and Catherine Cookson country where you can follow a six mile trail around the land where she set many of her popular novels.

The mystical island of Lindisfarne – the Holy Island – off the northeast coast is known as the Cradle of Christianity. It was here that St Aiden established the first English seat of Christianity in the 7th century. Cross to the island along the causeway to visit the evocative ruins of the Priory and the restored castle.

Raby Castle, Darlington, Co Durham

The Benedictine monks of Lindisfarne produced celebrated illuminated texts in honour of St Cuthbert who died in AD687 and is buried in Durham Cathedral. This cathedral, a World Heritage Site and over 900 years old, is the finest example of Norman church architecture in England, with its awesome columns and rounded arches. The fascinating city was home to the ancestors of George Washington – John Washington was one of Durham's 'Prince Bishops'; medieval bishops who ruled the whole region like kings. The Old Hall in the town of Washington, near Sunderland, was home to the family until 1613.

Go to the picturesque walled city of Chester, with its black and white buildings and extraordinary 14th-century two-tiered "Rows" of shops, and you'll see reminders of the Roman conquerors for whom this city was a fortress. The largest Roman amphitheatre in the world has been excavated here – and you may even bump into a centurion! Every five years, in the shadow of Chester's 900-year-old cathedral, 13th-century mystery plays are performed, but there are daily 'performances' from Chester's flamboyant town crier.

The network of canals that wend their way from town to city in the North Country are today given over to leisure and pleasure boats. But for centuries the canals, great feats of engineering, were alive with cargo barges carrying raw materials and finished goods. The world's largest collection of such narrowboats and barges is at Ellesmere Port in Cheshire, where life aboard is recreated in detail.

Climbers and potholers are drawn again and again to Derbyshire's Peak District, divided in two by the elegant spa town of Buxton. On one side lie the crags and moors of the northern Dark Peak, on the other, the green dales and limestone caves of the White Peak, both punctuated by vast hunks of Blue John stones, polished locally to make jewellery. Walkers love the peace of the Lancashire dales, the Forest of Bowland's silent hills and the deserted lanes which lead to eerie Pendle Hill, surrounded by stories and legends of the infamous Pendle Witches

Getting around England's North Country couldn't be easier either. Manchester Airport is one of the most civilised gateways in England. Facilities are second to none and the service is efficient and effortless. The airport rail link means the vibrant city of Manchester is only fifteen minutes away and the Roman city of Chester just forty minutes. In an hour and a half you could be standing on the shores of Lake Windmere, in the shadow of York Minster or in any one of numerous other places that can be reached directly by train.

English Tourist Board
Tel: 0181 846 9000

British Tourist Authority
Tel: 0181 846 9000

Cumbria
Tel: 015394 44444

East Of England
Tel: 01473 822922

Heart of England
Tel: 01905 763436

London
Tel: 0207 932 20007

Above: Highclere Castle, Berkshire

Below: Penshurst Place, Kent

North West
Tel: 01942 821222

Northumbria
Tel: 0191 375 3000

South East
Tel: 01892 540766

Central Southern
Tel: 01703 620006

West Country
Tel: 01392 425426

Yorkshire
Tel: 01904 707961

Bedford Tourist Information Centre.....
....you'd be amazed at what we offer!

- Discount Rail Tickets
- Monthly "What's on guide"
- Ghost Walks and Sunday Guided Walks
- Unique Bedfordshire Heritage Map (newly commissioned)
- Local lace, crafts and produce
- Coach & theatre bookings
- Local interest books & publications
  plus event & attraction information, local & national.

Come in or miss out!   See you soon!

10 St Pauls Square, Bedford MK40 1SL
T 01234 215226 F 01234 217932
E tic@bedford.gov.uk

Town Farm
Ivinghoe
Leighton Buzzard
Beds LU7 9EL

Set below the rolling Chiltern Hills, the cottages have panoramic views of Ivinghoe Beacon. Town Farm has been run by the Leach Family since the early 1930's. The cottages have 3 bedrooms and comfortably accommodate six guests. They have parking spaces and a garden area. All rooms are centrally heated. Linen is provided.
The cottages are well furnished and fully equipped. The kitchens have all the necessary appliances.

Please ring/fax 01296 668455 for rates,

HERTFORD HOUSE HOTEL
57 Deparys Avenue, Bedford, Bedfordshire MK40 2TP
Telephone: 01234 350007 Fax: 01234 535468
16 Rooms (8 en suite).
Hertford House Hotel is situated in a beautiful tree-lined avenue between the busy town centre leading to the river and embankment and Bedford Park tennis courts and indoor swimming pool. Family-run hotel, all rooms have TV and courtesy trays.

KNIFE & CLEAVER
The Grove, Houghton Conquest, Bedford MK45 3LA
Telephone: 01234 740387 Fax: 01234 740900
9 Rooms (all en suite).
AA ☆☆ ❀, RAC ☆☆ Restaurant Award, Michelin Two Knives and Forks.
Just off the A6, six miles south of Bedford. An atmospheric 16th century building with beamed and oak panelled bar. Modern en suite bedrooms in the quiet orchard. Award winning Victorian style conservatory restaurant with fresh seafood, meat and vegetarian dishes presented in the modern English style. Carefully selected wines, many by the glass. Flowery terrace with fountain.

MOORE PLACE HOTEL
The Square, Aspley Guise, Nr Woburn, Bedfordshire MK17 8DW.
Telephone: 01908 282000 Fax: 01908 281888
54 Rooms (all en suite).
AA ☆☆☆, RAC ☆☆☆ Dining Award Level 2.
Delightful Georgian Manor House, complete with duck pond, situated in the peaceful Bedfordshire village of Aspley Guise, yet only minutes from the junction 13 M1. Near to Woburn Abbey and Milton Keynes Ski Centre. Award winning Greenhouse Restaurant offering delicious food served by friendly professional staff. 54 bedrooms tastefully decorated with lots of thoughtful extras.

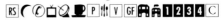

THE BEDFORD ARMS
George Street, Woburn, Milton Keynes MK17 9PX
Telephone: 01525 290441 Fax: 01525 290432
53 Rooms (all en suite), 1 Four Poster, 2 Suites.
RAC ☆☆☆☆, ETB ♛♛♛♛
This fine Georgian Coaching Inn, which dates back to 1678, has been tastefully modernised offering all the comforts and amenities of a first class modern hotel, but retaining all its old world charm and elegance. There are 53 luxurious bedrooms with private bathroom, conference facilities for up to 60 delegates, and renowned Victorian-style restaurant offering traditional English and international cuisine. Refurbishment completed Feb 1996.

OLD PALACE LODGE HOTEL
Church Street, Dunstable, Beds LU5 4RT
Telephone: 01582 662201 Fax: 01582 696422
AA ☆☆☆❀, ETB ♛♛♛♛
Converted from a large, victorian house, the hotel is full of charm and character, oak panelled, beams and an open fire all add to the Victorian ambience.

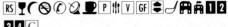

Woburn Abbey

Home of the Dukes of Bedford for over 350 years, the house is now lived in by the Duke's heir, the Marquess of Tavistock and his family. The house contains one of the most important art collections still in private hands. The State Apartments and galleries are hung with paintings by many of the great masters, notably 21 views of Venice by Antonio Canale in the beautiful Venetian Room and in the Long Gallery is the famous Armada portrait of Elizabeth I, by George Gower.

The furniture is mainly 18th century English and French and there are outstanding displays of English, Continental and Oriental porcelain. Also in the crypt can be seen superb examples of silver and silver gilt by renowned Huguenot silversmiths, together with a fine collection of miniatures.

Duchess Anna Maria is credited with the invention of Afternoon Tea as a light meal which was served in the Blue Drawing Room. 'Afternoon Tea' is a theme throughout the house where many teapots, tea services and related items are on display.

The beautiful 3,000 acre deer park was landscaped by Humphry Repton in the early part of the 19th century. It contains many lakes and much wildlife, including nine species of deer, the most famous of which is the Milu or Père David; once the Imperial herd of China and they were saved from extinction at Woburn.

The South courtyard is now devoted to the unique 40 shop Antiques Centre and the Catering Department. The former was established in 1967 and is probably the largest such centre in the U.K. outside London; most of the shops have genuine old frontages which were rescued over the years from demolition sites throughout Britain and restored and erected to form this attractive and imaginative centre.

The Sculpture Gallery, once used as a greenhouse and orangery was re-designed to accommodate the 5th Duke's collection of Sculptures and now, with its special situation overlooking the private gardens, offers a most elegant and prestigious venue for all manner of functions.

Address
Woburn Abbey
Woburn
Bedfordshire
MK17 9WA
Tel: 01525 290666

Location
On A4012 midway
between M1 (exit 13)
and A5 (Hockliffe)

Facilities
Coffee
Shop/Cafeteria
Antiques Centre

CANTLEY HOUSE HOTEL
Milton Road, Wokingham, Berkshire RG40 5QG.
Telephone: 0118 978 9912 Fax: 0118 977 4294
29 Rooms (all en suite), 1 Four Poster.
ETC ☆☆☆
A carefully restored 29 bedroomed Victorian country house
hotel set in 50 acres of parkland – yet only 10 minutes from
the M4 (junct. 10). The peaceful charm of the countryside
and the quality of the facilities and accommodation make
Cantley House an ideal retreat for conferences, weddings and
private functions. Fine English cuisine is served in the 17th
century converted barn restaurant.

RS (⊘ 🖿 ⌂ 💺 P ♨ V GF ☺ ✿ 🏠 1 2 3 4 C

THE MILL HOUSE
**Old Basingstoke Road, Swallowfield, nr Reading,
Berkshire RG7 1PU**
Telephone: 01189 883124 Fax: 01189 885550
10 Rooms, 1 Four Poster.
AA ☆☆, RAC ☆☆☆, ETB ♛ ♛
Our fine Georgian home, formerly the home of the 1st Duke
of Wellington, sits beside the river Loddon in the most
beautiful gardens. Sample traditional English cooking in the
garden restaurant. Being family-run you will receive a warm
welcome with service that is truly English tradition, so that
all your memories will be good ones.

RS ⊘ 🖿 💺 P ♨ V ✎ ✿ 🏠 1 2 3

Royal Windsor

Windsor conjures up images of castles and kings and all that is quintessentially English. Coupled with Eton, over the River Thames, its numerous historic buildings and delightful streets combine to make one of the most important visitor destinations in the country.

Windsor Castle dominates the surrounding landscape. It is one of three official residences of The Queen and has been home to The Sovereign for over 900 years.

The State Rooms, which range from the intimate rooms of Charles II's apartments to the vast area of the Waterloo Chamber, are all furnished with major pictures and works of art from the Royal Collection and are used by The Queen to entertain Her guests on ceremonial, State or official occasions.

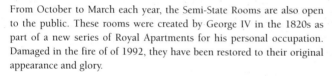

From October to March each year, the Semi-State Rooms are also open to the public. These rooms were created by George IV in the 1820s as part of a new series of Royal Apartments for his personal occupation. Damaged in the fire of of 1992, they have been restored to their original appearance and glory.

In Lower Ward of the Castle's precincts is St. George's Chapel, one of the most beautiful religious buildings in the country. Started by Edward IV in 1475, it took fifty years to build and is the shrine of the Most Noble Order of the Garter, Britain's highest order of chivalry. It is the burial place of many of England's Kings and Queens including Henry VII and his favourite wife Jane Seymour.

Windsor and Eton is just 30 miles West of central London yet boasts 1,000 years of history and heritage in a truly relaxing environment. The two heritage sites of Windsor Castle and Eton College are just 15 minutes walk apart and are complimented by a whole host of smaller attractions including river trips. Legoland Windsor is also less than 3 miles from the town centre. There are many internationally renowned events throughout the year along with smaller events all year round.

The serious shopper will find exciting names in fashion, specialist shopping and contemporary designs for the home, the towns boast no less than 14 different types of cuisine in a wide range of restaurants, all within easy walking distance and there is accommodation to suit all requirements, from country house hotels to friendly B&Bs.

With so much to discover, no matter what time of year, it is worth staying a couple of days.

For more information on Windsor and its surrounding area, contact:
Royal Windsor Information Centre
24 High Street
Windsor
Berkshire
SL4 1LH
Tel: 01753 743900
Fax: 01753 743904

Accommodation Hotline:
Tel: 01753 743907
Fax: 01753 743911

Windsor Castle Information:
Tel: 01753 831118
Email:
windsor.tic@rbwm.gov.uk

THE UPCROSS HOTEL

The Upcross is a small Country House Hotel set in a beautiful garden, with one of the best Restaurants in Berkshire.
Corporate events, private parties, weddings conferences. Special weekend rates.
The Hotel is ideally situated for business or leisure in the Thames Valley, within easy reach of M4 junctions 11 and 12. There are regular train services from Reading to London, Bristol and Oxford and a direct coach link to Heathrow and Gatwick.

THE UPCROSS HOTEL
68 Berkeley Avenue, Reading RG1 6HY
Tel: 0118 959 0796 Fax: 0118 957 6517

The GEORGE Hotel
"Right in the Heart of Reading"

The Walls of this former coaching inn are dated 1506. Its quaint cobbled courtyard, that has survived skirmishes between The Roundheads and The Cavaliers, is still a popular meeting place. The George is set in the centre of Reading within 8 minutes walk to the station. Heathrow coach link. Rail links across the UK, fast to London, 22 minutes. Excellent shopping exists in Reading. All rooms are en-suite with colour TV, tea/coffee, direct dial telephone, trouser press, hairdryer.

The GEORGE Hotel
10-12 King Street, Reading, Berkshire, England RG1 2HE.
Tel: 0118 9573445 Fax: 0118 9508614

CALCOT HOTEL

Peace and Quiet just a short distance from the M4 motorway and you have arrived at a central position to explore the Thames Valley and Beautiful Berkshire and only 1 hour from Central London, 35 minutes London Heathrow. A Hotel with character and personality, comfortable rooms, informal lively restaurant, Traditional Bars and Banqueting providing an ideal atmosphere in which to be entertained. Visit traditional England, places nearby, Royal Ascot, Henley, Royal Windsor, Newbury Races, Mapledurham, The White Horse of Uffingham, Railway Museum Didcot.

98 BATH ROAD CALCOT READING BERKSHIRE RG31 7QN
TEL: (01189) 416423 FAX: (01189) 451223
email: calcothotel@zoom.co.uk
www.calcothotel.co.uk

THE NATIONAL TRUST
for Places of Historic Interest or Natural Beauty
Basildon Park

A classical 18th century house by John Carr of York, in a beautiful setting overlooking the Thames Valley. The house contains an unusual octagon room, some of Graham Sutherlands studies for the tapestry in Coventry Cathedral as well as fine plasterwork, furniture and paintings. There are 19th century pleasure grounds and a 400 acre park with waymarked walks. The property opens in the afternoons between April and October from Wednesday to Sunday (closed on Good Friday).

Basildon Park, Lower Basildon, Reading RG8 9NR
Tel: 0118 9843040 Fax: 0118 984 1267

Reading – the welcoming Heart of the Thames Valley

Reading – the county town of Royal Berkshire – is a place of surprising contrasts. The town has existed since around 800 AD, and blends the very best of old and new – from coaching inns and Victorian gothic public buildings to imposing modern offices.

The town is ideally situated just 25 minutes drive from Heathrow, on the M4 corridor between London and South Wales. While we are surrounded by beautiful countryside, our excellent transport links put us in easy reach of Britain's most popular tourist attractions – Windsor, Oxford and London are under an hour, the Midlands and South Wales just 2 hours, whether you choose to travel by road or hi-speed train.

People come to Reading for all sorts of reasons – many to enjoy shopping in our attractive town centre. Others come to enjoy the beautiful riverside scenery and parkland (the town sits between the Thames and the Kennet), the nearby historic houses, exciting children's playparks, or our remarkable history.

The Museum of Reading is the perfect starting point if you want to discover the town – exciting and unusual exhibits tell the story of Reading from our earliest Saxon settlers. The Museum also features the important Silchester collection of Roman remains, and Britain's Bayeux Tapestry – a full-size Victorian replica of the world's most famous embroidery, and a hugely popular tourist attraction.

Next you can explore the beautiful Forbury Gardens and Abbey Ruins – the site of one of England's most magnificent Abbeys. Henry I, the Abbey's founder, is buried here. In an area saturated with history, two literary figures stand out – for here stands Reading Prison, made famous by inmate Oscar Wilde's great epic poem "The Ballad of Reading Gaol", and nearby is the Abbey Gateway where Jane Austen went to school.

Stroll along the Kennet, and just up from the prison you'll find Blake's Lock Museum, packed with exhibits from our recent industrial and social history.

For those who enjoy more lively entertainment, Reading's nightlife is varied and colourful – from live music in a wide choice of town centre pubs, to The Hexagon theatre, arts centres, open air cafes, nightclubs, casinos and more.

A crowded calendar of special events gives people more reasons to come back to our town. Highlights include the famous Rock Festival, Children's Festival, WaterFest, WOMAD International Festival... whenever you choose to stay in Reading we can guarantee you a choice of outstanding entertainment.

Contact us today for your free copy of our Visitor's Guide.
Reading Information Centre, Blagrave Street, Reading
RG1 1QH
Tel: 0118 956 6226
or E-Mail: s.brackley @beta.reading-bc.gov.uk.

A magnificent restored stately home, furnished with antiques and hung with fine paintings. Set among 90 acres of parkland with health spa and 46 elegant, individually decorated bedrooms and suites. Waddesdon Manor, Blenheim Palace and Woburn Abbey are all close by.

RELAIS & CHATEAUX

HARTWELL HOUSE

HOTEL, RESTAURANT AND SPA

Oxford Road Near Aylesbury, Buckinghamshire HP17 8NL

Tel: 01296 747444 Fax: 01296 747450

Fax toll-free from USA 1800 260 8338

THE FIVE ARROWS

WADDESDON • BUCKINGHAMSHIRE

Standing at the gates of historic Waddesdon Manor, THE FIVE ARROWS HOTEL is the perfect place from which to enjoy the beautiful gardens, walks, aviary and treasures of the Manor. The hotel has a reputation for delicious food, hospitable service and a relaxed, friendly atmosphere. There is an excellent choice of wines (including many Rothschild vintages), imported lagers, malt whiskies and real ales. Please telephone or fax for a brochure.

Tel: 01296 651727

Fax: 01296 658596

e-mail: thefivearrows@netscapeonline.co.uk C

Villiers Hotel

ETC ☆☆☆ Silver Award, AA ☆☆☆ 72%

Two AA Rosettes for exceptional food

A superbly renovated 400 year old coaching inn with 46 individually designed luxurious bedrooms and suites set around an original cobbled courtyard. "Henry's" Restaurant is an elegant air-conditioned restaurant serving quintessentially English cookery that has been awarded 2 AA Red Rosettes for its exceptional food. The Swan & Castle pub revives a Jacobean atmosphere. State-of-the-art conference & banqueting facilities for 2-250 people. Hotel guests can enjoy complimentary use of a nearby health & leisure club.

3 Castle Street, Buckingham MK18 1BS

Tel: 01280 822444 Fax: 01280 822113

Email: villiers@villiers-hotels.demon.co.uk

HATTON COURT COUNTRY HOUSE HOTEL

Bullington End, Hanslope, Nr Milton Keynes, Bucks MK19 7BQ

Telephone: 01908 510044 Fax: 01908 510945

20 Rooms (all en suite), 1 Four Poster. RAC ☆☆☆

Hatton Court is a splendid Victorian country house set in 6 acres of beautiful Buckinghamshire countryside. The 20 bedrooms, individually and tastefully decorated, offer guests all modern comforts and magnificent views. Our oak panelled dining room provides an elegant setting to sample our international modern cuisine.

RS P V GF SPECIAL 1 2 3 4 B

DANESFIELD HOUSE

Henley Road, Marlow on Thames, Bucks

Telephone: 01628 891010 Fax: 01628 890408

87 Rooms (all en suite), 10 Four Posters.

AA ☆☆☆☆, RAC ☆☆☆☆, ETB ♛♛♛♛♛ Highly Commended, 2 Red Star Oak Room Restaurant.

Danesfield House offers one of England's finest country house hotels in an idyllic setting within the Chiltern Hills near Henley-on-Thames/Windsor. Panoramic views of the River Thames from the luxurious bedrooms, a beautiful terrace brasserie and an award-winning restaurant make this a very popular destination.

RS P V GF SP SP SPECIAL 1 2 3 4 B

Waddesdon Manor
The Rothschild Collection

South Front & Parterre, courtesy of John Bigelow Taylor and the National Trust, Waddesdon Manor

Waddesdon Manor has won many awards including the Silver Award for Best Overall Property and the Europa Nostra Garden Award in 1999. This French Renaissance-style château was built (1874-89) for Baron Ferdinand de Rothschild to display his vast collection of works of art. The Collection includes French Royal furniture, Savonnerie carpets and Sèvres porcelain as well as important portraits by Gainsborough and Reynolds and works by Dutch and Flemish masters of the 17th century.

Waddesdon also has one of the finest Victorian gardens in Britain, famous for its landscape of specimen trees, parterre and striking displays of seasonal bulbs and bedding plants.

The Rococo-style aviary houses a splendid collection of exotic birds and thousands of bottles of vintage Rothschild wines are found in the wine cellars.

The gift shop was named best Gift Shop in 1999 and there is a wine shop and licensed restaurant. Many events are organised throughout the year including Collection study days, floodlit openings, wine tastings and events for children and families. For further information please phone 01296 653226, Mon-Fri 10am-4pm. Timed tickets to the House can be purchased on site or reserved in advance by ringing 01296 653226. Advance booking fee £3.00 per transaction.

Address
Waddesdon Manor,
Waddesdon, nr Aylesbury,
Buckinghamshire HP18 0JH
Tel: 01296 653211
(24 hr recorded information)
Fax 01296 653208
website:
www.waddesdon.org.uk

Opening Times
Grounds (including Garden, Aviary, Restaurant & Shops) 28 Feb-23 Dec, Wed-Sun & Bank Holiday Mondays 10am-5pm.

House (including Wine Cellars) 28 Mar-4 Nov, Wed-Sun & Bank Holiday Mondays 11am-4pm.
(Last recommended admission 2.30)
Bachelors' Wing open Wed, Thurs and Fri 11am-4pm (access cannot be guaranteed)

Admission
Adult: Grounds only £3.00, House and grounds £10.00.
Child: Grounds only £1.50, House and grounds £7.50.
Bachelors' Wing £1.00
National Trust members free.

Location
On A41 between Aylesbury and Bicester

Facilities
Aviary, Gift & Wine Shops, Licensed Restaurant and Parking

BEKONSCOT MODEL VILLAGE

Warwick Road, Beaconsfield,
Bucks HP9 2PL
Tel: 01494 672919 Fax: 01494 675284
Email: bekonscot@dial.pipex.com
www.bekonscot.org.uk

Be a GIANT in a miniature world where nobody grows up.

Gauge 1 model railway.

Children's parties.

'A little piece of England that is forever England'.

Junction 2 M40.

Rail: Marylebone/Beaconsfield, B'ham.

The Bell

MARKET SQUARE • AYLESBURY
BUCKINGHAMSHIRE HP20 1TX

*The Bell offers 17 bedrooms,
all en-suite with Full English
breakfast freshly cooked to order.
Home cooked food is the order of
the day with our new menu
tempting the diners in the evenings
for that more relaxing meal.
John, Diana and their Staff always
have a warm welcome be it for an
overnight stay, a hearty meal or to
sample one of our Traditional Ales.*

Tel: 01296 89835
(for further details)

C/D

Heritage Britain

Hotels, Inns, Bed & Breakfast
Historic Houses, Castles & Gardens,
Antiques & Curios,
Arts & Crafts, Books & Tours

Welcome to Heritage Britain, a brand new website with more than 2000 years of history and culture. Whatever your interest in Britain, we aim to help you find out more within these pages.

Visit the definitive heritage site and discover the history behind Britain and Ireland's long and colourful past.

Stay in a splendid country house hotel or a medieval inn and savour the delights of the British countryside or a historic British town.

Travel back in time by visiting the myriad of historic houses, castles and gardens or museums and galleries that adorn this Sceptred Isle

Scour the local shops or fairs for arts and crafts, antiques, collectables, curios or objets d'art.

You can even contact a genealogist to help you trace your family tree.

Heritage Britain - the essential website for domestic travellers and overseas visitors to Britain and Ireland.

**www.heritagebritain.com
mail@heritagebritain.com**

Wycombe District

Wycombe District is at the centre of the Chilterns and Thames Valley area – officially an Area of Outstanding Natural Beauty. The district stretches south to the river Thames at Marlow and north to the highest point in the Chilterns at Coombe Hill, beyond Princes Risborough.

High Wycombe, the largest town in Buckinghamshire has a wide Georgian High Street, dominated at its western end by the Guildhall where Benjamin Disraeli, who lived at Hughenden Manor nearby, addressed his public meetings. The Little Market House, known locally as the Pepperpot, built by Robert Adam is also situated here. Nearby lies the Rye, a wide expanse of grassland bordered by a lake and a Nature Trail through hanging beechwoods.

Set in the heart of the town in a delightful 18th century house with beautiful landscaped gardens, Wycombe Museum is a great place to discover the fascinating history of the district. Further to the west is West Wycombe House and Caves, part of the picturesque village belonging to the National Trust. Most of the buildings lining its main street are 17th and 18th century, with the Church and its golden ball dominating the village.

Princes Risborough lies in the lee of the Chiltern Hills forming a glorious backdrop with Whiteleaf Cross marking the route of the Ridgeway Path. This small market town is an ideal centre from which to explore the hundreds of miles of way-marked trails through the hills. For walkers, this area is one of the best in the country. The oldest part of the town is around the parish church of St Mary. Next to the church, surrounded by 17th and 18th century cottages is the Manor House which now belongs to the National Trust.

Marlow is a pretty Georgian Thames-side town famous for its 19th century suspension bridge and a fine High Street lined with tempting specialist shops. Many of the town's buildings are of architectural and historical interest with a number of famous writers having lived and worked in the town – the poet Shelley and his wife Mary, T. S. Eliot and Jerome K. Jerome.

Addresses

For further information please contact:

High Wycombe T. I. C.
Paul's Row
High Wycombe
Bucks
HP11 2HQ
Tel: 01494 421892

Marlow T. I. C.
31 High Street
Marlow
Bucks
SL7 1AU
Tel: 01628 483597

SWAN REVIVED HOTEL
High Street, Newport Pagnell, Buckinghamshire MK16 8AR

Tel: 01908 (Newport Pagnell) 610565
Fax: 01908 210995

Traditionally a coaching inn and providing excellent stabling and hospitality to travellers. The hotel has been extensively modernised and boasts 40 well-appointed guest rooms, a beautiful oak panelled restaurant and lounge and two bars.

The restaurant provides consistently good food – its menu changes quarterly and combines modern influences with traditional favourites. Look out for daily specials.

The public bar, the Frog and Nightgown, serves food at lunchtimes and evenings and the residents bar is open late for guests and diners.

AA ★★	ETB ♛♛♛ Highly Commended	**RAC** ★★

THE CROWN HOTEL
16 The High Street, Old Amersham, Bucks HP7 0HD
Telephone: 01494 721541 Fax: 01494 431283
23 Rooms (all en suite), 2 Four Posters.
AA ☆☆☆, RAC ☆☆☆☆.

In the popular movie "Four Weddings and a Funeral" Hugh Grant and Andie MacDowell find romance at the Crown Hotel in the Amersham countryside, a beguiling Forte Heritage Hotel with an Elizabethan interior complete with Inglenook fireplaces, four-poster beds, 16th century paintings and oak-beamed ceilings.

RS 🚭 🅿 ☕ P 🍴 V GF 🌸 🏨 🏨 SPECIAL
1 2 3 4 B/C

COMPLEAT ANGLER
Marlow Bridge, Marlow, Buckinghamshire SL7 1RG
Telephone: 01628 484444 Fax: 01628 486388
64 Rooms (all en suite), 4 Four Posters.
AA ☆☆☆☆, RAC ☆☆☆☆, ETB ♛♛♛, 2 Rosette.

The hotel is an English country house situated on the banks of the River Thames and within walking distance of Marlow – a beautiful Georgian town. The hotel has its own boats and private jetty and fishing in the grounds. Windsor, Henley, Ascot, Oxford all within easy reach and London is only 33 miles and London Heathrow 20 minutes away.

THE Roald Dahl CHILDREN'S GALLERY

Where marvellous things happen.

Step into the magical world of Roald Dahl with a visit to this exciting new hands-on museum for children.

- Discover Willy Wonka's inventions
- Go inside the Giant Peach
- Crawl along Fantastic Mr Fox's tunnel

.... and let your imagination run wild!

Part of the superb new Buckinghamshire County Museum and Art Gallery, Church Street, Aylesbury.

Telephone 01296 331441 for opening hours and booking details. Only an hour by train from London or 25 minutes off the M25 via A41. Fully accessible to our disabled visitors.

CAFE GARDEN SHOP

NOTICE BOARD
New Dialling Codes

Cardiff - (01222) xxx xxx
becomes (029) 20 xx xxxx

Coventry - (01203) xxx xxx
becomes (024) 76 xx xxxx

London - (0171) xxx xxxx
becomes (020) 7 xxx xxxx
(0181) xxx xxxx
becomes (020) 8 xxx xxxx

Portsmouth - (01705) xxx xxx
becomes (023) 92 xx xxxx

Southampton - (01703) xxx xxx
becomes (023) 80 xx xxxx

Northern Ireland - (01232) xx xxxx
becomes (028) 90 xx xxxx

Aylesbury Vale

If you are looking for a perfect setting for a restful short break or a fascinating daytrip in the heart of rural England look no further than Aylesbury Vale. Over 300 square miles of rolling North Buckinghamshire countryside sprinkled with enchanting villages, busy little market towns and magnificent country houses. Aylesbury Vale is just an hour's journey from both London and Birmingham, but the contrast with either could not be greater. Relax and take time to discover the charming tea shops, timeless thatched cottages, cosy country pubs and architectural gems that are the essence of Aylesbury Vale.

It was this natural beauty which first attracted the wealthy and influential Rothschild family to Aylesbury Vale in the 19th century, their legacy remains with the impressive, award winning French Renaissance-style chateau at Waddesdon.

Other hidden gems within Aylesbury Vale include Florence Nightingales old residence Claydon House and the magnificent landscape gardens at Stowe with its ornate temples, monuments and lakes, all of which are being restored to their original 17th century glory.

There's plenty too for the family to enjoy. Exciting motor racing at the world famous Silverstone Circuit, authentic steam days at the Bucks Railway Centre or a step into the magical world of Willy Wonka and James and his Giant Peach at the award winning Roald Dahl Children's Gallery at the Buckinghamshire County Museum.

The traditional English market towns of Aylesbury, Buckingham and Wendover offer shoppers a cheerful, friendly alternative to usual hustle & bustle of town centre shopping. In all three towns the market traders are joined by many fine independent stores offering a wide variety of wares.

Many visitors find that Aylesbury Vale provides the ideal base for touring in the Home Counties with the Chilterns, the Cotswolds and Oxford all nearby. Other major attractions within easy reach include Woburn Abbey, Xscape, Europe's largest indoor ski centre and the ever expanding Bicester Retail Village.

This is but a taste of what Aylesbury Vale has to offer, for a full information pack please contact:

Aylesbury Tourist Information Centre
8 Barbon Street
Aylesbury HP20 2RR
Tel: 01296 330559
Email: info@aylesbury-tourist.org.uk

Buckingham Tourist Information Centre
The Old Gaol
Market Hill
Buckinham MK18 1EN
Tel: 01280 823020

Wendover Tourist Information Centre
The Clock Tower
High Street
Wendover
Bucks HP22 6DU
Tel: 01296 696759
www.aylesbury.net

CHELWOOD HOUSE HOTEL

Chelwood, Nr. Bristol BS39 4NH

Telephone: 01761 490730 Fax: 01761 490072

Website: www.chelwoodhouse.co.uk

AA ☆☆ RAC ☆☆☆

Chelwood House, a 17th century Dower House, is situated in an area of outstanding natural beauty. The hotel enjoys an enviable location between Bristol, Bath and Wells – all renowned historical cities. The family-run establishment provides a high standard of accommodation and cuisine, complimented by friendly and efficient service.

THE GRAND, BRISTOL
A THISTLE HOTEL

The Grand Hotel is a distinguished Victorian property situated right in the heart of the city, ideally placed for the many local attractions, entertainments and within a few minutes walk of Bristol's historic harbour.

Having recently undergone a £5 million refurbishment programme it now includes 182 beautifully decorated en-suite bedrooms and a private, security monitored car park. Sports and leisure facilities are available for hotel guests at the nearby Welshback Sports Club.

The Grand Hotel
Broad Street, Bristol BS1 2EL
Tel: 0117 929 1645 Fax: 0117 922 7619

THORNBURY CASTLE HOTEL
Thornbury, Near Bristol, South Gloucestershire BS35 1HH
Telephone: 01454 281182 Fax: 01454 416188
21 Rooms (all en suite), 10 Four Posters.
AA ☆☆☆ (Red) ❀❀, RAC Gold Ribbon Award
This beautiful Grade I Tudor Castle, once owned by Henry VIII, stands in 15 acres of regal splendour, with its high walls, vineyard, and the oldest Tudor garden in England. Under the ownership of The Baron and Baroness of Portlethen, Thornbury Castle has become internationally renowned for its luxurious accommodation and award winning cuisine. Ideal base from which to explore the Cotswolds, Wales and Bath. Golf courses nearby.

RS 📞🅒🗄🎖 P 🍴 V GF ✒❀🚍🛏 SPECIAL
1 2 3 4 A/B

BERKELEY SQUARE HOTEL
15 Berkeley Square, Clifton, Bristol BS8 1HB
Telephone: 0117 925 4000 Fax: 0117 925 2970
42 Rooms (all en suite)
AA/RAC ☆☆☆, ETB 🐝🐝🐝🐝, AA ❀
Situated in a tranquil Georgian square within ½ mile of the city centre, the Berkeley Square is Bristol's most highly rated 3-star hotel. It has an exceptionally warm and welcoming atmosphere which, together with the unique Square Restaurant and Bar, ensures all guests enjoy a stay of the utmost quality.

RS 📞🚫🅒🗄🎖🎖 P 🍴 V GF ♥✒🚍🛏
1 2 3 4 B C B/C

SWALLOW ROYAL HOTEL
College Green, Bristol BS1 5TA
Telephone: 0117 925 5100 Fax: 0117 925 1515
ETB 🐝🐝🐝🐝🐝
The Swallow Royal Hotel has a splendid position next to Bristol's Cathedral on College Green in the heart of the City. It combines the best of Victorian style with all the modern comforts expected of a luxury hotel. According to the AA Guide: "The richly furnished bedrooms are exceptionally comfortable with luxurious bathrooms and thoughtful extras". Fully licensed. Fully air-conditioned.

RS 🍷📞🚫🅒🗄🎖🎖 P 🍴 V GF ♥↔🚍🛏
SPECIAL **1 2 3 4** B/C

INN LODGE AT THE BRIDGE
North End Road, Yatton, North Somerset BS19 4AU
Telephone: 01934 839100 Fax: 01934 839149
29 Rooms (all en suite), 1 Four Poster.
A warm welcome awaits you at the Bridge Inn, which is set in peaceful country surroundings. Located only 2 miles from junction 20 M5, we are an ideal break on route to Devon, especially for families, now boasting a fabulous childrens indoor play zone. Also an ideal holiday stop-over being only 15 mins from Bristol airport or simply as a base to enjoy Bristol, Bath, Weston Super Mare or the Mendips.

🍷🚫🅒🗄🎖🎖 P 🍴 V GF ✒🔗🚍🛏 **1 2 3**
4 D

Bristol

Bristol's history is both long and varied. Roman harbour remains can be seen at Sea Mills and traces of Bristol's once mighty castle can be found in Castle Park. Two splendid examples of medieval architecture remain.

Bristol Cathedral dates from 1140, and St Mary Redcliffe was described by Queen Elizabeth I as "the fairest, goodliest and most famous parish church in England". John Cabot sailed from Bristol in 1497 on his voyage of discovery to Newfoundland. The Cabot Tower, on Brandon Hill, was raised in celebration of his voyage.

A successful trading centre, Bristol grew in both size and stature. Some 17th century buildings still exist, notably the Christmas Steps, dating from 1669, a steep flight of stone steps flanked by charming shops and cafes.

The city's character really formed in the eighteenth and nineteenth centuries. Hotwells and Clifton were promoted as Spa's and the city became a centre for arts and literature. Row upon row of Georgian terraces were built, and Royal York Crescent is reputedly the longest terrace of its type in Europe. Other buildings of note are the Theatre Royal, built in 1766, the Georgian House, now a museum, and the Corn Exchange. Outside the Exchange are four bronze "nails" that were used for business transactions hence the saying "to pay on the nail".

The city has always tolerated non-conformist religions. John Wesley's New Room is the worlds first methodist chapel and still a place of worship today.

Another famous inhabitant was Isambard Kingdom Brunel, great genius of the Industrial Age and designer of the Clifton Suspension Bridge, the S.S. Great Britain, (which can be visited in her original dry dock), and the old Temple Meads station.

Bristol hosts the world famous annual International Balloon Fiesta every August, the International Kite Festival every September and many other distinctive events such as the Harbour Festival in June and Nightglow in July.

It is possible to take a themed walk around Bristol in the company of a professional guide. Please contact Bristol Tourist Information Centre for a brochure detailing accommodation and activities in Bristol, South Cotswolds and beyond.

Bristol Tourist
Information Centre
The Annexe
Wildscreen Walk
Habourside
Bristol BS1 5DB
Tel: 0117 926 0767
Fax: 0117 929 7703

E-mail: bristol@tourism.
bristol.gov.uk

Internet:
www.visitbristol.co.uk

Cambridge

The name "Cambridge" summons breathtaking images - the "Backs" carpeted with spring flowers, Kings College Chapel, punting on the river Cam, and of course the calm of the College buildings. The City known worldwide as a centre for academic excellence, retains much of the atmosphere of a bustling market town, with its narrow streets, and cobbled market place. Home to 100,000 people, it is also a centre for technological expertise, has a varied arts programme, and many good shops, including fine book shops.

Cambridge was however important long before the advent of the University; as the lowest reliable fording place across the river, there has been a settlement here since the first century B.C when an Iron Age Belgic Tribe is known to have settled at the point now called Castle Hill, followed by the Romans, Saxons and Normans.

The first Scholars arrived in 1209, fleeing from riots in Oxford; 75 years later, Hugh De Balsham, Bishop of Ely, founded the first College - Peterhouse. In the fourteenth Century, Clare, Pembroke, Gonville, Trinity Hall and Corpus Christi were founded, followed by 10 more Colleges in the fifteenth century including Christ's and King's.

Henry VI took over nearly one quarter of the medieval city to make way for King's College and Chapel. In the 19th century Girton - the first Women's College, Newnham and Selwyn were founded, followed this century by New Hall, Fitzwilliam, Churchill and Robinson.

The City, is richly served with museums and galleries, from the Fitzwilliam Museum, with a fine collection of paintings and works of art, the Cambridge Darkroom, showing exhibitions of photography, and many collections of scientific and classical interest, available in the University Museums.

Cambridge Tourist Information,
The Old Library,
Wheeler Street,
Cambridge, CB2 3QB.
Telephone:
Information:
01223 322640
Guided Tours:
01223 457574
Fax: 01223 457588

Cambridge with its' winding streets and splendid architecture has much to offer at any time of the year; it is also the ideal centre for visiting the surrounding country side - the historic houses of Wimpole Hall and Audley End are close by, Ely Cathedral - the "Ship of the Fens", peaceful villages with riverside pubs; the rolling wooded countryside made famous by the artist John Constable, are all a short drive away.

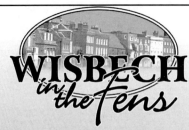

Peterborough - Cathedral City

Peterborough can boast a colourful history - from its Roman occupation to the burial of two Tudor queens. It has links with poet John Clare, nurse Edith Cavell and Hereward the Wake. Although the origins of the present-day City are Saxon, the Peterborough area has many prehistoric sites, proving people lived and farmed in this area some 6,000 years ago.

Today, Peterborough will prove a pleasant surprise to all new visitors. As your host, Peterborough has plenty to offer. A magnificent Cathedral steeped in history is the jewel of the City's colourful heritage while a multi-million pound shopping centre and excellent leisure facilities prove how easy it is to blend the old and new to produce a vibrant City with something for everyone.

Peterborough is ideally situated for day trips and is surrounded by some of the finest countryside and most interesting places to visit in the region. Throughout the area are stately homes, country houses, stone built villages, animal collections, museums and country parks.

With the majority of these attractions within 60 minutes travelling time, Peterborough provides the perfect base form which to explore.

Peterborough's Tourist Information Centre can help you with information about accommodation, where to go and what to do, events, travel and lots more.

Tourist Information Centre
3-5 Minster Precincts
Peterborough PE1 1XS
Tel: 01733 452336
Email:
tic@peterborough.gov.uk

CHESTER MOAT HOUSE
Trinity Street, Chester CH1 2BD
Telephone: 01244 899988 Fax: 01244 316118
152 Rooms (all en suite)
AA/RAC ☆☆☆☆ ✿, ETB ᴡ ᴡ ᴡ ᴡ Highly Commended.
Located within the city walls, this modern hotel offers style and luxury with many of the superbly equipped bedrooms having spectacular views over the hills of North Wales. The fully air conditioned facilities include Ranolph's Bar and our award winning Paddock's Restaurant. Also available is the well appointed leisure club.

RS 🕭 🚭 ✆ 🗖 🖳 P ⫻ V ⬍ ↔ 🛖
SPECIAL 1 2 3

THE QUEEN
City Road, Chester CH1 3AH
Telephone: 01244 350100 Fax: 01244 318483
128 Rooms (all en suite).
AA/RAC ☆☆☆☆, ETB ᴡ ᴡ ᴡ ᴡ ᴡ
Highly Commended.
Built in 1860 the Queen Hotel is one of Chester's more established hotels. Extensive refurbishment has brought rich colours and fabrics to this elegant and spacious Victorian hotel. All 128 rooms have been refurbished and executive and large superior rooms are available overlooking the secluded garden. Ample parking available.

RS 🕭 🚭 ✆ 🗖 🍳 ☕ P ⫻ V GF ⬍ ✤ 🚗 🛖
SPECIAL 1 2 3 4 C

THE PHEASANT INN
Burwardsley, Cheshire CH3 9PF
Telephone: 01829 770434 Fax: 01829 771097
10 Rooms (all en suite), 1 ½ tester.
AA ☆☆, ETB ᴡ ᴡ ᴡ Commended, Egon Ronay.
300 year old half timbered sandstone inn on top of Peckforton hills. Magnificent views to Chester, 10 miles. Close Beeston/ Peckforton Castles. Old world charm.

✆ 🗖 🖳 P ⫻ V GF ⟋ 🚗 🛖 SPECIAL
1 2 3 4 C

THE BRIDGE HOTEL
Prestbury, Macclesfield, Cheshire
Telephone: 01625 829326 Fax: 01625 827557
23 Rooms (all en suite). AA ☆☆☆, RAC ☆☆☆, ETB ᴡ ᴡ ᴡ ᴡ, Egon Ronay Johansens.
The Bridge Hotel is a 23 bedroom hotel set in one of the North's prettiest villages. The emphasis is on quality and the bedrooms are decorated to the highest standards. The 17th century charm of the restaurant combines with the culinary expertise of our kitchen and offers traditional English cuisine.

RS 🕭 ✆ 🗖 🖳 P ⫻ V GF 🚗 🛖 SPECIAL
1 2 3 4 C/D

Arley Hall

Arley Hall has been the historic home of the Warburton family for over 500 years and stands amidst some of the finest countryside in North Cheshire. The Hall, rebuilt by Rowland Egerton Warburton in the 1840s to a Victorian-Jacobean style is still very much a family home.

The current owner, Viscount Ashbrook, continues the family traditions taking a keen interest in horticulture and, indeed, Arley Hall and Gardens are famous throughout the world for their magnificent double herbaceous border, first laid out by Rowland in 1846. This breathtaking spectacle changes colour over the summer, from the early mauves and purples, through to the soft silvers and blues changing gently into the pale yellows before triumphantly bursting into hot oranges and reds of late summer.

Rowland Egerton Warburton planted many avenues of trees on his beloved estate. Of these the unique avenue of Quercus Ilex, modelled into 15ft cylinders, and the avenue of pleached limes that the visitor first encounters as they wander down to the stableyard merit special attention.

Over the years renovation and improvements have taken place both in the Hall and to the Gardens, including the renovation of the Vinery and glasshouses. These are situated in one of the Walled Gardens and still contain the original fig and peach trees that Rowland planted in the Victorian period. Extensive work has been carried out on the "hot walls" of the Walled Garden, constructed with a network of chimneys running along the course of the walls to ensure that the delicate fruit blossoms would not be frosted.

The Hall, open to the public one weekday and Sundays, has a magnificent library, wood panelling and plaster work in addition to family portraits and paintings. Guided tours are available and the Hall is available for functions, weddings and corporate events.

Arley Hall holds its annual Arley Garden Festival during the last weekend in June and welcomes visitors far and wide to two days of glorious gardening, with plant nurseries, horticultural accessories, celebrity gardener's question time and walks along the border. *A must for any garden lover!* Annual events also include antique and craft fairs, orchestral firework and brass band concerts.

The Gift Shop, Arley Plant Nursery and the Tudor Barn restaurant add up to make a visit to Arley Hall & Gardens special. A beautiful estate in beautiful surroundings giving the visitor a chance to sit and enjoy the magnificent views and enjoy the peace and tranquillity of one of the best gardens in England.

Arley Hall
Arley, near Northwich,
Cheshire CW9 6NA
Tel: 01565 777353/777284

Open
Tues-Sun, Easter to
end September.

Admission 2000
Gardens: Adults £4.40, OAPs
£3.80, Child (5-15) £2.20.
Hall charges extra.

Location
M6 (junctions 19 and 20)
signposted, M56 (junctions 9
and 10) signposted

Facilities
Gift shop, specialist plant
nursery, Tudor Barn
restaurant.
Local walks on the estate.

𝔅𝔯𝔢𝔡𝔟𝔲𝔯𝔶 ℌ𝔞𝔩𝔩 ℌ𝔬𝔱𝔢𝔩 𝔞𝔫𝔡 ℭ𝔬𝔲𝔫𝔱𝔯𝔶 ℭ𝔩𝔲𝔟

and Quaffers Conference & Exhibition Centre

Bredbury Hall Hotel is a family run independent hotel set in the beautiful Goyt Valley, yet located less than one mile off the M60 motorway and 7 miles from Manchester International Airport.

The hotel offers all the services and standards of a luxury hotel. The 120 bedrooms are tastefully decorated and have en-suite corner bath and shower, hair dryers, satellite TV and direct dial telephones, and a modern Conference Centre for up to 140 people.

We have an exclusive Country Club open Monday, Wednesday, Friday and Saturday evenings.

Leisure facilities are planned for early 2001.

GOYT VALLEY, BREDBURY, STOCKPORT, CHESHIRE SK6 2DH.
Tel: 0161 430 7421 Fax: 0161 430 5079

WHITE HOUSE MANOR
The Village, Prestbury, Cheshire
Telephone: 01625 829376 Fax: 01625 828627
11 Rooms (all en suite), 2 Four Posters.
ETB 👑👑👑, Which Hotel Guide, County Hotel of the Year 1994, Cheshire Life Restaurant of the Year 1996.
Luxuriously furnished 17th century manor house in the heart of Prestbury Village, only 15 minutes from Manchester Airport is the jewel in Cheshire's crown. Recently converted to an hotel using sumptuous fabrics and fine antiques and serving contemporary English cuisine and gaining national acclaim under the supervision of chef/proprietor Ryland Wakeham.

CROWN HOTEL AND RESTAURANT
High Street, Nantwich, Cheshire CW5 5AS
Telephone: 01270 625283 Fax: 01270 628047
18 Rooms (all en suite).
AA ☆☆. RAC ☆☆.
Situated in the heart of this historic town this 16th century former coaching inn retains many original features to complement the first class facilities required by todays guests. Offering lively bars popular with visitors and locals, the Crown Hotel is ideally located for the Cheshire countryside and Chester. Nantwich Jazz Festival held annually each Easter weekend.

THE ALDERLEY EDGE HOTEL
Macclesfield Road, Alderley Edge, Cheshire SK9 7BJ
Telephone: 01625 583033 Fax: 01625 586343
46 Rooms (all en suite), including Presidential Suite.
AA 🏵🏵 (Red), ETB 👑👑👑 Highly Recommended, Egon Ronay Commended Restaurant, 72% Hotel.
Surrounded by picturesque Cheshire countryside yet ideally positioned for motorway networks, mainline stations and Manchester Airport. The hotels restaurant offers extensive choice of menus with the bakery producing fresh breads, cakes, pastries and hot desserts daily.

THE MANOR HOUSE HOTEL
Audley Road, Alsager, Cheshire
Telephone: 01270 884000 Fax: 01270 882483
57 Rooms (all en suite). 2 Four Posters.
AA ☆☆☆ 🏵🏵. ETC ☆☆☆.
On the Cheshire/Staffordshire border, close to many attractions, this hotel has 57 comfortable en-suite rooms and an attractive indoor pool. The oak beamed restaurant, part of the original 17th century farmhouse, has 2 AA rosettes for its high standard of traditional and international cuisine. Six minutes drive from M6 junction 16.

HOLLY LODGE HOTEL
70 London Road, Holmes Chapel, Cheshire CW4 7AS
Telephone: 01477 537033 Fax: 01477 535823
43 Rooms (all en suite). 2 Four Posters.
AA ☆☆☆. ETB 👑👑👑 commended. Northern Tourist Board. Silver award - Small hotel of the year.
This large Victorian house has been extended in recent years to provide additional bedrooms located around a courtyard, overflowing with plants and hanging baskets. The rooms are nicely appointed, most with attractive colour co-ordinated fabrics and light wooden furniture. Warm hospitality is the cornerstone at this friendly hotel and can be enjoyed in the comfortable bar and adjoining Truffles Restaurant, where a selection of freshly prepared dishes are offered.

THE CROSS KEYS HOTEL
57 King Street, Knutsford, Cheshire WA16 6TD
Telephone: 01565 750404 Fax: 01565 750510
12 Rooms (all en suite). ETB ♦♦♦♦
A warm Cheshire welcome is guaranteed at the family owned and run Cross Keys Hotel. The eighteenth century coaching inn has been sympathetically converted to incorporate twelve luxury bedrooms, with all the facilities required by today's discerning traveller. Our cellar restaurant has an exclusive à la carte menu and fine wines.

Bramall Hall

Bramall Hall is an outstanding example of the black and white "magpie effect" Tudor style, England's distinctive contribution to world architecture. Dating back to the 14th century, the Hall has grown and evolved, and as a result, today's visitors can discover six centuries of fine examples of varied architecture, decoration, plaster ceilings, furniture and paintings as well as gleaning fascinating glimpses of social history.

The Hall stands in a park which was landscaped by its Victorian owner Charles Nevill after the style of Capability Brown, to give a grand vista over the terraces, lawns and lakes to the trees beyond.

The main rooms of the house, all of which are beautifully restored, include the Great Hall with its magnificent oak fireplace on either side of which are two stone felon's heads. These once stood at the gates of the Hall. The felon's head, the crest of the Davenport family, symbolises the traditional power of the Lord of the Manor to sentence local criminals to death.

In the Ballroom and Chapel are wall paintings which tell a story of life and religious turmoil in Tudor England.

The Hall's kitchen has been painstakingly and authentically restored to give a true flavour of Victorian life below stairs.

Bramall Hall's greatest treasure is a sixteenth century heraldic table carpet. Nearly twenty feet long it bears the Tudor shield and records family marriages back to 1397.

The Hall and Park are now owned and cared for by Stockport Metropolitan Borough Council. There are regular concerts, exhibitions and workshops to cater for a wide range of tastes. Licenced for civil marriage ceremonies and the perfect venue for wedding receptions and corporate entertainment.

Address
Bramall Hall,
Bramhall Park,
Bramhall, Stockport,
Cheshire SK7 3NX
Tel: 0161 485 3708
Fax: 0161 486 6959

Opening Times
Good Fri to Sept,
Mon-Sat 1pm-5pm.
Sun & Bank Holidays
11am-5pm.
Oct to New Year's Day, Tues-
Sat 1pm-4pm.
Sun & Bank Holidays 11am-
4pm. Closed 25th-26th Dec.
2nd Jan to Good Fri, Sat &
Sun 1pm-4pm.

Admission
Adult £3.50
Concessions £2.00
Family Ticket £8.50
(may be subject to review).

Location
10 miles South of Manchester

Facilities
Stables Tea Rooms,
Gift Shop, Car parking
(small charge)

Come, Stay and Visit the CONGLETON Area

Distinctive character and sheer variety are the essence of this attractive area which combines the beauty of our countryside and bustling market towns with a variety of attractions to suite every taste. We have historic houses, colourful gardens and scenic canals.

For further information and accommodation bookings please contact the:

Tourist Information Centre
Town Hall, High Street,
Congleton, Cheshire CW12 1BN
Tel: 01260 285257 Fax: 01260 298243

Discover...

QUARRY BANK MILL & Styal Country Park

- A great day out at a superbly restored working cotton mill
- Find out what daily life was like for the mill workers.
- Wonder at the 50 ton working water wheel
- Visit the Mill Shop and take home your own Styal Calico
- Enjoy a delicious home baked meal in the Mill Kitchen

Open all year
Styal, Wilmslow, Cheshire,
(Junction 5, M56)
Tel: 01625 527468

Registered Charity

QUARRY BANK MILL

BLAKEMERE CRAFT CENTRE

Blakemere is a large family attraction set around a restored Edwardian Stable block in the Cheshire countryside

OPENING TIMES
Tues - Fri: 10am - 5.00pm
Sat & Sun: 10am - 5.30pm
Bank Holidays: 10am - 5.30pm
Mondays closed

- 18 different Craft Shops
- Weekly Craft Fayres
- Various Craft Workshops
- Craft demonstrations
- Joe Crow's Indoor Playbarn
- Aquatic and Falconry Centre
- Birds of Prey Flying displays
- Excellent Restaurant and Coffee Shop

CHESTER RD, SANDIWAY, NORTHWICH CW8 2EB. TEL: 01606 883261

RODE HALL & GARDENS

Scholar Green, Cheshire.
Telephone: 01270 882961

An 18th Century house standing in a Repton landscape with extensive gardens including a woodland garden with a terraced rock garden and grotto. The formal garden was designed by Nesfield in 1860 and there is a large walled kitchen garden. House and garden open on Wednesdays and Bank Holidays from 5 April (£4.00). Garden only Tuesdays, Wednesdays and Thursdays (£2.50) 2-5pm. Location: 5 miles SW of Congleton between A34 and A50.

Heritage Britain

www.heritagebritain.com
mail@heritagebritain.com

The Hinton at Mobberley

Town Lane, Mobberley, Cheshire WA16 7HH
Telephone/Fax: 01565 873484

A warm welcome is extended to all our guests, whether on holiday or on business. All rooms are en suite, luxuriously furnished, offering all facilities. Meals by arrangement, all home cooking. Many awards. No smoking.
£44 single – £58 double/twin - £78 Family Suite inc. VAT

Tatton Park

 **CHESHIRE**

TATTON is one of the finest historic estates in Britain. Five separate features, special events and private functions attract around 700,000 visitors each year. A unique collection of features and buildings set amidst a thousand acres of landscaped Parkland depicts a vivid picture of this very important part of Britain's heritage. Perhaps Tatton is better equipped than anywhere else to convey the continuity of history in a most interesting and enjoyable way.

Man's occupation of Tatton began 10,000 years ago. The landscape History Trail guides walkers through time from a prehistoric camp to the wartime dropping zone for new recruits to the 1st Parachute Regiment based at Ringway (now Manchester International Airport). The trail's explanatory boards are also in the reception barn at Old Hall. Visitors are taken on an authentic journey through four centuries from the smokey shadows of the 15th century great hall lit by flickering candles. The tour ends with a visit to the home of a 1950s estate employee. The Old Hall was leased to his cousin by Thomas Egerton, Lord Chancellor of England during the reign of Queen Elizabeth I and James I.

At the other side of the park the Neo Classical Mansion by Wyatt is the jewel in Tatton's crown. The Egerton family collection of fine paintings, porcelain and furniture is found in the splendid setting of the magnificent staterooms. In stark contrast, the Victorian kitchens and cellars give a fascinating insight into life "downstairs". Much of the wealth to provide such a grand home and surroundings was created by agriculture.

The superb gardens are full of delightful surprises from all parts of the globe. Successive generations expanded the range of features and specimen plants according to their own taste and style of the times. Extending to 50 acres, including the arboretum, the gardens are considered to be amongst the most important in England. Attractions include the famous Japanese garden with a tea house and Shinto temple, orangery, New Zealand tree, fernery, Italian terraced garden and maze. There's also an African hut and a Greek monument.

Tatton Park is maintained, managed and financed by Cheshire County Council on lease from the National Trust to whom the Mansion and Gardens were bequeathed in 1958 by the late Right Honourable Maurice, Baron Egerton of Tatton, "for the benefit of the Nation".

Tatton Park Knutsford,
Cheshire WA16 6QN
Tel: 01625 534400

*Opening arrangements listed
are for the Mansion*
Tues-Sun, Apr-Sept
Weekends in October

Admission (2000 prices)
Park: £3.50 per car
Attractions:
£4.50 2 atts
or £3.00 each
Mansion or Gardens
£2.50 each Farm or Old Hall

Location
Junction 19 from M6
(signposted) Junction 7 M56

Facilities
Tatton Gifts, Garden and
Speciality Food Shop
Restaurant

Vale Royal

Vale Royal, situated in the heart of Cheshire, has some of the finest countryside and attractions in the country. Complemented by a wide range of high quality places to stay, Vale Royal is the ideal destination for day trips and longer stays.

The Vale Royal story begins in the 13th Century with a former king of England. During a violent storm at sea on his return from the crusades, Prince Edward, later King Edward I, vowed that on his safe return he would found an abbey in the county of Cheshire, of which he was the Royal Earl.

The abbey was founded in 1277 in what Edward declared to be "Vale Royal, the fairest vale in all England".

Vale Royal's history can be traced back to Roman times and beyond. There is much evidence of Iron Age settlement, although the influence of the Romans is more tangible. It was they who almost certainly first discovered brine springs along the Weaver Valley, thus founding an industry that remained the area's staple occupation for centuries. This industrial heritage can be traced in detail through fascinating displays at the Salt Museum and the Lion Salt Works at Northwich.

Crucial to the salt industry was the Anderton Boat Lift. The Lift is currently being restored and is one of Britain's most impressive pieces of Victorian engineering. It enabled boats to be lifted over 50ft between the Weaver Navigation and the Trent and Mersey Canal.

Additional reference to the past can be found at the Delamere Visitor Centre, Linmere. Visitors can learn about the Norman hunting forests of Mara and Mondrem which covered much of the Borough during the Middle Ages or enjoy woodland walks through the modern plantations which have replaced them.

Vale Royal has an abundance of meres, canals and rivers which means there is a wide variety of water based activities. Narrow boats can be hired for cruising the Cheshire Ring, while sailing and sailboarding are catered for along with the ever popular activities of angling and bird watching.

For those who like to walk, Vale Royal has an extensive network of footpaths to suit all abilities. Serious walkers can enjoy the more challenging long distance trails such as the Sandstone Trail.

Vale Royal is the ideal place to visit. Come and see for yourself.

For information contact the Tourism Officer, Vale Royal Borough Council
Tel: 01606 353534

Lanhydrock House

Lanhydrock is one of Cornwall's grandest houses set in a glorious landscape of gardens, parkland and woods overlooking the valley of the River Fowey.

The House dates back to the seventeenth century but much of it had to be rebuilt after a disastrous fire in 1881 destroyed all but the entrance porch and the north-wing, which includes the magnificent Long Gallery

with its extraordinary plaster ceiling depicting scenes from the Old Testament. A total of fifty rooms are on show today and together they reflect the entire spectrum of life in a rich and splendid Victorian household, from the many servants' bedrooms and the fascinating complex of kitchens, sculleries and larders to the nursery suite where the Agar-Robartes children lived, learned and played and the grandeur of the dining-room with its table laid and ready. You will want to allow plenty of time just for the tour of the house.

Surrounding the house on all sides are gardens ranging from formal Victorian parterres to the wooded higher garden where magnificent displays of magnolias, rhododendrons and camellias climb the hillside to merge with the oak and beech woods all round. A famous avenue of ancient beech and sycamore trees, the original entrance drive to the house, runs from the pinnacled seventeenth-century gatehouse down towards the mediaeval bridge across the Fowey at Respryn.

The park and woods, with a network of footpaths running through them, provide a variety of walks and a leaflet is available to help you to make the most of the estate which extends to nearly 1,000 acres.

THE CHURCH

Alongside the house is the largely fifteenth-century parish church of St Hydroc. The times of services are shown on the porch notice board and visitors are always very welcome. The church is generally open during house opening times.

EVENTS

A regular programme of events is held throughout the season and up to Christmas, including horse trials, Living History days and open-air concerts and theatre. For details, contact the Property Manager.

Address
The National Trust
Lanhydrock House
Lanhydrock
Bodmin PL30 5AD
Tel: 01208 73320
Fax: 01208 74084

Opening Times
Park & Gardens: 17th Feb to 31st Oct 2001. Gardens also open every day 1st Nov to 15th Feb 2002 during daylight hours, free of charge.
House: 1st April to 31st Oct 2001 Daily except Mondays (but open Bank Holiday Mondays), 11am-5.30pm (5pm in Oct). Last entry to House 1/2 hour before closing.

Admission 2000
House & Gardens: Adult £6.60; Children under 17 yrs £3.30.
Gardens & Grounds: Adult £3.60; Children under 17 yrs £1.60; Family Ticket (2 adults and 3 children) £16.50. Pre-arranged parties £5.50.
(Organisers please book visits through the Property Office and arrange for meals beforehand with the Catering Manager)

Facilities
Restaurant, shop, plant sales, parking, disabled facilities, special events

Location
2½ miles South East of Bodmin signposted from A30 and A38

Bude, Padstow & Bodmin Moor

Come to North Cornwall and meet the ghosts of Cornish Kings and celtic saints, of rebels, Royalists, tin miners and fishermen. Come to North Cornwall and walk the cliff paths worn bare by coastguards and smugglers. Stand on the quayside from which Cornish men and women embarked, bound to seek their fortunes in the New World.

The Atlantic Ocean has banged its fist on this 60 mile Heritage Coastline to produce the highest and most rugged cliffscape in Cornwall, complemented by some of the Country's top beaches for cleanliness, safety and surfing. Venture inland, deep into Bodmin Moor scene of Daphne Du Maurier's Jamaica Inn and witness an abrupt change in the landscape. Remnants of Bronze Age man, his stone circles, mounds, quoits and crosses stand as reminders of times gone by. Moorland legends abound including Dozmary Pool, King Arthur and the more recent and yet to be proved Beast of Bodmin Moor.

At Tintagel Castle high on the cliff face, relive the legends of Merlin, Guinevere, and the Knights of the Round Table at King Arthur's legendary home. Visit Thomas Hardy's Boscastle with its Elizabethan Harbour now protected by the National Trust, and the splendid seaside resort of Bude with it's Canal and unspoilt beaches. The poet and broadcaster John Betjeman loved North Cornwall. Launceston with its Norman Castle was his favourite inland Cornish town, and from his home in Daymer Bay he looked out over his beloved Camel Estuary, and of course Padstow. Each year on May 1st this bustling fishing port bursts into a pageant of colour and vitality for the annual "Obby Oss" celebrations, pagan festivities heralding the coming of summer, whilst in Stratton near Bude, on the summit of Stamford Hill, the Royalist Victory of 1643 is re-enacted annually.

Experience the great age of the Cornish gentry in the majestic homes of Pencarrow, Lanhydrock and Prideaux Place, whilst Wadebridge with its 17 arched bridge reputedly built on a foundation of woolsacks provides a perfect centre for touring the whole area. For the golf enthusiast North Cornwall has an abundance of high quality courses, the coastal path provides miles of unspoilt and spectacular walks, and cyclists have their own Camel Trail, 18 miles easy cycling on the former "Atlantic Coast Express" railway track, between Bodmin and Padstow.

Come to North Cornwall and, like poets, painters and musicians before you, be inspired at its grandeur, beauty and mystery.

For a free full colour guide to North Cornwall contact North Cornwall Tourism 3/5 Barn Lane Bodmin Cornwall PL31 1LZ or phone 01271 336072 (24hrs) quoting ref: HH

E-mail: Tourism@NCDC.gov.uk
www.North-Cornwall.com

TOURIST INFORMATION CENTRES

Padstow 01841 533449
Email: padstowtic@visit.org.uk

Wadebridge 01208 813725

Polzeath* 01208 862488

Bude 01288 354240
Email: budetic@visit.org.uk

Camelford* 01840 212954

Launceston 01566 772321

Bodmin 01208 76616
Email: bodmintic@visit.org.uk

Boscastle 01840 250010

*Denotes seasonal opening April to October

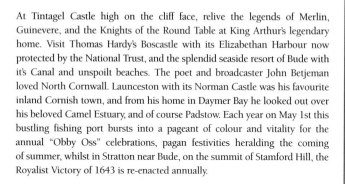

93

THE DAPHNE DU MAURIER FESTIVAL OF ARTS AND LITERATURE

Set in the beautiful Fowey Estuary and St Austell Bay on the Cornish Riviera, this 10 day annual Festival hosts a wide range of quality arts, literary and cultural events.

- ★ Star Names
- ★ Guided Walks
- ★ Music
- ★ Film Festival
- ★ Free Entertainment
- ★ Leading Writers
- ★ Talks
- ★ Theatre
- ★ Conferences
- ★ Exhibitions

130 events – SOMETHING FOR EVERYONE

11th-20th May 2001

For your free programme contact:
The Festival Office, Room 82, Restormel Borough Council, 39 Penwinnick Road, St Austell PL25 5DR

Tel (01726) 223535
(24 hour ansaphone)

South East Cornwall

Just beyond the River Tamar from England, lies the beautiful area of South East Cornwall. Steeped in Celtic tradition and over 6,000 years of human history, this region offers the visitor something special. Washed by the Atlantic Ocean in the south, the rugged and dramatic coastline contrasts sharply with the gently rolling hills, fields and quiet woodlands, before meeting the stark majesty of Bodmin Moor in the north.

In the east the Tamar Valley was once a hive of industry, producing fruit, flowers and vegetables for the London markets, as well as copper and tin from deep mines. The prosperous Tudor estates of Cothele and Antony, seats of the ancient Cornish families of Edgcumbe and Carew, were built on this trade. The magnificent houses and gardens of these estates still remain today, to be explored and enjoyed. To the west lies Polruan and the Fowey Estuary where St. Catherine's Castle stands dominant over this lovely natural harbour. The scenery here has inspired writers and artists alike; Daphne du Maurier's first novel was written here.

Along the coast are the busy ancient charter towns of East and West Looe, separated by a seven spanned bridge. Although a commercial fishing port with a lively daily fish market, the towns have much to offer; from the narrow streets, interesting shops and museums, to the many restaurants and fine cuisine. A short distance away is the typical Cornish fishing village of Polperro, its tiny harbour home to trawlers and crabbers. Nestling in a steep valley, the narrow streets contain picturesque cottages and houses that hold the secrets of the past. Once a centre for smuggling casks of brandy, silk and tobacco from France, in swift sailing luggers, the "free traders" made the most of Polperro's ideal location. Experience its unique charm or take the coastal path once trodden by smugglers and revenue men alike.

Shrouded in magic and mystery, Bodmin Moor holds abundant clues for those who want to delve into the past. Here you are re-treading the footsteps of Neolithic man, of Cornish Kings and of thousands of miners who once worked the area. Myths, legends and tales survive here and the surrounding countryside is full of traces of the Dark Age Celtic saints, in place names, churches and holy wells.

There are plenty of opportunities to sample local art, craft and food, as well as traditional Cornish events such as gig-racing and of course the local hospitality. Accommodation ranges from the Great British B&B to fine hotels, or outstanding self catering venues in traditional cottages or purpose built apartments.

Tourist Information:
Free Accommodation Guide
Dept. EE,
Tourism Office,
Caradon District Council,
Luxstowe House,
Liskeard,
Cornwall PL14 3DZ
Tel: 01579 341035
(24 hours)
Fax: 01579 341001
www.caradon.gov.uk

The Molesworth Arms Hotel

Although most of the coaches and carriages which once clattered across the cobbled courtyard of this 16th century Coaching Inn have long since disappeared, the tradition of hospitality and warm welcome are woven deep into the fabric of the Molesworth Arms. Old World charm is not just to do with the rich oak panelling in the hotel bar, the four poster bed or the deep, comfortable furniture, it is to do with the genuine hospitality which greets you at the door. The richly panelled hotel bar with its beamed ceilings and cheerful log fires provides an ideal meeting place for family and friends where you can soak up the real atmosphere of Cornwall, while the public bar is always alive with the hubbub of the day's events in this busy market town.

The hotel's own Coachhouse Restaurant offers a relaxed and elegant atmosphere where you can enjoy individual dishes, such as giant sizzling prawns in hot garlic butter, fresh local seafood and shellfish from the fishermen at Port Isaac and Padstow or Salmon straight from the River Camel while the locally famous Coachhouse Steaks appear as a regular feature on the restaurant's menu.

You'll enjoy the sort of welcome we call –
Proper Cornish

The Molesworth Arms Hotel
Wadebridge, Cornwall PL27 7DP
Tel: 01208 812055 Fax: 01208 814254

Kennacott Court

Set in the midst of 75 acres and overlooking the sea at Widemouth Bay, award winning Kennacott Court represents an outstanding collection of holiday cottages with unrivalled leisure and recreational facilities.

Every cottage is 'ETB 5 Keys', beautifully furnished and comprehensively equipped.

Enjoy our magnificent indoor swimming pool, sauna, solarium, snooker and other activities. We have a superb golf course with five full size holes, two all weather tennis courts and lots more.

Accommodation is on a weekly basis, commencing Friday or Saturday.

The memorable cottage holiday

Kennacott Court,
Widemouth Bay,
Bude, Cornwall EX23 0ND
Telephone: 01288 361766 Fax: 01288 361434
E-mail: maureen@kennacottcourt.demon.co.uk

Coombe Farm

WIDEGATES Nr LOOE CORNWALL PL13 1QN
(situated on the B3253 from Hessenford to Looe)

Tel No: 01503 240223 Fax: 01503 240895

AA QQQQQ Premier Selected, ETB ♕♕♕ Highly Commended

Experience the magic of Cornwall. Relax in a lovely Country House in a wonderful setting with superb views to the sea. Enjoy delicious food, candlelit dining, log fires, a heated outdoor pool and warm, friendly hospitality. Nearby many splendid National Trust houses and gardens and glorious walks and beaches. Coombe Farm is an excellent base to return to when touring Cornwall and Devon.

Bed & Breakfast from £28. Dinner from £16
RAC Small Hotel of the Year, S.W. England '96

The Ship Inn
Lerryn, Lostwithiel, Cornwall
Tel: 01208 872374 Fax: 01208 872614
Email: shiplerryn@aol.com www.lanista.co.uk/shipinn

The picturesque riverside village of Lerryn is noted as one of the most beautiful settings in Cornwall and is reputed to be the inspiration for Kenneth Grahame's children's classic *Wind in the Willows*. Lerryn's tranquil atmosphere and traditional charm is complemented by its pub, the 17th century Ship Inn, just a stones throw from the waters edge. All the comfortable bedrooms are en-suite and tastefully furnished. Walking, riding, golf and the coast are all within easy reach.

Pencarrow

The present Georgian House was completed by Sir John M o l e s w o r t h , 5th Baronet, circa 1770.

The East side has an imposing Palladian entrance; on the West can be seen part of an older house; whilst the back faces a courtyard, cottages, Tea Rooms and a Children's Play Area.

The interior contains an impressive inner hall and vaulted ceiling and a vast heating stove made in Plymouth in the 1830s. The music room has a fine plaster ceiling depicting the four seasons; with simulated birds-eye maple grained panelled walls. The panelled entrance hall has a secret door into the drawing room.

There is a superb collection of paintings with works by Arthur Devis, Samuel Scott, Richard Wilson, Henry Raeburn and many other well known artists, in addition to the family portraits by Sir Joshua Reynolds, set amongst some outstanding furniture and porcelain.

Here in 1882 Sir Arthur Sullivan composed much of the music for Iolanthe, while staying with Andalusia the widow of Sir William Molesworth, the Victorian statesman, who redesigned the gardens round the front of the House, and planted the rare conifer collection, made the lake, and planted the American gardens and mile long drive.

The House is still owned and lived in by the family.

Lt. Col. Sir Arscott Molesworth-St. Aubyn, Bt. MBE, DL, made a start in the early seventies on clearing much of the gardens that had become derelict during the second world war.

By 1993 he had planted out more than 200 different species of conifers from all over the world. He also planted more than 650 different species of hybrid rhododendron and more than 68 different camellias, and many other broadleaved trees and shrubs, often too tender to be grown except in the far West of Great Britain.

N.P.I. Award Winner 1997 & 1998. Voted "Best Property in the United KIngdom 1998

Address
Pencarrow
Bodmin
Cornwall PL30 3AG
Tel: 01208 841369

House Open
Easter – 15 Oct
Daily except Fri-Sat

Garden Open
Daily

Admission
(House and Gardens)
£4.50
(Gardens only) £2.00

Location
4 miles NW of Bodmin on
A389/B3266

Facilities
Tea rooms and
craft centre

MICHAELS NOOK
COUNTRY HOUSE HOTEL AND RESTAURANT
Grasmere, English Lakeland LA22 9RP
Telephone: 015394 35496

AA☆☆☆ (Red) ❀❀❀❀, Egon Ronay 80%
Cuisine ☆↑, Michelin Guide

A fine early Victorian stone-built Lakeland home with a wealth of mahogany panelling and elegant plasterwork. The name originates from William Wordsworth's poem "Michael" about a humble local shepherd.

The house was opened as an hotel in 1969 by former antique dealer, Reg Gifford, and enjoys an international reputation for the quality of furnishings and the excellence of the food and service. There are two suites, and twelve very comfortable bedrooms.

White Moss House Hotel
Water, Grasmere, Cumbria LA22 9SE
Tel: 015394 35295 Fax: 015394 35516
Email: sue@whitemoss.com
www.whitemoss.com

"Like a fair sister of the sky, unruffled doth the blue lake lie, the mountains looking on". William Wordsworth, who wrote these words about Rydal Water from White Moss viewpoint, once owned White Moss House. Now it is an intimate, highly rated hotel and restaurant run by Master Chef Peter Dixon and his wife Sue. Recommended by the Good Food Guide for 28 years, praised by all the leading hotel and restaurant guides and with AA Rosettes and Red Stars, this charming hotel is ideally placed overlooking Rydal Water in the heart of Lakeland.

THE WORDSWORTH HOTEL
Grasmere, English Lakeland LA22 9SW
Tel: 015394 35592
Email: enquiry@wordsworth-grasmere.co.uk
www.grasmere-hotels.co.uk

AA ☆☆☆☆, ❀❀ for food, Care and Courtesy Award 1999

The 35 bedrooms and 2 suites all have colour TV, radio, telephone and PC point. There are spacious lounges and cocktail bar, indoor heated pool, jacuzzi, sauna, solarium, minigym, terrace and garden. In the delectable "Prelude Restaurant" the finest seasonal produce is skilfully prepared and artistically presented. Non-residents most welcome. Exceptional facilities for conferences, banquets and civil weddings.

'Heart of the Lakes'

The Lake District's premier holiday home agency

We are proud to offer a wide range of holiday properties sleeping from two up to ten people - village centre homes, character country properties, luxury apartments and farm cottages - even some with lake frontage. Many have gardens and views and some take pets. If you are looking for a rural retreat or a cosy base for your Lakeland holiday at any time of the year we can help you to find the ideal holiday home from our wide selection.

English Tourist Board 3-keys to 5-keys up to de-luxe.

Fisherbeck Mill, Old Lake Road,
Ambleside, Cumbria LA22 0DH
Tel: 015394 32321 Fax: 015394 33251
Web site: http://www.leisuretime.co.uk

The Armitt Museum is a fascinating exhibition of Lakeland life and times. It is a treasure trove for Ambleside and presents an opportunity to explore the history of the area from Roman times to the twentieth century.

In particular, it proudly and lovingly recalls a remarkable time in the history of the Lake District a century ago when some of the nation's leading writers and artists including John Ruskin and Beatrix Potter lived nearby, drawing on local life as inspiration for their remarkable work The Museum display brings to life both their day to day lives and the way in which mutual acquaintanceship inspired their work, enriching an area already steeped in history and tradition.

Visitors can watch a 19th century lantern slide show, listen to John Ruskin, view Beatrix Potter's rarely seen exquisite natural history water colours and take an interactive 'birds-eye' view of Lakeland through the magic of photographer Herbert Bell.

Ambleside also nurtured and inspired the founder of the collection, Mary Louisa Armitt and two of the most advanced Victorian female thinkers of their time, Harriet Martineau and Charlotte Mason, whose lives are also celebrated in the Museum display. Items of interest from other ages gone by include artefacts from the Roman Fort of Galava, which is situated at the head of Lake Windermere, just a mile or so from the Museum.

For the researcher, the library upstairs contained many letters and books endowed by Beatrix Potter and others, among them a unique collection of early guide books, and fascinating documents and ephemera reflecting the life of Ambleside as a prosperous little market town during the past 400 years.

A visit to the Armitt Shop, which offers beautiful items exclusively produced for sale only at the Museum completes a delightful and rewarding experience to this beautiful new building which was formally opened by HRH Princess Alexandra during the summer of 1998.

The Armitt Ambleside Museum is situated close to the centre of the centre of town on Rydal Road just beyond the Bridge House opposite the main car park. Open daily throughout the year, 10am - 5pm, last admission 4.30pm.

Admission
Adults £2.50, Children £1.80,
Families £5.60.
Group reductions.

Ambleside Museum
Rydal Road, Ambleside
Tel. 015394 31212

Gilpin Lodge
Country House Hotel and Restaurant

**Crook Road, near Windermere
Cumbria LA23 3NE
Telephone: +44 (0)15394 88818
Fax: +44 (0)15394 88058
Toll free in USA: 800 323 5463**
Email: hotel@gilpin-lodge.co.uk
http://www.gilpin-lodge.co.uk

A friendly, elegant, relaxing hotel in 20 tranquil acres of woodland, moors and delightful country gardens. 12 miles from the M6 motorway and at the heart of the Lake District's wealth of sightseeing, history and activities. Sumptuous bedrooms – many with Jacuzzis, split level sitting areas and 4 poster beds. Three Rosette cuisine. A Pride of Britain Hotel.

THE BEECH HILL HOTEL
Newby Bridge Road, Windermere,
Cumbria LA23 3LR
Tel: 015394 42137 Fax: 015394 43745

Situated on the shores of Lake Windermere, the Beech Hill Hotel offers a peaceful and tranquil setting for a relaxing break. With award winning restaurant, terrace and lounge with panoramic views over the lake and fells. Indoor heated swimming pool, sauna and solarium, with private jetty on Lake Windermere.

58 Rooms (all en suite), 2 Four Posters.
AA ☆☆☆ ❀❀, ETB 👑 👑 👑 Commended.

MILLER HOWE
HOTEL AND RESTAURANT

Rayrigg Road, Windermere,
The English Lakes LA23 1EY
Tel: 015394 42536
Fax: 015394 45664
e-mail: lakeview@millerhowe.com

It is a well known fact that since Miller Howe opened in 1971 to visitors, Food and Travel writers have all boldly stated the hotel has the finest view of any property in the Western Lakes. The food is now in the capable hands of Susan Elliott who has been in the kitchen at the hotel for 11 years. The hotel was founded by celebrity chef John Tovey who remains a consultant now that Miller Howe is under the ownership of Charles Garside, a former international newspaper editor. The new approach to Food for the 21st Century is receiving critical acclaim. However, it is the warm, friendly, charming service from ALL the staff that has given Miller Howe the International reputation it enjoys.

NANNY BROW COUNTRY HOUSE HOTEL & RESTAURANT
Clappersgate, Ambleside, Cumbria LA22 9NF
Telephone: 015394 32036 Fax: 015394 32450
18 Rooms (18 en-suite), 4 Four Posters.
AA ☆☆ ❀❀ (Red) 75%, RAC ☆☆, ETB 👑 👑 👑 👑
Highly Commended, RAC: Restaurant, Hospitality, Comfort & Care, AA Romantic Hotel of the Year, Crystal Premier Britain Silver Shield Award.
Elegant and traditional Country House with spectacular views of the River Brathay, has direct access onto the fell. The award winning restaurant features superb cuisine and fine wines, charming lounges, fresh flowers, log fires, caring and attentive staff. Personally managed by resident owners.

SKELWITH BRIDGE HOTEL
Near Ambleside, Cumbria
Telephone: 015394 32115 Fax: 015394 34254
E-mail: skelwithbr@aol.com
29 Rooms (all en suite), 2 Four Posters, AA/RAC ☆☆
A former 17th century inn situated in the heart of the Lake District. This makes it an ideal centre for visiting the homes of Wordsworth, Ruskin, Beatrix Potter and many National Trust properties and gardens. The Hotel offers original atmosphere with oak beams and log fires and above all genuine English hospitality.

WORDSWORTH'S LAKE DISTRICT

Derwentwater and Skiddaw   Photo: National Trust Photographic Library/Joe Cornish

"Here the rainbow comes – the cloud – And mists that spread the flying shroud…"

WORDSWORTH HOUSE
Cockermouth

Birthplace of William Wordsworth in 1770

Open April to October, Monday to Friday and selected Saturdays. Closed remaining Saturdays and all Sundays.

Vegetarian Restaurant. Shop. Events during season. Parking in town centre car parks. National Trust.

TEL: 01900 824805

DOVE COTTAGE
Grasmere

Dove Cottage & Wordsworth Museum, Grasmere

Open Daily 9.30–5.30pm. Closed 24th–26th December

Parking next to Dove Cottage Tearoom & Restaurant immediately south of Grasmere village.

RYDAL MOUNT and GARDENS
Near Ambleside

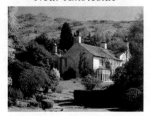

Rydal Mount Home of William Wordsworth from 1813–1850

Open:
Summer: Mar–Oct 9.30–5.00pm
Winter: Nov–Feb 10.00–4.00pm
(Closed Tuesdays in Winter)

FREE PARKING

TEL: 015394 33002

RECIPROCAL DISCOUNT OFFER – DETAILS FROM ANY OF THE ABOVE ATTRACTIONS

Abbot Hall Art Gallery
The Lake District's Heritage, History & Art

This impressive Grade I listed Georgian House is one of Britain's finest small galleries containing an extensive art collection. Overlooked by the ruins of Kendal Castle, the gallery is situated in Abbot Hall Park by the banks of the River Kent.

Downstairs you will find yourself in a fine 18th century town house surrounded by a superb collection of British art and furniture of the period. These restored Georgian rooms also contain lively ink drawings, portrait miniatures and paintings by Reynold's rival George Romney, who started his career in Kendal.

Abbot Hall is highly acclaimed for its stimulating changing exhibitions in the upstairs galleries. In addition, there is a large collection of watercolours, many of the Lake District, and a growing twentieth century collection.

People can walk, picnic or sit outside the gallery Coffee Shop and enjoy a freshly prepared meal or light snack. Adjacent to the gallery is the award winning Museum of Lakeland Life with Arthur Ransome, Victorian, toy, farming and traditional craft displays. Situated at the southern end of Kendal, Abbot Hall is just a 10 minute drive from the M6 (J36).

Address
Abbot Hall Art Gallery
Kendal, Cumbria
LA9 5AL
Tel: 01539 722 464
Fax: 01539 722 494
Email:
info@abbothall.org.uk
www.abbothall.org.uk

Opening Times
Open 7 days a week
10.30am - 5.00pm
(reduced hours in winter)
8 Feb to 21 Dec 2001

Admission
Adult £3.00
Senior citizen £2.80
Child £1.50
Family £7.50
Group £2.50

Facilities
Wheelchair access, WC's,
Shop, Coffee Shop, Free
Parking, Free Coach Parking

APPLEBY MANOR COUNTRY HOUSE HOTEL
Roman Road, Appleby-in-Westmorland,
Cumbria CA16 6JB
Telephone: 017683 51571 Fax: 017683 52888
30 Rooms (all en suite), 5 Four Posters.
AA ☆☆☆ (77%), RAC ☆☆☆, ETB ☆☆☆ Silver Award,
2 RAC Dining Awards, AA Courtesy & Care Award.
Probably the most relaxing and friendly hotel in the world. Pamper yourself in your luxury bedroom equipped with every convenience, relax in the sunny conservatory or magnificent lounges with log fires, enjoy a super meal in the award-winning restaurant, tone-up in the indoor leisure club and swimming pool. It's all yours to enjoy.

THE ROYAL OAK INN
Bongate, Appleby-in-Westmorland,
Cumbria CA16 6UN
Telephone: 017683 51463 Fax: 017683 52300
9 Rooms (7 en suite).
ETB ♦♦.
A lovely genuine old inn for many years, The Royal Oak Inn stands out for good food and drink and above all atmosphere. The bedrooms are particularly attractive. A warm welcome awaits you.

WHITEWATER HOTEL
The Lakeland Village, Newby Bridge, Cumbria LA12 8PX
Telephone: 015395 31133 Fax: 015395 31881
35 Rooms (all en suite).
AA ☆☆☆ RAC ☆☆☆ ETB ♕♕♕
Nestling on the banks of the River Leven, only minutes from Lake Windermere, our hotel can meet the many and varied needs of the discerning guest. This tastefully converted old mill offers you every modern comfort, superb hospitality and all the facilities expected of a hotel of its class.

HIGHFIELD HOUSE COUNTRY HOTEL
Hawkshead Hill, nr Ambleside, Cumbria LA22 0PN
Telephone 015394 36344 Fax: 015394 36793
11 Rooms (all en suite).
AA ☆☆, RAC ☆☆, ETB ♕♕♕♕ Highly Commended,
AA 75%, RAC Merit H&C.
A holiday to remember in a real country house hotel with splendid panoramic views, near to the picturesque village of Hawkshead, immortalised in Beatrix Potter's children's books, and scene of Wordsworths schooldays. Excellent bedrooms, with every comfort. Imaginative menus with delicious home-cooked food. A warm welcome from the Bennetts.

Carlisle and Hadrian's Wall

Historic Carlisle is a marvellous experience for the visitor, blending its unique heritage with all the modern day facilities of a traffic-free city centre environment. The Great Border City stands proudly at the gateway to one of the most fascinating areas of our country. The region, steeped in myth and legend possesses a rich and colourful past which includes some of history's most notable characters from ethereal Arthurian legend, to Emperor Hadrian, Rob Roy, Robert the Bruce and, of course, Bonnie Prince Charlie.

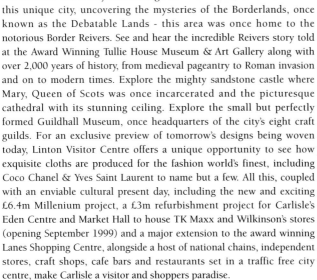

Carlisle has so much to offer with a variety of attractions, both historic and modern. In travelling to Carlisle, one can discover the beauty and heritage of this unique city, uncovering the mysteries of the Borderlands, once known as the Debatable Lands - this area was once home to the notorious Border Reivers. See and hear the incredible Reivers story told at the Award Winning Tullie House Museum & Art Gallery along with over 2,000 years of history, from medieval pageantry to Roman invasion and on to modern times. Explore the mighty sandstone castle where Mary, Queen of Scots was once incarcerated and the picturesque cathedral with its stunning ceiling. Explore the small but perfectly formed Guildhall Museum, once headquarters of the city's eight craft guilds. For an exclusive preview of tomorrow's designs being woven today, Linton Visitor Centre offers a unique opportunity to see how exquisite cloths are produced for the fashion world's finest, including Coco Chanel & Yves Saint Laurent to name but a few. All this, coupled with an enviable cultural present day, including the new and exciting £6.4m Millenium project, a £3m refurbishment project for Carlisle's Eden Centre and Market Hall to house TK Maxx and Wilkinson's stores (opening September 1999) and a major extension to the award winning Lanes Shopping Centre, alongside a host of national chains, independent stores, craft shops, cafe bars and restaurants set in a traffic free city centre, make Carlisle a visitor and shoppers paradise.

No trip is complete without a visit to the scenic beauty of our surrounding countryside and unique rural attractions including

Hadrian's Wall - World Heritage Site, comprehensively celebrated at Birdoswald Roman Fort & Visitor Centre. With an excellent range of quality accommodation both serviced and self catering, Carlisle is the premier touring base for the Lake District, Scottish Borders and Hadrian's Wall.

For a free information pack on what to see & do and where to stay, contact Carlisle Visitor Centre quoting reference **EE99** on:
Tel: 01228 625600,
Fax: 01228 625604
or in writing to:
Carlisle Visitor Centre
(EE99),
Old Town Hall,
Greenmarket, Carlisle,
Cumbria CA3 8JH.
email:
tourism@carlisle.city.gov.uk
or visit our web site:
www.historic-carlisle.org.uk

Aynsome Manor Hotel

Cartmel, nr. Grange over Sands,
Cumbria LA11 6HH
Tel: 01539 536653 Fax: 01539 360016
Email: info@aynsomemanorhotel.co.uk

Award winning family run manor situated in the tranquil and historic Vale of Cartmel. Renowned for hospitality, Cesar Award, Good Hotel Guide, Cuisine – AA Red Rosette and Log Fire Comfort. Aynsome Manor retains features dating to the 16th century and is wonderfully situated to explore South Lakeland and Morecambe Bay with many attractions close by. Dinner, bed and breakfast tariff from £45-£62 pp pn.

CROSBY LODGE

HIGH CROSBY, CROSBY-ON-EDEN,
CARLISLE, CUMBRIA CA6 4QZ
TEL: 01228 573618 FAX: 01228 573428
Email: crosbylodge@crosby-eden.demon.co.uk
www.crosbylodge.co.uk

Crosby Lodge is a beautiful country mansion. The Sedgwick family extend their enthusiasm for culinary excellence to the service and comfort in their hotel, with Head Chef James Sedgwick and his team creating the accolades with which the restaurant is renowned. The wine list by Philippa Sedgwick is exceptional, completing the personal attention to detail.
Eleven beautifully designed and appointed en-suite bedrooms. Four miles from Exit 44 on the M6, just off the A689.

AA ☆☆☆ ❀ **77%, Silver Award for Quality**

The Lake District Peninsulas, situated between the mountains of the Lake District and the shores of Morecambe Bay, are a perfect holiday destination with a wealth of intriguing visitor attractions and top quality accommodation. Rich in heritage and tradition, protective of the special historic sites and outstanding countryside, this secret corner offers quiet lanes, scenic strolls and pretty villages. For further information contact:

Furness Tourism Partnership
The Old Brewery
Ulverston, Cumbria LA12 7HU
Tel: 01229 580742 Fax: 01229 580870
Email: enquiries@lake-district-peninsulas.co.uk
www.lake-district-peninsulas.co.uk

The Pheasant

Brassenthwaite Lake, Nr. Cockermouth,
Cumbria CA13 9YE
Tel: 017687 76234 Fax: 017687 76002
Email: pheasant@easynet.co.uk
www.the-pheasant.co.uk

Set back from the lake, this 400 year old inn retains many of the features of bygone days – log fires, antiques, beams – and it has that combination of comfort, character and atmosphere that is almost impossible to find. Refurbished bedrooms and bathrooms, along with an excellent restaurant with a genuinely welcoming and smiling staff ensure a memorable stay.

Muncaster Castle CUMBRIA

Set in an idyllic corner of the English Lake District, with a breathtaking view of Eskdale from the Terrace … once described by John Ruskin as "Heavens Gate"…MUNCASTER CASTLE has something for

everyone. The castle has been the home of the Pennington family since the 13th Century.

The Pele tower stands on Roman foundations and was extended through the centuries to form the castle as it is seen today.

A walk through the castle brings you seven centuries of glorious history.

The 40 minute audio tour contains a wealth of interesting and humorous family anecdotes which add immensely to the enjoyment and create a unique atmosphere in which to view the superb antique furniture, portraits by famous artists, beautiful tapestries and many other articles of historical and artistic merit.

A walk through Muncaster's gardens will provide unceasing joy to anyone who loves nature. The gardens are spectacular, enjoying as they do a world wide reputation for their outstanding collection of azaleas and rhododendrons, with many varieties first raised here.

There is also a wide variety of rare and beautiful trees and exotic plants. A trip to our well stocked Plant Centre is a must. Here you can purchase top quality plants at modest prices. A mail order service is also available.

The gardens are home to the World Owl Trust, which strives to conserve owls and their habitat world-wide. Daily at 2.30pm (April to October) a talk is given on the work of the Trust and, weather permitting, the birds fly.

Light meals and refreshments are available at the stables cafe, and gift shops provide that special memento of your visit.

Muncaster Castle
Ravenglass,
Cumbria CA18 1RQ
Tel: 01229 717614
Fax: 01229 717010

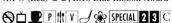

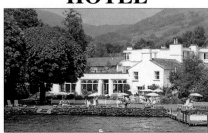

Brantwood

Home of John Ruskin 1872 - 1900

Brantwood is the most beautifully situated house in the Lake District. Enjoying the finest lake and mountain views in England. There is no other house in the district with such diversity of cultural associations, including Tolstoy and Gandhi.

The home of John Ruskin from 1872 until his death in 1900, Brantwood became an intellectual powerhouse and one of the greatest literary and artistic centres in Europe.

Today Brantwood still retains that special feeling which has given inspiration to so many, and Ruskin's thinking still has the keenest relevance.

Brantwood from Lake Coniston

Cloud study in Val D'Aosta by John Ruskin

★ Splendid collection of Ruskin watercolours and memorabilia

★ Video programme and bookshop

★ Glorious woodland walks

★ Ruskin lace demonstrations through the season

★ Seasonal programme of exhibitions and events

★ Jumping Jenny's restaurant and tea rooms

★ Coach House craft gallery

THE RUTLAND ARMS HOTEL
The Square, Bakewell, Derbyshire DE45 1BT
Telephone: 01629 812812 Fax: 01629 812309
35 Rooms (all en suite)
AA ✩✩✩ ❀, ETB ✩✩✩✩.
The Rutland Arms Hotel is a very famous coaching hotel, noted for the birth of the Bakewell Pudding and connected with Wordsworth and Turner. It is in the heart of the beautiful Peak District, Britain's first National Park, with Chatsworth House, Haddon Hall and superb hill walks all conveniently local.

RS 🆒 📠 🍺 P 🍴 V GF 🚗 SPECIAL **1** **2** **3** **4** C

FISCHER'S BASLOW HALL
Calver Road, Baslow, Bakewell, Derbyshire DE45 1RR
Telephone: 01246 583259 Fax: 01246 583818
6 Rooms (all en suite). 1 Four Poster.
AA ✩✩ (Red) ❀❀❀, ETB ♛♛♛ Highly Commended, Michelin starred dining room, UK Restaurant of the Year 1995, Egon Ronay. Restaurant with Rooms of the Year 1998, Good Hotel Guide.
Typical Derbyshire Manor House on the edge of the magnificent Chatsworth Estate. Surrounded by glorious countryside and stately homes including Haddon Hall. Egon Ronay UK Restaurant of the Year 1995. Good Hotel Guide Restaurant with Rooms of the Year 1998. Six individually styled bedrooms.
Price guide: single £80-£95, double £100-£130.

🆒 📠 P 🍴 V ❀ 🚗🚗 **1** **2** **3** **4** B

THE NEW BATH HOTEL
New Bath Road, Matlock Bath, Derbyshire DE4 3PX
Telephone: 01629 583275 Fax: 01629 580268
55 Rooms (all en suite). AA/RAC ✩✩✩
The New Bath Hotel is hidden away in a narrow twisting gorge of the River Derwent and is a spectacular retreat from the pressures of life. The leisure facilities include a large outdoor swimming pool and an indoor plunge pool – both fed by natural springs – a sauna, solarium and tennis court.

RS 🆒 📠 🍺 P 🍴 V GF 🆂🅿 SP ⏱ ❀ 🚗🚗
SPECIAL **1** **2** **3** **4** C

THE JARVIS PEACOCK HOTEL
Rowsley, nr Matlock, Derbyshire DE4 2EB
Telephone: 01629 733518 Fax: 01629 732671
14 Rooms (all en suite), 1 Four Poster, 1 Half Tester.
ETB ♛♛♛♛ Highly Commended. A Best Loved Hotel of the World, Johansens.
Nestling in picturesque countryside on the banks of the River Derwent, The Peacock, one of Derbyshire's most charming hotels, waits to greet you. This traditional 16th century building is full of character, providing true comfort and genuine hospitality. Our delightful restaurant offers a mixture of fine and traditional food. Fishing.

RS 🆒 📠 🍺 P 🍴 ⚓ ❀ 🚗🚗 SPECIAL
1 **2** **3** **4** B C B/C

Derbyshire & The Peak District

Take a breath of fresh air by visiting Derbyshire and the Peak District in the heart of England's green and pleasant land.

Escape the crowds and relax as you discover picture-postcard villages nestling amongst the rugged peaks and rolling countryside rich with woodland and neatly jigsawed together with Derbyshire dry-stone walls.

Heritage houses are around every corner. Chatsworth is the 'Palace of the Peak' housing an outstanding collection of fine art displayed in a variety of richly furnished rooms overlooking breathtaking gardens. A new Adventure Playground created in the Farmyard easily occupies the younger visitor's needs, and for food connoisseurs, the award winning Farm Shop is a culinary delight.

Neighbouring homes include such treasures as romantic medieval Haddon Hall with its sweetly scented rose garden, Elizabethan elegance at Hardwick Hall, and Eyam Hall, home to the Wright family for 300 years.

Towns bustling with lively market day activities are a great contrast. Chesterfield with its famous crooked spire, Ashbourne great for gingerbread, Bakewell proud of its puddings and Buxton flush with natural water springs, all heave with character as well as bargains! Derby's city scene offers a great shopping experience and is the proud home to fine porcelain producer, *Royal Crown Derby*.

Outdoor adventures are bountiful as Derbyshire's terrain is ideal for climbing, caving, cycling and hiking to name but a few.

If driving is more your style, take a cruise down the National Heritage Corridor® and discover England's original factories and the part Derbyshire played in the Industrial Revolution. Trundle along by tram at Crich, soar the skies by cable car at the Heights of Abraham, or sink underground to the Castleton caves – whatever your preference, Derbyshire and the Peak District has got the answer!

Quaint traditional customs are alive from May to September throughout all the towns and villages when the art of Well Dressing flourishes. Intricate artistic displays created from petals, bark, leaves and seeds offer thanks for the country's rich blessing of fresh water supplies.

Making your way to Derbyshire and the Peak District is simple as London is just 1 hour 40 minutes away by train (2 hours by car) and the main gateway airports of Birminham, East Midlands and Manchester offer doorstep services.

Address
Derby Tourism
Tourist Information Centre
Assembly Rooms
Market Place
Derby DE1 3AH
Tel: +44 (0)1332 256201
Fax: +44 (0)1332 256137
Email: tourism@derby.gov.uk

RIVERSIDE
HOUSE HOTEL
Ashford-in-the-Water, Bakewell, Derbyshire
Tel: 01629 814275 Fax: 01629 812873

Located in the heart of the Peak District by the tranquil banks of the Wye, Riverside House is a discovery to thrill to. You'll find a period country retreat perfectly in tune with the best traditions of hospitality, charming yet informal, professional yet intimate. With just 15 elegantly furnished bedrooms, one can savour the relaxed and private house party atmosphere, while, as with any good host, there's a high importance placed on all things culinary. The restaurant boasts top honours from the AA courtesy of its distinctive brand of modern English cooking – and it does a mean afternoon tea too! So seek, find and enjoy!

Royal Crown Derby
Visitor Centre
194 Osmaston Road, Derby, DE3 8JZ.
Tel: (01332) 712800/712841

Learn about the production of Royal Crown Derby china from clay through to the finished hand decorated product.

• Working Factory Tours (*Weekdays only – booking required*) • Demonstration Studio • Museum • Factory Shop • Duesbury Restaurant • Ample Parking Visitor Centre open seven days per week throughout the year. For further information or to book a factory tour call

Country House Hotel situated at the gateway to the Peak National Park, overlooking the Bentley Brook and vale of the river Dove.

Great care has been taken by the Spencer family, in transforming their home into an acclaimed hotel. The imaginative approach to modern English cuisine is complimented by a notable list of wines.

**Callow Hall
Mappleton, Ashbourne
Derbyshire DE6 2AA
Telephone 01335 343403
Fax 01335 343624**

RIBER HALL
Matlock, Derbyshire DE4 5JU
Telephone: 01629 582295 Fax: 01629 580475
Email: info@riber-hall.co.uk
www.riber-hall.co.uk
14 Rooms (all en suite), 9 Four Posters
AA ☆☆☆, RAC ☆☆☆, ETC Silver Award
Prestigious, historic Derbyshire Manor House set in very peaceful and picturesque countryside Gourmet cuisine, AA two rosettes, RAC two Blue Ribbons, excellent cellar. Recommended by all major hotel and restaurant guides. Experience in our old walled garden and orchard, that rarest of today's commodities – pure tranquility and wonderful bird life.

RS 🍷⊘🅒🖵 🍽 P ⑪ V ⊘🏨🛏 SPECIAL 1 2 3 4 B

TUDOR COURT HOTEL
Gypsy Lane, Draycott, Derby DE72 3PB
Telephone: 01332 874581 Fax: 01332 873133
30 Rooms (all en suite). 2 Four Posters.
AA ☆☆☆. ETB 👑👑👑👑.
A mock Tudor hotel set in 6 acres of grounds and woodlands in a peaceful rural setting between Derby and Nottingham easily accessible via Junction 25 of the M1. All bedrooms have recently been refurbished and offer all modern comforts. The hotel is an ideal base for touring Derbyshire and Nottinghamshire and offers special deals including tickets to Alton Towers.

RS ⊘🅒🖵 🍽 P ⑪ V ✂ 🦢 ❀🛏 SPECIAL 1 2 3

Haddon Hall

Built over 600 years ago close to the historic market town of Bakewell, this magical old manor house has triumphantly withstood the passage of time.

William the Conqueror's illegitimate son, Peverel, and his descendants held Haddon for a hundred years before it passed into the hands of the Vernons. The following four centuries saw the development of the existing medieval and Tudor manor house from its Norman origins.

In the late 16th century, it passed through marriage to the Manners family, later to become Dukes of Rutland, in whose possession it has remained ever since. The house has changed little since the reign of Henry VIII, whose elder brother was a frequent guest, although the time-worn steps are a constant reminder of its great age.

The terraced gardens, one of the chief glories of Haddon, were added during the 16th century. Roses, clematis and delphiniums, colourful and fragrant, soften the harshness of the great stone buttresses and ancient yellow and grey walls of the house itself. Believed by many to be the most romantic garden in all England.

The unique charm of this magnificent old house and idyllic rose gardens has made it a popular choice with film producers over the years. Recently, Franco Zerirelli transformed the house into "Thornfield" for his version of Jane Eyre which was filmed almost entirely on location at Haddon Hall. Other productions filmed at Haddon include the BBC's Prince and the Pauper, Moll Flanders and most recently the Oscar nominated film Elizabeth.

Above all else, Haddon remains a family home, lived in and cared for.

Whatever your reason for visiting Haddon Hall, there is one thing you can take for granted – you will not be disappointed. Make sure you visit the finest surviving Medieval house in all England.

Address
Haddon Hall, Bakewell,
Derbyshire
Tel: 01629 812855
Fax: 01629 814379
Open 1 April to
30 September (Daily)
Mon - Thurs in October

Admission
Adults £5.75
Children £3.00
Concessions £4.75

Location
1½ miles south of Bakewell
on A6

Facilities
Gift Shop
Restaurant

Eyam Hall

Eyam Hall is a small but charming 17th century manor house in the centre of the famous "plague village" of Eyam and has been the home of the Wright family for more than three hundred years. The present family opened their home to the public seven years ago but it retains the intimate atmosphere of a much-loved private home. Under the watchful gaze of the Wright ancestors you will see the impressive stone flagged hall, a unique tapestry room, the bedrooms with its magnificent tester bed and costumes and all manner of fascinating artefacts. You may even come across the ghostly apparation of Sarah Mills, a young servant girl who drowned herself in the well and still answers the night bell.

Eyam Hall garden, admired by Gertrude Jekyll as a fine example of a 17th century garden and still in the process of restoration, will open in 2002.

The picturesque Eyam Hall farmyard has been restored as a working Craft Centre attracting an astonishing variety of craftsmen. Visitors will find stencils, stencilled gifts and paints, attractive bowls and vases, beautiful hand-tooled leather goods and picture frames. Garden ornaments and metal fountains are designed and made in the fascinating Copper Mountain workshop. Stained glass windows and Tiffany lamps are created in Glasslights. One of our most unusual craftsmen makes violins and other stringed instruments. Consequently, music making plays an important part in the Craft Centre and on a sunny day in the yard visitors are frequently entertained by an impromptu folk trio.

A huge variety of gifts, cards and home accessories can be bought from the Aladdin's cave which is Saddlebacks Gift Shop.

Your visit to Eyam Hall will not be complete without sampling a delicious lunch or homemade cake from the licensed Buttery. Groups are catered for in the Art Gallery where they can enjoy a meal in the midst of contemporary paintings whilst admiring the 17th century roof trusses.

Eyam Hall runs a series of musical and drama events throughout the summer season.

Eyam Hall is also licensed for civil weddings which take place in the beautiful but intimate surroundings of the hall.

Eyam Hall,
Eyam,
Hope Valley,
Derbyshire S32 5QW
Tel: 01433 631976
Fax: 01433 631603

House open June, July &
August Tues, Wed, Thurs,
Sun, Bank Holiday Mons,
11am-4pm.
Guided Tours, Christmas
Tours, Weddings and
Events. Phone for details.

Craft Centre, Buttery and
Saddlebacks Shop open all
year every day except
Monday, 10.30am-5pm.

BOARS HEAD HOTEL

Litchfield Road, Sudbury, Derbyshire DE6 5GX
Tel: (01283) 820344 Fax: (01283) 820075

This 17th century house was lost from the famous Vernon estate through a game of cards! Guests arriving should be welcomed by the architectural beauty of this very old building. There is a warm bar, with natural brick walls, horse brasses and hunting horns. The residents' lounge looks onto a pretty patio where drinks are served in summer months. Much thought has been given to furnishing the delightful bedrooms which have every possible facility. There are two restaurants, the elegant Royal Boar with an imaginative à la carte menu and the less formal Hunter's Table Carvery and Bistro offering fresh fish, pasta dishes and splendid roasts, both at lunchtime and in the evening.

MAKENEY HALL

COUNTRY HOUSE HOTEL
Makeney, Milford Belper, Derbyshire DE56 0RU
Tel: 01332 842999 Fax: 01332 842777

Peace and tranquility are guaranteed at Makeney Hall, which is steeped in history and set in over six acres of glorious gardens overlooking the Derwent valley. Built as a Victorian country Mansion the house has been lovingly restored to a very high standard, while preserving its original charm and character. Many of the 45 bedrooms have panoramic views of the gardens and surrounding countryside. They are all traditionally furnished and decorated to the very highest standard in individual styles and have full en-suite facilities, trouser press, hairdryer, tea and coffee making facilities. Only twenty minutes drive from the M1 motorway, makes the ideal destination, with so many fascinating and famous places nearby, it would take a week-end just to sample a few of them!

AA
☆☆☆

AA 1993 Best Newcomer

AA

CALKE ABBEY

A great home with a big difference! No ordinary stately home, but a great house in a state of 20th century decline, set in a landscaped park. Walled garden and newly restored orangery, Pleasure ground and Church, Restaurant and Shop. Open daily except Thursdays and Fridays, April to October. 10 miles south of Derby on A514.

Telephone: 01332 863822

🌿 THE NATIONAL TRUST

MACKWORTH HOTEL
Ashbourne Road, Derby DE22 4LY
Telephone: 01332 824324 Fax: 01332 824692
14 Rooms (all en suite).
AA ☆☆☆, ETB 👑👑👑.
This much extended farmhouse, situated alongside the A52 Ashbourne Road, offers confortable accommodation. The carvery is very popular and there is a full à la carte menu available. Wedding receptions and other functions are catered for. Well tended gardens.

RS ((🛏 ⌲ 🍵 ♿ P ⅋ V GF ⌇ ❀ 🏠 **1 2 3** C

WIRKSWORTH HERITAGE CENTRE

Crown Yard, Wirksworth DE4 4ET
Tel: 01629 825225

"The Wirksworth Story". History for all the family. A former silk and velvet mill. Hear the quarryman's memories. See the contrast between the lead miner and the merchant. Find out how a well-dressing is made. Rescue the injured lead-miner on the computer. Find out about the regeneration of this historic market town.

Email: heritage@worksworth.fsbusiness.co.uk
www.gilkin.demon.co.uk

EAST LODGE COUNTRY HOUSE HOTEL
Rowsley, Matlock, Derbyshire
Telephone: 01629 734474 Fax: 01629 733949
15 Rooms (all en suite).
AA ☆☆☆, ETB 👑👑👑👑 Highly Commended.
Charming country house set in 10 acres of gardens amidst picturesque countryside, close to Chatsworth House, Haddon Hall, Bakewell and Matlock. The attractive lounge with log fire, elegant AA Rosetted restaurant with excellent cuisine and fine wines, and the 15 tastefully furnished en suite bedrooms combine to provide an idyllic location for relaxing breaks or small conferences.

RS (🛏 🍵 P ⅋ V GF ❀ 🏠 **SPECIAL 1 2** C

Amber Valley
the Heart of Derbyshire

DERBYSHIRE

Set in the heart of Derbyshire, Amber Valley offers glorious scenery which forms the background for tranquil villages and bustling market towns. Within the green fields and dense woodlands are a range of attractions that will appeal to all ages and interests. The River Derwent flows through Amber Valley forging the route of the National Heritage Corridor.

There are excellent transport attractions: At the Midland Railway Centre, enjoy the nostalgia of the era of steam and take in the numerous exhibits at the impressive Museum. Just a few miles away, the National Tramway Museum at Crich offers unlimited journeys along the tramway route with spectacular views across open countryside.

Wingfield Manor is set on the hillside overlooking South Wingfield village. This was the setting for the famous Babington plot involving Mary Queen of Scots, that changed the course of history. To the south is Kedleston Hall, which is one of the most important buildings associated with the Scottish architect Robert Adam.

There are beautiful gardens and parks throughout Amber Valley. In the early Spring and Summer visitors to Lea Gardens may enjoy one of the largest collections of rhododendrons and azaleas to be found anywhere in the country. Adjacent to the River Gardens at Belper, the Derwent Valley Visitor Centre is housed in the historic North Mill.

For a complete contrast, American Adventure offers an exciting day out for all the family. The theme park is situated close to Shipley Country Park with its miles of footpaths and bridleways.

Most people love a bargain and with Amber Valley's Individual Factory Shops Trail to guide you, visitors will be able to find the outlets for household name manufacturers. Amongst these are Denby Pottery with its superb Visitor Centre, where the skills handed down over the years can be witnessed.

The history and heritage of the Amber Valley links it with famous names worldwide. Samuel Slater was a Belper apprentice who travelled to Pawtucket in Rhode Island to establish America's cotton mass production. Another local man, Robert Watchorn became Commissioner of Immigration at Ellis Island in 1905. Whilst Florence Nightingale of Holloway was the daughter of a local landowner and became perhaps the most famous woman in the world.

Easily accessible from National and Regional airports or by rail or road, Amber Valley is well worth including in your visit.

For further information contact:
Sally Bruckshaw,
Tourism Unit,
Town Hall,
Market Place,
Ripley,
Derbyshire DE5 3BT
Tel: 01773 841482
Fax: 01773 841487
Email:
tourism@ambervalley.gov.uk
www.ambervalley.gov.uk

MILL END HOTEL
Chagford, Devon TQ13 8JN
Tel: 01647 432282 Fax: 01647 433106

A converted 18th century water mill beautifully situated on the banks of the River Teign on the edge of the Teign Gorge. The traditional English gardens flow down to the edge of the river and are an ideal spot for a pre-dinner drink or an afternoon cream tea. The relaxed country house atmosphere is enhanced by the slowly turning water wheel, the log fires and the peaceful views over the river and the gardens with Castle Drogo beyond. Ideal for walking, fishing or just relaxing.

The Restaurant at Mill End has a wonderful combination of superb award-winning food and a great atmosphere. The Restaurant has recently won two Red Rosettes and several other prizes for their modern British cuisine. Complemented by an extensive wine list and award-winning Westcountry Cheese Board.

EXETER CRAFTS GUILD
AT QUAYSIDE CRAFTS

The work of the Exeter Crafts Guild is displayed on the ground floor of this attractive 17th century building next to the Custom House on the city side of the River Exe. It was originally used as a bonded store. Quayside Crafts is run, and the shop manned, by members. Come and choose from our fine selection of work by over 50 local craftsmen and artists. Enjoy the riverside with its many features and lovely walks. Relax in our Coffee Shop and enjoy the home-cooked food. View our changing exhibitions by visiting artists.

Open 10am to 5pm Every Day (except Christmas Day and Boxing Day).

42 THE QUAY, EXETER, DEVON EX2 4AL
Telephone: 01392 214332

CASTLE DROGO
Near Drewsteignton, Devon

Extraordinary granite and oak castle which combines the comforts of the 20th century with the grandeur of a baronial castle with 'upstairs' and 'downstairs' rooms on display. Terraced formal garden with herbaceous borders and rose beds, and a huge circular croquet lawn. Delightful walks along the River Teign.

***Open** – Castle: 1 April to 31 Oct daily except Fri
(but open Good Fri) 11.00-5.30.
Garden: All year daily 10.30 to dusk.
House and Garden £5.40 adult, £2.60 child.
Located 4 miles south of A30 via Crockernwell.
Telephone: 01647 433306*

For details of other National Trust houses and gardens, please ring 01392 881691

 THE NATIONAL TRUST

ST OLAVES COURT HOTEL
Mary Arches Street, Exeter EX4 3AZ
Telephone: 01392 217736 Fax: 01392 413054
15 Rooms (all en suite), 3 Four Posters
AA ☆☆☆, RAC ☆☆☆, ETB ☆☆☆☆, Best Loved Hotels, Johansens, AA ❀❀.
Famous for its restaurant and home from home atmosphere. 400 yards from Exeter Cathedral. Lovely Georgian building with just 15 en suite rooms standing in own walled gardens. An oasis in the city centre. Central to the enjoyment of St Olaves is the excellence of the cooking. It is delicious!

 RS 🄲🄲🄳🄳 P 🍴 V GF ❀ 🏠🏠 SPECIAL 1 2 3 4 C

BARTON CROSS HOTEL
Huxham, Stoke Canon, Exeter EX5 4EJ
Telephone: 01392 841245 Fax: 01392 841942
9 Rooms (all en suite)
AA ☆☆☆ ❀❀, RAC ☆☆☆.
Inglenook fireplaces and heavily beamed ceilings all add to the charm of this small, thatched hotel which is run in a relaxed and friendly manner. Its setting in the Exe Valley in the midst of the Devon countryside is a peaceful one. Bedrooms are equipped with every modern creature comfort and the cooking skills of Paul Bending have won many awards, producing unique dishes from local produce.

RS 🍷🚭🄲🄲🄳🄳 P 🍴 V GF ↙↤↩❀ 🏠🏠 1 2 3 C

DEVON

City life seems a long way away when you explore the East Devon Area of Outstanding Natural Beauty. And you will be in for surprises in countryside which is little known, but incredibly beautiful and varied.

The Heritage Coast, stretching from Lyme Regis to Budleigh Salterton, shows the lush, highly coloured scenery of classic 'postcard Devon'. Devon red sandstone meets the sea in a coastline of sheer high cliffs, steep wooded combes and coves, its line startlingly broken by the white chalk of Beer Head. This coastline is familiar to those who prefer quieter, traditional holidays. Its character is gentler than the rugged coastlines that lie further west, but it is unmistakably Devon.

Inland, the landscape rises to high, flat and surprisingly remote plateaux, often topped by heathland commons, rich in wildlife. Cutting into the plateau the Rivers Axe, Sid and Otter flow north south through hedge bordered meadows. The smallest tributaries of these rivers create a web of small valleys or combes which arise, spring fed, in deep narrow 'goyles', forming inaccessible ancient places shrouded in woodland.

The AONB's estuaries, heaths and cliff top grasslands are important natural habitats and the 'Undercliffs' – the spectacular five mile landslip near Axmouth – is a National Nature Reserve of great geological and wildlife interest. Elsewhere, there are many wildlife and classic geological sites to discover. Hilltops are frequently characterised by remains of prehistoric settlements, often Iron Age forts, with spectacular views.

The AONB is well served with footpaths and bridleways and a wide range of self-guided routes are available from Tourist Information Centres. The Coastal Path is challenging in places, but with the variety of scenery and wildlife and the opportunity to stop off at the attractive coastal towns and villages, it is well worth the effort. Another long distance path, the East Devon Way, cuts through some of the best countryside in the AONB. Starting beside the Exe Estuary in Exmouth, the path continues across country for 40 miles to Lyme Regis. The more adventurous may choose to continue back to Exmouth, following the Coastal Path on a 65 mile circular route, thereby enjoying a combination of some of the country's most beautiful countryside and coast. Four circular paths link in with the East Devon Way and provide another option for those who wish to take their time and explore quiet more remote areas.

A number of cycle routes are also available from the TICs, free of charge. One of them, "The Buzzard Trail", is an 80 mile route which circles the Blackdown Hills AONB and passes through quiet country lanes and villages. It is possible to complete it all in one day, but it can be done in stages and thereby allow the cyclist time to savour the scenery.

The East Devon Way Guide is an excellent general guide to the area, well illustrated by a variety of local artists and photographers. Copies may be obtained from the Rural Affairs Officer, East Devon District Council, Knowle, Sidmouth, Devon EX10 8HL for £4.95+40p p&p.

Addresses

Tourism Department East Devon District Council The Knowle, Sidmouth, Devon EX10 8HL. Tel: 01395 516551

Exmouth TIC Tel: 01395 222299

Budleigh Salterton TIC Tel: 01395 445275

Sidmouth TIC Tel: 01395 516441

Ottery St. Mary TIC Tel: 01404 813964

Honiton TIC Tel: 01404 43716

Seaton/Beer/Colyton TIC Tel: 01297 21660

Axminster TIC Tel: 01297 34386

HOLNE CHASE HOTEL AND RESTAURANT
Nr Ashburton, Devon TQ13 7NS
Telephone: 01364 631471 Fax: 01364 631453
Internet: www.holne-chase.co.uk
Email: info@holne-chase.co.uk
17 Rooms (all en suite). AA ☆☆☆ ❀❀❀
"Being in a particularly secluded and Romantic Situation"
in a sheltered fold of the Dart Valley, some 350 feet above
sea level with a striking view. The Hotel is surrounded by its
own grounds of about 70 acres within Dartmoor National
Park. The last wilderness in Southern England, Dartmoor is
wonderful country to explore, either on foot or horseback.
There is a mile of salmon fishing in the grounds and more
extensive fly fishing on Dartmoor. Croquet and Putting in
the gardens. Excellent standard of cuisine and well stocked
cellar to complement.

GLAZEBROOK COUNTRY HOUSE HOTEL
Glazebrook, South Brent, Devon TQ10 9JE
Telephone: 01364 73322 Fax: 01364 72350
11 Rooms (all en suite), 4 Four Posters. AA ☆☆ ❀
The unique family run hotel within the heart of Devon,
which provides tradition, style and finesse to cater for your
every need from a wedding to a romantic meal for two. The
ideal location to explore the area in a totally relaxing
atmosphere and enjoying the finest food around.

BERRY HEAD HOTEL
Berry Head Road, Brixham, Devon
Telephone: 01803 853225
32 Rooms (all en suite). 1 Four Poster.
AA ☆☆☆. ETB ♛ ♛ ♛ ♛ commended.
Steeped in history, set in superb water's edge position,
enjoying spectacular views of Torbay and surrounded by six
acres of grounds in the seclusion of the National Park, yet only
a short walk from the picturesque fishing port of Brixham. A
super location for Walking, Sailing, Angling or simply
relaxing a warm welcome and a memory to Treasure...

THE EDGEMOOR
Haytor Road, Lowerdown Cross, Bovey Tracey,
Devon TQ13 9LE
Telephone: 01626 832466 Fax: 01626 834760
Email: edgemoor@btinternet.com
www.edgemoor.co.uk
17 Rooms (all en suite), 2 Four Posters.
AA ☆☆☆ ❀❀, RAC ☆☆☆, Which? Hotel Guide,
Johansens Recommended.
Romantically styled country house hotel on eastern edge of
Dartmoor National Park. Superb position for touring.
Beautiful gardens, lovely bedrooms (all en suite). Horseriding
nearby. Two AA Rosettes for food. "Epitomizes a gracious
English Retreat", *Dallas Morning News.* Friendly attentive
staff. Personally run by resident proprietors Rod and Pat Day.
Elegance without pretension.

Ugbrooke Park

Ugbrooke Park has been the Clifford family home for three hundred years. Nestled in the heart of beautiful Devonshire countryside, rolling hills and quiet parkland. Ugbrooke is a treasure in a unique setting awaiting discovery by the culturally inquisitive.

Robert Adam redesigned the original House and Chapel, dating from the 13th century, in 1750. At the same time Lancelot 'Capability' Brown landscaped the Park creating with his 'magic wand' lakes, swatches of majestic trees and views towards Dartmoor.

Fascinating tours of the House relate stories of Clifford Castles, Shakespeare's 'Black Clifford'. Henry II's 'Fair Rosamund'. Lady Anne Clifford who defied Cromwell, the Secret Treaty of Dover, the Cardinal's daughter, Charles II's Lord High Treasurer Clifford of the CABAL and tales of intrigue and espionage.

Since the early 1960s when the 13th Lord and Lady Clifford began a programme of restoration, Ugbrooke has been transformed. The present 14th Lord and Lady Clifford have continued that transformation to create a family home of authentic style balanced with charm and comfort. This unique, castellated manor house now provides elegant accommodation for special interest groups or executive conferences. While Lady Clifford has swept through the house with her style of interior design and decor, discovering treasures hidden away in the attics, restored and cared for, Lord Clifford has supervised the Park restoration including an extensive tree planting programme following Brown's parkland style.

The Lakeside walk, Spanish garden, the palm tree approach to the 18th century Orangery (now a tea room complete with elaborate *trompe l'oiel* painted by the Head Gardener) the 200 year old box parterre, the Rose Garden and Hydrangea Walk, provide tranquility and delight.

Ugbrooke Park is easily accessible, situated at the end of the M5 motorway, signposted off the A380. Exeter Airport is only twenty minutes away or there is ample landing space for helicopters.

Visitor Information
Ugbrooke House
Chudleigh,
Devon TQ13 0AD
Tel: 01626 852179
Fax: 01626 890729
www.historichouses.co.uk

Open
2nd Sunday in July to 1st Thursday in September, Tues, Wed, Thurs,,Sun and BH Mon, 1.00-5.30pm. Guided tours at 2.00 and 3.45pm.

Admission
Adults £4.80, Senior Citizens £4.50, Groups of 20 and over £4.50

Bickleigh Castle

A warm welcomes awaits at Bickleigh Castle where you can enjoy 900 years of history within the walls of this outstanding historic house, still a lived in and much loved home. Restoration projects both in the castle and grounds mean that there is always something new to see. Cars, coach parties, (by prior appointment), weddings or events are all welcome at Bickleigh Castle, so do come and enjoy some time with us, we would love to meet you.

Refreshments can be found at the Exe-Cargo licenced restaurant for lunches and tea or dinner by reservation. Tel: 01884 855731.

Bickleigh Castle is situated 4 miles south of Tiverton, 11 miles from Exeter, just off the A396. Follow the signs from Bickleigh Bridge

Bickleigh Castle
Nr Tiverton,
Devon EX16 8RP
Tel: 01884 855363

Opening times Easter Sunday to following Friday, then Sundays, Wednesdays and Bank Holidays till May Bank Holiday then daily (except Saturdays) until the first Sunday in October from 2pm. Last party at 4.30pm Adults £4.00. Children (age 5-15) £2.00. Family tickets (2 adults and 2 children) £10.00.

COOMBE HOUSE
COUNTRY HOTEL

Coombe House is an elegant Georgian Manor House nestling in 5 acres of a hidden valley in the rural heart of Devon. The house lies midway between Dartmoor and Exmoor, is equidistant from the north and south coasts and a 15 min journey by car from the cathedral city of Exeter. There are 7 National Trust properties, 4 castles and the Royal Horticultural Society's national garden at Rosemoor within a 20 mile radius.

Coombe House Country Hotel
Coleford, Crediton, Devon EX17 5BY
Tel: 01363 84487 Fax: 01363 84722
Email: coombschs@eurobell.co.uk
AA ☆☆☆
AA Rosette for Cuisine

A La Ronde

Summer Lane, Exmouth,
Devon EX8 5BD
Tel: 01395 265514

A unique 16 sided house built in 1796 for two Sainster cousins Jane and Mary Parminter, with stunning views over the Exe Estuary and beyond. Containing collections and pastimes put together by the cousins using feathers, sand and seaweed, cut paper and shells.

FAIRWATER HEAD HOTEL
Hawkchurch, Axminster, Devon EX13 5TX
Telephone: 01297 678349 Fax: 01297 678459
20 Rooms (all en suite)
AA ☆☆☆ ❀, RAC ☆☆☆, Country House Hotel, RAC 2 Dining Awards.
Where Dorset meets Devon. Welcoming country house hotel in peaceful landscaped gardens with glorious views across the Axe Valley. Enjoy friendly staff, award winning chefs and family hospitality. Near the coastal resorts of Lyme Regis and Charmouth. Coastal golf courses nearby.

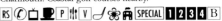

THE KINGS ARMS INN
Stockland, Honiton, Devon EX14 9BS
Tel: 01404 881361 Fax: 01404 881732
3 Rooms (all en suite).
A 17th century former coaching inn offering an extensive range of modern British and classic cuisine, complemented by an interesting wine list, well-kept ales, ciders, lagers, many malts, havannas etc. Hidden away but lively! From £20-£25 single

RED LION HOTEL
The Quay, Clovelly, Bideford, Devon EX39 5TF
Telephone: 01237 431237 Fax: 01237 431044
11 Rooms (all en suite). AA ☆☆, ❀ (Red)
Located on harbour front, overlooking the Quay at foot of picturesque fishing village with cobbled street and donkeys. Hotel has been sensitively renovated to provide modern en suite facilities. All rooms have sea/harbour views. Seafood a speciality. Vehicular access for hotel residents.

THE GRAND HOTEL
Elliot Street, The Hoe, Plymouth, Devon PL1 2PT
Telephone: 01752 661195 Fax: 01752 600653.
www.plymouthgrand.com
77 Rooms (all en suite).
AA ☆☆☆, ETB ♛♛♛♛ Commended.
The Grand Hotel is situated in an unrivalled location on Plymouth Hoe, with magnificent seaviews over the Sound. Just a few minutes' walk will see you in the city centre or at the Barbican, where the Pilgrim Fathers set sail for America. Acclaimed for its first class, friendly service, the Grand is a perfect combination of prime efficiency and old world charm.

Powderham Castle

DEVON

Powderham Castle is the historic home of the Earl of Devon and has stood beside the River Exe for centuries. This magnificent stately home is still lived in by the Courtenay family, whose ancestors built the Castle around 1390.

The fascinating tours around the State Rooms allow visitors to hear tales of the family history as well as the development of the Castle from its medieval origins to its 18th century transformation into a grand country house. Best known as the venue for the Merchant Ivory film The Remains of the Day, film fans will instantly recognise the Grand Staircase and Wyatt's beautiful Music Room.

In the last few years a great deal of work has gone on to improve and restore the gardens and grounds.

The tranquil Rose Garden is a favourite for many, not least it's senior resident, 155 year old Timothy the Tortoise, whose home it has been since the 1930's. This garden, with it's views over the Park to the Exe Estuary is filled with a fantastic display of older English roses whose scent and colour is memorable.

The lake below the castle walls provide an easy circular walk and is a great opportunity to spot local wildlife. For those with more time, a visit to the Woodland Garden is a must. Originally planted in the mid 18th century, it was allowed to go wild after about 50 years. Over the last two years, with help from the Countryside Commission, the garden has gradually been cleared, fenced and now replanted.

From here also the Belvedere Walk leads up through lovely woodland to the ruined Belvedere Tower. It is a steep climb but well worth it for the fabulous views from the top of the Exe estuary, from Exeter to the sea.

With the opening of the Farm Shop and Plant Centre visitors can enjoy the castle grounds 364 days a year. Sample wonderful shopping, the centre specialises in West Country and Estate grown produce.

Families and children will enjoy Powderham's Children's Secret Garden. Open a door in an old brick wall and a wonderful surprise greets you. Under an apple tree wallow three happy pigs. Jemima puddle ducks paddle the ponds and tiny rabbits, guinea pigs, chicks and chinchillas peer out from the old cold frames. Whilst grown ups sit in this sunny garden, admiring the doves in their dovecote and the peafowl strutting the lawns children can run around in full view and complete safety making new friends around every corner.

Powderham Castle
Exeter
Devon EX6 8JQ
Tel: 01626 890243
Fax: 01626 890729
www.powderham.co.uk

Open
2 April-29 Oct
10am to 5.30pm

Farm Shop Centre
Open 364 days a year (closed Christmas day), daily 9am-6pm (Sunday 11am-5pm).

Admission 2000
Adults £5.85, Senior Citizens £5.35, Children £2.95

Facilities
Courtyard Restaurant, Gift Shop, Farm Shop, Plant Centre, Bothy Restaurant.

Two Bridges Hotel

Two Bridges, Dartmoor, Devon
Tel: 01822 890581 Fax: 01822 890575

Dartmoor's warmest welcome awaits at our delightful 18th century former Coaching Hotel set on the banks of the West Dart River in 60 acres of private grounds. 29 very well-appointed en suite rooms, many with four poster beds and jacuzzi baths. AA 2 Red Rosette Tors Restaurant with menus reflecting a wide range of imaginatively presented dishes using only the finest of local fresh produce. Comfortable lounges with blazing log fires and our traditional Saracens Head Public Bar (don't miss our own home brewed Jail Ale).

"…a fabulous find at the heart of the Moor"

WHITE HOUSE HOTEL

Chillington, Kingsbridge, Devon TQ7 2JX
Tel: 01548 580580 Fax: 01548 581124
AA ☆☆ ETC ☆☆ Silver

The White House is a Grade II listed building set in an acre of lawned and terraced gardens. A small Country House Hotel of seven en-suite rooms which has a magical atmosphere reminiscent of a quieter and less hurried age. The Copper Beech Restaurant, overlooking the garden offers excellent home cooked food using fresh local produce. An ideal base for a relaxing holiday in the beautiful South Hams.

The Bedford Hotel

1 Plymouth Road, Tavistock PL19 8BB
Tel: 01822 613221
www.warm-welcomehotels.co.uk

Built in 1820 in a castellated style, the Bedford Hotel was originally a private home to the Dukes of Bedford. Occupying the site of a Benedictine Abbey, the 15th century gateway and ancient stone of the Abbey still remain. Situated in the ancient market town of Tavistock on the edge of Dartmoor National Park. Renowned for some of the finest food in the west country. A warm welcome awaits all.

While in Devon
visit the
MUSEUM OF DARTMOOR LIFE
Okehampton

Step back in time in this attractive Victorian Courtyard.

Explore the three galleries that tell you the story of life on Dartmoor throughout the centuries

★ **Award Winning Displays** ★
★ **Local walks starting point** ★
★ **Tea Rooms and Crafts shop** ★

Open 10am-5pm Monday to Saturday from Easter to October, plus Sundays June to September. For Winter opening times please ring.

All at the Museum Courtyard, 3 West Street, Okehampton 01837 52295

PROMOTING AWARENESS OF DARTMOOR'S HERITAGE

West Devon

West Devon is an area of great beauty and tranquillity. At its heart is Dartmoor National Park. Here, the land rises to over 2000 feet in places and is characterised by its distinctive granite tors, huge open moorland and its most famous inhabitants – the Dartmoor ponies.

Surrounding Dartmoor is a gentler mix of countryside blending perfectly with the moorland skyline. You'll find very different and varied scenery here that's well worth exploring. Bronze Age settlements, traditional Devon longhouses, medieval churches and abandoned tin mines are scattered throughout the area.

Tavistock, the largest town in West Devon, is a thriving market town rich in history. A benedictine abbey was founded on the banks of the river Tavy in 974 and before the dissolution by Henry VIII it had become the largest and wealthiest abbey in South West England. Ruins of the abbey can be seen close to Bedford Square in the centre of the town.

Tavistock is a must for shoppers with its wide range of local and specialists shops. The Pannier Market, first held in 1105 takes place every Friday.

Sir Francis Drake, the town's most famous citizen is commemorated in a bronze statue at the end of Plymouth Road. You can also visit his home at Buckland Abbey and see his famous drum.

Okehampton, situated at the northern edge of Dartmoor has the oldest castle in Devon. It was built by the Normans and is well worth a visit. The Museum of Dartmoor life in West Street has award winning displays telling the story of the people who have shaped the landscape from the earliest hunter-gathers to modern farmers. A variety of exhibitions are held in the Museum and there are also extensive archives which can prove extremely useful if you are tracing your family tree.

Next door, Okehampton Tourist Information Centre is a valuable source of information on things to see and do in the area.

A wide range of shops are centred on Fore Street and the Victorian Arcade and Red Lion Yard feature specialist shops in pedestrian-only surroundings.

Information Centres:
Okehampton Tourist Information Centre
West Street
Okehampton
Tel: 01837 53020
Fax: 01837 55227

Tavistock Tourist Information Centre
Bedford Square
Tavistock
Tel: 01822 612938
Fax: 01822 618389

SHERBORNE CASTLE

Built by Sir Walter Raleigh in 1594, the Castle contains a fine collection of pictures, porcelain and furniture. Set in glorious lakelands and gardens it has been the home of the Digby family since 1617.

Gardens: Every day except Wednesdays from 10.00am.
Last admission 5.00pm.
Tearoom and Shop: Every day except Wednesdays from 12.30pm.
Last admission 5pm.
Castle: Tuesdays, Thursdays, Sundays and Bank Holiday Mondays from 12.30pm; Saturdays from 2.30pm. Last admission 4.30pm.
Throughout the season we will be pleased to make arrangements for party bookings (15+) during normal opening hours or private views at other times and days.

Telephone: 01935 813182
Email: enquiries@sherbornecastle.com
www.sherbornecastle.com

Purbeck House Hotel

"An oasis of relaxation and enjoyment"
ETB ♛♛♛ Highly Comm., AA ☆☆☆

A family-run hotel steeped in history, combining a country house with a modern hotel. The hotel nestles in expansive gardens in the centre of Swanage yet only 300 yards from the beaches.
Many rooms have views over the Purbeck Hills and Swanage Bay. All rooms en-suite with direct dial telephones, colour and satellite television, hospitality tray, ground floor bedrooms, disabled bedroom. Meals available in our restaurant or conservatory.
Fully licenced. Conferences, functions, wedding receptions and ceremonies catered for. Private car park. Children welcome.

Purbeck House Hotel
91 High Street, Swanage, Dorset BH19 2LZ
Tel: 01929 422872 Fax: 01929 421194
Email: purbeck.house@easynet.co.uk

The Eastbury Hotel
Long Street, Sherbourne, Dorset DT9 3BY
Tel: 01935 813131
Fax: 01935 817296
Proprietors: Tom & Alison Pickford
AA ☆☆☆ RAC

A beautiful townhouse which was built in 1740. During it's refurbishment great care was taken to preserve it's character. In fine weather guests can enjoy the seclusion of the Hotels tranquil walled garden. The bedrooms are individually decorated and each equipped with a full range of modern comforts and facilities.
The merited Eastbury Restaurant very tastefully presents a range of traditional English and Continental dishes which are completed by an extensive list of the worlds finest wines.

North Dorset with its peaceful, largely unspoilt countryside embraces the five small market towns of Blandford Forum, Gillingham, Shaftesbury, Stalbridge and Sturminster Newton. The many small thatched villages and quiet back roads would still be recognised by Thomas Hardy who lived here and the area featured strongly in his work.

In the south and east of the District are the Dorset Downs and Cranborne Chase, both officially recognised as areas of outstanding natural beauty. A feature of the expansive landscape is the high chalk land with hills approaching 1,000 feet and panoramic views of the Isle of Wight, the Purbeck Hills in the south and the Mendips in the north, suitable for walking, riding, cycling or just picnicking and admiring the view from one of the many grassy areas to which the public have access. The Blackmore Vale occupies the western part of the District. In summer this is a lush pastoral landscape and the visitor can spend days meandering through the maze of small roads, footpaths and bridleways.

North Dorset is still one of the most peaceful and genuinely unspoilt parts of rural England. For those who really appreciate the English countryside and our heritage of history and fine buildings, this is a wonderful place for a holiday or a short break. The market towns within the District are all worthy of a visit. Shaftesbury is one of the oldest towns in England, standing at a height of more than 700 feet, overlooking the Blackmore Vale, Shaftesbury's Abbey was founded in 888 AD by King Alfred the Great, whose daughter was the first Abbess. The Abbey ruins are now open to the public and provide a tranquil and peaceful haven.

Blandford Forum is delightfully situated in the wooded valley of the River Stour and is an ancient crossing point of the river. The town is unique in having been almost totally re-built after the 'Great Fire' of 1731. The local architects, the Bastard Brothers, co-ordinated re-building in the Georgian style and produced the distinctive and beautiful town centre which we see today. To the southwest of Blandford lies Milton Abbas with its superb Abbey Church. Two hundred years ago, the Earl of Dorchester cleared the original town of Milton Abbas and rehoused the occupants in the 'new' thatched village. This is one of England's finest examples of a complete estate village.

Sturminster Newton stands on the northern end of a fine six arched medieval bridge over the River Stour. On the south side of the bridge lies Sturminster Mill. The mill is driven by a water turbine and open to the public. Sturminster Newton was the home of Thomas Hardy for years and he would still recognise much of the local architecture.

Address
For more information on North Dorset please contact the Tourist Information Centre at the Marsh and Ham, West Street, Blandford Forum, Dorset
Tel/Fax: 01258 454770
or Bell Street, Shaftesbury, Dorset
Tel: 01747 853514
www.ruraldorset.com

BEECHLEAS
Hotel & Restaurant
17 Poole Road, Wimborne Minster, Dorset

Award-winning Hotel & Restaurant, a beautifully restored Grade II listed Georgian House. All en-suite accommodation, elegant Georgian bedrooms or cosy Coach House and Lodge bedrooms. Delightful restaurant with open fire autumn and winter. Lovely Conservatory for summer and spring. Family-run with a warm welcome and a feel of quality about everything. Ideal to explore Thomas Hardy country, Purbeck Hills, New Forest, National Trust properties such as Corfe Castle, Kingston Lacey, Badbury Rings Iron Age Encampment, Bournemouth and Poole.

RAC Blue Ribbon, AA ★★ ❀❀, Good Hotel Guide.

ETB ☆☆ Silver Award

Contact Josephine McQuillan
Tel: 01202 841684 Fax: 01202 849344

KINGSTON LACY HOUSE
Wimborne, Dorset BH21 4EA
Tel: 01202 883402 Fax: 01202 882402
Email: wklgen@smtp.nttrust.org.uk

Beautiful 17th century house containing outstanding collection of paintings, including works by Van Dyck, Titian and Brueghel and exhibition of Egyptian artefacts from 3000 BC. The garden changes through the seasons. Walks through 250 acres of wooded parkland. Herd of Red Devon cattle. Shop and Restaurant. Events leaflet available.

THE NATIONAL TRUST

CHETTLE HOUSE is a fine example of English Baroque architecture, designed by Thomas Archer and built c. 1715.
Open: Sundays only 11am-5pm, Easter to end September.
Stay at the Castleman Hotel and Restaurant in the village, which is in the heart of Cranborne Chase. Chettle House, Chettle, Dorset, DT11 8DB.
Tel: House 01258 830209, Hotel 01258 830096

♣THE♣
MANOR
HOTEL

16th century Manor House 500 yds Chesil Beach. Jacobean oak panelling and flagstone floors. Fully licensed, 13 en-suite bedrooms all with TV, direct dial telephone, room service, Children welcome, baby listening, panoramic views of Dorset coast from most bedrooms. Bar meals. Last orders 10pm. Special diets. Excellent reputation for cuisine and service. Three real ales. Character cellar bar. Log fires. Conference facilities, max 60. Sea bathing. Golf 5 miles. Riding 2 miles. Open all year. Credit cards accepted.

THE MANOR HOTEL
West Bexington, Dorchester, Dorset DT2 9DF
Telephone: 01308 897616 Fax: 01308 897035

LA FOSSE AT CRANBORNE
London House, The Square, Cranborne, Wimborne, Dorset BH21 5PR
Telephone: 01725 517604 Fax: 01725 517778
3 Rooms (all en suite).
◆◆◆ commended, AA ❀
A charming, family-run restaurant with rooms all 'en-suite' in the village of Cranborne, on the edge of the Chase. Fantastic value, £65.00 for a double room including F. E. breakfast, dinner from £12.00.

¶□☕ P ⑪ V ⤬ ⟶🏥 SPECIAL 1 2 3 C D

THE LANGTON ARMS
Tarrant Monkton, Nr Blandford, Dorset DT11 8RX
Telephone: 01258 830225 Fax: 01258 830053
6 Rooms (all en suite).
Other awards: Good Pub Guide.
Village England at its best: idyllic countryside and picturesque thatched cottages, 17th century and thatched the Langton Arms is a free house with a very good name for food. Six guest rooms around an attractive flowered courtyard. 2 night break £50.00 p.p.

RS ⓒ□☕ P ⑪ V GF ⤬ ⟶🏥🏥 SPECIAL 2 3
C/D

Purbeck

Purbeck is one of Dorset's best kept secrets. Its superb coastline has been declared a heritage coast for its stunning beauty and amazing geological formations and is a proposed World Heritage Site. Explore hidden coves, secret caves, Jurassic cliffs and majestic rock formations populated by a wide variety of wildlife including puffins and birds of prey and, in the waters around, playful dolphins.

However, the coastline is not Purbeck's only star attraction! Much of the countryside inland has been officially designated as an Area of Outstanding Natural Beauty. Nestled amongst these stunning hills and vales are outstanding attractions such as the dominating and romantic ruins of Corfe Castle, Durlston Country Park perched dramatically on the cliff top and an 18th century Castle at Lulworth complete with magnificent grounds.

Purbeck is also the ideal place to discover more about Lawrence of Arabia, its famous son. Close by to his house is the world famous Tank Museum which amuses children of all ages for hours with its exciting and unique exhibits. Or for a different form of escapism, Monkey World, a famous monkey sanctuary, is situated nearby.

Purbeck is delightful with small villages of stone, cob and thatch. It also has one of Britain's favourite seaside resorts, Swanage, whose charming beach and bay can be enjoyed by all. Also to be discovered is the ancient town of Wareham, once one of the most important towns in the country in Saxon times, and now a peaceful town that is gaining a reputation as a centre for locally produced food.

There are also so many ways to explore Purbeck! A steam railway travels through spectacular scenery from Corfe Castle to Swanage. There are also many bus links enabling you to enjoy your holiday without using your car. However, if you really want to discover the secrets of the countryside, there are many walking routes which take in hidden rock formations, sightings of rare wildlife, spectacular beaches and views over the second largest harbour in the world!

Accommodation is plentiful and can suit all types of visitors. From historic farmhouses to small guesthouses, camping and caravanning to self catering and some large hotels in the town and countryside, Purbeck has it all.

So, what are you waiting for? Purbeck will offer you a warm welcome, whenever you come.

Address
Purbeck Tourist
Information Centre,
Holy Trinity Church
South Street, Wareham,
Dorset BH20 4LU
Tel: 01929 552740
Email:
purbecktic@compuserve.com

THE BRIDGE TOBY HOTEL
Croxdale, County Durham DH1 3SP
Telephone: 0191 378 0524 Fax: 0191 378 9981
46 Rooms (all en suite).
The hotel is set on the outskirts of Durham, one of Britain's most historic cities. Relax and enjoy a drink in the traditional Lounge Bar before dining in the Toby Carving Room, which offers an excellent range of starters, main courses and desserts. The hotel is perfectly placed on the A167 being only 3 miles south of the town centre and close to the A1.

RS ⊘ ⊘ 🛏 🍽 P ⅲ V GF ✂ 🚗 SPECIAL
1 2 3

THREE TUNS SWALLOW HOTEL
New Elvet, Durham City DH1 3AQ
Telephone: 0191 386 4326 Fax: 0191 386 1406
AA/RAC ☆☆☆, ETB 👑 👑 👑 👑
50 Rooms (including 2 suites).
The Three Tuns is a former 16th Century coaching inn which has been discreetly modernised to retain much of its original character. The hotel is situated in the heart of Durham City, only 15 minutes from the Cathedral and Castle. Free use of Leisure Club facilities at our sister hotel, the Royal Country, only 200 yards away, is available for all our residents.

RS ⊘ ⊘ 🛏 ⚲ 🍽 P ⅲ V ✂ 🚗 🚗 SPECIAL
1 2 3 4 C

KENSINGTON HALL HOTEL
Kensington Terrace, Willington, Co Durham DL15 0PJ
Telephone: 01388 745071 Fax: 01388 745800
10 Rooms (all en suite), AA ☆☆, ETB 👑 👑 👑, Les Routiers
Small cosy hotel – friendly staff – excellent food. Eight miles from Durham City on A690. Perfect for Wear Dales, Beamish Museum, Raby Castle or Bowes Museum. Was originally an old 'Parish Hall' built in 1914.

RS ⊘ 🛏 🍽 P ⅲ V ✂ 🚗 🚗 1 2 3 4 C

Teesdale

The River Tees is one of England's great rivers and is the heart of Teesdale, a beautiful, unspoiled world in County Durham, Land of the Prince Bishops. Access to Teesdale is from the A1(M) at Scotch Corner, the M6 at Penrith and Tebay and from Darlington with its high-speed rail services. The important A66 cross-Pennine route passes through the District.

Although Teesdale is relatively easy to reach it has not suffered from the pressures of large numbers of visitors and is an ideal area for those in search of peaceful countryside, heritage and the outdoor life.

The starting point for many trips in Teesdale is the historic market town of Barnard Castle, a bustling little place which is full of fascinating old shops and a wonderful centre for antique collectors. It is also home to the Josephine and John Bows Museum, a magnificent French style chateau housing art collections of international importance and set in beautiful gardens. There are also lovely gardens open to the public at Eggleston Hall close to the River Tees between Middleton-in-Teesdale and Barnard Castle. Then there are the beautiful gardens at Raby Castle, near Staindrop built by the Nevill family in the 14th century and one of the country's most impressive medieval castles, set in an extensive deer park.

Another attractive base for touring is Middleton-in-Teesdale which grew up as the main centre of lead mining in the 19th Century and which retains its historical character. It is an ideal base for walking and is situated on the well-known Pennine Way and new Teesdale Way long-distance footpaths. The countryside around here is all included in the North Pennines Area of Outstanding Natural Beauty, the highlights of which are the magnificent waterfalls on the River Tees, upstream of Middleton – Low Force, High Force and Cauldron Snout. There are also many walks in Hamsterley Forest in the north of the District, which also has facilities for picnicking, cycling and nature studies and is ideal for families. As an alternative, there is the popular Whorlton Lido situated beside the River Tees, 4 miles east of Barnard Castle. The Otter Trust reserve near Bowes Village is also ideal for families.

The beauty of the countryside of Teesdale has long been an attraction for visitors and has inspired artists and painters, including Cotman and Turner, as well as the writers Sir Walter Scott and Charles Dickens. Teesdale formed the basis of the novel "Nicholas Nickleby" and you can visit the sites associated with the story on The Dickens Drive – leaflets are available from the T.I.C. in Barnard Castle.

Barnard Castle Tourist
Information Centre
Woodleigh
Barnard Castle
Co Durham
DL12 8AA
Tel: 01833 690909

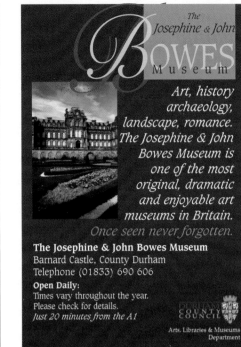
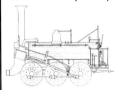
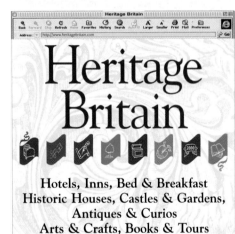

Wear Valley

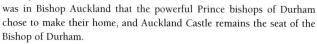

The Wear Valley is a "District of Contrasts", with a subtle blend of ancient and modern. Over the centuries man has shaped the landscape and environment, resulting in picturesque stone-build villages, miles of dry-stone walls and dramatic features carved into the countryside, a legacy of the long-gone lead mining industry in Weardale. The heritage of the past blends with a modern range of attractions and activities. Wear Valley offers something for everyone.

A journey from the head of Weardale takes the visitor from England's highest tourist attraction at Killhope Lead Mining Centre, through an area with a rich Methodist tradition and down via Dales villages to the wider plains of the River Wear. Fine examples of a Saxon Church at Escomb and a Roman Hypocaust at Binchester remind us that this has been an important settlement for centuries. It was in Bishop Auckland that the powerful Prince bishops of Durham chose to make their home, and Auckland Castle remains the seat of the Bishop of Durham.

Visitors can enjoy outdoor pursuits – fishing, golf and riding are popular, and walkers and cyclists are well catered for. The Coast to Coast cycle route passes through Weardale and other local routes are equally testing. Walkers can choose to tackle challenging paths such as the Weardale Way, or enjoy more leisurely rambles, including routes specifically designed for the disabled and small children.

Crafts and rural arts, culture and creativity are represented through the Wear Valley with interpretative displays and exhibitions at the Durham Dales Centre in Stanhope, the Weardale Museum and Bishop Auckland Town Hall. Browse in the local shops, markets and fairs. Traditional annual agricultural shows draw crowds back to the Dale year after year.

Accommodation and hospitality range from hotels to cosy local pubs, farmhouse bed & breakfast, self-catering cottages and caravan sites, to suit all tastes and budgets. Our hosts take pride in serving local produce and supporting the Dale's agricultural community.

Extending into the heart of the North Pennines, Wear Valley offers the opportunity to relax and sample northern English countryside – and hospitality – at its best.

Further information can be obtained from:

Economic Development & Tourism Department,
Wear Valley District Council,
Civic Centre,
CROOK,
DL15 9ES
Tel: 01388 761575/761579
Fax: 01388 766660
Email:
b.burdess@wearvalley.gov.uk
www.wearvalley.gov.uk

Tourist Information Centres:

Durham Dales Centre,
Castle Gardens,
Stanhope
Tel: 01388 527650

Town Hall,
Market Place,
Bishop Auckland
Tel: 01388 604922

Chelmsford

ESSEX

Chelmsford can trace its origins to Roman times, when a settlement called "Caesaromagus" grew up near the River Can. Little is known about the Roman settlement, but sited on the main road from London (with the equivalent of a motel!) it was an important site – and the only place in Britain honoured by the imperial prefix in its name.

The Saxons settled nearby, and one of them, possibly called Ceolmaer, may have given his name to the river Chelmer, its ford and the town. He may even have been related to the 7th century Saxon King of Essex whose rich burial was discovered nearby.

In 1199 a new town was established on the site of the modern town centre and King John granted it the right to hold a weekly market. By 1250, Chelmsford was acknowledged as County Town of Essex, a position it holds to the present day.

Gradually Chelmsford became an important industrial and techno-

Great Waltham – one of Chelmsford's outstanding villages

logical centre. Most famously, Guglielmo Marconi established the world's first radio factory here in 1896. In 1920 Chelmsford was the venue for the world's first public broadcast entertainment with Dame Nellie Melba singing from an improvised studio. Many aspects of Chelmsford's fascinating history are displayed in an excellent local museum.

Today, Chelmsford is a modern, bustling town, surrounded by Essex's finest countryside with a wealth of attractive villages, historic buildings, churches and characterful local pubs. Its continuing importance as an administrative, industrial and technological centre is easily forgotten among the parks, pedestrianised High Street shopping area, and the interesting streets that make up the older parts of the town.

Chelmsford Cathedral dates from the 1400s – one of many attractive, historic buildings. It is also the venue for the annual Chelmsford Cathedral Festival each May, a week of musical events featuring artistes of international standing. Nearby are the town's two theatres, which together with award-winning outdoor events, and many amateur groups make up a thriving cultural scene.

One of Chelmsford's most famous sons was Thomas Hooker (1586-1647), one of the founding fathers of the USA. He emigrated to America, founded Newton (now Cambridge, Mass), Hartford, Connecticut and a new state. He was also credited with the institution of the Fundamental Articles, the forerunner of the modern Constitution.

Tourist Information Centre
County Hall
Market Road
Chelmsford
Tel: 01245 283400
or visit us on
www.chelmsfordbc.gov.uk

Mon – Fri
9.30am – 5pm
Sat 9.30am – 4pm

Hedingham Castle

Castle
Hedingham,
Nr. Halstead,
Essex CO9 3DJ.

Telephone:
01787 460261

Facsimile:
01787 461473

Hedingham Castle, Castle Hedingham:
Splendid Norman keep built in 1140 by the
famous de Veres, Earls of Oxford. Approached
by lovely Tudor bridge. Visited by Kings
Henry VII and VIII and Queen Elizabeth I,
and besieged by King John. Magnificent
Banqueting Hall with Minstrels' Gallery and
finest Norman arch in England. Beautiful
grounds, peaceful woodland and lakeside
walks. Beside medieval village with fine
Norman Church.
Open from Easter to October 10.00am-5.00pm
Enquiries telephone: 01787 460261

Maison Talbooth Hotel

Stratford Road, Dedham, Essex CO7 6HN
Tel: 01206 322367 Fax: 01206 322752
Email: mtreception@talbooth.co.uk
www.talbooth.com

Tranquility is the essence of this Victorian country house,
which enjoys a superb position on a bluff overlooking the
river valley, stretching away to the medieval church of
Stafford St. Mary. Ten spacious bedrooms are decorated
with a sure sense of colour and the luxurious bathrooms
are a special pleasure. Breakfast and light meals are
available in the hotel, but for lunch or dinner guests dine
at the internationally known Le Talbooth Restaurant,
which is within walking distance or a minute away in the
hotel courtesy car.

Saffron Walden and the Uttlesford District

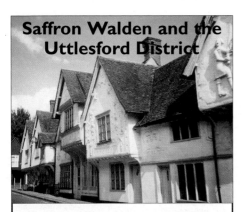

Historic country towns with a wealth of
timber-framed thatched cottages in a
beautiful unspoilt undulating countryside,
yet with easy access from London and
Cambridge. Ideal for a short break or a
longer stay to explore East Anglia.

*Contact for a free brochure and
comprehensive Accommodation Guide:*

**Tourist Information Centre (HH)
1 Market Place, Saffron Walden
Essex CB10 1HR. Tel: 01799 510445
Email: tourism@uttlesford.gov.uk**

INGATESTONE HALL

Hall Lane, Ingatestone, Essex CM1 3QF
(Half a mile from Ingatestone High Street via Station Lane)
Tel: 01277 353010 Fax: 01245 248979

Sixteenth-century manor house with two priests' hiding-
places. On display are furniture, family portraits and
memorabilia accumulated over the centuries. There is a tea
room and gift shop.

Open to visitors (1pm to 6pm) on Saturdays, Sundays and
Bank Holidays from Easter until the end September.
Also, during the school summer holidays on Wednesdays,
Thursdays and Fridays. Guided tours for groups booked in
advance are also available at other times.

THE HEYBRIDGE HOTEL
Roman Road, Ingatestone, Essex CM4 9AB
Telephone: 01277 355355 Fax: 01277 353288
22 Rooms (all en suite)
AA ☆☆☆, RAC ☆☆☆, ETB 🏨🏨🏨 Highly Comm.
We offer guests accommodation in a number of highly
appointed deluxe garden rooms, all located on the ground
floor. The Tudor style restaurant is acclaimed for its excellent
cuisine and the newly revised à la carte menu is ideally
complemented by a comprehensive wine cellar.

RS 🍽 🕾 🕐 🖵 🕮 🖬 P 🍴 V GF 1 2 3 4 B

Layer Marney Tower is the tallest Tudor gatehouse in Britain. Visitors may climb the Tower and enjoy the views over the Essex countryside as far as the River Blackwater estuary. The 80 ft tall Tower is the principal feature of the 300ft long range of buildings that Henry 1st Lord Marney constructed in the middle years of the reign of Henry VIII. There are further outbuildings and the Long Gallery that may be visited, together with the Church that has the fine tombs of both Henry Marney and his son John.

The gardens are both beautiful and peaceful, featuring some unusual trees and shrubs and having very attractive roses. In addition there is a farm walk of approximately 2.5 km which afford marvellous views of the buildings as well as the deer in the surrounding paddocks. The medieval barn houses part of the collection of rare breed farm animals, many more of which may be seen on the short walk around the pond. Visitors may bottle feed the lambs and goats in April and May, and feed the other animals throughout the season.

There is a gift shop with guides, postcards, souvenirs and some local produce and it also sells meat from the farm. The Tea Room is situated in the old Stables and has a fine range of hot and cold drinks and cakes. Lunches and afternoon teas are our speciality. Above the gift shop and Tea Room is the Corsellis Room – originally part of retainers accommodation. It is now used for wedding ceremonies, concerts and other functions. It has a magnificent oak roof with pincer beams and ogee wind braces and houses the Manderley Dolls House.

Special events are arranged throughout the year, including outdoor theatre, craft fairs, workshops etc. Layer Marney Tower may be hired for wedding ceremonies, receptions, concerts, conferences and other events.

Location
Layer Marney Tower,
Mr. Colchester, Essex CO5 9US
Tel: 01206 330784
Fax: 01206 330784

Opening Times 2001
Every day except Saturday,
1st April-7th October,
12 noon-5pm
(22nd July to 7th September
11am-5pm).
Bank Holidays 11am-6pm.
Group visits and Guided tours
may be arranged throughout
the year.

Admission
Adults £3.50, Children £2.00,
Family (2 Adults + 2 Children)
£10.00.

BUCKLAND MANOR
Country House Hotel
Buckland, Gloucestershire, WR12 7LY
Tel:(01386) 852626 Fax: (01386) 853557
E.Mail: Buckland-Manor-UK@msn.com

Situated near the Cotswold village of Broadway, Buckland Manor retains an exquisite charm which beckons those seeking a luxurious break or holiday - whatever the season.

Surround yourself with the comfort and splendour which is eminent from the 14 beautifully furnished bedrooms, log fires, immaculate gardens and fine cuisine.

The hotel has been ecommended by Relais Routier, Egon Ronay and Michelin whilst maintainsing an AA Three Red Star rating with three rosettes for cuisine

THE SWAN HOTEL
Bilbury, Gloucestershire G17 5NW
Tel: +44(0)1285 740695 Fax: +44 (0)1285 740473
Email: swanhot1@swanhotel-cotswolds.co.uk

A luxurious hotel with cosy parlours, elegant dining room, sumptuous bedrooms (a few with four poster beds) and lavish bathrooms (some with double jacuzzi/baths).
Our 2 AA Rosette dining room boasts menus created by Head Chef Shaun Naen and his brigade in a Modern English style. While for a more informal meal we have Jankowski's Brasserie. An ideal base for touring the Cotswolds, visiting Shakespeare's Stratford, Roman Baths, antiques in Brford and the Oxford Colleges. Relax in our private garden on the banks of the River Coln or soak up the ambience of one of England's prettiest villages or fish for your own trout.

Laverton Meadow House
Nr. Broadway WR12 7NA
Tel: 01386 584200
Fax: 01386 584612
Email: andrea@lavertonmeadows.demon.co.uk
www.accommodation-cotswolds.co.uk/andrea.html

A beautiful Cotswold house with stunning views set in lovely gardens with large outdoor pool surrounded by tranquil meadows. In an area of outstanding beauty, near Broadway. Winchcombe, Cheltenham, Stratford-upon-Avon are nearby and we are in easy reach of all the attractions that make the Costwolds a delight to visit.

Large romantic rooms with king size canopied beds, antique furniture and spacious bathrooms provide luxury accommodation. Full English breakfast is served in the farmhouse kitchen warmed by the Aga. Superb candlelit dinners are served in our beautiful private dining room.

A warm welcome and relaxed friendly atmosphere. A log fire and a sherry awaits you in the delightful sitting room and the promise of a perfect treat.

Cotswold Tourism

Anyone in search of the true English Countryside need look no further than the Cotswolds, considered by many to be amongst the most beautiful areas in England. Two things above all give the Cotswolds their special warmth and richness: the soft, natural limestone and the wealth of the wool trade in days gone by which has left a heritage of superb buildings. The Cotswold Hills rise gently from the green meadows of the Upper Thames and its tributaries in the east to the great western escarpment where the hills plunge dramatically into the Vales of Severn and Evesham. The river valleys cutting through the plateau form the setting for many of the small towns and villages, which are the great delight of the Cotswolds and seem almost to 'grow' in the surrounding landscape.

Several of the Cotswold villages such as Bibury and Bourton-on-the Water are world famous as the quintessence of the English rural scene. Less well known are the smaller villages away from the main road, each with its own secrets waiting to be discovered by the more adventurous traveller with time to go deeper into the real Cotswolds – perhaps an unspoilt historic church set on an older, iron age rampart, an unassuming pub with a log fire in the hearth, serving locally brewed real beer and good food, or a stone bridge spanning a crystal clear stream – each one in its unique setting, given harmony by picturesque cottages and imposing manor houses of Cotswold stone.

Exploring the real Cotswolds at any time of the year is a rewarding experience, each season throwing a different light on the changing scene. An Area of Outstanding Natural Beauty an interest in itself, the Cotswolds are an excellent centre for visiting nearby heritage towns – the university City of Oxford, Stratford-upon-Avon, the Regency Spa Towns of Cheltenham and Bath.

For more information contact:

Cotswold Information Centre,
Hollis House,
The Square,
Stow-on-the-Wold
Gloucestershire
GL54 1AF
Tel: 01451 831082
Fax: 01451 870083

For Free Accommodation Guide
Tel: 01285 643812
Fax: 01285 641345
Email:
tourism@cotswold.gov.uk

THE GREENWAY

Shurdington, Cheltenham,
Gloucestershire GL51 5UG
Tel: 01242 862352 Fax: 01242 862780

Set in 10 acres of formal gardens and grounds, this 16th century Manor House is renowned for it's warm welcome, fine food and friendly service. With 19 luxury bedrooms and its outstanding restaurant, it is perfect for all occasions whether on business or for pleasure. Special breaks and activity weekends are available all year.
19 Rooms (all en suite), 1 Four Poster,

AA ☆☆☆ (Red), ❀❀❀ for Restaurant, RAC
☆☆☆ Blue Ribbon for Excellence.

ACANTHUS COURT is a lovingly restored handsome Regency house. It has been transformed into a private luxury hotel full of period character.

ALL ROOMS ARE PROVIDED WITH:
Direct line telephone
Colour television and radio
Tea & Coffee making facilities
Trouser press • Fresh fruit
Mineral water • Luxury toiletries

PLEASE CALL FOR A BROCHURE AND TARIFF:
59 Leckhampton Road, Cheltenham GL53 0BS
Telephone 01242 576083 Fax: 01242 224579
Website: www.acanthus-court.co.uk
ETC ♦♦♦♦ GUEST HOUSE ACCOMMODATION **GOLD AWARD 2000**

CHARLTON KINGS **HOTEL** & RESTAURANT

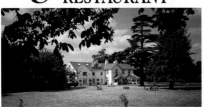

Situated in an area of outstanding natural beauty on the edge of Cheltenham Spa in an acre of award winning gardens. We are ideally placed to tour the Cotswolds. (Ask for your free 'Romantic Road' Guide when checking-in).

The AA recognised the culinary skills of our Chef and awarded us a Rosette in 1997. The hotel itself has recently been totally refurbished, no detail has been overlooked. All bedrooms are ensuite with bath and shower – some are reserved for non-smokers. Although we have high standards the hotel is run informally, providing for the needs of each guest individually. Whether you stay for a night or a week you will be well cared for at the Charlton Kings Hotel.

AA, RAC & ETC ☆☆☆ Silver Award for Quality

**Charlton Kings, Cheltenham
Gloucestershire GL52 6UU**
Telephone: 01242 231061 Fax: 01242 241900

THE PRESTBURY HOUSE HOTEL AND RESTAURANT

The Burgage, Prestbury, Cheltenham, Gloucestershire GL52 3DN
Telephone: 01242 529533 Fax: 01242 227076
www.SmoothHound.co.uk/hotels/prestbur.html
17 Rooms (all en suite), 2 Four Posters.
AA/RAC ☆☆☆, ETB ♛♛♛♛ Comm, Ashley Courtney. 300-year-old Ancestral Country House situated in 5 acres of grounds in the tranquil Cotswold village of Prestbury. Only 1½ miles from beautiful Regency Cheltenham Town Centre. House is steeped in history. Ideal for touring Shakespeare's country, Bath, Oxford and Warwick. Acclaimed oak panelled restaurant. Log fires, golf, horseriding, shooting and hill walking.

HOTEL ON THE PARK

Evesham Road, Cheltenham, Gloucestershire
Telephone: 01242 518898 Fax: 01242 511526
12 Rooms (all en suite), 1 Four Poster and 2 suites.
AA ☆☆☆ (Red), RAC ☆☆☆, ETB ♛♛♛ deluxe. The nationally acclaimed On the Park is an exclusive town house hotel, overlooking Cheltenham's Pittville Park. All 12 individually styled bedrooms and suites blend antique furniture and designer fabrics with every modern comfort found in a small, luxury hotel. The Restaurant offers some of the finest in modern British cooking today.

The Pittville Pump Room and Park

Cheltenham's beautiful Pittville Pump Room not only gives visitors the chance to step back in time and "take the waters", there's also a wide range of recreational and sporting facilities to enjoy within the splendid grounds of Pittville Park. With its fine Regency architecture, and the world famous Racecourse on its doorstep, the Pump Room and Park provide a fascinating insight into a bygone age, alongside excellent modern leisure facilities.

Built between 1825 and 1830 the Pump Room was planned as the centrepiece of a grandiose estate, belonging to wealthy landowner, politician and entrepreneur, Joseph Pitt. During its Regency heyday it was the largest and most magnificent of several buildings where the renowned Cheltenham Spa Waters could be taken.

The spa waters can still be tasted today from the original marble and scagliola pump, although now they are pumped electrically from the well, 80 feet below, rather than by the traditional handpump

method. Medical men in the 19th century considered Cheltenham's waters as something of a cure-all, prescribing them to their wealthy clients for a variety of disorders. The Pittville spa water is unique in that it is the only natural alkaline water in Great Britain – but be warned, it is salty!

The Pump Room is a regular venue for hire to classical and contemporary live music bands in the park and private dinners, as it was traditionally intended.

A walk around Pittville Park is a delight in any season, with its open lawns, gracious trees, shrubs and attractive lakes.

You can also enjoy a game of golf on our 18 hole pitch and putt course, play tennis, skateboard and rollerblade, mess about in boats on the lake, or go fishing. An orienteering track takes the active all the way around the Park.

Pittville Pump Room
Pittville Park
Cheltenham
Gloucestershire
Tel: 01242 523852
Fax: 01242 526563
Email:
jayneb@cheltenham.gov.uk

Open Times
11am-4pm
Closed Tuesday

Sudeley Castle

The Cotswolds is the largest Area of Outstanding Beauty in Britain and represents traditional England at its best. The beautiful countryside is complemented by the villages of honey-colored stone, which retain their unique style and character.

Set against the beautiful backdrop of the Cotswold hills Sudeley Castle is regarded as one of England's most romantic castles. It has royal connections spanning a thousand years and has played an important role in the turbulent and changing times of England's past.

Sudeley was once the magnificent palace of Queen Katherine Parr, Henry VIII's last and surviving wife who is buried in the castle church. Henry VIII, Anne Boleyn, Lady Jane Grey and Elizabeth I stayed at Sudeley. Charles I resided here while his nephew, Prince Rupert, established Sudeley as his garrison headquarters during the English Civil War.

After its desecration by Cromwell's troops the castle lay sadly neglected, much of it in ruins. Sudeley's fortunes were however to change some 200 years later when it was acquired by the Dent brothers, famous glove manufacturers from Worcester. They set upon an ambitious programme of restoration. Upon their death this task was taken up by their nephew John Croucher Dent and his wife, Emma Brocklehurst. Today Sudeley is home to the Dent-Brocklehurst family.

Surrounding Sudeley Castle are ten magnificent gardens each with their own special beauty and charm. Centrepiece is the Queen's Garden, named after Katherine Parr and famous for its magnificent collection of old fashioned roses interspersed with fragrant herbs and surrounded by yew hedges and fine examples of topiary. A Knot Garden was opened in 1995 to commemorate a visit by Queen Elizabeth in 1592, the design of which was inspired by the fabric from the Queen's dress depicted in a painting which hangs in the Castle.

Sudeley is located a quarter of a mile from the Saxon town of Winchcombe, once the ancient capital of the Kingdom of Mercia. The town has retained many features of its long history yet is still largely uncommercialised and unspoilt – features which appeal to the discerning visitor and resident alike.

Open daily 3rd March to 28th October, 10.30am-5.30pm.

Admission
Castle & Gardens:
Adults £6.20,
OAP's £5.20,
Children £3.20

Gardens & Exhibition Centre:
Adults £4.70,
Concessions £3.70,
Children £2.50

Special discounted rates for groups

Free Parking, Castle Apartments, Church and Gardens, Exhibition Centre, Castle, Gift Shop, Plant Centre, Restaurant and Tea Rooms, Picnic Area, Adventure Playground.

Call 01242 602308 for list of special events.

Sudeley Castle & Gardens
Winchcombe,
Gloucestershire
GL54 5JD.
Tel: 01242 602308
Fax: 01242 602959

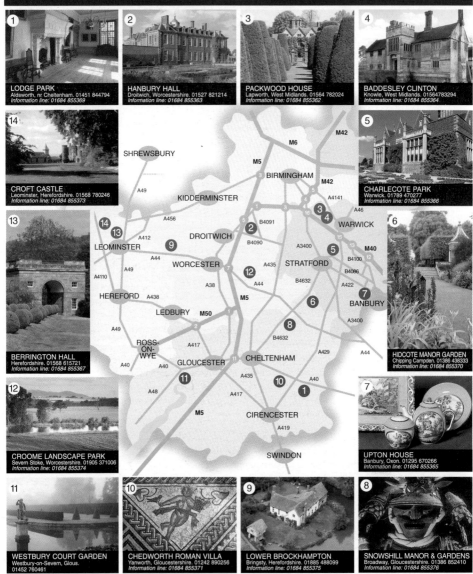

Berkeley Castle

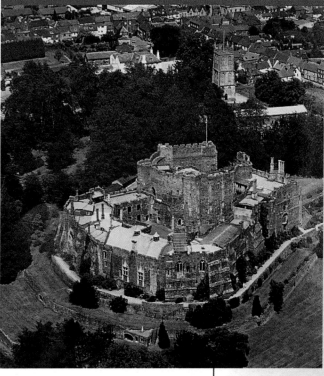

This beautiful and historic Castle begun in 1117 still remains the home of the famous family who gave their name to numerous locations all over the World, notably Berkeley Square in London, Berkeley Hundred in Virginia and Berkeley University in California.

Scene of the brutal murder of Edward II in 1327 and besieged by Cromwell's troops in 1645, the Castle is steeped in history. The state apartments contain magnificent collections of furniture, tapestries and rare paintings by primarily English and Dutch masters. Part of the famous Berkeley silver is on display in the dining room. Many other rooms are equally interesting, particularly the Great Hall where the Barons of the west country met in 1215 before going to Runnymede to force King John to put his seal to Magna Carta.

Just off the A38 midway between Bristol and Gloucester, England's oldest inhabited castle and most historic home. Since 1153 twenty four generations of Berkeleys have transformed a savage norman fortress into a truly stately home full of treasures and history.

The Castle is surrounded by sweeping lawns and Elizabethan terraced gardens. The butterfly Farm is a tranquil oasis with hundreds of exotic butterflies in free flight. There is a plant centre at the butterfly farm stocked with outdoor plants, shrubs, house plants, china and earthenware

Berkeley Castle,
Gloucestershire
GL13 9BQ
Tel: 01453 810332

Free Car Parking,
Picnic Lawn, Tea Rooms,
Gift Shop.

2000 Opening Times
April & May, Tues to Sun
2pm-5pm.
June, Tues to Sat 11am-5pm,
Sun 2pm-5pm.
July & Aug, Mon to Sat
11am-5pm, Sun 2pm-5pm.
September, Tues to Sat 11am-
5pm, Sun 2pm-5pm.
Oct, Sundays only 2pm-
4.30pm.
Bank Holiday Mondays
11am-5pm.
Enquiries: 01453 810332

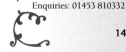

The Stroud Valleys

Imagine the vibrant green of English countryside – a quiet corner where the march of time seems to have stood still. Imagine a tranquil spot on the edge of the Cotswold Hills – where land falls away giving views across the Berkeley Vale to the Horseshoe Bend of the majestic River Severn, with the Welsh Hills on the skyline beyond. Imagine leafy green tunnels sprayed with sunlight breaking through the branches. Imagine the Stroud Valleys.

This is England at its very best – unspoiled, unhurried, undiscovered. This is Gloucestershire – the Stroud Valleys – a veritable treasure trove. Trace the remains of ancient civilisations. Walk in the footsteps of the Romans. See the scars of the Civil War. Hunt out Stroud's industrial legacy – a fascinating tribute to an era which thrived on the wool of the Cotswold sheep and the power of the waterwheel.

Walk in the superb countryside; take a flight in a glider; visit a Rococo garden; fly in a balloon; play a round of golf; feed the birds in a wildfowl sanctuary; explore a castle; eat lunch in a converted mill or a timeless rustic pub; enjoy a home-made ice-cream; marvel at a unique Gothic mansion; browse in Painswick, the 'Queen of the Cotswolds'; fly a kite on National Trust land; take the children to a picnic site; ride a horse; take dinner in a first-class restaurant, the possibilities are literally endless.

Easily reached by train or motorway, the Stroud Valleys offer quality accommodation, whether you choose self-catering, bed and breakfast or a luxury hotel. You will remember 'good value for money', and the friendliness of the local people.

Whilst staying in and around Stroud you can make use of its close proximity to Cheltenham, Gloucester, Bath or Stratford for excursions. Or you can simply relax and unwind: re-discover a leisurely pace of life you may have thought had gone forever.

For FREE colour brochure/ accommodation list – please contact: Subscription Rooms, George Street, Stroud, Glos. GL5 1AE
Tel: 01453 765768
Fax: 01453 755658
Email: stroud.tic@dial.pipex.com

TEWKESBURY PARK HOTEL GOLF & COUNTRY CLUB

Lincoln Green Lane, Tewkesbury,
Gloucestershire GL20 7DN
Tel: 01684 295405 Fax: 01684 292386

Just 5 minutes drive from the hectic M5 motorway and you'll find yourselves in the medieval town of Tewkesbury. Situated high on a hill with breathtaking views across the Malvern Hills sits Tewkesbury Park Hotel Golf & Country Club. This charming Victorian Manor house has been tastefully extended to provide comfortable accommodation and exquisite dining. Take advantage of our challenging 18 hole par 73 parkland course and the 6 hole par 3 course, or simply relax and enjoy some pampering in our Beauty salon!

Your visit is complemented by full Leisure facilities to include:
• *indoor heated swimming pool* • *fully equipped gymnasium* • *fitness centre* • *tennis and squash courts* • *jacuzzi* • *sauna* • *solarium*

Local attractions include the medieval town itself with famous Abbey and the "bloody meadow" battlefield. Sudeley Castle, the Cotswold villages, Stratford-upon-Avon & Cheltenham Spa are all within easy reach.

The Lamb Inn

Great Rissington, Cheltenham,
Glos. GL54 2LP
Tel: (01451) 820388 Fax: (01451) 820724
Paul & Jacqueline Gabriel

The Lamb Inn is situated sitting beside the Village Green in a quiet, unspoilt Cotswold Village. This award-winning 17th Century Inn boasts an attractive bar, with an excellent choice of home-cooked bar meals. We also offer a variety of good wines and real ales. Alternatively, the candlelit restaurant with it's antique pine tables offers an à la carte menu using fresh local produce. The 14 delightful bedrooms are individually furnished including two new garden suites, "Millies House" and "Jemmimas House", both king size beds. Why not pay us a visit? Open Christmas and New Year.

THREE WAYS HOUSE
Mickleton, Chipping Campden, Gloucestershire
Telephone: 01386 438429 Fax: 01386 438118
41 Rooms (all en suite).
AA ☆☆☆, RAC ☆☆☆.
This charming Cotswold village hotel is close to Chipping Campden Broadway and Stratford-upon-Avon, and is renowned as the "Home of the Pudding Club", an institution for devotees of the great British Pud! With 40 comfortable bedrooms and a restaurant serving some of the best food of its kind, make Three Ways House a must in your Cotswold itinerary.

RS 🚭 📞 🖨 🛏 ☕ P ⅰↀⅰ V GF ⚓ 🏨 🏨 SPECIAL 1
2 3 4 C

PETTY FRANCE HOTEL
Dunkirk, Badminton, Avon GL9 1AF
Telephone: 01454 238361 Fax: 01454 238768
20 Rooms (all en suite), 2 Four Posters.
AA ☆☆☆❀ RAC ☆☆☆ and Merits ETB 🍷🍷🍷 Comm.
Petty France Hotel is a small Georgian and Regency house set in extensive private gardens located at the edge of the Cotswolds and run by the owners in an informal manner. Modern French and English food is served in the light and airy Regency dining room. A large lounge and small cosy bar both with fireplaces offer guests a place to meet and relax. Twelve rooms which are built in the old stables offer unusual charm.

RS 🚭 📞 🖨 🛏 ☕ P ⅰↀⅰ V GF ⚓ ❀ 🏨 🏨 SPECIAL
1 2 3 4 C

HILTON PUCKRUP HALL HOTEL AND GOLF CLUB
Puckrup, Tewkesbury GL20 6EL
Telephone: 01684 296200 Fax: 01684 850788
112 Rooms (all en suite). Please quote 'Essence of England' Guide. Situated between the Cotswold and Malvern Hills in over 140 acres of secluded wood and parkland, Puckrup Hall Hotel combines the elegance of a former 17th Century Georgian Mansion with the amenities of a modern luxury hotel. The hotel offers extensive conference and leisure facilities and is surrounded by its own par 70, 18 hole championship golf course. Located just 3 miles north of Tewkesbury on the A38, or 2 miles from Junction 8 of the M5. Puckrup Hall is an ideal location for an overnight stay or weekend break.

RS 🚭 📞 🖨 🛏 Q ☕ P ⅰↀⅰ V 🍴 SP ⚓ ↦ ⚓ ❀
🏨 🏨 SPECIAL 1 2 3 4 C

TUDOR HOUSE HOTEL
High Street, Tewkesbury, Glos GL20 5BH
Telephone: 01684 297755 Fax: 01684 290306
21 Rooms (15 en suite), 1 Four Poster.
AA ☆☆, RAC ☆☆, ETB ☆☆☆☆
A 15th century Coaching Inn steeped in history and still retaining a lot of it's original features. We pride ourself on good food and hospitality served in comfortable surroundings. The Tudor is an ideal place to relax and get away from it all and is near to major tourist destinations.

📞 🖨 🛏 ☕ P ⅰↀⅰ V 🏨 🏨 SPECIAL 1 2 3 4 C

Cotswolds & Severn Vale
Tewkesbury & Winchcombe...
Discover a compendium of secrets

GLOUCESTER SHIRE

The historic mediaeval town of Tewkesbury contrasts beautifully with the traditional Cotswold wool town of Winchcombe. Explore the rivers and valleys of the Severn and Avon or enjoy the rolling countryside of the Cotswold Hills. You'll be bewitched by Tewkesbury, a town renowned as having one of the best mediaeval black and white townscapes in the country. Discover the hidden charms along narrow alleyways where the eaves of crooked timber buildings nearly touch. There is plenty to see and do. Explore the famous Norman Abbey which will fascinate those interested in the historical. Enjoy adventures along the rivers by renting a boat or taking a leisurely cruise.

Winchcombe makes the perfect base to explore the mysteries of the Cotswolds. When you've admired its handsome, timeless honey coloured stone buildings, visit the Folk and Police Museum and the secret Railway Museum. Take time to discover Hailes Abbey, the romantic ruin of an ancient Cistercian Abbey and of course, Sudeley Castle with its glorious gardens and 1,000 years of Royal connections. See a traditional Jacobean Cotswold manor house at Stanway, a collectors paradise at Snowshill Manor, the Gloucestershire Warwickshire Railway where you can relive the days of steam, and if aircraft inspire you more, find the Jet Age Museum at Staverton.

Take a short break... for a relaxing weekend, enjoy a leisure break or special interest break throughout the year or over one of our special event weekends such as the Mediaeval Fayre or Water Festival. If you live life at a more leisurely pace, enjoy some of our beautiful countryside by walking or cycling. The area is also a golfer's paradise with many high quality golf courses. For those interested in arts and crafts, Winchcombe, Conderton and Bredon potteries are perfect for watching craftsmen at work. Nature in Art is the perfect gallery for nature lovers and the Beckford Silk Mill or Elaine Rippon can delight you with their original hand printed silks.

Accommodation ranges from working farms to high quality hotels, many offering golf and leisure facilities. Our wide range of comfortable guest houses and self catering establishments can be found in the centres of our historic towns or set amidst our beautiful countryside. The region also has excellent caravan and camping sites. There's plenty to tempt you to stay in our beautiful and historic area.

For more information on short breaks, places to visit and accommodation send for our free Visitor Information Pack.
Tel: +44 1684 272096 and quote heritage.
Tewkesbury Tourist Information Centre
Tel: +44 1684 295027
Winchcombe Tourist Information Centre
Tel: +44 1684 602925
Email:
coxa@tewkesburybc.gov.uk
www.tewkesburybc.gov.uk

NATURE IN ART

The world's first museum dedicated exclusively to art inspired by nature!

Twice specially commended in the National Heritage Museum of the Year Awards, in scope, appeal and stature Nature in Art offers an unrivalled experience in its ever-changing collection of work in any medium from any period and any country. From life-size sculptures to Picasso, David Shepherd to ethnic art, tapestries to ceramics, there is something for everyone? International wildlife artists demonstrating February to November. Art courses and events.

**OPEN: Tues-Sun 10am-5pm & Bank Hols.
Free parking • Cafe • Shop • Garden • Full
wheelchair access • Artists at work**

Telephone: 01452 731422

Find us 2 miles north of Gloucester on main A38

www.nature-in-art.org.uk

WESTONBIRT ARBORETUM

DISCOVER THE TRANQUIL BEAUTY OF ONE OF THE WORLDS FINEST TREE & SHRUB COLLECTIONS. SET IN 600 ACRES OF LANDSCAPED GROUNDS, A PLACE TO VISIT AT ANY TIME OF THE YEAR.

SPRING – Magnificent displays of rhododendrons, magnolias and bluebells. SUMMER – Tranquil walks in leafy glades. AUTUMN – Breathtaking kaleidoscope of autumn colour. WINTER – Wonderland of evergreen foliage. GROUNDS – Open all year 10.00-20.00hrs (or dusk if earlier). 17 miles of paths. VISITOR CENTRE – Open Mar to Dec 10.00-17.00hrs. Video presentation. Exhibition. Country gift shop. PLANT CENTRE – Open all year 10.00-18.00hrs. COURTYARD CAFE – Open as Visitor Centre. TOILETS – With disabled facilities. PICNIC AREAS.

**WESTONBIRT ARBORETUM
Telephone: 01666 880220
3 miles south of Tetbury on A433** Forest Enterprise

PRINKNASH ABBEY POTTERY

Prinknash Abbey, Cranham, Gloucester GL4 8EX
Telephone: 01452 812239
Open all year

A visit to Prinknash Pottery, situated in one of the beauty spots of England, is of unique interest. The Benedictine community welcomes visitors to the abbey church and grounds. These offer relaxation in a tranquil atmosphere with a breathtaking view of the Vale of Gloucester. Guides are available to conduct visitors on a tour of the pottery viewing gallery. It is the ideal venue for UK and worldwide visitors. Most of the articles that can be seen being made in the pottery are on sale in the shop which is open every day, excluding Christmas Day, Boxing Day and Good Friday.

FRAMPTON COURT

Frampton-on-Severn, Gloucester
Telephone: Mrs Clifford 01452 740698 (office), 740267 (home)

Listed Grade I, Vanburgh 1732. Stately family home of the Cliffords who have lived at Frampton since granted land by William the Conqueror, 1066. Fine collection of original period furniture, tapestries, needle work and porcelain. Panelled throughout. Fine views over parkland to extensive lake. A famous Gothic orangery, 1750, stands reflected in Dutch ornamental canal. Open all year by appointment, £4.50. Accommodation. Near jct. 13 of M5 motorway.

**FOR A JOURNEY
THROUGH BRITAIN**
Daily 10am-5pm
• Historic Boats
• Working Engines
• Blacksmith
• Hands-on displays

*A GREAT DAY OUT
Fun for all*

QUEEN BOADICEA II
**Daily 45 minute cruises Easter to
October
Departs Merchants Quay
For information:
Tel: 01452 318054
Llanthony Warehouse, Gloucester
Docks, Gloucester GL1 2EH**

Gloucester

The City of Gloucester is a compact and exciting City full of contrasts and surprises, where each period of history has left it's mark – whether it be the Saxon Priory of St Oswald, the magnificent Norman Cathedral or Blackfriars, the best preserved Priory in Britain.

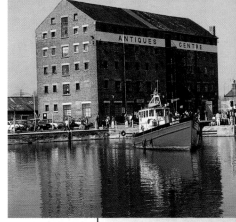

Nestling in College Court, next door to the Cathedral, is Beatrix Potters 'House of the Tailor of Gloucester', the very house Beatrix Potter used as the tailors house in her favourite book "The Tailor of Gloucester". Today, it is a unique gift shop, with displays of Beatrix Potters life and work, and is open to visitors all year.

The historical development of Gloucester unfolds in the City Museum, with views of the original Roman City Wall and the social evolution can be traced at the Folk Museum, which is housed in a splendid 16th century building. A visit to these two museums gives an insight into the complete Gloucester story, from its extraordinary history to its people, their lives and livelihoods.

A short walk from the Cathedral, are the Historic Docks – Britain's most inland port, first granted a charter in the reign of Elizabeth I and developed as a bustling commercial centre by the Victorians. Today, the imposing warehouses have been sympathetically restored, and house visitor attractions, shops and offices.

The Docks are home to 3 museums, the National Waterways Museum, where the history of inland water navigation throughout the country is portrayed in a fascinating and imaginative mixture of tableaux and exhibits, the Museum of Advertising and Packaging and the Soldiers of Gloucestershire Museum, which brings to life the outstanding career of the Gloucestershire Regiments.

Also in the Docks are the Antiques Centre with 4 floors of antiques and collectibles and boat rides, along the Gloucester – Sharpness canal, on board the Queen Boadicea II.

Events and Festivals play an important part in Gloucester throughout the year, with open air concerts, a carnival procession, street theatre and historical pageants, live music, both classical and contemporary, amateur dramatics, special exhibitions and the Cathedral hosts the Three Choirs Festival once every three years.

For further information contact
Vicki Rowan
Tourism Manager
Gloucester Tourism
28 Southgate Street
Gloucester GL1 2DP
Tel: 01452 500706
Fax: 01452 309788
email:
tourism@gloucester.gov.uk

The City of Gloucester also has a wide variety of stores, numerous eateries and superb pedestrian areas, both in the City centre and waterside in the Historic Docks, making a visit to Gloucester a positive joy!

The City of Gloucester offers a warm welcome and a wealth of interest, we harbour a long and proud tradition of welcoming visitors as strangers and bidding them "bon voyage" as friends. Little wonder then, that people return time after time to experience the warmth of our City's unique hospitality!

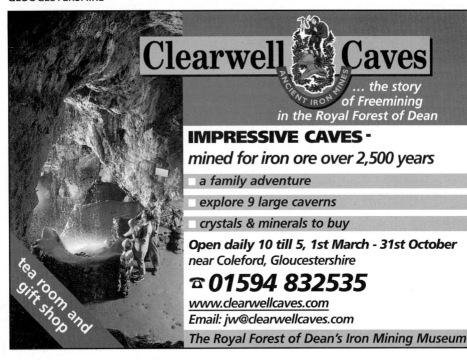
THE DEAN HERITAGE CENTRE

GATEWAY TO
THE MAGICAL
FOREST OF DEAN

The Dean Heritage Centre offers an introduction to the unique history of the Forest of Dean. From Romans to the present day, an area steeped in the history and tradition of a Medieval Forest; Freeminers, Sheepbadgers, Ironmining, the Industry of the area, all in the rich wooded landscape of the Forest today.

The Museum offers a wide variety to cater for visitors of all ages, whether you want to learn about the history of this unique area, explore the woods, along with temporary exhibitions for local artists, on local people like Dennis Potter or just enjoy a good cup of tea. There are pigs, ducks, animals, and an adventure playground for children, a beam engine, a miners cottage, and a nationally important collection of longcase clocks. Free attractions include a Blacksmith, a Potter, a Glazier and a Café. During the Summer we are one of the few places in the country where you can see charcoal burning done with the traditional wood and turf stack, other events. Open all year with both indoor and outside facilities.

Super opening: April to September 10.00–18.00. Winter opening: October–March 10.00–16.00 (1999), 11.00–16.00 (2000).

Year 2000 Admissions: Adults £3.50, Children £2.00, Senior citizens/ concessions £3.00. Family ticket £10. Ring for further information on the special evenings.

The Dean Heritage Centre, Camp Mill, Sudeley, Forest of Dean, Gloucestershire, GL14 2HR.
Telephone: (01594) 822170.

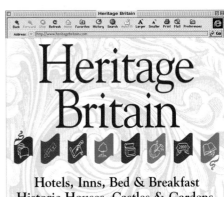

Royal Forest of Dean

The Royal Forest of Dean is one of England's few remaining ancient forests. Once a hunting ground for Norman Kings the area is now enjoyed for its natural beauty.

Over 24,000 acres of ancient woodland remain, stretching from the Wye Valley on the border of South Wales, known for its outstanding natural beauty, to the River Severn on the Eastern border. This is internationally known for the "Severn Bore", a natural phenomenon. To the north of the Royal Forest of Dean is the Vale of Leadon, with its black and white timbered buildings, market gardens, vineyards and rolling farmland hills.

The beauty of the landscape has inspired many famous writers. The play writer Dennis Potter was born in the Forest of Dean and based much of his work on the area, he referred to the Forest of Dean as "This Heart Shaped Land". Dymock in the Vale of Leadon was home to the Dymock Poets who lived in the area just before the First World War. The poets were Lascelles Abercrombie, Rupert Brook, John Drinkwater, Wilfred Gibson, Edward Thomas, and the American poet Robert Frost.

Such a widely contrasting landscape make the Royal Forest of Dean the perfect place for a wide range of outdoor activities such as walking, cycling, canoeing, rock climbing and caving.

The changing seasons make the forest a delight to enjoy these activities all year round. In the spring you can see the daffodil woods, bluebells, and other spring flowers, enjoy the beautiful summer days to the burning colours of autumn, and crisp winter days.

The history of the Royal Forest of Dean is as rich, varied and exciting to discover as the landscape it has shaped. Formerly a royal hunting ground, and later an important industrial centre with the mining of iron ore and coal.

Traces of the area's industrial past are still evident and there is a wealth of historic attractions where you can discover more about the history and culture of the area. Traditional crafts such as iron sculptures, and creative pottery still survive. Craft outlets can be found throughout the Royal Forest of Dean and are well worth a visit when shopping for that special gift!

The Royal Forest of Dean is ideal for a short break or long holiday. A wide selection of accommodation is available from hotels, guest houses, bed & breakfasts, self catering and camping.

Address
For more information please contact:
Dept, HHB
Tourist Information Centre
High Street
Coleford
Glos GL16 8HG
Tel: 01594 812388
Fax: 01594 812330
e-mail: tourism@fdean.gov.uk
Internet:
www.fweb.org.uk/fddc/tourist

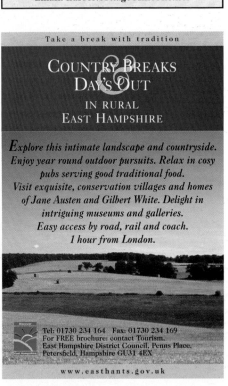

NEW PARK MANOR HOTEL
Lyndhurst Road (A337), Brockenhurst, SO42 7QH
Telephone: 01590 623 467 Fax: 01590 622 268
24 Rooms (all en suite), 1 Four Poster.
AA ☆☆☆❀❀, RAC ☆☆☆, ETB HR.
The New Park Manor is a prestigious and romantic Country House Hotel, dating back to the 16th century, in a wonderful setting of gardens, lawns and beautiful parklands in the heart of the New Forest. The rosetted Stag Restaurant offers excellent French influenced cuisine. Log fire ambiance, quality and service with a smile. Charming designed en-suite bedrooms. Own Equestrian Centre, seasonal heated swimming pool and tennis court. Wedding receptions and ceremonies, conferences and all other celebrations.

RS ⊘ ✆ ⌷ ⚲ ⚑ P ⋔ V SP ⊘❀ 🏠🏚 SPECIAL
1 **2** **3** **4** A B

The New Forest

We are in a remarkable corner of the English countryside set aside as a special place more than nine centuries ago by William the Conqueror. At that time William named it the "New" hunting forest, to be jealously guarded against any possible threat to his Chase of Royal Deer. Over the centuries too many places have changed almost beyond recognition yet the New Forest's ancient woodlands and wilderness heaths remain largely intact, earning the area national and international status.

As we enter the New Forest today, we appear to step backwards in time. The landscape is unique and traditions exist here that haven't changed since mediaeval times.

This most English of forests continues to be a living and working community where ponies and cattle still have the right of way as they freely graze the land. Deeper in the Forest wild deer browse beneath canopies of mighty oak and beech – natural scenes unchanged by the modern world.

It is remarkable that this way of life has survived as a remnant of ancient England along with the unmistakable landscape it created, when so much of our heritage has been lost elsewhere.

Whatever your preference, be it peace and solitude, visiting local places of interest, or participating in your favourite sport; the New Forest offers the visitor the ideal holiday location. A host of activities await in the great outdoors. Fishing, golf, riding or sailing in the Solent are possible but the New Forest is particularly renowned for walking and cycling.

Taking a New Forest Encounter offers you the opportunity to experience the real forest in the company of people who have lived and worked there throughout their lives. Your host's recollections and anecdotes will bring the history and heritage of the New Forest alive.

In addition to its fascinating and unique heritage, the New Forest has a wealth of places to visit right at its heart, including Beaulieu National Motor Museum (home of Lord Montagu) and Exbury Gardens, world famous for its azaleas and rhododendrons.

You are sure to find the New Forest is the ideal 'get away from it all' holiday destination yet connections couldn't be better; only 90 minutes from London by road and main rail services into Brockenhurst from London Waterloo.

The New Forest
T.I.C.
New Street
Lymington
Hampshire
General Enquiries
Tel: 01590 689000
Where to Stay Guide
Tel: 01590 689090

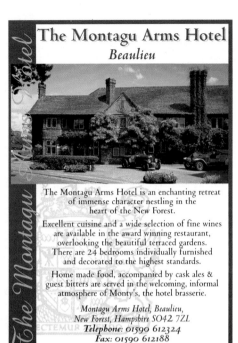

Beaulieu
A Truly Historic Experience

Set in the heart of the New Forest on the South Coast, Beaulieu is a unique day out where you can enjoy 800 years of history and heritage in one day.

Overlooking the Beaulieu River, Palace House has been the ancestral home of the Montagu's since 1538. The House was once the Great Gatehouse of Beaulieu Abbey and its monastic origins are reflected in such features as the fan vaulted ceilings. Many treasures, which are reminders of travels all round the world by past generations of the Montagu family, can also be seen. Walks amongst the gardens and by the Beaulieu River can also be enjoyed.

Beaulieu Abbey was founded in 1204 and although most of the buildings have been destroyed, much of beauty and interest remains. The former Monks' Refectory is now the local Parish Church. The Domus, which houses an exhibition of monastic life, is home to beautiful wall hangings and 15th century beamed ceilings.

Beaulieu is also home to the world famous National Motor Museum which traces the story of motoring from 1894 to the present day. 250 vehicles are on display including legendary World Record breakers such as Bluebird and Golden Arrow plus Veteran, Vintage and Classic cars.

The modern Beaulieu is very much a family destination where there are various free and unlimited rides and drives on a transportation theme to be enjoyed by everyone including a mile long monorail and replica 1912 London open topped bus.

When visiting Beaulieu arrangements can also be made to view the Estate's vineyards. Visits, which can be arranged between April and October, must be pre-booked at least one week in advance with the Beaulieu Estate Office.

Address
The National Motor Museum
Palace House & Gardens
Beaulieu Abbey Ruins,
Beaulieu, Hampshire
SO42 7ZN
Tel: 01590 612345
Fax: 01590 612624
website: www.beaulieu.co.uk

Opening Times
Open all year (except Christmas Day)
Apr-Sep: 10am-6pm
Oct-Mar: 10am-5pm
Last admission
40 mins before closing

Admission (2000 prices)
Adults £9.25
Child (4-16) £6.50
Senior Citizens £8.00

Facilities
Restaurant, Rides & Drives,
Parking, Disabled Facilities,
Special Events

Free additional services for educational visits
*Prices correct at time of going to press.

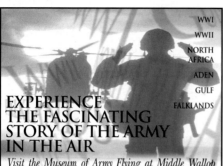

Highclere Castle & Gardens

Nestling between rolling hills where the Berkshire Downs merge into Hampshire, Highclere Castle and its beautiful gardens offer a wealth of interest to be discovered by its many visitors.

Designed by Sir Charles Barry, Highclere Castle bears more than a resemblance to the Houses of Parliament which he built at the same time. The family home of Lord and Lady Carnarvon, the 7th Earl and Countess, Highclere Castle, with its ornate exterior complemented by striking interior design is rich in treasures yet retains the warmth of a family home.

An informative tour of the historical state rooms includes an exhibition giving the history of the Highclere Stud, highlighting the success of its horses. The present Earl is Racing Manager to Her Majesty the Queen and for over 100 years the Earls of Carnarvon have owned and raced horses.

The Egyptology exhibition portrays the experiences of and discoveries made by the Fifth Earl of Carnarvon who in 1922, together with the Egyptologist, Howard Carter, discovered Tutankhamun's Tomb. This was one of the most important discoveries in the history of archaeology. Part of the Carnarvon collection remained undetected at Highclere until the late 1980s when it was once again discovered and is now on display.

The Highclere Castle Tea Room is licensed and opens between 11.00am and 5.00pm. Hot meals are served between 12 noon and 2pm. Admission to the Castle and Gardens for adults is £6.50, OAPS £5.00, children £3.00. To the Gardens only the adult price is £3.00, children £1.50. The Castle will open from 1st July to 2nd September, everyday from 11am to 5pm (except Saturday 11am to 3.30pm). Last admission one hour prior to closing. For information on group bookings or details of special events held in the grounds during the year, telephone 01635 253210. There is a gift shop and ample free parking. The house is occasionally subject to closure.

Highclere Castle
Highclere, Nr. Newbury
Berkshire RG20 9RN
Tel: 01635 253210
Fax: 01635 255315
email: theoffice@
highclerecastle.co.uk
website: www.highclere
castle.co.uk

Open
1 July to 2 Sept, Mon-Sun
11am-5pm, Last admission
into house 4pm (last
admission Sat at 2.30pm).

Admission
Castle & Garden £6.50
Adult, £3.00 Children, £5.00
OAPs, Gardens only £3.00
Adult, £1.50 Children

Facilities
Licensed tea-room, Gift Shop,
Free Parking

For information on group
bookings or details of special
events held in the grounds
during the year, phone 01635
253210. The house is
occasionally subject to closure.

ESSEBORNE MANOR HOTEL
Hurstbourne Tarrant, Andover, Hants SP11 0ER.
Telephone: 01264 736444 Fax: 01264 736725.
14 Rooms (all en suite), 1 Four Poster.
AA ☆☆☆, RAC ☆☆☆, Egony Ronay, Which Good Food
Guide, AA Best Restaurants Guide.
This cosy country house hotel located high on the north Wessex downs has fourteen individually designed bedrooms, a snug bar, comfortable lounge and pretty dining room. French/English cuisine is complemented by a celebrated cellar. Delightful gardens and many walks make this an ideal place for relaxing and exploring the south.

THE WELLINGTON ARMS HOTEL
Stratfield Turgis, Near Basingstoke, Hampshire
Telephone: 01256 882214 Fax: 01256 882934
35 Rooms (all en suite), 1 Four Poster.
AA ☆☆☆ ETB ☆☆☆.
The hotel is ideally situated on the A33 midway between Reading and Basingstoke, only 10 minutes from both the M4 and M3 motorways yet in the heart of Rural Hampshire on the Duke of Wellington's estate. Originally a 17th century farmhouse, this Grade II listed building has 15 individually furnished rooms in the main building and 20 in a new courtyard wing.

The Test Valley

Test Valley is situated in the beautiful rural landscape of north west Hampshire. This picturesque location is an ideal touring base for the south of England. Excellent road and rail links make Test Valley easy to reach, yet nestled between Salisbury and Winchester it remains a secluded alternative destination with its own treasures and is ideal for short breaks.

Test Valley's beautiful historic houses are amongst the best in the country and include Mottisfont Abbey, which hosts the national collection of old-fashioned roses. Romsey Abbey is one of the great parish churches of England and is an excellent example of Norman and early English architecture. This historic market town also boasts the Palladian manor house of Broadlands, the former home of Lord Palmerston, situated in its own grounds on the banks of the River Test.

The Test Valley is also rich in Iron-age history, a walk up the huge 2000 year old ramparts of Danebury hill fort is rewarded by views across the beautiful surrounding countryside and Stonehenge is just a short drive away.

Discover the history behind Test Valley's bustling market towns of Andover and Romsey, brought to life by the Heritage Trails. Wind through the medieval streets, passing a variety of shops and boutiques, or follow the 'Poetry in Motion' trails to the quieter parts of town, discovering words of verse, as you wander alongside the river.

The variety of landscape provides interesting routes for visitors on foot, with something to suit all tastes, from riverside ambles and woodland walks to rolling hillsides. With hills sweeping down to the river valley, the miles of bridleways give cyclists a variety of options from challenging downhill tracks to gentle rural rides, travelling on quiet country lanes and tracks passing thatched cottages in pretty villages. We have compiled 25 of the best of the cycling and walking routes in the area for you, on handy weatherproof route cards.

Our wide variety of visitor attractions is sure to keep you entertained. Test Valley has an excellent range of accommodation and beautifully located country inns serving excellent food and a variety of traditional ales.

For a free visitors guide please contact, quoting ref HE2, Tourist Information Centres at:

Andover
Tel: (01264) 324320

Romsey
Tel: (01794) 512987

Rownhams
Tel:(01703) 730345

or write to:
Tourism Officer,
Leisure Services,
Test Valley Borough Council,
Beech Hurst,
Weyhill Road,
Andover SP10 3AJ

Tel: 01264 368836
Fax: 01264 368899
Email:
tourism@testvalley.gov.uk

Pencraig Court
Country House Hotel

A fine Georgian country house set in three and a half acres of gardens, lawns and secluded woodland overlooking the river Wye with unforgettable views across the valley to the Royal Forest of Dean and the distant hills.

Pencraig Court offers guests the opportunity to unwind in a totally relaxed atmosphere and enjoy first class food cooked to the highest quality and complemented by an excellent wine cellar.

Pencraig, Ross-on-Wye, Herefordshire HR9 6HR
Tel: 01989 770306 • Fax: 01989 770040
Email: mike@pencraig-court.co.uk

The GRAFTONBURY GARDEN *Hotel*

The Graftonbury Garden Hotel, set in 18 acres, has been very carefully refurbished in a modern style that retains the character of the building but creates the bright comfortable ambience of a private country house. The Hotel provides bedrooms ranging from the spacious double, twin, family and single rooms to modern garden rooms with patio doors onto a terrace – all with en suite bathrooms, colour TVs, telephone, tea and coffee making facilities.

The Bistro & Terrace Bar with patios overlooking the beautiful country-side, caters for all tastes. Particular care has been taken to create a warm and intimate atmosphere with interesting and varied menus.

THE GRAFTONBURY GARDEN HOTEL
Grafton Lane, Hereford HR2 8BN
Tel: 01432 268826 Fax: 01432 354633
AA ☆☆☆, Les Routier, BHAB Landing Site, Conference Facilities

THE TALBOT HOTEL
West Street, Leominster, Herefordshire HR6 8EP
Telephone: 01568 616347 Fax: 01568 614880
20 Rooms (all en suite).
AA ☆☆, RAC ☆☆, ETB ♛♛♛

Town Centre Hotel, originally a 15th century coaching house sympathetically updated offering modern facilities and en suite bedrooms. Leominster, an undiscovered corner of England, memorable for beautiful countryside, black and white timbered villages and wealth of antique shops. Ideal touring location for Mid-Wales, Herefordshire and Shropshire. Locally arranged golf and sporting holidays.

RS ⊘ ⌂ 🍵 P 🍴 V ✈ 🐾 1 2 3 4 C

THE OLD COURT HOTEL
Symonds Yat West, Ross on Wye, Herefordshire HR9 6DA
Telephone: 01600 890367 Fax: 01600 890964
RAC ☆☆, 20 Rooms (14 en suite), 3 Four Posters.

15th Century Manor House set in three acres of gardens, oak beamed bars with roaring log fires in winter. Baronial Hall restaurant serving award-winning cuisine and wines. Set amongst some of the most beautiful scenery in England in the Wye Valley and Royal Forest of Dean and yet easily accessible via the M50/A40 motorway network.

⊘ ⌂ 🍵 P 🍴 GF ✈ 🌸 🏨 SPECIAL 1 2 3 4 D

THE VERZONS COUNTRY HOTEL
Trumpet, Nr Ledbury, Herefordshire HR8 2PZ
Telephone: 01531 670381
9 Rooms (all en suite), 1 Four Poster.
AA ☆☆, ETB ♛♛♛ Commended.

Our Georgian hotel, built in 1788 retains the original period features yet combines modern comforts in this relaxed heart of England. See glorious views, visit the many historic sights nearby and meet the locals in our farmhouse bar. Large en suite rooms, log fires and a warm welcome from resident owners.

RS ⊘ ⌂ 🍵 P 🍴 V ✈ 🌸 🏨 SPECIAL 2 3 4 C

Eastnor Castle

Eastnor Castle, some two and a half miles from Ledbury on the Tewkesbury road, is a superb example of the great Norman and Gothic revival of the medieval fortress. Built in 1812, it is popular with film producers. Two recent productions have been Sherlock Holmes and the BBC's Little Lord Fauntleroy.

The Castle sits serenely overlooking the Malvern Hills in an estate of some 5,000 acres. Much of it is farmed, but it also includes a deer park with a herd of about 200 red deer.

The first Earl Somers commissioned the building and had the courage to give the undertaking to an original and inspired young architect, Robert Smirke. The Result was a magnificent baronial castle exactly as Lord Somers had requested.

The interior of the castle is equally impressive. A vast sixty foot hall leads to a series of state rooms. The Gothic Drawing Room is spectacular. Pugin designed it and must have been exalted by the task. It still has much of the original furniture. The Octagon Saloon, along with the Gothic Drawing Room and Long Library, has magnificent views over the lawned terraces to the lake and the Malvern Hills beyond.

The pair of coal fires is welcoming on winter days. The Library is different again with a wonderful collection of books and tapestries decorated in the style of the Italian Renaissance. Many other rooms are open to the public including the Grand Dining Room with many family portraits, dominated by the first Earl.

In the grounds there is also much to see. The trees are wonderful and include some mature cedars, one variety of which was introduced by the third Earl into the UK in the 19th century. Visitors are welcome to picnic in the grounds or visit the old kitchen, now a tea room, for homemade teas and ice cream.

The deer park is home during much of the season to visiting caravans and many special events. This doesn't seem to bother the deer, nor do the walkers on their way to or from the Malvern Hills or Ledbury.

The Castle is now owned and occupied by James and the Hon. Sarah Hervey-Bathurst and their three young children. In addition to the public opening the family welcomes corporate entertainment, wedding ceremonies and receptions as well as filming.

All in all, Eastnor is a most dramatic historic house which still remains something of a secret to many people living in the outlying towns and counties.

The Castle is open to the public from 11am to 5pm (last admission 4.30pm) every Sunday from Easter to the end of September; every Bank Holiday; and Sunday to Friday during July and August.

Address
Eastnor Castle
Eastnor
Nr. Ledbury
Herefordshire
HR8 1RL
Tel: 01531 633160
Fax: 01531 631776

Opening Times
Sunday and Bank Holidays
Monday from Easter to end
September
Every day in July and August
except Saturdays 11am-
5.00pm (last admissions
4.30pm)

Admission
Castle and Grounds
Adults £5.00, Children £3.00

Facilities
Deer Park and Arboretum,
gift shop, tea room/restaurant,
parking, exhibition room,
children's adventure
playground, garden centre,
maze, special events

Hatfield House & Gardens

This celebrated Jacobean house, which stands in its own great park, was built between 1607 and 1611 by Robert Cecil, 1st Early of Salisbury and Chief Minister to King James I. It has been the family home of the Cecils ever since.

The main designer was Robert Lyminge and, it is thought, young Inigo Jones. The interior decoration was the work of English, Flemish and French craftsmen, notably Maximiliain Colt. The State Rooms are rich in world-famous paintings including The Rainbow Portrait of Elizabeth I, and The Ermine Portrait by Nicholas Hilliard. Fine furniture from the 16th, 17th and 18th centuries, rare tapestries and historic armour can be found in the State Rooms.

Within the delightful gardens stands the surviving wing of The Royal Palace of Hatfield (1497) where Elizabeth I spend much of her girlhood and held her first Council of State in November 1558. Some of her possessions can be seen in the House.

The National Collection of Model Soldiers is located in an attractive exhibition in the Stable Yard. The 3,000 model soldiers, from BC to the present day, are deployed in panoramic display cases.

The West Gardens contain a formal garden, a scented garden with a herb garden at its centre, and a knot garden, planted with plants and bulbs which would have grown there in the 15th, 16th and 17th centuries.

**Address
Information & Bookings**
The Curator, Hatfield House,
HATFIELD, Herts. AL9 5NQ
Tel: 01707 262823
Fax: 01707 275719.
Functions, Weddings &
Banqueting, tel: 01707 262055

Opening Times
24 March to
23 September 2000.
(closed Good Friday, but open Bank Holiday Mondays).
House: Tuesday to Friday, guided tours only, 12-4.
Saturday & Sunday, no guided tours, 1-4.30.
Bank Holidays, no guided tours, 11-4.30.
Park: daily, except Friday, 10.30-8, (Friday 11-6).
West Gardens: Tue to Sun 11-6.
East Gardens: Friday, (Connoisseurs' Day) 11-6.
Shop: Tuesday to Saturday, 11-5.30; Sunday, 1-5.30
Restaurant: Tuesday to Sunday, 10.30 - 5.30.

Location
21 miles North of London - M25 Junction 23, seven miles.
A1(M) Junction 4, two miles.
Signed off A414 and A1000.
Opposite Hatfield railway station (Kings Cross 25 minutes).

Admission
(except Fridays and during Major Events)
House Park & West Gardens: adult £6.60, child £3.30, booked party (20+) £5.60.
Park only: adult £2, child £1.
CONNOISSEURS' DAY
(Fridays only, but not during Major Events)
Park & Gardens (East & West) £6 (no concessions).
House Tour, Park & Gardens: £10.
MAJOR EVENTS:
(changing the above admission details)
Living Crafts
10-13 May, £7 (pty. £6)
Festival of Gardening: 23 & 24 June, £7.50 (pty. £6.50)
Art In Clay (7th Pottery & Ceramics Festival) 3-5 August £5.50
Country Homes & Gardens Show 7-9 September £5.50

LETCHWORTH GARDEN CITY ‧ HERITAGE ‧ FOUNDATION

FIRST GARDEN CITY HERITAGE MUSEUM

296 Norton Way South
Letchworth Garden City
Hertfordshire SG6 1SU
Telephone: 01462 482710
Facsimile: 01462 486056

The Museum is housed in the drawing offices of the towns original architects Barry Parker and Raymond Unwin.

It provides a fascinating insight into the vision of one of the world's great social reformers, and his concept of a "social city".

Ebenezer Howard, social reformer and founder of the Garden City Movement, believed that the problems of overcrowding, pollution and poor living conditions could be solved through the marriage of town and country.

His vision was realised by the building of Letchworth Garden City and the story of this unique town is told at the First Garden City Heritage Museum.

Apart from the many exhibits demonstrating the development of the World's First Garden City, the Museum also holds regular special exhibitions and events relating to the different aspects of the towns history.

The Museum also provides many talks and guided tours of the town.

Open Monday to Saturday, 10am-5pm. Closed Christmas Day and Boxing Day.

Admission: Residents 50p, Non-Residents £1, Students 50p, Under 16s FREE.

NOTICE BOARD
New Dialling Codes

Cardiff - (01222) xxx xxx
becomes (029) 20 xx xxxx

Coventry - (01203) xxx xxx
becomes (024) 76 xx xxxx

London - (0171) xxx xxxx
becomes (020) 7 xxx xxxx
(0181) xxx xxxx
becomes (020) 8 xxx xxxx

Portsmouth - (01705) xxx xxx
becomes (023) 92 xx xxxx

Southampton - (01703) xxx xxx
becomes (023) 80 xx xxxx

Northern Ireland - (01232) xx xxxx
becomes (028) 90 xx xxxx

THE BOBSLEIGH INN

On the outskirts of the Chiltern countryside and situated approximately 8 miles from St. Albans, The Bobsleigh Inn, privately owned, is an ideal venue for both business or pleasure.

The award-winning restaurant offers excellent cuisine with extensive à la carte and table d'hote menus.

44 en-suite bedrooms, two with Jacuzzi baths and one four poster, heated swimming pool (open nine months of the year), Golf nearby. Easy access M1 Junction 8 Hemel Hempstead or M25 Junction 20. Luton and London Heathrow airports 25 minutes.

AA ☆☆☆ ❀, ETB 👑 👑 👑 👑 Commended.

Hempstead Road, Bovingdon, Herts HP1 HP3
Tel: 01442 833276 Fax: 01442 832471

EDGWAREBURY HOTEL
Barnet Lane, Elstree Herts WD6 6RE
Telephone: 0181 953 8227 Fax: 0181 207 3668
47 en suite bedrooms – Suites, Executive and Standard.
AA ☆☆☆, RAC ☆☆☆, ETB 👑 👑 👑 👑 Highly Comm.
Elegant Tudor style Manor House set in 10 acres of woodland with stone fireplaces, carvings and oak beams. '2 Rosette' awarded restaurant, 6 conference/meeting rooms, private dining, wedding ceremonies, terrace bar, tennis courts and panoramic views.

RS 🚭 ♨ ⌂ ⚲ ☕ P ⑪ V GF ⊘ ⌃ ❀ 🚗 🛏
SPECIAL **1** **2** **3** A B C

WHITE HORSE HOTEL
Hertingfordbury, Hertfordshire SG14 2LB
Telephone: 01992 586791 Fax: 01992 550809
42 Rooms (all en suite).
AA ☆☆☆, RAC ☆☆☆, ETB 👑 👑 👑 👑
The Doomsday Book mentions the peaceful little village of Hertingfordbury. Later the Manor House was built and has since become the White Horse Hotel. A Coaching Inn set in its own attractive gardens offering the very best traditional English hospitality.

RS 🚭 ♨ ⌂ ☕ P ⑪ ⌃ ❀ 🛏 SPECIAL
1 **2** **3** **4** C

Knebworth

Knebworth has been the home of Lord Cobbold's family, the Lyttons, for over 500 years. The house was built in 1490 by Sir Robert Lytton, who fought with Henry Tudor at the Battle of Bosworth and served the new King as a trusted friend, courtier and Privy Councillor.

Successive generations have made their mark on the house. The most drastic was in 1811 when Mrs Bulwer Lytton had three of the four sides demolished. Following this in 1843, her son, the romantic novelist and statesman, Edward Bulwer Lytton, added the spectacular turrets, domes, gargoyles and other mythical beasts to realise his 'Gothic Fantasy'.

Despite the efforts of Sir Edwin Lutyens, the architect, to subdue Edward's flamboyant creation, the High Gothic décor remains the most striking feature of the house today.

Inside the house there are many beautiful rooms to see, all richly furnished and containing exquisite works of art evoking the lifestyle and splendours of bygone ages. There is important early-classical 17th century panelling in the Banqueting Hall, Crace's work is particularly evident in the fantastical State Drawing Room, whilst the Entrance Hall and Bulwer Lytton's Library were among alterations done by Lutyens who married Emily, daughter of the 1st Earl.

Charles Dickens acted here in private theatricals and Winston Churchill painted at his easel in the Banqueting Hall. Knebworth was the home of Constance Lytton, the suffragette and also of Robert Lytton, Viceroy of India. Lord Lytton's Vice-Royalty and the Great Delhi Durbar of 1877 are commemorated in the British Raj Exhibition.

The magnificent formal Gardens adjoin the house and contain many features including the recently restored Maze, the Rose Garden, Gold and Blue Gardens, a Jekyll Herb Garden, a Victorian Wilderness area and pleached lime avenues.

The 250 acres of Rolling Parkland contain herds of Red and Sika Deer, a large Adventure Playground, and they provide the setting for a wide variety of special events each summer.

Knebworth is one of only a handful of historic houses open to view in Hertfordshire. Located just north of London and accessed direct from Junction 7 of the A1 Motorway.

Address

Knebworth House
Knebworth
Herts SG3 6PY
Tel: 01438 812661
Fax: 01438 811908
Email:
info@knebworthhouse.com
www.knebworthhouse.com

Opening Times

Open to the public from 7 April to 30 September inclusive (but not every day). Open for pre-booked groups all year.

Admission 2001

|House, Gardens, Park & Playground
Adults £7.00, Child*/ OAPs £6.50
Groups (min 20)
Adults £6.00, Child*/ OAPs £5.50 (Subject to Special Events)
Gardens, Park & Playground
All Persons £5.50,
Family (2+2) £19.00
Groups (min 20)
All Persons £4.75
Supplement tickets to House (individuals) Adults £1.50
Child*/OAPs £1.00
*Age 4-16
Season Tickets available

Facilities

Gift Shop in House and Information Centre, Licenced Tea Room, Unlimited Parking, Toilets (inc Disabled), Ground Floor of House only accessible for wheelchairs, Guide Dogs only in House

City of St. Albans

St. Albans has been welcoming visitors for centuries. Medieval pilgrims came to the shrine of Britain's first Christian martyr, St. Alban. Today's visitor comes not only to explore the inspiring Cathedral, but also the site of Roman Verulamium, now protected in 100 acres of beautiful parkland. The award-winning Verulamium Museum tells the story of the Roman city and displays fabulous mosaics and wallplasters. Nearby are the remains of the best preserved Roman theatre in Britain.

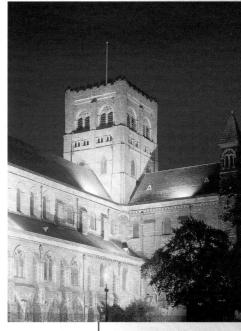

St Albans is easy to get to by road or rail. There are ample car parks and two railway stations. It is a city easily explored on foot, offering contrasts of old and new. Walk down historic Fishpool Street and you find yourself in the delightful village of St. Michael's with its 16th century water mill. Back in the city centre regular walks are available.

The 15th century Clock Tower, a rare example of a town belfry, is just a short step away from a wealth of attractive shops and restaurants. This mixture of past and present provides a unique atmosphere in which to linger, gaze and enjoy. Every Saturday and Wednesday see the lively street market. Established over 1000 years ago, it is now one of the largest in the South East, offering goods of every kind from fruit and vegetables to antiques, records and books.

The story of St. Albans is explored further at The Museum of St. Albans in Hatfield Road. Here you will find lively exhibitions and a wildlife garden where you can relax for a while, before resuming your tour.

On the edges of the city are the Organ Museum with its working instruments and the famous Gardens of the Rose. Home of the Royal National Rose Society, it presents a magnificent show of colour and scent throughout the summer.

St. Albans offers a real day out – priceless heritage, original shops, and a unique and welcoming atmosphere. Ideal for a weekend break, St. Albans offers a world of choice and boasts over 100 places to eat and drink in the city centre alone. It hosts three theatres and enjoys a lively nightlife. By contrast, quiet lanes, delightful villages and enticing pubs can be found only minutes away from the centre.

Come and explore St. Albans – you won't be disappointed.

For further information please visit or write to:

St. Albans Tourist
Information Centre
The Old Town Hall
Market Place
St. Albans
Hertfordshire
AL3 5DJ

Tel: 01727 864511

Fax: 01727 843167

Please quote ref: HH.97

St. Albans Internet Home Page:

http://www.stalbans.gov.uk.

The Sevenoaks District
a world of history

In 1528 he came to sample our delights...

...nearly 500 years later, we have even more to offer our visitors.

Knole Park • Chartwell • Hever Castle • Penshurst Place • Lullingstone Castle • Lullingstone Roman Villa • Chiddingstone Castle • Riverhill House and Gardens • Squerryes Court • Quebec House

Sevenoaks
DISTRICT COUNCIL

Hever Castle & Gardens

Hever Castle is a romantic, double moated castle set deep in the heart of the Kent countryside. Its rich and varied history stretches back over seven centuries when the impressive stone gatehouse and outer walls were constructed. However the castle is best known as the childhood home of Anne Boleyn, the second wife of Henry VIII and mother of Queen Elizabeth I. It was her family who added the comfortable Tudor manor house within these walls in about 1500. Henry VIII is thought to have wooed Anne at Hever and there are exhibitions in the castle celebrating this romantic part of English history. Henry VIII later gave Hever Castle to his fourth wife, Anne of Cleves.

The American millionaire, William Waldorf Astor, acquired the estate in 1903 and invested a great deal of time, money and imagination in restoring the castle, building the Tudor Village and creating the glorious gardens. Inside the Castle, the walls were covered with magnificent carving and panelling and the rooms were filled with wonderful antiques and works of art, most of which can still be enjoyed by visitors today. Recent attractions include the 'Book of Hours' Exhibition and the Queens Chambers. The Tudor Village adjoining the castle, with its historic interiors and modern facilities provides a unique setting for residential and day conferences with accommodation suitable for both corporate and private clients.

The award winning gardens surrounding Hever Castle have now reached their full maturity and are a blaze of colour for most of the year. The spectacular Italian Garden contains William Waldorf Astor's collection of antique sculpture and statuary set amongst the shrubs and herbaceous plants. The formal gardens include a walled rose garden, fine topiary, a 110 metre herbaceous border and a yew maze. There is also a 35 acre lake and a unique water maze on 'Sixteen Acre Island'.

The Castle's current owner, John Guthrie, has further added to its charms by opening a collection of miniature model houses in a purpose built exhibition centre in the grounds. This exquisite collection contains three one-twelfth scale period houses, a number of room views and two formal miniature gardens. The 'From Castles to Country Houses' exhibition tells the history of English country houses from Norman to Victorian times.

Address
Hever Castle & Gardens
Nr. Edenbridge
Kent TN8 7NG
Tel: 01732 865224
Email: mail@hevercastle.co.uk
www.hevercastle.co.uk

Opening Times
Open 1st March to 30th November 11-5pm
(4pm Winter)

Admission (2001 prices)
Adult: Castle & Gardens £8.00, Gardens only £6.30, Family Tickets available

Location 30 miles from London & 3 miles S.E. of Edenbridge, junction 5 & 6 of M25

Facilities
Licensed self-service restaurants, gift, book & garden shops

SQUERRYES COURT

Experience the warm welcome of this beautiful lived-in 17th century manor house which has been the Warde family home since 1731. Fine collection of Old Master paintings, furniture, porcelain, tapestries acquired or commissioned by the family in the 18th century. The attractive gardens are interesting all through the seasons. Lake, restored formal garden and 18th century dovecote. Delicious home-made teas served in the Old Library or on the Tea Lawn.

SQUERRYES COURT
MANOR HOUSE AND GARDENS
Westerham, Kent TN16 1SJ
Telephone: 01959 562345 or 563118
Fax: 01959 565949
e-mail: squerryescourt@pavilion.co.uk

OPEN: 1st April to 30th September
Wednesday, Saturday, Sunday, Bank Holiday Mondays
Gardens: 12 noon. House: 1.30pm. Closed 5.30pm

Lullingstone Castle
Eynsford, Kent DA4 0JA.
Telephone: 01322 862114.

The original manor and gatehouse were built by Sir John Peche in the reign of King Henry VII. A regular royal visitor was Queen Anne, a friend of the Hart family who owned the estate until 1738 when it passed to the Dyke family, whose descendants, the Hart Dykes, live their today.

BELMONT
Belmont Park, Throwley, Faversham, Kent ME13 0HH. Telephone: 01795 890202

BELMONT is a charming 18th century House containing fine Indian and English furniture and paintings. It also houses the magnificent clock collection formed by the 5th Lord Harris. Set in delightful grounds, the house is a joy to visit. The gardens are particularly attractive in the spring and early summer.

Opening Times: Easter Sun to end of Sept on Sats, Suns and Bank Holiday Mons. Guided tours 2pm to 5pm. Last admission 4.30pm. Tues & Thurs pre-booked groups (min 20) 2pm to 5pm. Tea Room.

Directions: 4½ miles south south west of Faversham and 1½ miles west of the A251 Faversham-Ashford road. From the A2 or M2 exit 6, take the A251 South towards Ashford. At Badlesmere follow the brown tourist sign.

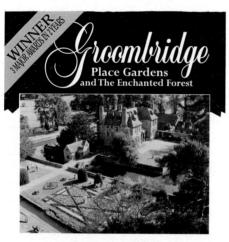

WINNER 3 MAJOR AWARDS IN 2 YEARS

Groombridge
Place Gardens
and The Enchanted Forest

* *The Best Family Day Out*
* *Let Your Imagination RUN WILD*
* *700 Years of History*
* *200 Acres of Excitment*

OPEN DAILY APRIL - OCTOBER 9.00AM - 6.00PM

Groombridge, Nr. Tunbridge Wells, Kent, TN3 9QG.
Tel: 01892 861444. Fax: 01892 863996.
Website: www.groombridgeplace.com

Chislehurst Caves
Old Hill, Chislehurst,
Kent BR7 5NB
Tel: 020 8467 3264
Fax: 020 8295 0407
Email: thecaves@cwcom.net

Take a 45 minute lamplit guided tour through the darkness of these unique man-made caves, deep beneath Chislehurst. You will hear of the Druids, Romans and Saxons, see the tunnels made famous as a shelter during World War II, the Haunted Pool and more! Cave, Gift shop, Free Car Park.

BEXLEYHEATH MARRIOTT
1 Broadway, Bexleyheath, Kent DA6 7JZ
Telephone: 0181 298 1000 Fax: 0181 298 1234
138 Rooms (all en suite). AA/RAC ☆☆☆☆
A luxury four star hotel located just minutes from Junction 2 of the M25 giving easy access from all points of the country via the National Motorway Network. Central London is only 14 miles – 34 minutes by train.

RS ▮ (⊘ ⊙ ▱ ⦶ ▮ ▮ P ⋔ V GF ⬍ ⬍ ↲ ↦

🏠 SPECIAL 1 2 3 4 C

Penshurst Place and Gardens KENT

The history of Penshurst Place stretches back more than six and a half centuries. The first recorded owner, Sir Stephen de Penchester, a distinguished royal servant, who died in 1299, was followed by Sir John de Pulteney, a wealthy wool merchant and four times Lord Mayor of London. Later, King Henry VIII stayed at Penshurst, whilst he wooed Anne Boleyn. It has remained the ancestral home of the same family, the Sidneys, for nearly 450 years. The present owner, Philip Sidney, 2nd Viscount De L'Isle succeeded his father in 1991 and now lives at Penshurst with his wife and their two children.

Situated in the medieval village of Penshurst, and surrounded by rolling countryside, this splendid manor house with its acres of gardens and parkland, embodies the finest and most complete example in England of 14th century domestic architecture.

The Great Hall, with its vast sunlit arching chestnut roof has been described as one of the world's grandest rooms. Today, the house reveals at least eight architectural periods, and the state rooms contain family collections of portraits, tapestries, furniture and armour from the 15th, 16th and 17th centuries. They chart the history of the family whose forbears include the Elizabethan courtier poet, Sir Philip Sidney who, on his death in 1587, was accorded the honour of a state funeral at St Paul's cathedral, the first commoner to receive such a tribute, not to be repeated until the death of Nelson and later, Sir Winston Churchill.

The gardens, another of Penshurst's treasures, date from 1346, and retain the Elizabethan formal framework, destroyed in most other great houses in Georgian times. The writer Ben Jonson praised them for: "thy Orchard Fruit, thy Garden Flowers, /Fresh as the Air, and new as are the Hours." The subject of a programme of restoration and replanting instigated by the late Lord De L'Isle, they consist of a series of garden 'rooms' divided by yew hedges, each delighting and surprising the visitor in turn by its individual character and atmosphere.

Guided tours of the house are available in the mornings; guided tours of the gardens by appointment.

Address

Penshurst Place and Gardens, Penshurst, Tonbridge, Kent TN11 8DG Tel: 01 892 870307

Prices & opening times for 2000

Weekends from 3rd March. Daily from 31st March until 31st Oct.
Grounds open from 10.30am to 6pm. House open from 12 noon to 5pm. Shop and Plant Centre 10.30am to 6pm

(House and Grounds): Adults £6.00, OAPs £5.50, Children (5-16) £4.00, Family Ticket £16.00, Adult Party (20+) £5.30.

(Grounds only): Adults £4.50, OAPs £4.00, Children (5-16) £3.50, Family Ticket £13.00 (2 adult + 2 children), Garden Season Ticket £25.00

Pre-booked Guided Tours House Tours: Adults £6.00, Children £3.20
Garden Tours: Adults £6.50, Children £4.00
House & Garden £8.00

Location
35 miles SE of London

Facilities
Tea Room, Gift Shop, Venture Playground, Toy Museum, Picnic Site, Nature Trail, Garden Exhibition & Plant Centre

Chiddingstone Castle

Although only thirty-five miles from London, Chiddingstone Castle enjoys a completely rural situation in the dramatic countryside of the Weald. It is ten miles from the enchanting small town of Sevenoaks, and ten from the spa town of Tunbridge Wells. In its immediate neighbourhood are a number of other historic houses.

The Castle itself stands at the head of the single street of medieval houses of the tiny National Trust village of Chiddingstone, reputed as the loveliest in Kent. Once it was the home of the Streatfeilds, lords of several manors hereabouts. From 1550 they occupied a house here, and then, about 1805, Squire Henry Streatfeild decided to transform his ancestral home into a Castle. It was the fashionable thing to do, but the place was expensive to run, and in 1938 the Streatfeilds sold it.

The mansion was occupied by the Army during the War, and then by a school, and was on the verge of ruin when the art connoisseur and collector, Denys Bower, saw it, fell in love with it, and bought it. He did his best to restore it but was hampered by lack of cash – he spent his all on acquiring works of art, particularly Japanese swords and lacquer, Egyptian antiquities, Royal Stuart pictures and mementoes. When he died in 1977 he left the Castle and its contents to the Nation. It is now run by a private charitable Trust.

Restoration of house and grounds has just been completed, with the help of English Heritage. The house is still lived in – it is not a museum, but a home, crammed with Denys Bower's treasures, arranged just as he had them. It is completely non-commercial, a reminder of what old England used to be like.

The interior of the house centres, like a medieval Castle, round the Great Hall, a fine Romantic representation of an ancient Hall. Civil marriages can now be celebrated here, and it is extremely popular – a happy development for the old house.

A stroll round the grounds – parkland, with three acres lake – completes the tranquillity of a visit to the Castle, with vista after vista opening up before the visitor.

Chiddingstone Castle
Nr. Edenbridge
Kent TN8 7AD.
Tel: 01892 870347
(ENGLISH HERITAGE
LISTED GRADE II*
GROUNDS: LISTED
GARDEN OF KENT)

Hours of Opening
June-Sept: Wed, Thurs, Fri
and Sun. April, May,
Open Easter, Spring Bank
Hol.

Hours Sun and Bank Hols,
11.30am-5.30pm; weekdays
2.00pm-5.30pm. Last
admission 5pm.

The Trustees reserve the right
to close the house at any time
for private functions.

The Spa Hotel

The Spa Hotel is an elegant country mansion set in 15 acres of beautiful gardens overlooking historic Tunbridge Wells. Family owned, The Spa is renowned for its high standards and friendly service. The Chandelier Restaurant serves traditional English dishes and French cuisine. Real ales and a wide selection of wine are served in the Equestrian Bar. The Sparkling Health Club invites guests to sample the gymnasiums, sauna, steam rooms, jogging track, indoor swimming pool and beauty salon. The Spa is ideally located for shopping in Tunbridge Wells, visiting the many local historic attractions and playing golf.

THE SPA HOTEL
Mount Ephraim, Tunbridge Wells, Kent TN4 8XJ
Tel: 01892 520331 Fax: 01892 510575
Internet: http://www.spahotel.co.uk Email: info@spahotel.co.uk

AAA ☆☆☆, RAC ☆☆☆☆, ETB ✿ ✿ ✿ ✿ ✿ Commended

KENNEL HOLT HOTEL

Goudhurst Road, Cranbrook, Kent TN17 2PT
Tel: 01580 712032 Fax: 01580 715495
AA ★★   *Sets the standard*
www.kennelholt.co.uk

Kennel Holt is 300 yards from the road, an Elizabethan manor house with 10 individually furnished rooms all with en-suite bathrooms. Restaurant, Library and Drawing Room are all filled with antique furniture and pictures. Log fires prevail whenever the air chills.
Kennel Holt is independently owned and run by Sally and Neil Chalmers. The restaurant specialises in fresh local ingredients, imaginatively cooked. An ideal base for visiting the historic houses and gardens of Kent and Sussex.

The Shant Hotel and Prince of Wales

Rural Hotel and Freehouse, owned and managed by Colin and Sue Botley. 16 comfortable bedrooms with en-suite facilities, tea/coffee-making facilities, colour TVs. Good reputation for a wide variation of luncheons, Dinners and snacks available every day. Situated in a rural position just off the A274, 6 miles from Maidstone & M20 Junction 8. Close to Leeds and Sissinghurst Castles.

THE SHANT HOTEL & PRINCE OF WALES
East Sutton, Nr. Maidstone, Kent ME17 3DT
Telephone: 01622 842235 Fax: 01622 844278

Bedgebury Pinetum
Goudhurst, Cranbrook,
Kent TN17 2SL
Tel: 01580 211044
Fax: 01580 212423

Bedgebury Pinetum, started in 1925, originally designed by William Dallimore, a notable botanist from Kew. The collection is set in 300 acres containing the National Conifer Collection, with 5000 specimen trees. It includes rare, endangered and historically important trees.

The Forestry Commission have been responsible for the Pinetum since 1965.

FINCHCOCKS LIVING MUSEUM OF MUSIC
Fine 18th century manor in beautiful garden housing famous collection of period keyboard instruments played in entertaining musical tours whenever the house is open.
OPEN DAYS: Sundays, BH Mondays, Wednesdays & Thursdays in August, 2-6pm. By appointment: most days April-October.
Concerts, fairs & other special events.
All details from:
Finchcocks, Goudhurst, Kent TN17 1HH
Tel: 01580 211702 Fax: 01580 211007
New website: www.finchcocks.co.uk

Royal Tunbridge Wells

Come and stroll through the charming streets of Royal Tunbridge Wells and you will soon discover why this delightful spa town has retained its appeal as one of the most attractive and fashionable spa towns of Georgian and Victorian England.

After the chance discovery of the Chalybeate Spring by Lord North in 1606, shops and lodging houses quickly sprang up around the Spring. Today Royal Tunbridge Wells is most noted for its attractive colonnaded walks, known as the Pantiles, where visitors still come to admire the stylish architecture, to shop at the many intriguing antique and other specialist shops, or just to enjoy a stroll along the Walks, or to "take the waters" served from the Spring in the traditional manner by a "dipper".

Experience the sights, sounds and smells of Royal Tunbridge Wells in its Georgian heyday at the visitor attraction "A Day at the Wells", as you walk through six life-like sets recreating life in Tunbridge Wells over two centuries ago.

Lying at the heart of some of England's most scenic countryside, and with a wide range of attractive accommodation in the area, Royal Tunbridge Wells could not be better situated for a relaxing short break or as a base for touring the surrounding Weald. It provides a delightful retreat for walkers, cyclists, history and garden enthusiasts and nature lovers alike.

Nearby Hever Castle, with its stunning grounds, dates back to the 13th century and was once the childhood home of Anne Boleyn (second wife of Henry VIII). Visitors to Finchcocks, near the pretty village of Goudhurst, are treated by the owner of this beautiful Georgian manor house to informal recitals on a wonderful collection of clavichords and harpsichords. Chartwell, once the charming country residence of Sir Winston Churchill, now houses memorabilia and other articles from the statesman's life. The writer Rudyard Kipling lived at nearby Batemans until 1936, and Vita Sackville-West grew up at Knole and spent her later years at nearby Sissinghurst Castle, famous for its spectacular gardens. The area also boasts several other marvellous gardens such as those at Scotney Castle, Great Dixter and 17th century Groombridge Place.

Royal Tunbridge Wells has something for everyone. If you would like more information on what the area has to offer you, please contact the Royal Tunbridge Wells Tourist Information Centre.

Address
Royal Tunbridge Wells TIC
The Old Fish Market
The Pantiles
Royal Tunbridge Wells
Kent TN2 5TN
England
Tel: 01892 515675
Fax: 01892 534660

TAKE A BREAK IN THE MED

Not the Mediterranean but Medway, named after the river along which are the 'Dickensian' City of Rochester, and the towns of Chatham and Gillingham.

Famed for its Cathedral, Norman Castle and many connections with Charles Dickens, Rochester also offers antiques, rare books, crafts and other gifts on its attractive high street. New for 2001 will be the first fresco to be painted in an English cathedral since the 12th century.

Chatham grew up around its famous dockyard, now a prospective World Heritage Site along with its defences, including Napoleonic Fort Amherst and Elizabethan Upnor Castle. The historic dockyard will also have many new features in 2001, including the dockyard railway and new visitor centre.

The Royal Engineers have long been based in the area and their Gillingham Museum tells of their skills, bravery and heroism, with the largest collection of Victoria crosses in the country.

Naturally the river has many attractions in its own right, with leisure sailing and bird watching both popular. The country's last remaining coal-fired paddle steamer 'Kingswear Castle' provides guided river tours, which are particularly popular during Medway's famous events, such as the Dickens and Sweeps Festivals, and Navy Days.

MEDWAY (COUNCIL)
VISITOR INFORMATION CENTRE
95 HIGH STREET, ROCHESTER, KENT ME1 1LX
Tel: 01634 843666 Fax: 01634 847891
Email: *visitor-centre@medway.gov.uk*
Website: *www.medway.gov.uk*

Maidstone

Recorded in the Domesday Survey as land held by the Archbishop of Canterbury at 'Meddestane' – Maidstone, the County Town of Kent, is a historically captivating area. Situated almost midway between London and Dover the town was a main route for pilgrimages and a bustling centre for local and national trade. Despite many changes throughout the centuries, the ambience of old Maidstone can still be captured when walking through the town in the unusual and intriguing buildings.

Possibly the oldest known inhabitant of Maidstone was the Iguanodon – the fossilised remaiuns were found in 1834. The dinosaur is incorporated in the town's coat-of-arms – the first time in the history of heraldry that a dinosaur has been used. The replica Iguanodon can be seen in the Maidstone Museum & Bentlif Art Gallery in the centre of Maidstone. Also in the Town Centre is the Tyrwhitt-Drake Museum of Carriages, situated in the medieval stables of the Archbishop's Palace – this wonderful collection of vehicles from royal state carriages to horse drawn sledges offers an intriguing visit.

Spanning the River Medway, Maidstone is surrounded by picturesque countryside and villages with a range of delightful accommodation, ideal to enjoy a refreshing and relaxing short break or as a base to explore and tour the Heart of Kent.

Maidstone – Kent's County Town is a reasture trove of hidden delights waiting to be discovered. If you would like more information on what Maidstone has to offer, please contact our award-winning Tourist Information Centres.

Address
Maidstone Tourist
Information Centre
The Gatehouse
Palace Gardens
Mill Street
Maidstone
Kent ME15 6YE
Tel: 01622 602169
Fax: 01622 673581

M20 Tourist Information
Centre
Maidstone Motorway
Service Area
Junction 8, M20
Hollingbourne
Kent ME17 1SS
Tel: 01622 739029
Fax: 01622 738985

Brooklands Museum

Brooklands, the birthplace of British motorsport and aviation, opened in 1907 as the first motor racing track in the world. Features include part of the famous banked circuit and many original buildings plus an amazing collection of historic racing cars and aeroplanes. The famous Loch Ness Wellington aircraft plus the giant Napier-Railton car raced by John Cobb make it a great day out. Visit www.motor-software/brooklands for more details.

Brooklands Museum, Brooklands Road, Weybridge, Surrey KT13 0QN
Tel: 01932 857381 Fax: 01932 855465
Email: brookland@dial.pipex.com

The Powell-Cotton Museum
Quex House and Gardens

This purpose-built internationally important Museum was added on to Major Powell-Cotton's Regency Country home. There are eight galleries in all – three of them built by the Major himself. The Major created huge dioramas showing 500 African and Asian animals, mostly mounted by Rowland Ward, in scenes re-creating their natural habitats.

He assembled one of the largest private collections of African ethnography gathered on his 28 expeditions, and displayed it at the Museum, together with extensive weapon collections, cannon, local archaeological material and outstanding fine arts from many countries of the Orient.

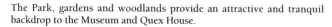

The Park, gardens and woodlands provide an attractive and tranquil backdrop to the Museum and Quex House.

Quex House was built as a Regency gentleman's country residence and grew to become the Victorian mansion we see today. Still home to the Powell-Cotton family, it has a mellow atmosphere with many of the rooms still arranged much as they were during the Major's lifetime and contain fine early and period furniture.

- One of Kent's finest Regency Country Houses (approved for Civil Weddings).

- Home to Generations of Powell-Cotton Families.

- 14 acres of extensive mature gardens, including a Victorian Walled Garden.

- Some of the finest exotic animal displays in the world set in their natural habitat.

- Extensive Museum Galleries housing Oriental Porcelain, African and Asian Fine Arts, Weaponry, Cannon etc.

- Gift Shop

- Restaurant and Banqueting Suite – Cream Teas, Lunches, Snacks etc.

- Conference Room.

Please ring for further details:
The Powell-Cotton Museum
Quex House and Gardens
Quex Park
Birchington, Kent
Tel: 01843 842168
Fax: 01843 846661
Email: powell-cotton.museum@
virgin.net

Charity No. 307757

Open
April-end Oct, Tues, Weds, Thurs, Sundays & Bank Hols, 11am-6pm
(House opens 2.30pm).
March, Nov, Dec, Sunday only 11am-5pm (Museum only).
Jan-Feb, Closed.
Adults £3.50, Concessions £2.80, Family Ticket (2 adults and up to 3 children) £11.

Location
Signed from the A28 into and out of Margate.

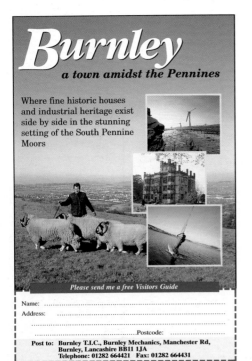

Lancaster Tourism

The historic county town of Lancaster is one of the highlights of any tour of England's North Country. Lancaster enjoys a picturesque setting on the River Lune and is dominated by the hill-top Castle owned by Her Majesty Queen Elizabeth II in her right as "Duke of Lancaster". Close by is the ancient Priory Church of St Mary the Virgin, which has just celebrated its 900th Anniversary.

The Castle is open to the public for guided tours, which include the dark, ancient dungeons, a Grand Jury Room magnificently arrayed with the renowned Gillow furniture, the ghoulish " Drop Room", Hanging Corner, and a stunning Shire Hall decorated with the shields of English monarchs stretching back to Richard I. Part of the Castle still serves as a prison and important law courts.

Next to the Castle, the Priory Church is the finest mediaeval church in the County of Lancashire, with extraordinary wooden carvings and architecture of surpassing beauty.

Sharing the historic Castle Hill site, with its cobbled streets and fine Georgian town houses is a Museum of Gillow Furniture and a Museum of Childhood, both contained in the Judge's Lodgings House. Almost opposite, is the Cottage museum, giving a glimpse of everyday life in the 1840s.

The riverside Custom House, now an award winning Maritime Museum, and the splendid Sessions House, now containing the City Museum and Regimental Museum are short strolls away. High on the opposite hill is the eye-catching Ashton Memorial in Williamson Park, a vast Folly known as the "Taj Mahal of the North" and a Palm House containing tropical butterflies in a natural, free-flying setting.

Historic Lancaster is brought alive throughout the year with its famed historical festivals and promotions. The four day Easter Maritime Festival, when 18th Century costumed "press gangs" rove the quayside seeking recruits for the Royal Navy of Good King George, is a popular gathering of sea shanty singers, Pace Egg dances and other traditional events - many centred on the hospitality of the town's characterful inns. In the summer the Georgian Legacy Festival re-creates scenes from 200 years back and features the unique National Sedan Chair Championships.

Spectacular Fireworks light the November skies on the Saturday nearest "Guy Fawkes Night" and there are torchlit costumed walks around the historic streets and inns throughout the year.

Lancaster Tourist Information Centre,

29 Castle Hill,
Lancaster LA1 IYN

Tel: 01524 32878
Fax: 01524 847472

Pendle
On the Trail of the Pendle Witches

Pendle Hill rises above the ancient hunting ground called the Forest of Pendle. Once the home of wolves and wild boar, it is still an untamed place, full of mystery.

Beneath Pendle Hill are the tiny hamlets and farms which played a part in the true story of the Pendle Witches. It is a story which still haunts the traveller today. How did nine villagers come to be found guilty of witchcraft? And why does mystery still surround them even though their trial is one of the best documented in the world?

On the Trail you will find out about that fateful year of 1612. You will explore the old villages under Pendle Hill where events took place. Then you'll follow the lonely road the Pendle Witches took through the Ribble Valley to Lancaster Castle where they stood trial.

Along the way there are historic places to visit including villages, castles and an ancient abbey which help piece together a mystery which is almost 400 years old.

The wild beauty of the landscape makes this one of the most unspoilt journeys in England. You won't forget the breathtaking drive up the narrow Trough of Bowland and the dramatic descent into the historic City of Lancaster.

There are an astonishing variety of views which span the hills above the River Hodder and take in the Lake District mountains and the sea.

The 45 miles can be followed by car, minibus or bike. Make the most of the experience by taking at least three days, staying at historic pubs, guest houses, hotels or farmhouses along the way. There are also many hikes to enjoy including the classic climb up Pendle Hill.

Addresses

For a complimentary Pendle Witches Trail guide and further information contact:
Tourist Information Centre, 29 Castle Hill, Lancaster LA1 1YN
Tel: +44 (0)1524 32878 (24 hours)

Tourist Information Centre, 12-14 Market Place, Clitheroe Lancashire BB7 2DA
Tel: +44 (0)1200 425566 (24 hours)

Pendle Borough Council Business Centre
Trafalgar Court
Nelson
Lancs BB9 9BT
Tel: +44 (0)1282 661685

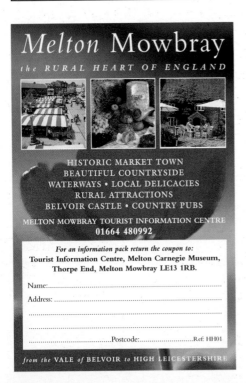

Leicestershire

Leicestershire encompasses all that is precious about the heart of England. There is a wealth of beautiful countryside ranging from the secluded valleys and rocky summits of Charnwood Forest to the sweeping slopes and far off horizons of the Wolds.

There is a county where timeless villages really do exist and market towns actually live up to the name. There are also some of the most tranquil and scenic sections of waterway in Britain. Above all Leicestershire is a place to relax and unwind.

The country is also steeped in history and rich in heritage. Bradgate Park contains the ruins of Bradgate House, birthplace of Lady Jane Grey, the tragic Nine Day Queen of England. Ashby Castle was under siege for over a year during the Civil War and later inspired the famous tournament scene in Sir Walter Scott's novel 'Ivanhoe'.

Bosworth Battlefield is a special place, for the course of English history was changed foreve when the armies of Richard III and Henry Tudor came to an end and the prosperous Tudor era began.

Bosworth Battlefield has an award winning Visitor Centre, which includes artefacts from the Mary Rose, and a well interpreted Battle Trail. A re-enactment of the Battle of Bosworth takes place annually. Narrowboats on the Ashby Canal and steam trains on the Battlefield Railway offer trips from the edge of the Battlefield.

For a free information pack, including 'Cream of Leicestershire & Rutland', which contains 100 places to visit, write to:

Leicestershire Tourism
County Hall
Glenfield
Leicester LE3 8RJ
Tel: 0116 265 7039
Email: tourism@leics.gov.uk

Burghley House

Burghley House is the largest and grandest house of the first Elizabethan Age. Built and mostly designed by William Cecil, Lord High Treasurer of England, between 1565 and 1587, the House is a family home for his descendants to this day. At present it is occupied by Mr. Simon and Lady Victoria Leatham, well-known as one of the experts on 'The Antiques Roadshow'.

Eighteen State Rooms, including many decorated by Antonio Verrio in the 17th century, house a huge collection of great works of art, including one of the most important private collections of 17th century Italian paintings, the earliest inventoried collection of Japanese ceramics in the West, rare examples of European porcelain, and wood carvings by Grinling Gibbons and his followers. There are also four magnificent State Beds, fine examples of English and continental furniture, and important tapestries and textiles.

The Orangery was designed and built by 'Capability' Brown in the 18th century, and is now a licensed restaurant overlooking the rose beds and gardens. The Orangery is open from 11am to 5pm – lunch is served between 12 noon and 2.30pm. Coffee, tea and light refreshments, including traditional cream teas, are available all day.

The Parkland that surrounds the House was laid out by 'Capability' Brown and extends to 160 acres. Visitors are able to walk throughout the Park and enjoy the results of Brown's vision, together with many newly planted trees. The Park is home to a large herd of Fallow deer, established in the 16th century. The deer can be observed at close quarters and provide great enjoyment for children and adults alike.

The House is open daily from Sunday 1st April until Sunday 7th October between 11am and 4.30pm. The House is shown by guided tour only, except on Saturday and Sunday afternoons and Bank Holidays when there are guides in each room. The House will be closed for one day on Saturday 1st September, the cross-country day of the Burghley Horse Trials.

The Sculpture Garden is open between 11am and 4pm every day. The South Garden is open between Saturday 1st April and Monday 1st May. In early April there is usually a splendid display of spring flowers.

(Opening times may be subject to change and alteration at any time).

Enquiries and Party Bookings, contact:
The Manager,
Burghley House,
Stamford,
Lincolnshire PE9 3JY
Tel: 01780 752451
Fax: 01780 480125

Admission charges
The charge covers a tour of the House, car parking and admission to the Park and Sculpture garden. Please telephone for details

Facilities
Licensed Restaurant, Gift Shop, Sculpture Garden, Deer Park, Disabled Access, Ample Car Parking and Coach Park.

Lincolnshire

Lincolnshire lies on the east side of England less than two hours north of London. It is a very attractive rural county but with a vibrant history which has produced many famous sons and daughters – people like Captain John Smith and Sir Isaac Newton to name just two.

The City of Lincoln boasts one of England's loveliest Cathedrals, surprisingly one of the least well known. There are some magnificent country houses and the fertile soils of Lincolnshire mean that we have some splendid gardens too. We have developed a series of themed brochures on such diverse subjects as antiques, churches, aviation heritage, crafts and gardens – all designed to help you make the most of your visit.

The County has strong connections with America – from Captain John Smith, to the 'Separatists' who worshipped in secret at the beautiful mediaeval Gainsborough Old Hall. They eventually managed to escape to become members of the Mayflower Pilgrims. A later exodus left Boston, England to found Boston, Massachusetts. Religion also played a prominent part at Epworth – a pretty little town in the north of the county. It was here, through the sons of Samuel and Susannah Wesley, that Methodism was born and adjacent to the inspiring church of St Andrew where they all preached, you can visit the Old Rectory where John and Charles grew up.

For a free Information Pack call 01522 526450 or Fax: 01522 526431

Lincolnshire Tourism,
Dept Ess,
The Castle,
Lincoln LN1 3AA

Eltham Palace & Gardens

more

style

Spencer House

From its conception, Spencer House was recognised as one of the most ambitious aristocratic private palaces ever built in London and is, today, the city's only great eighteenth-century private palace to survive intact. It is, without question, one of the most important buildings in London; an extraordinarily beautiful house in its picturesque setting overlooking Green Park.

The house was built 1756-66 for John, 1st Earl Spencer. Designed by John Vardy and James 'Athenian' Stuart, the house is one of the pioneer examples of neo-classical architecture and marks a turning point in English architectural history from Palladianism to neo-classical.

Spencer House has regained the full splendour of its late eighteenth-century appearance, after a painstaking ten-year programme of restoration undertaken by RIT Capital Partners plc.

Eight state rooms are now open to the public for viewing on Sundays, and are available for corporate and private entertaining during the rest of the week. These magnificently restored rooms were amongst the first neo-classical interiors in Europe. Vardy's Palm Room, with its spectacular screen of gilded palm trees and arched fronds, is a unique Palladian setpiece, while the elegant mural decorations of Stuart's Painted Room reflect the eighteenth-century passion for classical Greece and Rome.

Stuart's superb gilded furniture has now been returned to its original location in the Painted Room by courtesy of the Victoria & Albert Museum and English Heritage. Visitors can also see a fine collection of eighteenth-century paintings and furniture, specially assembled for the house, including five major Benjamin West paintings graciously lent by Her Majesty the Queen.

Advance booking for group tours may be reserved by applying in writing to the Administrator.

For information on private and corporate entertaining telephone: 020 7514 1964.

Spencer House
27 St James's Place
London SW1
Tel: 020 7499 8620
www.spencerhouse.co.uk

Open Sundays (except Jan & Aug) 10.30am-5.30pm (last tour 4.45pm) (tickets may be purchased from 10.30am)

Admission
Adults £6.00
Concessions £5.00
Children under 16 £5.00
No children under 10

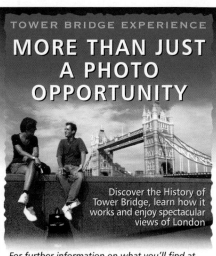

Hampton Court Palace stands majestically on the banks of the River Thames. Its rich red brick Tudor front cannot fail but impress the twentieth century visitor, just as it did when Henry VIII acquired it from Cardinal Wolsey in 1528.

In 1689 Christopher Wren was commissioned by William III to re-design Hampton Court and the result of his work is probably England's best and most famous expression of the baroque style.

With nearly 500 years of royal history Hampton Court has something to offer everyone, a living tapestry of history from Henry VIII to George II.

The Banqueting House is the only surviving part of the Palace of Whitehall, which was the Sovereign's main London residence from the days of Henry VIII, until it was destroyed by fire in 1698. It now stands as the lone testament to the speldours of a regal past.

Charles I commissioned the Flemish painter Rubens to paint the ceiling. Just as the Banqueting House featured in his early career as King, so it was to feature at the end of Charles's reign. On 30th January 1649, on a high platform outside the north end of the building, Charles was beheaded – the only British monarch ever to suffer such a fate.

Kensington Palace is an oasis of tranquillity in the heart of one of London's most prestigious areas.

It's history goes back to 1689 when the newly crowned William III and Mary II commissioned Sir Christopher Wren to convert the then Nottingham House into a royal palace.

This beautiful historic building has seen such momentous events as the death of George II and the birth of Princess Victoria who began her long reign as Queen in 1837, with a meeting of her Privy Council in the Red Saloon.

The Tower of London was first built by William the Conqueror, for the purpose of protecting and controlling the city. Over the ensuing 900 years The Tower of London has served as a royal palace, armoury, fortress, royal mint and more infamously a prison and place of execution.

The Tower remains home to the magnificent Crown Jewels. To many these represent the most potent symbols of the British monarchy.

Hampton Court Palace
Surrey KT8 9AU
Tel: 020 8781 9500
Open mid March to mid Oct:
Tues-Sun 9.30-6 pm
Mon 10.15-6 pm
Mid Oct-mid March:
Tues-Sun 9.30-4.30
Mon 10.15-4.30
Last admission 45 mins
before closing
Closed Dec 24-26 incl.

The Banqueting House
Whitehall Palace
Tel: 020 7930 4179
Open Mon-Sat
10am-5pm
Closed Dec 24-Jan 2

Kensington Palace
Tel: 020 7937 9561
Open mid March-mid Oct
10am-6pm, Mid Oct-mid
March 10am-5pm
Last admission one hour
before closing

The Tower of London
Open March-Oct:
Mon-Sat 9am-6pm
Sun 10am-6pm
Nov-Feb:
Tues-Sat 9am-5pm
Sun-Mon 10am-5pm
Closed Dec 24-26 and Jan 1st.
Last admission one hour
before closing.
Tel: 020 7709 0765

St. John's Gate

Discover the rich history of the Knights Hospitaller, a monastic order dedicated to serving the sick and defending the faith, dating back to the time of the Crusades. The Museum of the Order of St. John is found inside St. John's Gate, built in 1504 and once the entrance to the Knights' English Priory. Treasures on show include arms and armour, a 15th century Flemish altar piece and decorative drug jars from the monks' pharmacy. On the tour, visitors see fine collections of painting, furniture and silver from the order's time on Malta, and the Library which contains manuscripts dating back to the 12th century. The tour continues in the 16th century Priory church with its remarkable Norman

Crypt, where a dramatic tomb effigy shows Prior Weston wrapped in his shroud.

The Priory has an interesting history independent of the Order. After the dissolution of the monasteries, Henry VIII used its precincts for storing army supplies and under Elizabeth I, it housed the Revels Office where thirty of Shakespeare's plays were registered. In the Gate's east tower, Hogarth's father ran a coffee house and Edward Cave's Gentleman's Magazine was published, with a young Dr Johnson writing the articles.

In Victorian times, St. John Ambulance was founded here, inspired by the medical traditions of the Knights. A new interactive exhibition uncovers its surprising history from 19th century mining disasters to London in the Blitz. Ceremonial attire, 1920s Cadet uniforms and an ARP gas suit are among exhibits on display. Visitors can explore multimedia touchscreens, see early film footage and listen to the stories of ordinary members and their extraordinary experiences.

This impressive building, its beautiful contents and museum galleries portray a fascinating and wide-ranging history that should not be missed by anyone visiting London.

St. John's Gate
St. John's Lane
Clerkenwell London EC1M 4DA

Tel 020 7253 6644

Open
Museum
10am-5pm Mon-Fri, 10am-4pm Sat

Tours of St. John's Gate (including Grand Priory Church and Crypt). 11am & 2.30pm Tues, Fri & Sat

Admission
Admission Free,
Donations Welcome

Facilities
Sales Point, Disabled toilet (limited disabled access – please advise before visit)

Transport
Farringdon or Barbican Underground Stations

Syon House and Park

A unique and beautiful house standing in 200 acres of Capability Brown parkland. The London home of the Dukes of Northumberland since 1597, Syon House stands on the banks of the Thames surprisingly only eight miles from Marble Arch and seven miles from Heathrow.

Still the residence of the Percy family, (see feature on Alnwick Castle), Syon is one of London's great stately homes and the house features Robert Adam's designs from 1760 and contains much of the original furnishings. Remodelled from its Tudor original, Syon House is considered to be one of Adam's finest works. The ceiling by Cipriani (Red Drawing Room) and the magnificent Scagliola floor (Ante Room) in particular, attract visitors from all over the world.

The forty acres of garden include the restored Great Conservatory, a huge and beautiful building of glass and stone, now replanted with a succession of plants with a scented theme throughout the summer. You will also discover the minature steam railway (additional to cost of the garden entrance), it operates at weekends only April-October.

Syon Park includes many attractions for a real family day out. The Butterfly House, Art Centre, Cafeteria, Restaurant, National Trust Shop and one of the most extensive Garden Centres in the country, followed by a picnic by the lake and we think you'll agree that there is something to please everyone from the oldest to the youngest.

Syon Park is recognised as a Grade I landscape in the *English Heritage Register of Parks and Gardens of Historic Importance in England.* It is one of Britain's oldest landscapes, and it was started in the 1430s by the Bridgettine nuns.

Address
Syon House and Gardens,
Brentford,
Middlesex TW8 8JF
Tel: 020 8560 0883

Opening Times
Syon House:
14 March – 31 October
Wed, Thurs, Sun & B.H.
Monday 11am–5pm
(open Good Friday &
Easter Saturday)
Gardens:
Daily 10am–5.30pm/dusk

Admission
|Adults £6.00,
Concessions £4.50

Location
A4 Westbound from central
London (8m)

Facilities
National Trust Shop, Cafeteria

MELIÁ WHITE HOUSE
Albany Street, Regents Park, London NW1 3UP
582 Bedrooms (all en suite)
Telephone: 020 7387 1200 Fax: 020 7388 0091
AA ☆☆☆☆ ETB ♛ ♛ ♛ ♛ Commended.
Centrally located adjacent to Regents Park, an ideal location for Oxford Street, the West End and City. This listed building offers a wide selection of bedrooms and suites. A fine choice of dining including an award-winning restaurant, leisure and business centre.

CRESCENT HOTEL
49-50 Cartwright Gardens, Bloomsbury,
London WC1H 9EL
Telephone: 020 7387 1515 Fax: 020 7383 2054
Email: general.enquiries@crescenthoteloflondon.com
www.crescenthoteloflondon.com
27 Rooms (21 en suite)
ETC ♦♦♦, BHA member.
Features: friendly, family-run period furnished townhouse in quiet Georgian garden crescent, high quality housekeeping, individually cooked breakfasts, tennis and rackets, direct-dial telephones in every room. Advice: Antique markets. Walking distance to Russell Square underground, Euston and Kings Cross rail/underground stations, British Museum, Covent Garden. Easy access from Heathrow, Gatwick and Stansted airports; Eurostar terminal.

CAMELOT HOUSE HOTEL
18-20 Sussex Gardens, London W2 1UL
Telephone: 020 7723 2219 Fax: 020 7402 3412
25 Rooms (15 en suite). Highly Commended.
We seek to provide a comfortable and clean home away from home. We are located just five minutes walk from Marble Arch. Our 25 rooms are equipped with televisions and tea/coffee making facilities. Also direct dial telephones. We hope to welcome you soon.

Hogarth's House

Just 50 yards from the busy Hogarth Roundabout lies this charming early 18th century house which was once the country home of William Hogarth, the famous painter and engraver. It is now a gallery where most of his well known engravings are on display. These include: "Harlot's Progress", "Rake's Progress", "Marriage a la Mode", and also "Gin Lane" and "Beer Street" both of which can be bought at the house, together with books and postcards of Hogarth's works. The house was restored with funds from many sources for the Hogarth Tercentenary in 1997.

In nearby Chiswick Mall are houses of a similar period, and in the graveyard around St. Nicholas' Church, is Hogarth's tomb. World famous Chiswick House is only 10 minutes walk away.

Address
Hogarth's House
Hogarth Lane
Great West Road
London W4 2QN
Tel: 020 8994 6757

Opening Times
Tuesday to Friday
1pm-5pm
(November to March
1pm-4pm)
Saturday and Sunday
1pm-6pm
(November to March
1pm-5pm)
Closed Monday
(except Bank Holidays)
Closed Good Friday,
Christmas & Boxing Day
& the month of January
Parking: Axis Business
Centre, named spaces to
the right of the entrance -
just before the house and
Chiswick House Grounds
car park.

Admission
Free Parties by
arrangement.

Buckingham Palace

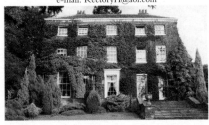

Norwich, Norfolk Broads & Countryside

Just a short journey, 100 miles north east from London lies the heart of quintessential, unspoilt England – Norwich, Norfolk Broads & Countryside.

Set amidst the Norfolk countryside the Norwich area is the perfect base from which to explore and discover the many small market towns, villages, historic homes, the famous Norfolk Broads and at its centre the City of Norwich.

Constructed around a 900 year old Norman cathedral, the centre of Norwich remains perhaps the most intact Medieval city in England. Here, fine merchants' houses, half-timbered shops and elegant Georgian townhouses line cobblestone lanes beneath a skyline that bristles with the bell towers and spires of over 30 flint-built churches dating from the middle ages – more than those of London, Bristol and York put together. Towering over them all is Norwich Castle, one of Britain's great treasure houses.

Set in the tranquil confines of the Cathedral Close, rising to 315 feet, Norwich Cathedral's impressively ornate spire crowns one of the country's most beautiful buildings.

Norwich's Medieval city centre boasts England's largest open air market, together with a great many charming speciality shops and even a museum completely devoted to Mustard whilst the best in antiques and unusual gifts can be found alongside antiquarian books and displays of art.

The city's many theatres, art galleries and music venues provide it with a cultural scene to rival those of England's other main centres.

For boating and wildlife enthusiasts alike the Norfolk Broads (lakes formed with Medieval peat-diggings filled with water) are a very special attraction indeed. Connected by rivers they provide over 200 kilometres of navigable channels, Britain's largest inland lock-free waterway. It is a land of mysterious fens, wet tangled woodlands and acres of march – an enchanted land. A fine city amidst great lakes.

FREE BROCHURE
Tel: +44 (0)1271 336033
(quote ref: 126)
or visit our website:
www.visitnorwich.co.uk

211

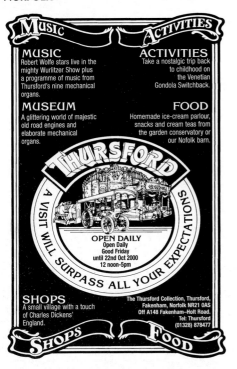

North Norfolk

North Norfolk Coast and Countryside is an area of outstanding natural beauty steeped in heritage and history and yet complimented by a host of attractions and places to visit. Getting to North Norfolk is easy. Norfolk has a good road network connected to Britain's motorways with coach and rail links from most parts of the country and air connections via Norwich Airport.

As soon as you reach North Norfolk you can turn your back on the hustle and bustle, relax and enjoy this unspoilt part of England.

Take time to explore the tranquil countryside where traditional Norfolk flint cottages slumber in sleepy villages along its seemingly endless coastal stretch of wide sandy beaches, reaching north from Horsey to Holkham where boats moor in sheltered harbours and cliffs command views never to be forgotten.

Venture inland to the Norfolk Broads where miles and miles of waterways weave their way through an enchanted watery landscape of reed beds full of wildlife under immense expanses of sky.

No visit to North Norfolk is complete without a visit to one of its magnificent stately homes. Visit Holkham Hall, the palladian style mansion built between 1734 and 1762 by Thomas Coke, 1st Earl of Leicester, one of Britain's most majestic stately homes. Felbrigg Hall, owned by the National Trust, with its original 18th century furniture, or nearby Sandringham, a favourite countryside home of the royal family.

For a summer holiday, short break, summer, autumn or winter, whatever the season North Norfolk has so much to offer.

For free accommodation and attractions guide for North Norfolk, write to:
Coast Countryside & Boating Holidays,
Dept. EES,
1 Upcott Avenue,
BARNSTAPLE
EX31 1HN
or telephone 0870 2410312
or find us on the web:
www.north-norfolk.gov.uk

HOLKHAM
ENJOY 300 YEARS OF HISTORY

Holkham Hall, home of the Earls of Leicester, is one of Britain's most majestic Stately Homes. A classic 18th century Palladian style mansion it has magnificent state rooms with ancient statues and fine paintings and furniture. A Bygones Museum has over 4,000 domestic and agricultural items. Also a History of Farming Exhibition, Restaurant and Pottery Shop. 20001 OPEN: April 15 & 16, May 6, 7, 27 & 28, 11.30am-5pm. Then May 29 to Sept 30, Sun-Thurs (inc) 1pm-5pm.
Holkham Country Fair July 21 & 22, Hall & Museum closed.

Holkham, Wells-next-the-sea, Norfolk NR23 1AB
Tel: 01328 710227 Fax: 01328 711707

Heritage Britain

Hotels, Inns, Bed & Breakfast
Historic Houses, Castles & Gardens,
Antiques & Curios
Arts & Crafts, Books & Tours

Heritage Britain - the essential website for domestic travellers and overseas visitors to Britain and Ireland.

www.heritagebritain.com
mail@heritagebritain.com

SANDRINGHAM HOUSE
MUSEUMS & GARDENS
Country retreat of HM The Queen

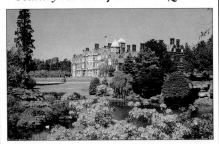

Set in 60 acres of glorious gardens, lakes and woodlands glades, Sandringham House is neither a palace nor a castle but a cherished country home. Built in 1870 by Edward and Alexandra and loved by successive generations of British Monarchs, Sandringham is filled with family portraits, fine furniture and exquisite collections of porcelain, jade and crystal figures and bronzes. A large Museum of Royal mementoes adds to the attraction for all ages. Open from Easter to mid-July and early August to October. Closed Good Friday.

Telephone: 01553 772675

DUKES HEAD HOTEL
Tuesday Market Place, Kings Lynn, Norfolk PE30 1JS
Telephone: 01553 774996 Fax: 01553 763556
71 Rooms (all en suite). AA ☆☆☆, RAC ☆☆☆,
ETB 👑👑👑👑 Commended.
A classical Georgian building overlooking the ancient marketplace, it sits in pride of place at the centre of town. Whilst retaining all its original elegance the hotel has been beautifully refurbished to a high standard. In the restaurant the beautiful decor is complemented by the fine menu.

ABBEY HOTEL
10 Church Street, Wymondham, nr Norwich NR18 0PH
Telephone: 01953 602148 Fax: 01953 606247
23 Rooms (all en suite).
AA ☆☆, ETB 👑👑👑 Commended.
The Abbey Hotel is a mix of 16th to 19th century architecture giving charm and character. Located in a peaceful spot opposite the 12th century Abbey (voted Tourist Church of the Year 1996 and 1997). Wymondham with a streetscape spanning three centuries is an ideal touring base. Come and enjoy a genuine Norfolk experience.

Dating back to the 12th century, this historic port was originally Bishop's Lynn, until Henry VIII renamed it Lynn Regis – King's Lynn – during the reformation. Fine 14th century merchant's houses stretch back to the River Great Ouse and a sense of maritime history pervades among the cobbled lanes, elegant streets and town inns.

At the southern end of Lynn is the Saturday Market Place, shadowed by the beautiful 12th century Church of St Margaret. This area houses some of the finest examples of ancient architecture in England, among them the magnificent chequered-fronted Trinity Guildhall, housing the 'Tales of the Old Gaol House' attraction; the 15th century Hanseatic Warehouse and the Saxon Church of All Saints.

Lynn's second market, the Tuesday Market Place, is a vast and elegant square of mainly Georgian-fronted buildings, from which St George's Guildhall, the largest surviving medieval guildhall in England, and St Nicholas' Chapel, which boasts the country's largest chapel of ease, are within easy walking distance. From here, the famous Custom House is only a short walk away. Built by Henry Bell in 1683, this monument to maritime prosperity overlooks the river from its vantage point on Purfleet Quay and houses the town's Tourist Information Centre and Maritime Display. Close by, along the recently refurbished waterfront is the new Green Quay exhibition, housed in a restored 14th century barn. Other attractions include the Town House Museum, the Lynn Museum and True's Yard Fishing Museum.

While the Queen's Norfolk home at Sandringham ranks as the area's most famous estate, there are many other fine properties scattered across West Norfolk. Just north of King's Lynn is Castle Rising, a Norman hall keep set amidst massive defensive earthworks. Holkham Hall is a classic and imposing 18th century mansion on the coast, and to the south is Houghton Hall, one of the finest Palladian houses in the country, built by Sir Robert Walpole and with lavish interiors by William Kent.

South east of King's Lynn is Oxburgh Hall, a 15th century moated mansion featuring an 80 foot Tudor gatehouse, priest's hole, and panels of embroidery by Mary Queen of Scots. From here the breathtaking ruins of 12th century Castle Acre Priory are a twenty-minute drive away through the West Norfolk counrtyside. With so much to see and do, King's Lynn is ideal for short breaks.

Address
King's Lynn Tourist
Information Centre
Dept. ESS 101
The Custom House
Purfleet Quay
Kings Lynn
PE30 1HP
Tel: 01553 763044

South Northamptonshire Council

SOUTH NORTHAMPTONSHIRE

There are fascinating views, whether you travel by boat or walk beside the Oxford and Grand Union Canal. You can walk past seven locks to Stoke Bruerne, where there are craft shops, two pubs and places to eat, as well as boat trips in summer. Why not try a narrow boat holiday, there are even en-suite rooms on a Hotel Boat! For more information contact:

**BRACKLEY TOURIST INFORMATION H20
2 BRIDGE STREET, BRACKLEY,
NORTHANTS NN13 5EP
Tel: 01280 700111 Fax: 01280 700157**

Rockingham Castle
2 miles north of Corby, Northants, off A6003

Built by William the Conqueror, a Royal fortress for 450 years, Rockingham offers the best remaining visible ground plan of a Norman castle in Britain. For the last 450 years it has been home to the present family who offer visitors a warm welcome. Set in a panoramic location, with views over five counties, the Castle has magnificently furnished rooms of several periods, and is surrounded by 12 acres of superbly contrasting gardens. An Exhibition sets out the Castle's fascinating history, home-made teas, lunches and light refreshments are available. **Open 1 April to 30 September.**
For details Tel: 01536 770240 Fax: 01536 771692

NOTICE BOARD
New Dialling Codes

Cardiff - (01222) xxx xxx
becomes (029) 20 xx xxxx

Coventry - (01203) xxx xxx
becomes (024) 76 xx xxxx

London - (0171) xxx xxxx
becomes (020) 7 xxx xxxx

THE GLOBE HOTEL
High Street, Weedon, Northampton NN7 4QD
Telephone: 01327 340336 Fax: 01327 349058
18 Rooms (all en suite). 2 Four Posters.
AA ☆☆, RAC ☆☆, ETC ☆☆.
The Globe Hotel is a characterful old coaching inn conveniently located on the junction of the A5 and A45, close to Daventry and Northampton. It is the ideal place for business and social occasions. Whether you are looking for accommodation, conference facilities or a place for a family gathering.

COURTYARD BY MARRIOTT HOTEL
Bedford Road, Northampton NN4 7YF
Telephone: 01604 622777 Fax: 01604 655454
104 Rooms (all en suite)
ETB ♛♛♛
A modern 104 bedroomed hotel located close to historic attractions, the theatre, galleries and just 15 minutes from Silverstone and Althorp House. The hotel has a relaxed friendly atmosphere and specialises in group travel. Only 5 minutes from J15 off the M1, making the hotel an ideal base to leisure travellers.

THE CROWN HOTEL
20-22 Market Place, Brackley, Northants NN13 7DP
Telephone: 01280 702210 Fax: 01280 701840
19 Rooms (all en suite).
AA ☆☆, RAC ☆☆.
The Hotel is a 13th century Coaching Inn situated in the heart of the market town of Brackley. Minutes from the M40 and only 7 miles from Silverstone Grand Prix racing circuit. Fully licensed with Egerton Restaurant open 7 days. Conference & Banqueting facilities available.

Northampton

Northampton combines a rich heritage and distinguished history with all the energy and vigour of one of the fastest growing towns in the country. Located in the heart of England, halfway between London and Birmingham, the town offers visitors the highest quality and range of accommodation and a strong portfolio of places to see and visit.

Statues and carvings on the town's magnificent Victorian Gothic Guildhall depict events and people in the town's fascinating history. Other buildings of architectural interest include the Church of the Holy Sepulchre, one of only four Norman round churches remaining in England, and 78 Derngate a terraced house remodelled by the celebrated art-nouveau architect Charles Rennie Mackintosh. Fascinating glimpses of Northampton's past can be seen on the Historic Town Trail, or find out more on a guided walk around the town centre.

In the past Northampton enjoyed a worldwide reputation as the centre of the English shoe industry. Today the Central Museum and Art Gallery in Guildhall Road boasts the largest museum collection of boots and shoes in the world and visitors can see shoe fashions across the centuries and the machines that made them.

Dating back to 1235, the town's impressive Market Square has a bustling traditional market with over 260 stalls, ideal for browsing and bargain hunting. The Square leads off to vibrant pedestrian streets and shopping malls which have all the well-known names, as well as many specialist shops for those who are looking for something just that little bit different.

Church of the Holy Sepulchre

Visitors are spoilt for choice when it comes to entertainment. The elegant Royal Theatre, a gem of Victorian architecture is cleverly linked to the Derngate, a multifaceted entertainment centre. The town also boasts a cosmopolitan range of café bars, pubs, restaurants and nightclubs. Annual events include the Music & Arts Festival (June), Town Show (July), Hot Air Balloon Festival (August), Heritage Open Days (September) and the St. Crispin Street Fun Fair (October).

Northampton is perfectly placed for exploring notable attractions nearby including Althorp (family home and burial place of Diana, Princess of Wales); Sulgrave Manor (home of the ancestors of George Washington) and Rockingham Castle.

Address
Tourist Information Centre
Mr Grants House
St Giles Square
Northampton
NN1 1DA
Tel: 01604 622677
Fax: 01604 604180
e-mail:
tic@northampton.gov.uk
www.northampton.gov.uk/
tourism

Tourism Development Unit
Northampton Borough
Council
Tel: 01604 238775
Fax: 01604 238988

Alnwick District
The Heart of Northumberland

★ Magnificent castles – including Alnwick, family home to the Duke of Northumberland.

★ Award winning rural beaches

★ Breathtaking countryside and Northumberland National Park

★ Historic market towns and villages

★ An area rich in history

. . . *everything for a perfect break*

For a FREE brochure Tel: 01665 510665

TILLMOUTH PARK
Country House Hotel

Built in 1882 by the famous architect Charles Barry, Tillmouth Park typifies a more leisurely age. A secluded mansion set in fifteen acres of mature parkland and gardens. You will feel yourself relax into it's atmosphere of a bygone age. With 14 individually styled, en-suite bedrooms and award-winning cuisine, Tillmouth Park is ideally located for visiting the many stately houses and historic sites in the Scottish borders as well as a venue for shooting, fishing, riding and golf.

For reservations write to:
**Tillmouth Park Hotel,
Cornhill-on-Tweed,
Northumberland TD12 4UU
Tel: 01890 882255 Fax: 01890 882540**

The Blue Bell
at Belford, Northumberland
**Tel: 01668 213543 Fax: 01668 213787
Email: bluebel@globalnet.co.uk**

A **17th century Royal Mail Coaching Inn** offering delightful en-suite bedrooms, excellent cuisine and award winning hospitality in this timeless and unspoilt area. Ideally located for discovering the best of Northumbria's magnificent Coastline and the National Parks of the Cheviot Hills. The Hotel represents some of the finest accommodation in the region with 17 individually designed bedrooms and three superb **Self Catering Apartments**.
The Blue Bell specialises in short breaks for Golf, Birdwatching and Walks and is open all year round.

WHITE SWAN HOTEL
Bondgate Within, Alnwick, Northumberland
NE66 1TD
Telephone: 01665 602109 Fax: 01665 510400
58 Rooms (all en suite)
AA☆☆☆, RAC ☆☆☆, ETB ♛♛♛, Highly Comm.
Former 18th century Coaching Inn with many fittings from the sister ship of the Titanic Liner, the *SS Olympic*. Situated just off the A1 in the heart of the old capital of Northumberland, offering fine fayre with feature bedrooms in a graceful setting. Only ten minutes' walk from the historic Alnwick Castle.

[RS] [symbols] [P] [symbols] [V] [GF] [symbols] [SPECIAL]
[1][2][3] [C]

CHARLTON HOUSE
2 Aydon Gardens, South Road, Alnwick, Northumbria
Tel: 01665 605185
5 Rooms (all en-suite)
ETB ♦♦♦♦ Highly Commended, AA QQQ
Recommended, Which? Consumer Guide Recommended.
Charlton House, delightful Victorian town house where guests are always welcome. First class en-suite bedrooms, ideally situated in the historic border town of Alnwick, home of the Duke of Northumberland. **From £20 pp pn.**

[symbols] [P] [V] [TB]

Chillingham Castle

Situated in a spectacular setting, Chillingham Castle is possibly the finest surviving example of fortified domestic architecture in the county. The same family have owned the castle since the mid-1200s. 13th and 14th century monarchs rested here on their way to Scottish campaigns.

Here are fortifications, courtyards, a Minstrel's Hall, even dungeons and Torture Chambers. We have hidden passages through which Castle defenders escaped.

The Avenues and Gardens were laid out by Sir Jeffrey de Wyatville fresh from his Royal Windsor triumphs. The best specimen trees in Northumberland form a backdrop to the formal topiary gardens and England's longest herbeaceous border. Astonishing drifts of snowdrops, daffodils, bluebells give way to rhododendrons and then the glory of the summer gardens.

Near to hand the famous Chillingham Wild Cattle have their own separate venture and, with luck, you may see red squirrels and fallow deer as well as badger and even otter up by the lake.

The Castle has seven self-contained apartments and is a wonderful base for visits to the sea, fishing resorts, mountainous walks and several golf courses. It is a unique venue for weddings, seminars and small conferences.

Chillingham Castle,
Northumberland NE66 5NJ
Tel: 01668 215359
Fax: 01668 215463

Opening Times
Easter, May through September (closed Tuesdays May, June and September). Parties by arrangement at any time.

Admission (2001)
Adults £4.50, Senior Citizens £4.00, Children aged 3 to 13 50p. Group rate £3.80

Facilities
Shop, Tearoom, Woodland, Formal Gardens, Parking, Accommodation and Catering. No Dogs.

LANGLEY CASTLE

Langley-on-Tyne, Hexham,
Northumberland NE47 5LU
Tel: 01434 688888 Fax: 01434 684019

Langley is a genuine 14th Century, fortified Castle hotel, offering every modern comfort, within a charming medieval setting. The eight bed-chambers are luxuriously appointed, with private facilities, some boasting features such as four-poster beds, sauna, spa-bath and window seats set into 7 feet thick walls.

The CastleView development within the grounds, offers an additional eight bedrooms, all with private facilities and stunning views up to the Castle itself.

The magnificent drawing room compliments an intimate restaurant.

Langley extends a unique exclusivity, perfect for discovering the riches of Northumberland.

THE PHEASANT INN
By Kielder Water, Stannersburn, Falstone,
Northumberland NE48 1DD
Telephone: 01434 240382 Fax: 01434 240382.
8 Rooms (all en suite).
AA/ETB ◆◆◆◆ Commended, Staying off the Beaten Track, Egon Ronay, Circle (Ind. Hotels), Ashley Courtenay Highly Commended.
The Pheasant is a 375-year-old Country Inn which offers superior en suite accommodation, as well as retaining its old worlde charm of beamed ceilings, exposed stone walls, open fires and a collection of rural antiques. All meals are prepared by your hosts, to a high standard, most of which are traditional dishes. An excellent centre for touring.

BATTLESTEADS HOTEL
Wark, nr Hexham, Northumberland
Telephone: 01434 230209 Fax: 01434 230730
e-mail: info@Battlesteads-Hotel.co.uk
Web page: http://www.Battlesteads-Hotel.co.uk
10 Rooms (all en suite). ETB ♛♛ Commended.
18th century Inn, formerly a farm house, in the heart of rural Northumberland. Close to the Roman wall and Kielder Water. An ideal centre for exploring the border country and for relaxing.

Castle Morpeth

Castle Morpeth, 'The Gateway to Northumberland', is the ideal base for exploring Northumberland and the Scottish Borders. Nestling between Holy Island, Hadrian's Wall and the Scottish Borders, Northumberland's historic towns, magnificent castles and beautiful beaches are within easy reach. Bisected by the A1 and served by other major roads, it's open, unspoilt countryside, magnificent beaches and mellow sandstone villages are easily accessible to visitors from any direction.

MORPETH, County Town of Northumberland, combines specialist shopping facilities, plentiful accommodation and an excellent Wednesday market. Within 20 minutes journey of the Metro Centre shopping complex and Newcastle upon Tyne with its superb nightlife, restaurants and theatres, you can 'shop till you drop'.

The Normans sited a castle here above the River Wansbeck and 12th century Cistercians built an abbey nearby. Though these have largely gone, much of the old Morpeth does remain and is outlined in an excellent town trail. There's new pride too in the 13th century Chantry, restored to prove a home for a splendid Bagpipe Museum, Northumbrian Craft Centre and the Tourist Information Centre. Thus blending old and new, Morpeth remains at heart what it has always been – a market town of great character, the focal point of villages around.

DRURIDGE BAY stretches in one magnificent curve from the old village of Hauxley in the north to Cresswell in the south. Mature sand dunes and miles of beautiful white sand, Druridge has now been recognised as part of Northumberland's 'Heritage Coast'. Druridge Bay Country Park, the largest country park in Northumberland, combines the country pursuits of birdwatching, walking and angling with the excitement of water-skiing, canoeing and sailing.

BOLAM LAKE COUNTRY PARK near Belsay. Created in 1818 by John Dobson, with woodlands, lakeside meadows, paths and picnic areas. An excellent location for birdwatching.

BELSAY HALL CASTLE & GARDENS, Belsay, one of the most remarkable estates in the Border Country. Here you can visit the medieval castle, a Jacobean manor house, a Georgian hall and breathtaking gardens (English Heritage).

WALLINGTON HALL, Cambo an elegant 17th century home of the Trevelyan family, set in 100 acres of lawns, lakes and woodland including a walled garden with large conservatory (National Trust).

Accommodation and Tourist Information
Morpeth Tourist Information Centre,
The Chantry,
Bridge Street,
Morpeth NE61 1PD
Tel: 01670 511323
Fax: 01670 511326
Open Mon-Sat, 10am-5pm

Druridge Bay
Open all year, daily

Belsay Hall Castle & Gardens
Open all year, daily

Wallington Hall
House: 1st Apr-30th Sept daily except Tuesday 13.00-17.30;
1st Nov daily except Tues 13.00-16.30
Walled Garden:
1st Apr-end Sept daily 10.00-19.00; 1st Oct-1st Nov daily 10.00-18.00;
Nov-March daily 10.00-16.00 or dusk

Nottingham
The city of legends

A wealth of attractions, events and superb shopping await exploration in the historic city of Nottingham. With many areas conveniently pedestrianised, the compact street layout makes it easy to discover the full city picture.

Attraction treasures include The Caves of Nottingham, a unique insight of Nottingham's 700 year old man-made sandstone cave network where you can visit a World War II air-raid shelter, medieval tannery and beer cellars.

The beautiful Lace Market area is home to a spine chilling visitor experience, Condemned!... at the Galleries of Justice. Based in a magnificent 19th Century court-room and county gaol, visitors can assume the identity of past prisoners and see the site of the hangman's gibbet. The neighbouring Lace Hall offers more gentle appeal with exhibits researching the history of Nottingham's lace industry in the beautiful setting of a former Unitarian chapel.

Other attractions all within easy walking distance of each other are Nottingham Castle Museum, Brewhouse Yard (situated next to the famous Ye Old Trip to Jerusalem pub), The Tales of Robin Hood and the medieval timbered Lace Centre (opposite the famous Robin Hood statue).

Newstead Abbey

Newstead Abbey (pictured) is just 11 miles north of the city – a magnificent, fully furnished former ancestral home of Lord Byron. Displays of original manuscripts are also available.

Events to look out for include Goose Fair, (now in its 704th year) traditionally held over the first Thursday, Friday and Saturday in October – the largest travelling fun fair in Europe with the unique combination of old Victoria side stalls lying in the shadow of the latest white-knuckle rides.

Colourful medieval celebrations take place at the end of October during the Robin Hood Pageant at Nottingham Castle. Spectacular floodlit jousts highlight this golden opportunity to re-live the life and times of the world's most famous outlaw.

For further information, please contact:

Arts, Tourism & Heritage Division
Nottingham City Council
Castle Gate House
24-30 Castle Gate
Nottingham NG1 7AT

Tel: 0115 915 1418
Fax: 0115 915 1414

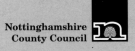

Newark and Sherwood

The delightful District of Newark and Sherwood, famed for its connections with Robin Hood, extends a warm welcome to you.

Sherwood Forest and Robin Hood are well-known throughout the world but the District has an abundance of other attractions to offer.

Two very interesting market towns, historic Newark-on-Trent with important Civil War connections and the pretty little town of Southwell with its beautiful Norman Minster.

Markets, antiques fairs and good shopping can be enjoyed throughout the District as well as friendly pubs and restaurants.

Visitors will discover a wealth of attractive villages, many of which have retained their special traditions. Famous names such as Charles I, Byron and Darwin are associated with the District of Newark and Sherwood

A wide variety of interesting attractions, ranging from fine halls, splendid gardens to lively farm parks enhance and make Newark and Sherwood an area truly worth exploring.

Visitors interested in sport will not be disappointed. The District includes an all weather horseracing track, excellent golf courses, good horse riding, fishing and boating. Passing through the area are two long distance footpaths, the Robin Hood Way and the Trent Valley Way.

Newark is the proud home of Sherwood Forest Holiday Village - Centre Parcs' first holiday village in the united Kingdom - an all-season holiday complex with excellent sporting and leisure facilities.

Many events take place within the District throughout the year including the very popular Robin Hood Festival at Sherwood Forest Country Park and the International Antiques Fairs at Winthorpe near Newark.

The District's accommodation addresses range from good hotels, guest houses, B and B's, inns and farmhouses to delightful self-catering cottages, an excellent holiday village and an award winning caravan park. All of them will give you, the visitor, a warm and friendly welcome.

To make the most of your visit to our area why not telephone or call in at one of our Tourist Information Centres. Staff at the Centres will be able to assist you in a friendly and efficient way with the information you need to make your holiday truly special.

Newark Tourist Information Centre
The Gilstrap Centre
Newark
Nottinghamshire NG24 1BG

Telephone: Newark
(01636) 78962

Ollerton Tourist Information Centre
Sherwood Heath, Ollerton Roundabout
Ollerton, Newark
Nottinghamshire NG22 9DR

Telephone: Mansfield
(01623) 824545

The Oxfordshire Cotswolds

Warm golden stone, meandering streams, historic houses, peace and tranquillity. An area of gently contoured hills, patches of woodland and sheep grazing; unexpected glimpses of hidden valleys containing cottages whose gardens overflow with flowers, and churches and stately homes reflecting the power and splendour of England's past. This is the Oxfordshire Cotswolds.

The principal towns for visitors are Burford, often known as "The Gateway to the Cotswolds", Chipping Norton, Witney and Woodstock. Of more recent origin is the bustling town of Carterton, the home of RAF Brize Norton.

Although a rural area road and rail communication are good with easy access from Oxford, Gloucester, Cheltenham and Stratford upon Avon. Airports at Heathrow and Birmingham are less than 90 minutes away.

However, the narrow country lanes over rolling hills linking the beautiful golden villages with the countryside provide the key to the Oxfordshire Cotswolds.

The influence of water is ever present. From the mighty Thames coursing its way along the southern fringe of the district to its meandering tributaries – the evocatively named Windrush, Evenlode, Glyme, Dorn and Cherwell.

The traveller is offered a plentiful supply of hotels, inns and guest houses with an excellent range of bed and breakfast establishments. Pubs offer good real ales, good food and traditional games of darts, dominoes plus Oxfordshire's Aunt Sally. During the summer months the colourful groups of Morris Dancers perform in the centuries old traditional manner of the Oxfordshire Cotswolds.

Visit the fine heritage of country houses including Rousham, Kelmscott, Stanton Harcourt and the splendours of Blenheim Palace. See the ruins of Minster Lovell Hall by the tumbling Windrush and North Leigh Roman Villa whilst the Rollright Stones spread an aura of mystery and magic about them.

If you are a fairly active person the extensive network of well signed field paths invite you to travel the old way and discover the unspoilt villages and hamlets by foot, cycle or horse staying at inns unearby. Whichever way you travel you will see and hear England at its most glorious.

Truly the Oxfordshire Cotswolds are made for exploring.

Visitor Information Centres

The Brewery,
Sheep Street,
Burford
Oxon OX18 4LP
Tel: 01993 823558
Fax: 01993 823590

The Guildhall,
Chipping Norton,
Oxon OX7 5NJ
Tel/Fax: 01608 644379

51a Market Square,
Witney,
Oxon OX8 6AG
Tel: 01993 775802
Fax: 01993 709261

The Oxfordshire Museum,
Park Street,
Woodstock, Oxon OX20 4SN
Tel: 01993 813276
Fax: 01993 813632

Email:
tourism@westoxon.gov.uk
www.oxfordshirecotswolds.org

227

THE BEAR HOTEL
Park Street, Woodstock, Oxon
Telephone: 0870 400 8202 Fax: 01993 813380

This charming old 13th century coaching inn is located in the centre of the historical Cotswold town of Woodstock. By the gates of Blenheim Palace and only 8 miles from the centre of the university town of Oxford. Whether business or pleasure the Bear with a reputation for hospitality and cuisine is the perfect choice. 52 Rooms (all en suite). 6 Four Posters

AA ☆☆☆ ❀❀, RAC ☆☆☆, RAC Merit Award for Comfort.

FEATHERS HOTEL
Market Square, Woodstock, Oxfordshire OX20 1SX
Telephone: 01993 812291 Fax: 01993 813158
E-Mail: enquiries@feathers.co.uk
21 Rooms (all en suite).
AA ☆☆☆ ❀❀❀.
This privately owned 17th century town hotel, with individually decorated rooms is centrally situated in picturesque Woodstock within walking distance of Blenheim Palace, on the edge of the Cotswolds and eight miles from Oxford. The fine cuisine, which has received much critical acclaim, the friendly staff and relaxing atmosphere contribute towards an enjoyable stay.

VICKERS HOTEL & RESTAURANT
7 Market Place, Woodstock
Telephone: 01993 811212 Fax: 01993 811030
6 Rooms (all en suite). 2 Four Posters.
The 16th century Vickers Hotel & Restaurant is perfectly situated right in the centre of Woodstock overlooking the ancient market place. We offer the greatest modern comforts in truly historic surroundings. Lunch or dinners are served in the large and timbered restaurant. The bedrooms are tastefully decorated individually to suit all tastes.

The Black Prince
**2 Manor Road
Old Woodstock
Oxfordshire OX20 1XJ
Tel/Fax: 01993 811530**

Traditional English Pub serving real ales. Home cooked food in restaurant or bar. Sunday roasts a speciality. Varied vegetarian menu. Real fires in the winter in our beautiful Cotswold stone fireplaces.

Occasional live music. In the summer enjoy the garden on the banks of the River Glyme, overlooking Woodstock's ancient Watermeadows.

Entrances to Blenheim Palace and Park close by.

The Crown Inn
**31 High Street
Woodstock
Oxfordshire OX20 1TE
Tel: 01993 811117
Fax: 01993 813339**

Beautiful, lively 17th century inn in the heart of the ancient town of Woodstock. Bed & Breakfast. Eight guest rooms, all with showers. Family room. Tea/coffee making facilities. Sky TV in every room.

Real ales and high quality cuisine available in our comfortable, convivial bars and conservatory restaurant.

Private functions and conferences catered for.

The Marlborough Arms Hotel
**Oxford Street, Woodstock, Oxfordshire OX20 1TS
Tel: 01993 811227
Fax: 01993 811657**

Dating back to 1649 with cobbled courtyard, oak beams and welcoming log fires, the Marlborough Arms Hotel evokes the atmosphere of the heyday of the coaching era. 16 bedrooms, most with en-suite bathrooms, tea/coffee making facilities, TV, four poster beds available. Conferences and private celebrations expertly catered for.
Relax in comfortable lounges and bar. Eat in Winston's Restaurant, with its collection of Churchill memorabilia. Blenheim Palace, Churchill's birthplace and 'Capability' Brown's Park within walking distance.

Blenheim Palace

Blenheim Palace, home of the 11th Duke of Marlborough and birthplace of Sir Winston Churchill was built for John Churchill, 1st Duke of Marlborough, by Sir John Vanbrugh between the years 1705 and 1722.

The land and a sum of £240,000 were given to the Duke by a munificent sovereign, Queen Anne, and a grateful nation in recognition of his great victory over the French and Bavarians at the Battle of Blenheim 1704.

Apart from Vanbrugh, who designed the Palace in the Baroque style, other famous architects, craftsmen and landscape gardeners have been involved in the construction and development of Blenheim. The original gardens were designed by Queen Anne's gardener Henry Wise with later (1760s) alterations by Lancelot 'Capability' Brown which included the creation of one of Blenheim's most outstanding features, the lake. In more recent times the French architect, Achille Duchene, built the formal gardens to the east and west of the palace. Hawksmoor, Grinling Gibbons, Yenn and Chambers also contributed to the Palace and gardens as we see them today.

WORLD HERITAGE LIST
Blenheim Palace was recommended by H.M. Government and accepted by UNESCO's World Heritage Committee for inclusion in the World Heritage List as a site of special Heritage value.

SANDFORD AWARD
Blenheim has held the Sandford Award for an outstanding contribution to Heritage Education since 1982.

BLENHEIM VISITORS
View Sir Winston Churchill's Birth Room and the Churchill Exhibition. Admire tapestries, paintings, sculpture and fine furniture, set in magnificent gilded State Rooms, and the outstanding beauty of the Long Library, containing over 10,000 volumes in a room 183ft. in length.

The inclusive ticket covers the Palace tour, gardens, motor launch, train, butterfly house, lavender and herb gardens and adventure play area, and there are also restaurants, cafeterias, gift shops and a garden shop. Optional extras are the Marlborough Maze and Rowing Boat Hire.

Address
Blenheim Palace
Woodstock, Oxon
OX20 1PX.
Tel: 01993 811325
(24hr recorded info)

Opening Times
Open Daily 10.30am-4.45pm
mid March to 31st October

Location
8 miles North of Oxford on the A44

Facilities
Guided tours, Gift Shops,
Restaurant, Cafeterias

The Oxford Story Exhibition
900 Years of Oxford University History in 1 Hour!

OXFORDSHIRE

The Oxford Story Exhibition captures the very essence of Oxford University's fascinating 900 year history which is brought to life as you travel through the exhibition's impressive recreated scenes, events and even smells of a bygone era!

Learn about the University's early beginnings and the interesting facts behind its record breaking discoveries.

Meet the famous faces who came through Oxford to make their impact on our world in the fields of sport, medicine, literature and politics.

Relax on The Oxford Story's amazing dark 'ride' and enjoy the excellent commentary which is available in a number of foreign languages, with a specially recorded version for children.

Excellent for group visits, The Oxford Story offers special group rates, based on 20 or more in a party. Advanced booking for groups is always advisable and there is a coach drop off/pick up point in Beaumont Street.

At the end of the Oxford Story Exhibition, enjoy our excellent Gift Shop – one of the finest in the city. The shop is an official stockist of the 'University of Oxford Collection' and also stocks unusual items such as miniature versions of Oxford's famous stone gargoyles and hand painted chess sets.

College Guest Pass

This package ticket offers admissions to The Oxford Story and 2 University colleges. The Pass can be purchased at The Oxford Story during spring and summer.

"The Student Life" – a new film at the beginning of the exhibition which gives a fascinating insight into a student's university life at Oxford.

The Oxford Story Exhibition is located at the heart of Oxford. Follow the city centre signposts.

Address
The Oxford Story
6 Broad Street
Oxford
OX1 3AJ
Tel: 01865 728822
Fax: 01865 791716

Opening Times
April – October
9.30 – 5.00pm
July – August
9.30 – 5.30pm
November – March
10.00am – 4.30pm
(weekends 5.00pm)
Closed Christmas Day

Admission
(valid until 31.1.2001)
Adult £5.20
Child £4.70
Senior £4.70
Student £4.70
Family £17.50 (2+2)

Recreating the Golden Age of the Great Western Railway

Open weekends all year
daily Easter to September

See the steam locomotives in the engine shed • stations and signalling • Brunel's broad gauge trackwork and much more.

STEAM DAYS WITH RIDES ON TRAINS and special events throughout the year

DIDCOT 2000 – the steam event of the millennium

Please write or telephone for a programme
Entrance at Didcot Parkway rail station
on A4130, signed from A34 and M4 (junction 13)

DIDCOT RAILWAY CENTRE
DIDCOT • OXFORDSHIRE
Tel: 01235 817200
www.didcotrailwaycentre.org.uk

THE MANOR HOUSE AND GARDENS STANTON HARCOURT
**9 miles west of Oxford,
5 miles SE of Witney off B4449**

Unique mediaeval buildings in tranquil surroundings – Old Kitchen, (Alexander) Pope's Tower and Domestic Chapel. House maintained as family home, containing a fine collection of Pictures, Silver, Furniture and Porcelain. 12 acres of Garden with Great Fish Pond and Stew Ponds.

Open: Apr 23, 24, 30; May 1, 11, 14, 25, 28, 29; Jun 8, 11, 22, 25; Jul 6, 9, 20, 23; Aug 3, 6, 17, 20, 24, 27, 28; Sept 7, 10, 21, 24.

Admission: *House and Gardens*, Adults £5.00, Children & OAPs £3.00. *Garden only*, Adults £3.00, Children & OAPs £2.00.

Waterperry
GARDENS

Eight acres of stunning gardens famed for the 200ft herbaceous border, flowering continuously from May to October. Plant enthusiasts will love the tree and shrub borders, the alpines and the formal garden.

Open all year round, 7 days a week. Closed during Christmas week and Art in Action Festival. Superb teashop facilities, plant centre and craft gallery.

Waterperry Gardens Ltd
Waterperry, Nr. Wheatley, Oxon OX33 1JZ
Just off M40 junction 8
Tel: 01844 339226

NOTICE BOARD
New Dialling Codes

Cardiff - (01222) xxx xxx
becomes (029) 20 xx xxxx

Coventry - (01203) xxx xxx
becomes (024) 76 xx xxxx

London - (0171) xxx xxxx
becomes (020) 7 xxx xxxx
        (0181) xxx xxxx
becomes (020) 8 xxx xxxx

Portsmouth - (01705) xxx xxx
becomes (023) 92 xx xxxx

Southampton - (01703) xxx xxx
becomes (023) 80 xx xxxx

Northern Ireland - (01232) xx xxxx
becomes (028) 90 xx xxxx

ROUSHAM HOUSE
Steeple Aston, Oxfordshire OX6 3QX.
Tel: 01869 347110/0860 360407
Owner: Charles Cottrell-Dormer Esq.
Contact: Charles Cottrell-Dormer Esq.
Rousham represents the first stage of English landscape design and remains almost as William Kent (1685-1748) left it. One of the few gardens of this date to have escaped alteration. Walled garden with herbaceous borders, rose garden and pigeon house.

Bring a picnic and its yours for the day.
Location: E of A4260 S of B4030.
Opening Times: House; Apr-Sept, Wed, Sun and BH Mons 2.00pm-4.30pm. Garden; All year, daily, 10.00am-4.30pm last entry.
Admission: Garden: Adult £3.00. House: Adult £3.00
No children under 15.

KINGS HEAD INN & RESTAURANT
The Green, Bledington, Oxon OX7 6XQ
Telephone: 01608 658365 Fax: 01608 658902
Email: kingshead@orr-ewing.com
12 Rooms (all en suite), 1 Four Poster. AA QQQQ Selected, ETB ♛♛♛ Commended, Johansens, Egon Ronay. Quintessential Cotswold Inn located on the village green with brook and attendant ducks. Retains olde world charm, inglenook fireplace, pews, settles and beams. Delightful bedrooms complement, with full facilities and thoughtful extras. Award winning restaurant offering bar fayre, table d'hôte, á la carte. Ideal base for Stratford, Blenheim, Warwick etc.

C

North Oxfordshire
The Cherwell Valley

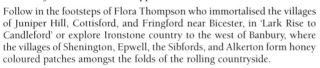

Beautiful North Oxfordshire is adjacent to the Oxfordshire Cotswolds, and remains a reassuringly rural, gentle harmony of grassy meadows, cornfields, ancient hedgerows and quiet streams.

Banbury is probably best known for its Cakes, Cross and Nursery Rhyme – a good place to get a feel for this lovely area is the Museum and Tourist Information Centre opposite the Cross.

When you're out and about in North Oxfordshire, you'll discover Bicester and Kidlington – as well as an abundance of picturesque villages. Adderbury, celebrated for the glory of its medieval church, Hook Norton with its brewery, Deddington with its ancient market square and interesting local shops and Bloxham with its charming village museum – these are just a few to wet the appetite!

Follow in the footsteps of Flora Thompson who immortalised the villages of Juniper Hill, Cottisford, and Fringford near Bicester, in 'Lark Rise to Candleford' or explore Ironstone country to the west of Banbury, where the villages of Shenington, Epwell, the Sibfords, and Alkerton form honey coloured patches amongst the folds of the rolling countryside.

The River Cherwell runs the length of the valley, and is accompanied by the beautiful and tranquil Oxford Canal where life slows down to a gentle pace. The towpath is a long distance walk, and there are a series of seven circular walk leaflets and guided walks. The area also forms part of the Oxfordshire Cycleway.

North Oxfordshire is abound with attractions to suit young and old alike. Enjoy the chance to handle chicks, ducklings and rabbits at the Waterfowl Sanctuary and Children's Farm at Wigginton Heath, near Hook Norton. Burton Dassett Hills and Country Parks offer masses of space for picnics and magnificent views over the surrounding countryside.

For grand historic houses and castles try Broughton Castle, a moated 14th Century Manor House, home of the Saye and Sele family since 1451 and set in countryside as beautiful now as it must have been all those years ago. Rousham House near Steeple Aston is an uncommercialised 17th Century house with a unique William Kent landscape garden. Upton House, Farnborough Hall, Canons Ashby and Stowe Landscape Gardens are all National Trust properties and quite distinct, ideal for garden lovers.

Sulgrave Manor was home of the ancestors of George Washington and stages events throughout the year. For attractions with a difference try some special shopping at Bicester Village, where outlets sell top of the range designer brands at discount prices or visit the Motor Heritage Centre at Gaydon to see over 300 classic and historic British cars.

Oxford, Warwick, Stratford and the Cotswolds are all within half an hour's travelling time and surround the area, making North Oxfordshire such an ideal location for a touring base.

For our FREE Visitor and Where to Stay Guide please contact:
Banbury TIC
8 Horsefair, Banbury, (opposite Banbury Cross)
Tel: 01295 259855
Fax: 01295 270556
email: banbury.tic@cherwell-dc.gov.uk

Opening Times
April-September,
Mon-Sat, 10am-5pm,
(closed Sunday)
October-March, Tues-Sat, 10am-4.30pm,
(closed Sun and Mon).

Bicester TIC
Unit 6A, Bicester Village, Pingle Drive, Bicester, (Look for information sign in shopping village)
Tel: 01869 369055
Fax: 01869 369054
email: bicester.tic@cherwell-dc.gov.uk

Opening Times
All year: Daily,
10am-6pm.

Cherwell Valley TIC
Motorway Service Area, Junction 10 M40, Northampton Road, Ardley Nr. Bicester.
Tel: 01869 345888
Fax: 01869 345777
email: cherwell.tic@cherwell-dc.gov.uk

Opening Times
April-Oct 9.30am-4.45pm
Nov-March 10am-3.45pm

Sulgrave Manor

Sulgrave Manor is a superb example of a modest manor house and garden of the time of Shakespeare, and was home to the ancestors of George Washington. First mention of the Manor occurs in the Doomsday Survey of 1086; it later belonged to the Priory of St Andrew, Northampton. It was surrendered to the Crown in 1539, and sold by Henry VIII to Lawrence Washington, who built the present house. His descendants were to live here for the next 120 years.

In 1656, Colonel John Washington left England to take up land in Virginia which later became Mount Vernon. Col. Washington was the great grandfather of George Washington, first President of the United States of America.

In 1914, Sulgrave Manor was presented by a body of British subscribers to the Peoples of Great Britain and the United States of America, in celebration of the Hundred Years Peace between the two nations.

The House

Each room in the house is furnished to suit either the Tudor or the queen Anne Period, and the difference between these two styles is particularly striking when stepping from the stone flagged, Tudor Great Hall to the cosy, wooden panelled 18th century Parlour.

One of the most fascinating rooms is the fully furnished 18th century Kitchen, complete with open hearth and a huge array of pots, pans and other curious equipment.

Upstairs, the two 18th century bedrooms are elegantly furnished with exquisitely embroidered bed hangings and period items. The third bedroom the Tudor Great Chamber; a large, high ceilinged room with a broad fireplace and sparce furnishing.

Beyond this room is a collection of fascinating items relating to the house and its famous connections. Outside the house, the Washington coat of arms, said to have been the inspiration for the American flag, can be seen above the main porch.

Gardens

One of the many attractive features of the Manor is the garden. To the East is the Rose Garden with its 16th century sundial. Beyond a yew hedge is the Kitchen Garden which would have supplied fresh vegetables for the household. On either side of the porch are herbaceous borders which in summer, are a riot of colour, brimming over with flowers which threaten to engulf the ground floor window. Stretching southwards is the well kept lawn with its fine topiary work.

On the terrace lawn there is a herb garden in the form of an Elizabethan Knot. The orchard, beyond, is underplanted with bulbs which provided a magnificent display each spring.

The Buttery and Courtyard Range

Here visitors may enjoy light refreshments whilst viewing the delightful setting of the Manor House and the old 18th century Brewhouse. The latter now houses exhibitions relating to the life of George Washington. The well stocked Gift Shop also forms part of the Courtyard Range.

Sulgrave Manor
Nr Banbury
Oxfordshire OX17 2SD
Tel: 01295 760205
Fax: 01295 768056
Email:
sulgrave-manor@talk21.com
www.stratford.co.uk/sulgrave

Normal Opening Times
Weekdays - every day except Wednesdays:
1st April -31st October
2.00pm - 5.30pm
Bank holidays & the month of August 10.30am - 1.00pm, 2.00pm - 5.30pm December 27th - 30th 10.30am - 1.00pm, 2.00pm - 4.30pm
Weekends: Apr - Oct 10.30am - 1.00pm, 2.00pm - 5.30pm March, November & December 10.30am - 1.00pm, 2.00pm - 4.30pm
Note: Last admissions are one hour before closing times. All visitors on non-event days are taken round the manor House in regularly organsied guided tours.
Closed: Christmas Day, Boxing Day and the whole of January. Occasionally access to house restricted during wedding ceremonies.

KELMSCOTT MANOR

KELMSCOTT MANOR, KELMSCOTT,
LECHLADE, GLOUCESTERSHIRE GL7 3HJ
TEL: 01367 252486 FAX: 01367 253754

Kelmscott Manor was the country home of William Morris – poet, craftsman, and socialist – from 1871 until his death in 1896. The house which is open to the public, contains a collection of the possessions and works of Morris and his associates, including furniture, textiles, carpets and ceramics.

The Manor is open to the public every Wednesday from the beginning of April to the end of September, 11am-1pm & 2pm-5pm and the third Saturday in April, May, June and September, and first and third Saturday in July and August 2pm-5pm.

Price of Admission:
★ Adults £7 ★ Children aged 16 and under £3.50
★ Students in full-time education £3.50

KINGSTON BAGPUIZE HOUSE & GARDENS
Nr. Abingdon, Oxfordshire OX13 5AX
Tel: 01865 820259 Fax: 01865 821659
Owners: Mr & Mrs Francis Grant

Beautiful family owned manor house originally dating from 1660's but substantially altered in early 1700's. Panelled rooms, cantilevered staircase. Large garden with collection of rare trees, shrubs and plants.

Location: South of A420/A415 junction.
Opening Times: Bank Holiday weekends and other selected weekends and weekdays, 2.30-5.30pm. Telephone for details. Groups by written appointment only. Tea room and small gift shop.
Admission: House and Garden Adults £3.50, OAP £3.00, Child £2.50, Garden only £1.50.

FARINGDON HOTEL
1 Market Place, Faringdon, Oxon SN7 7HL
Telephone: 01367 240536 Fax: 01367 243250
20 Rooms (all en suite), 2 Four Posters..
AA ☆☆, RAC ☆☆, ETB ☆☆
Situated on the edge of the Cotswolds, the Faringdon Hotel is the ideal touring base for Oxford, Blenheim Palace, the Cotswolds and the Thames Valley. Offering comfort and relaxation in peaceful surroundings plus authentic Thai Restaurant.

THE JERSEY ARMS
Middleton in Stoney, Oxfordshire
Telephone: 01869 343234 Fax: 01869 343565
16 Rooms (all en suite), 1 Four Poster.
AA ☆☆, RAC ☆☆, AA ✿, RAC Merit Award.
An Egon Ronay Recommended, 16th century Inn only 10 miles from the centre of Oxford. Perfectly positioned on the edge of the Cotswolds for touring, Blenheim, Waddlesdon Manor, Stratford, Warwick Castle. Privately owned and managed by the Livingston family. A warm welcome is always assured.

THE BIRD IN HAND
Whiteoak Green, Hailey, nr Witney, Oxon OX8 5XP
Telephone: 01993 868321 Fax: 01993 868702
16 Rooms (all en suite).
RAC ☆☆☆, ETB ♛♛ Highly Commended,
Michelin Guide, Egon Ronay, Which Guide to Country Pubs, Les Routiers Inn Of The Year 1998.
A popular hostelry with both locals and visitors specialising in quality home cooked food and fresh fish. Set in peaceful rural surroundings, the Inn rambles through a number of rooms, one with a huge Inglenook fireplace. The bedrooms surround a quiet private courtyard and are designed to the highest modern standard.

GEORGE HOTEL
High Street, Wallingford, Oxon, OX10 0BS
Telephone: 01491 836665 Fax: 01491 825359
39 Rooms (all en suite).
AA ☆☆☆, RAC ☆☆☆, ETB ♛♛♛ Egon Ronay
An historic coaching inn set in the picturesque market town of Wallingford. The Hotel's 39 bedrooms boast evry modern facility the visitor requires, and Wealh's Restaurant has a well deserved local reputation for quality and service. With two bars, the George is an ideal venue for a relaxing break.

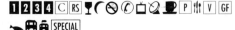

White Horse Country
and its three distinctive towns

Only 100 kilometres from London, White Horse Country stretches from the edge of Oxford to the threshold of the Cotswolds. Its enchanting landscape is marked by a mysterious Pagan past – the very name comes from the oldest chalk figure in Britain, dating back over 3000 years.

The landscape's calm undulating beauty has inspired poets, painters and musicians. It offers the choice of two national trails for walking: the prehistoric Ridgeway slips across open downland under big skies. Alternatively mile upon mile of the Thames Path leads you on lush willowy walks to the rewards of waterside pubs, hidden villages, elegant houses and an unhurried atmosphere that belongs to another time.

Abingdon on Thames is White Horse Country's largest town and can claim to be the oldest continually occupied settlement in England. Nearby, the engaging market town of Wantage, birthplace of Alfred the Great, nestles at the foot of the Downs under the ancient Ridgeway. Faringdon, the smallest town, perches on the golden limestone ridge between the two beautiful river valleys of the Ock and Thames.

For free Visitor Information and Accommodation Guide contact:

Abingdon Tourist
Information Centre
Tel: 01235 522711

Faringdon Tourist
Information Centre
Tel: 01367 242191

Wantage Tourist
Information Centre
Tel: 01235 760176

HISTORIC HOUSE & MUSEUM MARIAN FATHERS

FAWLEY COURT, HENLEY-ON-THAMES, OXON RG9 3AE
Tel: 01491 574917

HOUSE OPEN: March to October, Wednesday, Thursday and Sunday 2-5pm.
CLOSED: Easter Sunday and Whitsuntide.
Groups also by appointment during closed season.
ADMISSION: Adults £4, OAPs £3, Children/from 11 years/£1.50.
VISITOR FACILITIES: Car park, souvenir shop, refreshments and toilets. Some disabled access. Dogs not allowed.
Splendid historic and cultural Polish collections: paintings, books in several European languages, manuscripts and documents of the Polish Kings with their signatures, 16th-18th century/ 15th-19th century arms and armour and domestic items. The museum is housed in a building, designed in 1684 by Sir Christopher Wren and decorated by Grinling Gibbons and James Wyatt.
EVENTS: July 25th – Mozart Festival; September 24th-26th – Home Design and Interiors Exhibition; November 20th-21st – Christmas Craft and Gift Fayre.

Stonor Park

Henley-On-Thames, Oxfordshire RG9 6HF
Telephone: 01491 638587

Stonor has been owned by the Stonor family for over 800 years. Situated five miles north of the River Thames, the house is hidden in a valley in the beech woods of the Chiltern Hills surrounded by extensive deer park.

The house contains many rare items of furniture, tapestries, bronzes, sculptures, drawings,and family portraits from Britain, Europe and the USA.

Extensive walled gardens at the rear of the house offer commanding views over the rolling hills that form the park in which a large herd of fallow deer roam freely. A tranquil setting portraying historical English countryside.

Open 2-5.30pm April-Sept, Sundays & Bank Holiday Mondays. July-August, Weds also Sats 27 May and 26 Aug.

Cottage Holidays

A delightful selection of self-catering holiday homes in central/middle England. Town or rural, modern or traditional – something for everyone!

Properties close to London in the Thames Valley, an extensive Cotswold choice, pretty 'black & white' towns of Worcestershire & Herefordshire & last, but not least the beautiful countryside of Shropshire, Staffordshire & Welsh Borders.

Includes some of Englands finest historical towns: Windsor, Henley, Oxford, Stratford, Malvern to name but a few.

Free brochure: Karen Spiers, Forest Gate, Frog Lane, Milton under Wychwood, Oxon OX7 6JZ. Tel: (01993) 831495/831743. Fax: (01993) 831095 e-mail: cottage@cottageinthecountry.co.uk www.cottageinthecountry.co.uk
Member of Heart of England Tourist Board.

Mapledurham

Mapledurham, a beautiful late 16th century Elizabethan manor houses set in tranquil surroundings alongside the River Thames, has been the house of the Blount family and their descendants for over 500 years.

Richard Blount purchased the old manor (now tea-rooms) in 1490 and building of the present manor houses was commenced by Sir Michael Blount, lieutenant of the Tower of London, in 1588 and completed by his son Sir Richard in 1612. Original plasterwork ceilings and grand oak staircases can still be admired by visitors, as can the fine collections of pictures and family portraits of the 16th, 17th and 18th centuries. The family chapel built in the late 1700s, decorated in Strawberry Hill Gothic and still in regular use, is one of the rooms viewed by the public.

The great 18th century poet, Alexander Pope, spent much time at Mapledurham visiting his friends, Martha and Theresa Blount and was probably responsible for landscaping the grounds.

Mapledurham also has literary connections with John Galsworthy and "The Forsyte Saga" whilst lovers of Kenneth Garham's "Wind in the Williows" constantly question whether or not Mapledurham House was the original Toad Hall or the Watermill the setting of Mole and Ratty's memorable picnic.

There has been a Watermill at Mapledurham since Saxon times and present structure dates from the 15th century. The traditional wooden machinery is fully restored and the undershot waterwheel can be seen in action powering the great French burr milestones to produce flour on open afternoons each weekend during the summer.

The great sense of continuing history and the idyllic setting add to pleasure of either an afternoon visit to the House or a longer holiday in one of the estate's self-catering cottages. These are all historic houses in their own right with tiny 500-year-old thatched cottages sleeping two to oak-beamed farm cottages sleeping up to six.

In all there 34 listed buildings on this small country estate, a veritable feast of English Heritage.

Mapledurham Estate
Mapledurham
Reading RG4 7TR
Tel: 01189 723350

Open
Easter to End September

(Pre-booked parties by arrangement)

Admission
Please ring for admission prices

Facilities
Tearooms Gift Shops

Location
4m NW of Reading
Signposted off A4074

Town Hall: 01491 835373

Wallingford is a pleasant country market town in the upper Thames Valley. The wooded Chiltern Hills and the beautiful Berkshire Downs form a unique setting.

Historically, Wallingford is hard to surpass. One of the oldest towns in England with a charter dated 1155, its long history is well represented with Saxon Earthworks, the remains of a great castle, a magnificent medieval bridge, an elegant Town Hall (1670) and fine Georgian buildings.

Wallingford stands on the Thames in an Area of Outstanding Natural Beauty.

Explore the beautiful countryside that rural South Oxfordshire boasts throughout the year in an area of outstanding natural contrasts.

With over 80 villages and the four main towns of Henley-on-Thames, famous for the Royal Regatta – a highlight in the British social calendar; Wallingford with its award winning market place and antiques and craft arcade; Didcot with its links to the Great Western Railway and Thame, home to the largest one day agricultural show in the country, South Oxfordshire is an area to discover and enjoy.

In the northern part of the area lies Waterperry where there has been a House since before the Doomsday Book was written over 900 years ago. Today there are 83 acres of trees, shrubs and gardens with the River Thame flowing gently through the grounds. The grounds include a walled kitchen garden, alpine nursery, a formal garden, a rose garden, the Virgin's Walk and the rock garden as well as a Saxon Church, an extensive centre, an 'Art in Action' Gallery and a tea room.

In the southern part of the area is Mapledurham which consists of a house, watermill and a country park. The house has been the home of the Blount family since Elizabethan times. Visit the manor house and the last working corn mill on the river situated between the Chilterns and the Thames. Scattered on the estate are 12 self-catering holiday cottages available for those who wish to stay longer.

Come back for a weekend and discover Stonor Park where craft fairs are sometimes held, and take children of all ages to Didcot Railway Centre for a special steamday where you can ride in the 1930s carriages.

Alternatively, whether walking, cycling or boating, you will delight in the rurality of the Chilterns, the Ridgeway, the Icknield Way, the River Thame, the Thames Path and Wittenham Clumps. The Oxfordshire Cycleway passes through the district, which also boasts many attractive and not too strenuous walks, together with trails which help you discover the arts and crafts of this multi-faceted area of the country.

South Oxfordshire
District Council
PO Box 140,
Council Offices,
Crowmarsh, Wallingford,
Oxon OX10 8QX.
Tel: 01491 823726
Fax: 01491 823015

THE BOULTONS
Country Town House
HOTEL & RESTAURANTS
4 Catmose Street, Oakham,
Rutland LE15 6HW
Tel: 01572 722844 Fax: 01572 724473

A family Country Town House Hotel with much charm and character. In the historic market town of Oakham. After a leisurely day in scenic Rutland or a visit to Geoff Hamilton's Barnsdale Gardens, relaxing in our Cobbler Brasserie, one of the oldest cottages in the area built from local stone around 1604, or dining in our award-winning dining room before retiring to the comfort of your superb en-suite bedroom will make your day complete.

Rutland Water Cottages
Edith Weston

Designated THE BEST SELF CATERING HOLIDAY 1997 by the Heart of England Tourist Board, overall winners for second time.

Four delightful 19th century stone cottages in quiet village by Rutland Water. Log fires and antiques, period charm and welcome baskets. Fresh flowers and a personal welcome. Come and relax, play golf, celebrate in style. Special gourmet weekends, short breaks.

Children and disabled always welcome. We offer the ultimate "Home from Home"

RUTLAND WATER COTTAGES
Dormer Cottage Ryhall Stamford PE9 4JA
Tel: 01780 764001 Fax: 01780 482808
E-mail WalmsleyT@aol.com
www.rutland-on-line.co.uk/rutlandwatercottages

HAMBLETON HALL
Hambleton, Oakham, Rutland LE15 8TH
Telephone: 01572 756991 Fax: 01572 724721
17 Rooms (all en suite), 2 Four Posters, 1 suite.
AA ☆☆☆ (Red) ❀❀❀❀ Relais et Chateaux. Michelin ❀ Good Food Guide 8/10.
In the old county of Rutland 100 miles north of London and 2 hours by car with good rail service via Peterborough. The house has a spectacular rural setting overlooking a huge lake, Rutland water. Since opening in 1980 Hambleton has established itself as one of the very best in terms of food, wine, comfort and friendly but professional service.

RS 🕐 🛏 🍵 P 🍴 SP ⊘ ⌒ ❀ 🏨 🏨 SPECIAL
2 3 4 B

LAKE ISLE HOTEL
High Street East, Uppingham, Leics LE15 9PZ
Telephone: 01572 822951 Fax: 01572 822951
12 Rooms (all en suite).
AA ☆☆ ❀❀, RAC ☆☆, ETB ♛♛♛ Highly Commended, Johansons, Egon Ronay, Michelin Good Holiday Guide.
Nestling amongst the shops of this pretty market town you'll find a warm welcome, thoughtful extras including decanter of sherry, homemade biscuits and fruit bowl. Menus using fresh produce and an interesting wine list of 300 wines.

RS 🕐 🛏 🍵 P 🍴 V ⌒ SPECIAL 1 2 3 4 C

KINGS ARMS INN AND RESTAURANT
Top Street, Wing, Rutland LE15 8SE
Telephone: 01572 737634 Fax: 01572 737255
8 Rooms.
ETB/AA ♦♦♦ Recommended by Which? and main entry in Good Food guide.
The Inn has eight individually designed letting bedrooms all very spacious and decorated with little touches to make them a home from home. Food can be as elaborate or simple as you wish. The atmosphere is friendly and typical of an old coaching inn. Visit it once and you will return.

🚫 🕐 🛏 🍵 P 🍴 V GF ⌒ ❀ 🏨 🏨 SPECIAL 1
2 3 C

Rutland
England's Secret County

"Multum in parvo" says the motto of Rutland – so much in so little. England's secret county, just twenty miles across, is packed with interesting places to visit, enjoyable things to do and different ways to relax.

Walk or cycle on 25 miles of safe, off-road paths around Rutland Water. Fish for trout, observe rare birds or simply ramble and relax on the shores of the lake. Sail or windsurf on the 3,100 acres of Rutland Water, or cruise on the Rutland Belle pleasure boat. Beside the shore, find a modern butterfly centre, visit the historic church they saved from drowning and uncover the history of Europe's largest man-made lake.

Explore the two towns, Oakham and Uppingham, and more than fifty villages of Rutland. Discover how the mellow golden and grey stone has been used for hundreds of years to create charming townscapes and simple country cottages which are quintessentially English in their appeal.

Find historic buildings in and around Rutland. Big stately homes such as Burghley House, Belvoir Castle and Rockingham Castle are all open to visitors, as is the 400-year-old public school at Uppingham. Tour the elegant Bishop's Palace at Lyddington which became an almshouse for the local poor. Look at scores of horseshoes inside Oakham's ancient Castle and find out why Peers of the Realm were forced to hand them over to the Lord of the Manor. See the stocks on the green at Market Overton, where Sir Isaac Newton played as a child. Climb into the church porch at Stoke Dry, where the gunpowder plot is said to have been hatched.

Find real shops in Oakham, Uppingham and Rutland villages which have carried the same family name for generations, where traditions of service, quality and value are as important today as ever before. Stroll through the weekly markets in both towns which have been held here since medieval times.

Along the way, enjoy Rutland's inviting pubs, hotels and restaurants where character, good food and a warm welcome are the rule rather than the exception.

For a visitor guide, please phone or fax the number in the panel (right).

Rutland Tourist
Information Centre
Flore's House,
34 High Street,
OAKHAM,
Rutland LE15 6AL
Telephone and Fax:
01572 724329

OVERTON GRANGE HOTEL

Ludlow, Shropshire SY8 4AD
Tel: 01584 873500 Fax: 01584 873524

Located just one and a half miles from the distinguished county town of Ludlow, this Edwardian mansion stands in two and a half acres of tranquil landscaped gardens overlooking the spectacular Shropshire countryside. A delicious experience awaits you in our award winning Les Marches restaurant, where the chefs use only the freshest of produce. A carefully selected wine list will fascinate you and your palette with the finest wines from around the world. The perfect venue for a weekend away!

AA & RAC ☆☆☆ ❀❀❀   ETB ♛♛♛

Burford House Gardens

Tenbury Wells, Worcestershire WR15 8HQ
(off A456, 1m west of Tenbury Wells, 8 m from Ludlow)
Tel: 01584 810777 Fax: 01584 810673
email:treasures@burford.co.uk

The sweeping lawns and plantsman's paradise of Burford House Gardens are set in the picturesque valleys of the River Teme and Ledwych Brook. The late Georgian bridge over the Ledwych has been restored, leading to a new wildflower gardens down to the heavenly spot where the two rivers meet. The grass garden has been redesigned, a bamboo collection planted, and the National Collection of Clematis of over 200 varieties continue to grow. The nursery of Treasures of Tenbury grows over 300 varieties of clematis and many of the unusual plants that can be seen in the gardens, which are also on sale in the Garden Centre.

Also on site is the **Burford House Gallery**, contemporary and botanical art shows; **Treasure's Café Bar**, serving a wide selection of homemade cakes, hot and cold meals; **Mulu**, exotic plants; Jungle Giants, bamboos.

Open all year daily 10.00-17.00 or dusk if sooner.
Adults £3.50; Children £1.00; Groups of 10+ £3.00.
Evening parties by appointment.

HAWKSTONE PARK

Hawkstone Park, originally built in 1752, is a fine example of a large Country House Hotel set in over 400 acres of Grade 1 Listed Landscape with panoramic views of the famous Hawkstone Golf Course and beyond to the "Forgotten Masterpiece" An historic Park & Follies with breathtaking wooded cliffs and spectacular lush valleys. Location for BBC Television "Chronicles of Narnia" and "One Foot in the Past".

Nestled quietly amidst the foothills of the delightful Shropshire countryside Hawkstone Park is ideally situated being close to the main routes to many of the major towns and cities including Chester, The Potteries, Shrewsbury, Telford and a mere 30 minutes drive off the M54 link from M6.

Rooms with en suite bathrooms/showers, colour satellite TV, tea-making facilities, hair dryer, radio, trouser press, ironing facilities, direct dial telephone, restaurants, bar. 2 x 18 hole golf courses, 6 Hole Par 3 Academy Golf Course, Practice Ground, Teaching Academy, and Golf Shop.

Hawkstone Park, Weston-under-Redcastle,
Shrewsbury, Shropshire SY4 5UY
Tel: 01939 200611   Fax: 01939 200311

ETC ☆☆☆ (Silver)

SEVERN VALLEY RAILWAY

The best way to see the beauty of the River Severn is from a steam-hauled train on the Severn Valley Railway.

Bridgnorth – Bewdley – Kidderminster

Open every weekend throughout the year, DAILY from mid May until the end of September, plus school holidays and half-terms.

**THE RAILWAY STATION
BEWDLEY, WORCESTERSHIRE DY12 1GB
Tel: 01299 403816
www.svr.co.uk**

The Ironbridge Gorge

 SHROPSHIRE

The Ironbridge Gorge in Shropshire, some 150 miles north west of London, is a stunningly beautiful valley. Today, visitors browse in its small shops, enjoy its riverside pubs and are fascinated by the range of Monuments and Museums in the 6 square miles of the Severn Gorge. Yet over 200 years ago the scene was very different. Coalbrookdale, as it was then known, was the most industrialised area in the world: blast furnaces, ironworks, lead smelters, china works, foundries, cannon boring mills all lined the river banks and constantly lit up the smoke-filled skies with their constant flaring fires.

Visitors flocked here from all over the world to see the most advanced technology of its day. For the Industrial Revolution was born here, begun by a Quaker ironmaster called Abraham Darby I, who pioneered a better way of making iron. This led the way to many 'firsts' in the Ironbridge Gorge – the first iron rails, the first iron wheels, iron steam engine cylinders, steam railway locomotive and, of course, the world's first great Iron Bridge from which the valley took its name. Abraham's grandson, Abraham Darby III, built the Bridge in 1779 and it has come to symbolise the industrial innovations of this English valley.

In the nineteenth century the Coalport china works was one of the largest porcelain factories in the world, its ornate wares presented to the crowned heads of Europe, and at Jackfield, the largest decorative tile works in the world exported their beautiful tiles all round the globe. Yet by the 20th century industry had largely moved elsewhere and the transport systems and factories were abandoned, nature gradually reclaiming the landscape.

In 1968 the Ironbridge Gorge Museum Trust was set up and the history of this 'most extraordinary district in the world' is now interpreted through a series of fascinating Museums based on original sites: Blists Hill Victorian Town – a recreated Victorian community, with shops, cottages and machinery all operated by costumed staff. Coalport China Museum – housed in the original riverside works. Jackfield Tile Museum – wonderful arrays of colourful tiles and production revived. Museum of Iron – in the Coalbrookdale Company's great warehouse and close to Abraham Darby's excavated furnace. Rosehill & Dale House – restored homes of the ironmasters and their families. Museum of the Gorge – an introduction and a stunning 40ft model of the Gorge as it was in 1796. Broseley Clay Tobacco Pipeworks Museum - a preserved time capsule.

All these Museums and more, can be visited by the simple purchase of an Ironbridge Passport Ticket, incredibly good value, it is undated and is valid indefinitely until each Museum has been visited. The Ironbridge Gorge is a United Nations designated World Heritage Site and is ideal for a short break. The Museum's Tourist Information Centre can help with accommodation, currency exchange, and planning your stay in Shropshire, one of England's best kept secrets.

Address
Ironbridge Gorge Museums
Ironbridge, Telford
Shropshire
Tel: 01952 433522
Web site:
www.ironbridge.org.uk
7 day line
Tel: 01952 432166
Freephone: 0800 590258
for full details

Admission
Adult: £10.00
Senior Citizen: £9.00
Family (2 adults
& 5 children): £30.00
Child & Student: £6.00

Location:
Junction 4 off the M54.
Follow signs to Telford

Facilities
Tourist Information Centre,
Gift Shops,
Cafeterias, Restaurants

Shifnal Manor Properties

Shifnal Manor, Shifnal TF11 9PB
Tel: 01952 411412 Fax: 01952 463336
Email: naughtynells2000@aol.com
www.shifnalmanor.com

Holiday Lets and Weekend Breaks. Shifnal Manor Properties has invested in an extensive range of exclusive accommodation at affordable prices in and around the rural location of Shropshire. Steeped in history, these impressive locations are second to none. The manor grounds date back to the 16th century when they were laid out by the Earl of Shrewsbury and were considered to be the most important gardens in the whole of Shropshire.

OAKLEY HALL

Market Drayton, Shropshire
Tel: 01630 653472 Fax: 01630 653282

OAKLEY HALL is situated in magnificent countryside on the boundary of Shropshire and Staffordshire. Built in 1710, the Hall is a fine example of a Queen Anne Mansion house.

Oakley Hall provides the perfect location for corporate events, private parties or wedding receptions.

We would be delighted to discuss your individual requirements in more detail. Please contact at the numbers shown above.

The Crown at Hopton

Hopton Wafers, Cleobury Mortimer, Shropshire SY8 3DE
Tel: 01299 270372 Fax: 01299 271127
Email: desk@crownathopton.co.uk
www.crownathopton.co.uk

ETC ◆◆◆◆/Silver Award

A privately owned, warmly hospitable, 16th century coaching inn of authentic character and ambience with inglenook fireplaces, oak beams, AA Rosetted Restaurant and delightfully furnished, individually decorated, en-suite bedrooms.
Set in the rolling hills of South Shropshire The Crown is the ideal base from which to explore the beauty and history of Ludlow and the Welsh Marches and provides easy access to The Severn Valley Railway, Ironbridge and Stokesay Castle. 35 minutes from M5/M42

WALCOT HALL

**Lydbury North
Shropshire SY7 8AZ
Tel: 020 7581 2782
Fax: 020 7589 0195**

Georgian House built for Lord Clive of India. Exceptional arboretum with pools to rear, mile-long lake in front. Simple yet comfortable self-catering accommodation available all year. Marriage licence and ballroom for weddings, celebrations and conferences. Food, caravan site and bed & breakfast also available at Powis Arms (01588 680 254) at main entrance. Superb base for perusal of Shropshire's secrets.

Open: Bank Holidays, Sunday & Monday (except Christmas and New Year) 2.15-4.30pm. All other times by appointment.
Admission: Adults £3.00, children (under 15) free.

BATH POSTAL MUSEUM

Illustrates the history of written communication from the clay tablets of Babylon to the present day.
Life-size Victorian model post office.
The building from which the FIRST STAMP was sent on 2 May 1840.
Dynamic presentation of the "Story of the Post".
Airmail room, Film room, Children's activities room.
Souvenir shop. Tea and coffee facilities.

**Bath Postal Museum
8 Broad Street, Bath
Tel/Fax: 01225 460333**

Open all year Mon-Sat 11am-5pm, Sun (Mar-Dec) 2-5pm

Hodnet Hall & Gardens

Hodnet Hall, a large red-brick house in the later Elizabethan style, was built around 1870, and was reduced in size in 1967 by removing the original roof, tower and top floor to make it more manageable to live in.

It commands a prominent position at the top of a flat plateau facing south above a large pool. When the garden was started in 1922 none of these pools were in existence. The large one in front of the house was a marshy hollow with the banks a mass of elders, laurels and rushes. The late Brigadier A.G.W. Heber-Percy, then a young man, took over and started on his gardening career with the grudging approval of this father. This interest in gardening continued with the years, and became not only a full-time hobby but a full-time job as well.

The gardens, with their series of lakes and pools of varying sizes occupy some sixty acres. They were planned and developed by the late Brigadier with a staff of only three; their maintenance and development are continued today by a staff of four under the direction of the late Brigadier's son, Mr A. E. H. Heber-Percy. The small size of the staff is most surprising when the vast extent of the gardens, the continuing large scale development, and the high standard of maintenance are considered. This economy of personnel is, no doubt, due to the inspired enthusiasm, energy and skillful planning of the late owner and the excellence of his staff, an inspiration that persists to the present day.

It is supposed that the pools which are fed by numerous underwater springs have a great deal to do with the moderation of the temperature as they seldom freeze over, and there is often a blanket of warm mist which keeps off severe frosts. Be that as it may, the range of plants grown is certainly a surprising one for northern Shropshire, and many more tender shrubs have been introduced experimentally.

Hodnet Hall is of great interest as an example of a garden which has been carefully planted to provide a show of colour throughout the seasons. All has been planned and over and above the general effect there are many interesting and unusual plants as well.

Visitors come to the gardens time after time throughout the year, knowing that each season brings its fresh attractions, and that there is always something new and interesting to see.

Address

Hodnet Hall Gardens,
Hodnet,
Nr Market Drayton
Shropshire TF9 3NN
Tel: 01630 685202

Opening Times

April – September,
Tuesday to Sunday and
Bank Holiday Mondays
12 noon – 5.00pm

Admission

|Adult £3.00
OAP £2.50
Child £1.20
Party Rate (1999 prices).

Facilities

Refreshments: delicious light lunches and afternoon teas in half-timbered Tearooms with Big Game trophy collection.

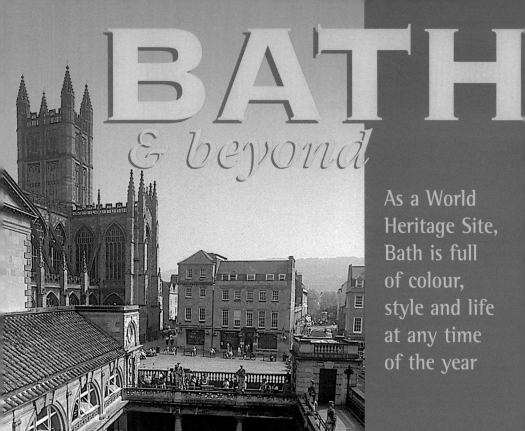

BATH

& beyond

As a World
Heritage Site,
Bath is full
of colour,
style and life
at any time
of the year

- World Class Heritage and Architecture
- Theatres, Festivals and Entertainment
- Great Shopping and Restaurants
- 37 Attractions and Museums
- Beautiful Countryside

Roman Baths & Museum of Costume - Bath

The City of Bath is designated by UNESCO as a World Heritage Site. A visit will soon reveal the reasons.

Central to Bath, the very reason for its existence, is the natural hot spring which has flowed for as long as man can tell through the heart of the city.

At 46°C (115°F) it rises at a temperature which is almost too hot for bathing, but Roman settlers living at the very limits of their extensive empire quickly solved the problem by channelling this unique resource – the only hot spring in Britain – to flow through an extensive suite of bathing pools as it cooled. They added changing rooms, hot saunas and cold plunge pools to complete the ultimate in first century leisure experiences.

The Great Bath still flows with natural hot water and the Roman site has been extensively excavated to reveal not only the Roman Baths but also a magnificent 2000 year old Temple. Sulis Minerva, Goddess of Wisdom and Healing, was worshipped next to the Sacred Spring by both the Roman conquerors and native Celts until at least 360 AD. A wealth of treasure and many everyday objects have been discovered and are now on display in the museum which is part of the site. The entire site is interpreted by personal audio guides which are available to visitors at no extra charge, in any of six languages.

After the visit, browse in the Museum Shop or take lunch or tea in the Pump Room above the Roman Baths. There, you can also taste the spring water which was so popular in Georgian times as a cure for all ailments.

If you are in Bath for a full day or more, a joint ticket for the Roman Baths Museum and Museum of Costume is very good value. Housed ten minutes' walk away in Bath's magnificent Georgian Assembly Rooms, the Museum of Costume is one of the finest collections of fashionable garments in the world. Special exhibition "Fashion in the Fifties", the flowering of fashion design in the glamorous decade following the War, from 7 Dec 2000 to 4 Nov 2001.

Address
ROMAN BATHS
Pump Room
Stall Street
Bath BA1 1LZ
Tel: 01225 477785
Fax: 01225 477743

Opening Times
Open daily: Jan-Feb 9.30am-5.30pm; Mar-June 9am-6pm; Jul-Aug 9am-10pm; Sep-Oct 9am-6pm; Nov-Dec 9.30am-5.30pm. Last admissions 1 hour before closing. Closed 25 & 26 Dec.

Admission (2000 prices)
Adult £6.90, Child £4.00, Family ticket (2 adults and up to 4 children) £17.50.

Group rates for parties of 20 or more.

Facilities
Restaurant with live chamber music, Museum Shop.

Address
MUSEUM OF COSTUME
Bennett Street
Bath BA1 2QH
Tel: 01225 477785
Fax; 01225 444743

Opening Times
Open daily: 10am-5pm; Last admission, 30 minutes before closing; Closed 25 & 26 Dec.

Admission (2000 prices)
Adult £4.00, Child £2.90. Family ticket (2 adults and up to 4 children) £11.00.

Group rates for parties of 20 or more.

Facilities
Combined tickets to both Museums offer best value.

The American Museum in Britain - Bath

Claverton Manor, Bath is the home of the American Museum in Britain, the first museum of Americana to be established outside the United States. It is a museum of the decorative arts illustrating domestic life in America from colonial times to the end of the nineteenth century.

The primary collection is arranged as a series of period rooms many of which are fitted with original panelling and floorboards brought from houses in the United States and furnished with fine examples of American furniture and decorative art. They extend in date from the late seventeenth century to the eve of the Civil War, and in cultural tradition from the English Puritans to the Spanish colonists of New Mexico.

Complimentary galleries represent the work of American craftsmen and women in pewter, silver, glass and textiles including examples of quilts, woven coverlets, hooked rugs, and Navajo weavings. Special exhibits are devoted to maritime history, westward expansion and cultures of North American Indians, Shakers and Pennsylvania-Germans.

The grounds and gardens include three exhibits: a colonial herb garden with a dye-plant border, a replica of part of George Washington's garden at Mount Vernon, and an arboretum devoted to American trees and shrubs. Dispersed through the grounds are various displays, including a Conestoga wagon and a milliner's shop filled with colourful band boxes. There are also two separate galleries in the grounds: one houses the impressive folk art collection, and the other, the New Gallery, houses temporary exhibitions.

Throughout the summer months the American Museum is host to a number of groups who will demonstrate a variety of events and lifestyles from America's past. These vary from displays of Native American dancing and 18th-century military drills to very realistic re-enactments of engagements in the French and Indian War and the American Civil War.

The American Museum in Britain
Claverton Manor, Bath
North Somerset
BA2 7BD
Tel: (01225) 460503

Opening Times
Open from April to Nov each day (closed Mondays) from 2pm to 5pm.

Admission
Museum, Grounds and Galleries
Adults £5.50, Senior Citizens/students £5.00, Children £3.00

Grounds, Folk Art and New Gallery only
Adults £3.00, Senior Citizens/Students £2.50, Children £2.00
Location
The Museum is well signed from the City centre up Bathwick Hill and from the A36 Warminster Road.

Facilities
Gift Shop, Tea Rooms (famous for the American Cookies), Picnic Area, Free Parking.

Villa Magdala Hotel

Henrietta Road, Bath BA2 6LX

Tel: 01225 466329 Fax: 01225 483207
Email:villa@btinternet.com
Website: www.btinternet.com/~villa

ETC ◆◆◆◆ (GOLD AWARD) AA, RAC ◆◆◆◆

The Villa Magdala built in 1868,
a charming Victorian town house hotel
with its own car park, is ideally situated for
those wishing to explore this famous City.
It enjoys a tranquil location overlooking
the beautiful Henrietta Park, but is only a
5 minute level walk to the City centre
and Roman Baths. The delightful bedrooms
are spacious, comfortable and have private
bathrooms, television, direct-dial telephone,
hairdryers and tea/coffee making facilities etc.
Enjoy our speciality – the Magdala Full
English Breakfast – in our sunny dining room
with views of the park.

*For the comfort of all our guests, the Villa
Magdala is entirely non-smoking.*

**SPECIAL MID-WEEK SHORT BREAKS AVAILABLE
NOVEMBER – MARCH**

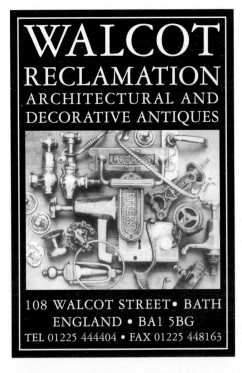

Holburne Museum of Art - Bath

Described by Hugh Scully as "one of the most perfect small museums in Europe in such a fine classical setting" the Holburne Museum of Art displays sone of the finest art collections in the West Country. Originally the famous Sydney Hotel, it played an integral part in Bath's history during the fashionable Georgian period when artists and artisans made their fortunes here. The building is surrounded by the Sydney Pleasure gardens frequented by Jane Austen, who lived nearby in Sydney Place, where Queen Charlotte also stayed for the water-cure, with a fine vista of the city's elegant Great Pulteney Street, named after Sir William Pulteney. He was responsible for the building of Robert Adam's Pulteney Bridge, Bath's great tourist attraction with its boutiques and coffee shops leading to Laura Place. Sir William's daughter was the heiress and colourful personality Henrietta Laura Pulteney, Countess of Bath, and Angelica Kauffman's charming portrait of her as a young girl can be seen in the museum.

Sir William Holburne (1793-1874) was renowned for his superb silver, particularly the rosewater dish dated 1616 given by Queen Charlotte to the Duke of York. His collections also include Dutch and Italian Old Masters, a bronze statue by Susini, originally owned by Louis XIV, fine porcelain, glass, furniture, rare portrait miniatures and Italian maiolica. His legacy has been enriched over the years, most significantly in 1955 by Ernest E Cook of the Thomas Cook travel firm, whose bequest to the museum included Zoffany's portrait of Queen Charlotte, Gainsborough's portrait of Dr Rice Charleton and a family group by George Stubbs. Other treasures include works by Guardi, Turner, Ramsay and Raeburn. Hone's miniature of Master of Ceremonies Beau Nash, Paintings by the Barker brothers of Bath, and Italian-born Bath sculptor Guiseppe Plura's beautiful marble masterpiece of Diana and Endymion. A new addition to the Top Gallery, Gainsborough's masterpiece 'The Byam Family' will be unveiled to the public in February.

The museum is a popular venue for prestigious fine art exhibitions, concerts and lectures. Home-made lunches and teas can be enjoyed either in the Museum Teahouse or in the authentic 18th century gardens.

Address
Holburne Museum of Art
Great Pulteney Street
Bath BA2 4DB
Tel: 01225 466669
Fax: 01225 333121
www.bath.ac.uk.holburne

Opening Times
Tues-Sat 11am-5pm (inc. Bank Holidays), Sun 2.30-5.30pm,
Mon open for Group Bookings only – by appointment.
Closed mid Dec-mid Feb.

Admission
Adult £3.50, Children £1.50,
Family £7.00. BANES residents £2.50 plus a range of concessions.
Special rates for group bookings.
Guided Tours by request.

Facilities
Free parking (max 2 coaches),
Licensed Teahouse open Tue-Sat 11am-5pm, Sun 2.30-5.30pm.
Lovely gardens.
Tel: 01225 420465

Location
Rail: Bath Spa Railway Station.
Car: From London, M4 Exit 18 to the A4 and follow brown signs.
From Bristol via A4 or A431. From Warminster via A36. Local Bus:
No.4 or 18 from Bus Station, Town Centre to Great Pulteney Street.

Above: Forde Abbey, Chard, Somerset
Below: Wells Cathedral, Wells, Somerset

Taunton Deane

At the Heart of Somerset, Taunton Deane is an area steeped in mystery, history and legends. Explore the rich countryside peppered with picturesque villages, secret gardens, beautiful historic houses and an abundance of rural attractions. Visit a traditional country pub, perfect for relaxing and recharging the batteries. Sample some local brew, a drop of cider perhaps!

The focal point of the area is Taunton, Somerset's county town, which has found itself at the centre of many bloody rebellions, the most notorious was the Monmouth Rebellion of 1685. Explore the town's architectural gems by following the Taunton Heritate Trail. Shopping is a pleasure with an intriguing mix of specialist shops and High Street names. The town prides itself on its parks and gardens and no visit would be complete without an excursion to Vivary Park to admire its extensive floral displays. Seven miles west of Taunton is the small town of Wellington, whose name is synonymous with the famous "Iron Duke". Prominent on the surrounding hills is the 175ft Wellington Monument, a landmark for miles around.

Village Life – Take time to explore the country lanes and discover dream cottages, ancient churches, charming tea rooms or see a game of cricket on the green and skittles in the pub.

Food & Drink – Good food and drink are essential ingredients of any holiday and in Taunton Deane you are in for a feast. Historically this is apple country famous for its eating apples and cider production, but you can sample local wine, cheese and enjoy a unique blend of traditional and innovative gastronomic delights using local produce in our many restaurants, inns and hotels.

The Countryside – Discover the eerie stillness of the Somerset Levels, a land of legends and mystery, and the majestic hills of the Quantocks, Brendons and Blackdowns. Together with the rich farmland they all combine to create the rich tapestry of landscape that is Taunton Deane.

Local Attractions – Recapture the era of the branch line country railway in the days of steam, experience the nostalgia of traditional Somerset country crafts, including cider making and basket weaving. Enjoy a leisurely walk through an orchard or by the canal or wander through the Deane's secret gardens. If history is where you interest lies, there is a rich variety of museums housed in equally impressive buildings.

Or simply escape and enjoy the peace and tranquillity that is Taunton Deane.

For Free Visitors Guide and Accommodation Service, please contact: Taunton Tourist Information Centre, Paul Street, Taunton, Somerset TA1 3DP Tel: 01823 336344 www.tauntondeane.gov.uk/ tourism e-mail: tourism@ tauntondeane.gov.uk

HUNSTRETE HOUSE
Pensford, Nr Bristol BS39 4NS
Telephone: 01761 490490 Fax: 01761 490732
23 Rooms (all en suite).2 Four Posters.
AA ☆☆☆ ❀❀❀ 1997 best hotels of the world.
Michelin 1 star.
Hunstrete House is a beautiful 18th century Georgian manor
House set in 92 acres of beautiful grounds, including
woodland deer park and traditional Victorian walled garden.
23 individually furnished bedrooms and suites, two four
posters, open fires, croquet, tennis court & heated outdoor
swimming pool.
Exceptional cuisine served in our terrace restaurant. £170.00
for bed and English breakfast.

RS 🌊 📺 🛏 P 🍴 V SP 🕐 🏊 ❀ 🚗 🚗 SPECIAL 1 2 3 4 A

SIMONSBATH HOUSE HOTEL
Simonsbath, Exmoor, Somerset TA24 7SH
Telephone: 0164 383 1259
7 Rooms (all en suite), 3 Four Posters.
AA ☆☆, ❀, ETB ♛ ♛ ♛ Highly Commended.
The first house to be built within the Royal Forest of
Exmoor in 1654. Simonsbath House is now a small and
friendly family-run country house hotel, situated in an ideal
position for exploring the Exmoor National Park, whether
on foot or by car. Unstinting comfort, generous and
interesting food, rooms with log fires, panelling and some
four poster beds. Dogs welcome to stay in our hotel kennels.

RS 🌊 🛏 P 🍴 V 🎣 ❀ 🚗 🚗 1 2 3 4 C

THE REST AND BE THANKFUL INN
Wheddon Cross, Exmoor, Somerset TA24 7DR
Telephone: 01643 841222 Fax: 01643 841222
5 Rooms (all en suite).
AA QQQQ, RAC Acclaimed, TB ♦♦♦♦
Former Coaching Inn, now offering superior accommodation
on Exmoor. Excellent views of Dunkery Beacon and the
moors. Well stocked bar including real ales. Full restaurant
and bar meals available 7 days a week. Ideal location to
explore Exmoor and North Devon either by foot or car.
Horse riding and golf nearby.

🍴 🚭 🕐 🌊 🛏 🍺 P 🍴 1 2 3 4 C

South Somerset

Discover South Somerset … soft landscapes, hidden farmsteads, architectural gems, glorious gardens, historic towns with a village atmosphere, all cradled in the gentle hills and vales south of Bath and the Mendip Hills. This is England at its very best – a part of the country that appeals to the discerning and inquisitive visitor.

South Somerset is full of contrasts, from the ancient and isolated hilltop fort at South Cadbury – reputedly King Arthur's 'Camelot' – to bustling towns like Yeovil and Chard with their excellent shopping facilities and attractions. Predominantly it is an unspoilt agricultural area, an intimate tapestry of fields, orchards and woods, but its towns are full of historic and architectural interest. Be sure to visit Castle Cary, a charming little town of thatch and golden stone, and see its market house and famous 18th century 'pepper pot' jail, one of only four in England.

More than a hundred towns, villages and hamlets, with such evocative names as Hardington Mandeville, Isle Abbotts and Pen Selwood, are waiting to be explored. Many are built of local stone and have churches with the handsome towers for which Somerset is famous – those at Crewkerne, South Petherton and Kingsbury Episcopi are especially memorable.

Cosy village inns offer hospitality as they have done for centuries – a pint of refreshing ale or traditional Somerset cider, a wholesome meal and a chance to chat with the locals. Many also offer inexpensive overnight accommodation and a hearty English breakfast, or you can stay at one of the many farms and country cottages which welcome visitors from overseas.

Tucked away in the narrow lanes of the tranquil South Somerset countryside are some wonderful estates where you can capture something of the essence of the classic English garden, whether it be an informal cottage garden as at East Lambrook Manor, a small formal garden as at Tintinhull House and Lytes Cary Manor or an extensive landscaped estate as at Barrington Court and the medieval Forde Abbey. At many of them you can also explore the house.

Best known of all is Montacute, one of the finest Elizabethan houses in England, where formal gardens provide a grand setting for the architectural splendour of the house. Montacute village and the sweeping driveway to the house have achieved worldwide fame as locations in the acclaimed Emma Thompson film 'Sense and Sensibility'. Come to South Somerset and experience them yourself.

Address
South Somerset Tourist
Information Centre
Petters House
Pettera Way
YEOVIL
Somerset BA20 1SH
Tel: 01935 471279 (24 hrs)
Fax: 01935 434065
e-mail: tourism@
southsomerset.gov.uk
Website: www.southsomerset.
gov.uk

THE MUSEUM OF CANNOCK CHASE

A delightful Museum reflecting the history of Cannock Chase – through Seven Centuries of Coal – from Royal Hunting Forest to Coalfield Community.

• **Special Events Diary • Exhibitions • Gift & Coffee Shops • Picnic Areas • Nature Reserve • Way Marked Walks • Touring Caravan Site • Disabled Access • Guided Tours & Group Bookings • Tourist Information Point.**

Opening hours 2000 Easter to end of September: Daily 11am-5pm. October to Easter: Monday to Friday 11am-4pm. Closed Dec 24-Jan 5. **ADMISSION FREE** except for pre-booked guided tours and some special events.

The Museum of Cannock Chase at The Valley Heritage Centre Valley Road, Hednesford, Cannock, Staffs WS12 5TD Telephone 01543 877666
for further details or booking enquiries.

EAST STAFFORDSHIRE

Situated in the Heart of England you will find
BURTON UPON TRENT
The largest town in the National Forest and the Brewing Capital of Britain.
UTTOXETER
Friendly Market Town with its popular National Hunt Racecourse.
TUTBURY
Historic Village with its imposing castle and where the ancient craft of crystal glassmaking survives.

Further information on the area from

East Staffordshire Borough Council

EAST STAFFORDSHIRE BOROUGH COUNCIL Regeneration & Partnerships Midland Grain Warehouse Derby Street, Burton upon Trent Staffs DE14 2JJ Tel: 01283 511942

Stafford

The Ancient High House has dominated Greengate Street, the main north-south road in the centre of Stafford, for over 400 years. An excellent example of Elizabethan architecture, it is the largest timber-framed town house in England.

The house was built by the Dorrington family at a time when Stafford was developing as a centre of trade and commerce. The Sneyd family were the occupants when King Charles I stayed in Stafford during 1642. His nephew, Prince Rupert, is believed to have fired a new German gun at the weathercock of St Mary's Church, Stafford to demonstrate its accuracy. The following year, the town was taken over by the Parliamentarian forces and the High House became a jail for Royalist officers.

Many alterations were carried out to the building over the years. The most damaging was the removal of a corner post during the Victorian period. By the early 1970's, rain was leaking through cracks in the structure and major repairs became essential. Stafford Borough Council was eventually able to carry out this work and the house was opened as a heritage centre and Tourist Information Centre.

In 1993, the Staffordshire Yeomanry Museum was opened on the top floor. This tells the 200-year history of this proud regiment. Ex-members and their families continue to donate items to this important collection and an archive is being developed to enable researchers to have access to information.

In 1996, the High House received full museum registration status, which demonstrated the high standards maintained by heritage staff. The Friends of the High House work to raise funds for the improvement of the displays and they have recently paid for a beautiful stained glass window depicting the Sneyd coat-of-arms. The Borough Broderers work in the House every Tuesday on embroidery projects. They are currently starting a counterpane for a tester bed. The temporary exhibition gallery provides a showcase for the talent of local artists and craftspeople.

The success of the partnership of the work of Stafford Borough Council and local volunteers will ensure that the High House has always got something new to see. The House will hopefully continue for at least another 400 years to be a fascinating landmark in the town.

Address
Stafford Tourist Information Centre The Ancient High House, Greengate Street, Stafford, Staffordshire ST16 2JA
Tel: 01785 619619

Ancient High House
Open all year
Mon – Sat

Admission
Adult £2.00
Child £1.20
Family £4.00

The World of

Spode

Visitor Centre

Take a closer look...

For over 200 years, Spode's beautiful and original designs have become amongst the most collectable and sought after in the history of ceramics.

Come and enjoy the unique experience at the Spode Visitor Centre with Craft Demonstrations, Factory Tours, Museum, Factory Shops and Restaurant.

Spode, Church Street, Stoke-on-Trent ST4 1BX
Telephone 01782 744011 Fax 01782 744012
E.mail: visitorcentre@spode.co.uk http: www.spode.co.uk

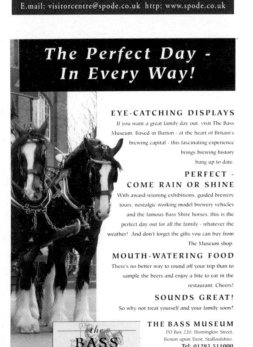

The Perfect Day - In Every Way!

EYE-CATCHING DISPLAYS
If you want a great family day out, visit The Bass Museum. Based in Burton - at the heart of Britain's brewing capital - this fascinating experience brings brewing history bang up to date.

PERFECT - COME RAIN OR SHINE
With award-winning exhibitions, guided brewery tours, nostalgic working model brewery vehicles and the famous Bass Shire horses, this is the perfect day out for all the family - whatever the weather! And don't forget the gifts you can buy from The Museum shop.

MOUTH-WATERING FOOD
There's no better way to round off your trip than to sample the beers and enjoy a bite to eat in the restaurant. Cheers!

SOUNDS GREAT!
So why not treat yourself and your family soon?

THE BASS MUSEUM
PO Box 220, Horninglow Street,
Burton upon Trent, Staffordshire.
Tel: 01283 511000

Open every day, except Christmas Day,
Boxing Day and New Years' Day.

ROYAL DOULTON
VISITOR CENTRE
Home of the Royal Doulton Figure

Take a look "behind the scenes" at Royal Doulton – the World's leading fine china company.

Open seven days a week, the Visitor Centre houses the World's largest public collection of Royal Doulton figures, live demonstrations of the arts and skills which go into all Royal Doulton pieces, a video theatre, factory shop and the Sir Henry Doulton Gallery – both a museum and a restaurant.

Working factory tours are available twice daily during the week where you can see how tableware and figures are created – from raw clay right through to the hand decorated finished piece (not available during factory holidays).

Factory tours and groups by appointment only, please contact:

Royal Doulton Visitor Centre
Nile Street, Burslem, Stoke-on-Trent ST6 2AJ
Tel: 01782 292434

LICHFIELD
England's best kept secret

Lichfield Cathedral

Treasures include 8th century Gospel
& 16th century Flemish glass.

International music festival-July

Dr Johnson Birthplace

Georgian House dedicated to
Dr Johnson's life and work with
tableaux and video.

Lichfield Heritage
Exhibition & Treasury

Treasury, 2 audio visual
presentations, view from spire and
Social History Gallery.

For Information Pack and Discount Voucher contact Dept BT:
Tourist Information Centre, Donegal House, Bore Street, Lichfield,
Staffordshire, England WS13 6NE

Tel 01543 252109   Fax 01543 417308

Lavernham Priory

Water Street, Lavenham,
Sudbury CO10 9RW
Tel: 01787 247404
Fax: 01787 248472
Email: mail@lavenhampriory.co.uk
www.lavenhampriory.co.uk

Benedictine monks originally owned this "Grade I listed house, one of Lavenham's finest. Bed chambers feature crown posts, wall paintings and oak floors, with four poster, lit bateau and polonaise beds. Visitors can relax by inglenook fires in the 13th century Great Hall or sitting room. Breakfast and pre-dinner drinks can be enjoyed in the sheltered courtyard herb garden. A relaxed family atmosphere, good humour and a memorable visity are Gilli and Tim's objectives. Lavenham is often described as one of the finest mediaeval villages in England with its historic buildings and streets. Within easy walking distance of The Priory are the Guildhall, Wool Church, antique and gift shops, tea rooms, restaurants and country strolls. Abandon your car for the day.

The Plough Inn

Brockley Green, Hundon, Sudbury, Suffolk
Tel: 01440 786789 Fax: 01440 786710
Email: enquires@hundonplough.co.uk
www.hundonplough.co.uk

Delightfully situated in a rural hamlet commanding spectacular views over the Stour Valley – a charming country inn with soft red brickwork and oak beamed interior.
The guest rooms are all en-suite and individually themed to local places of interest such as Cambridge, Newmarket, Bury St. Edmunds, Lavenham etc. all within a half-hours drive. After a day's sightseeing one can sample the delights of Simms Restaurant then relax on the terrace and enjoy the sunset.

SWAN HOTEL
High Street, Lavenham, Sudbury, Suffolk CO10 9QA
Telephone: 0870 400 8116 Fax: 01787 248286
51 Rooms (all en suite), 4 Four Posters. AA ☆☆☆☆
RAC ☆☆☆☆
The Four Star Swan Hotel is a wonderful timber building dating back to the 14th century. Situated in the centre of the Tudor village of Lavenham in the heart of the Suffolk countryside, just two hours from London. The hotel offers five lounges, beautiful gardens, open fireplaces, an excellent restaurant with a Minstrel Gallery and two bars.

RS 🚭 🄫 🖥 🍺 P 🍴 V GF ✒ ❀ 🏨 🏩 SPECIAL 1 2 3 4 B

Suffolk Coast

The unique Suffolk Coastal area of the county of Suffolk extends from Felixstowe in the south to Walberswick and Blythburgh in the north. With 40 miles of Heritage Coast set in an Area of Outstanding Natural Beauty, there is a feeling of peace and tranquillity even at the height of summer and it is an ideal place to unwind and explore the many attractive towns, villages and rivers. There is a constant presence of water from the coast and the five rivers, which gives a romantic and mysterious atmosphere to the district. The inland areas have many secrets to be discovered; churches, castles, gardens, windmills, museums, tide mills, vineyards and Anglo-Saxon sites. All of these provide the visitor with many happy hours of visiting and finding new interests.

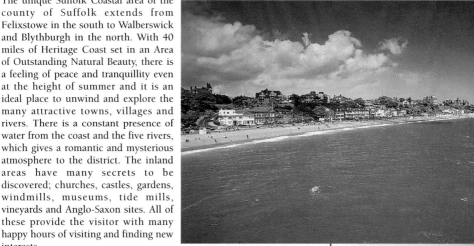

Aldeburgh is a small fishing town, unspoilt by modern times. You will still find fishermen pulling their boats up onto the beach and selling their fresh catch.

Felixstowe is an Edwardian resort that has retained its charm over the ages and has a seafront over 4 miles long, with an excellent paved promenade local museum and historic fort.

An attractive town steeped in history on the banks of the river Deben, Woodbridge has many fine buildings, a local museum with changing exhibitions and a picturesque Tide Mill, probably one of the most photographed scenes in England! Close by is the famous Anglo-saxon burial ground of Sutton Hoo.

You will find a good range of places to stay, from luxury hotels to simple bed and breakfasts in private homes and if you prefer self-catering, there are cottages, farms, flats, and houses. Whatever style of accommodation you require, you should have no difficulty in finding something suitable, along the Suffolk Coast.

Tourist Information Centre
Seafront
Felixstowe
Suffolk
Tel: 01394 276770

High Street
Aldeburgh
Suffolk
Tel: 01728 453637

The Station

Woodbridge 01394 382240

Ipswich
County Town of Suffolk

Visitors to Ipswich are constantly surprised at the diversity of the town, its heritage and how much there is to see and do.

The town's streets, the pattern of which has changed little for centuries, are lined with many buildings with history and character. The Ancient House (dated 1670, with older parts) is renowned for its beautiful plasterwork and is just one gem among a wealth of timber framed buildings. Twelve mediaeval churches offer testimony to the importance of the town as it developed in the middle ages. Stroll to Christchurch Park, just off the town centre. In the heart of this tranquil parkland is Christchurch Mansion, a beautiful tudor building which dates from 1548. Open to the public and furnished as a country house, its superb art collection includes work by local artists John Constable and Thomas Gainsborough.

In fact, you can follow in the footsteps of many famous people connected with the town. Thomas Wolsey, who was to become one of the most powerful men in the country as cardinal to Henry VIII, was born here.

Charles Dickens stayed in the town, where local events and characters helped to inspire his writing – notably in *Pickwick Papers*.

More recently, Giles, the much loved cartoonist, worked in the town and lived nearby. Many local scenes are instantly recognisable in his work and today his immortal 'Grandma' is commemorated by an impressive statue in Princes Street.

The Victorians left symbols of their civic pride in the town. Notable is the Town Hall (1878), adjacent to the town's main square, and the Old Custom House (1844) which grandly watches over the Wet Dock as a reminder of the town's maritime heritage. Nearby is the splendid Tolly Cobbold Brewery (1896) which it is possible to explore as part of a guided tour. The Brewery Tap Public House next door makes a good refreshment stop.

Ipswich today is a centre of regional importance offering excellent hotels, an extensive pedestrianised shopping centre, and a wide choice of places to eat, drink and be entertained.

For further information, including Ipswich Heritage Trails:
Ipswich Tourist Information Centre
St Stephen's Church
St Stephen's Lane
Ipswich
Suffolk IP1 1DP
Tel: 01473 258070

Named The Summer Country by the Vikings who were its first 'visitors', Bury St Edmunds and its beautiful surroundings still offer a warm welcome to today's visitors. Rich in legend and history, this is one part of East Anglia that will linger in your memory.

Bury St Edmunds was home to one of the most powerful Abbeys in medieval Europe, and has seen glory, turmoil and scandal over the centuries that few small towns could boast. It is named after King Edmund of the East Angles, who was martyred by invading Danes in 869 AD and laid to rest in Bury. From a small settlement, the town became a centre for pilgrimage and grew rapidly until the dissolution of the monasteries. The Abbey Church was where 25 barons swore an oath in 1214 to force King John to ratify the Magna Carta, the basis of democracy as we know it in Britain. Today, Bury remains a busy and picturesque market town, surrounded by the tranquil villages and countryside of rural West Suffolk.

Friendly shops and market stalls, charming pubs and restaurants greet visitors with old-fashioned hospitality and goodwill. You can take your time exploring the many sights, from Cathedral, Art Gallery, stately homes and museums to leisure centres, country parks and the prize-winning Abbey Gardens.

There is also a year-round programme of events from an Anglo Saxon Fair and a major arts festival to Christmas markets, with cricket, chariot racing, street fairs, carnivals and open air theatre along the way. The summer months are a riot of colour as the towns and villages put on their floral finery for the 'Britain in Bloom' judges who have awarded so many prizes to the area over the last decade.

Loved by Charles Dickens, Bury St Edmunds has lost none of its appeal. Step back in time and enjoy life the way it ought to be lived.

Please respond to:
Bury St. Edmunds
Tourist Information
Centre
6 Angel Hill
Bury St. Edmunds
Suffolk
England IP33 1XB

Tel: 01284 764667

Painshill Landscape Garden
Cobham

158 acre Painshill, created by the Hon. Charles Hamilton between 1738 and 1773, contemporary with Stourhead and Stowe, is one of Europe's finest 18th century landscape gardens. Europa Nostra Medal winner for "exemplary restoration". The 14 acre lake, filled by a massive waterwheel, gives a perfect setting for a Gothic temple, ruined abbey, Turkish tent, Chinese bridge, crystal grotto, replanted 18th century shrubberies, magnificent Cedars of Lebanon and much more. Open April to October: Tuesday to Sunday and Bank Holidays, 10.30am-6pm (last entry 4.30pm). November to March: Tuesday to Thursday, Saturday, Sunday and Bank Holidays, 11am-4pm (last entry 3pm). Closed Christmas Day and Boxing Day.

Teas, Light Refreshments, Gift Shop, Guided Tours.

Adults £4.20, Concessions £3.70, Children 5-16 £1.70, Under 5s free. Pre-booked Groups of 10+ £3.30pp and Coaches welcome.

Please call 01932 864674 for opening times or 01932 868113 for further information.

Painshill, Portsmouth Road, Cobham, Surrey
Close to M25 – junction 10 on A3-A245 towards Cobham

CLAREMONT
Claremont Drive, Esher, Surrey, KT10 9LY
Telephone: 01372 467841

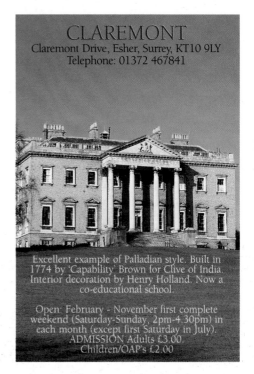

Excellent example of Palladian style. Built in 1774 by 'Capability' Brown for Clive of India. Interior decoration by Henry Holland. Now a co-educational school.

Open: February - November first complete weekend (Saturday-Sunday, 2pm-4.30pm) in each month (except first Saturday in July).
ADMISSION Adults £3.00.
Children/OAP's £2.00

LOSELEY PARK
Home of the More-Molyneux family for over 400 years

The mansion is a fine example of Elizabethan architecture, dignified and beautiful, set amid 1,400 acres of rolling countryside. The house contains many fine works of art, including paintings, carvings, tapestries and panelling from Henry VIII's Nonsuch Palace.

Glorious Walled Garden featuring a stunning collection of roses, herbs, flowers and fountains. Also idyllic Moat Walk.

• Estate Tours • Courtyard Tea Room • Gift Shop (selling the famous Loseley dairy and bakery products) • Chapel • Picnic Area • Children's Play Ground •
Guildford, Surrey GU3 1HS (off B3000)
Telephone 01483 304440

CHASE LODGE HOTEL
10 Park Road, Hampton Wick, Kingston-upon-Thames, Surrey KT1 4AS
Telephone: 020 8943 1862 Fax: 020 8943 9363
10 Rooms (all en suite), 3 Four Posters.
AA QQQQ Selected, RAC Highly Recommended, ETB ♛ ♛ ♛ ♛, Winners of a British Tourist Authority Trophy.
Chase Lodge Hotel is situated in a quiet conservation area, walking distance to Hampton Court Palace, River Thames nearby and Kew Gardens. 22 mins from the centre of London. Beautiful food and accommodation. Highly Recommended.

RS ⊘ 🕭 ⌂ ⚲ 🍺 P ⵌ V GF 🛏 SPECIAL **1** **2** **3** **4**

OATLANDS PARK HOTEL
Oatlands Drive, Weybridge, Surrey KT13 9HB
Telephone: 01932 847242 Fax: 01932 842252
130 Rooms (all en suite), 1 Four Poster.
AA ☆☆☆☆.
Oatlands Park is a country house hotel with a wealth of history. A recent refurbishment has provided luxury accommodation and impressive public areas complete with gallery and glazed dome. This is a good touring base 2 miles from the M25, 10 miles from Heathrow and 25 miles from London. Hampton Court Palace, Windsor Castle and family attractions such as Thorpe Park and Chessington World of Adventures are all local.

RS ✆ ⊘ 🕭 ⌂ ⚲ 🍺 P ⵌ V GF ⇕ ◷ ◞ ⚘ 🛏
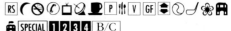
🛏 SPECIAL **1** **2** **3** **4** B/C

Surrey

Only 30 miles from London, Surrey has an abundance of lovely countryside and areas of natural beauty which capture the essence of the traditional English landscape – river valleys, leafy lanes, picture-book villages, vibrant market towns, beautiful gardens and historic country houses. Wherever you roam in Surrey, discover history and legends.

The ever-changing landscape of Surrey offers thousands of acres of open countryside. Well-known beauty spots nestle in the famous North Downs and have stunning views of the surrounding countryside.

An alternative way to experience the splendour of Surrey is from one of its waterways. Old Father Thames himself winds through the north of the county, where pleasure boats cruise past the sights of Hampton Court Palace and Runnymede. It was on the banks at Runnymede that King John sealed the Magna Carta in 1215, marked by a simple memorial. The Thames joins the River Wey at Weybridge, which then meanders south through the Wey Valley to Guildford and Godalming, where brightly painted traditional narrowboats are a familiar sight.

The county town of Guildford with its cobbled High Street and historic buildings was once frequented by Lewis Carroll, who is buried here, and today offers excellent shopping in a traditional setting.

Experience the treasures of Surrey's magnificent historic houses and gardens. Originally a Regency villa, Polesden Lacey is now the regional headquarters of the National Trust. Loseley Park is an inviting Elizabethan mansion which has recently become well-known for its delicious ice cream. With a garden by Gertrude Jekyll, Hatchlands has a fascinating collection of early keyboard instruments that visitors can often hear being played.

A stroll through the world renowned Royal Horticultural Society garden at Wisley is not to be missed. Or enjoy the beautiful 18th century landscape garden at Painshill Park, winding your way through exquisite scenes featuring a gothic style temple, ruined abbey and a magical crystal grotto set around an islanded lake.

For further information on the delights and attractions of Surrey, contact:
Surrey Tourism,
Room 404, County Hall,
Kingston upon Thames,
Surrey KT2 2DY.
Tel: 020 8541 8092
Fax: 020 8541 9172
Email:
surreytourism@surreycc.gov.uk
www.surreytourism.org.uk

Guildford

Guildford is the county town of Surrey in the South East corner of England. The town has been an important staging post for travellers throughout its long history, being mid-way between London and the coast at Portsmouth.

From May to September volunteer guides conduct walks which give visitors a flavour of this historic town. They visit the Norman castle keep with its splendid municipal gardens and Guildford Museum which has displays relating to Lewis Carroll, who often spent holidays in Guildford and is buried here. Memorabilia of another famous resident, Gertrude Jekyll the landscape gardener, is also on display and there are many examples of her gardens in Surrey. The tour also takes in the cobbled High Street and the Guildhall which is mainly Tudor and has a magnificent overhanging clock.

Guildford is excellent for shopping, both in the High Street and the lanes and alleyways leading from it and in modern shopping arcades where well-known stores complement the many individual retailers.

Although Guildford is proud of its history it has a modern outlook. This is exemplified by the Cathedral of the Holy Spirit, which dominates the town from an imposing position on Stag Hill, one of only four built this century and it's near neighbour, the University of Surrey, which contributes greatly to the life of the town.

The surrounding countryside is dotted with picturesque villages and within a few miles of Guildford there are almost 250 acres of wonderful gardens at Wisley, one of the Royal Horticultural Societies Gardens. The three National Trust properties here include two 18th century houses and a restored barge building centre on the River Wey, which can be reached by a river bus service. Loseley, a beautiful Elizabethan mansion which is still a family home, is open to visitors during the summer months.

Accommodation in Guildford ranges from guest houses to town centre and country hotels and its proximity to London, together with an excellent road and rail network, make it the ideal base for touring the area.

Guildford Tourist
Information Centre
14 Tunsgate
Guildford
Surrey GU1 3QT
Tel: 01483 444333
Fax: 01483 302046
www.guildfordborough.co.uk

Goodwood House - Chichester

SUSSEX
(WEST)

The ancestral home of the Dukes of Richmond is lived in by the heir to the estate, the Earl of March, with his young family. Lord and Lady March have just completed a three year refurbishment of the State Apartments, returning them to the Regency splendour of earlier times. As a photographer, Lord March supervised the decorations personally while as an historian, Lady March was keen that the recreated interiors should be historically correct.

The Egyptian Dining Room, which was covered up and painted over in the early 1900s, is once again alive with bronzed crocodiles and gilded cobras. It is the largest faux marble hall in England and contains all its original Regency furniture. 350 metres of glowing yellow silk was specially woven for the Yellow Drawing Room, and the original curtain scheme was recreated. The room had lain empty in order to be used for events, but although still much frequented for weddings and parties, is now once again fully furnished as a grand Regency drawing room of the sort in which Jane Austen's heroines would have paraded in their grander moments.

The Card Room is of interest not just to art lovers but also to ornithologists. The Duke of Richmond's famous blue and green Sèvres dinner service is on display. The bird paintings on it were copied by the china painters from the Duke's own bird books. There are also chic neo-classical vases.

The Royal English and Scottish and French ancestry of the Dukes of Richmond, Lennox, Gordon and Aubigny are all fully represented in this elegant but lively family home. There is a large and representative collection of British portraits as well as brilliant paintings of hunting, shooting and racing at Goodwood by George Stubbs, and sensational views from the family's London house by Canaletto. The newly restored tapestry drawing room creates a sense of 19th century Paris and is set off by fine French furniture.

Opening Times
From Easter Sun and Mon, open on Suns and Mons until the end of Sept and on Suns through to Thurs in August, 1-5pm. Closed on certain event days, call recorded information for details. Groups welcome. Special Guided Tours available (min 20) on Mon by arrangement (£8.50), all groups please book in advance. Afternoon Tea. Free car and coach park, shop, picnic area at Gooodwood racecourse. Suitable for disabled. Adults admission £6.50, Children 12-18 £3, Under 12s Free. Group rate £5.50. Tel: 01243 755048: or 01243 755040 for recorded information.

Chichester

Chichester has been a Cathedral city since 1075, and the great building, erected by the Normans, with its majestic spire rising above the Sussex plain, has for centuries been the focal point of the city.

The history of Chichester dates back to Roman times, when the Romans camped in the area under the supervision of King Cogidubnus about AD43. The Roman Palace at nearby Fishbourne is believed to have been built for Cogidubnus. The Roman road to London, called Stane Street, can still be walked in places, through the countryside, and there is a Roman Villa at Bignor.

Surrounding Chichester are the City Walls, originally built on Roman foundations, but today these are medieval or later works. In the late AD200's circular bastions were added mainly as sites for stone throwing catapults used for defence, and these can be seen on the Walls Walk.

At the centre of Chichester, where the four main streets meet, is the magnificent Tudor Market Cross, given by Bishop Story in 1501. There are many historic buildings in the city; the Georgian Pallant House is a fine art gallery; there are museums in an 18th century cornstore and 13th century priory, while the modern Festival Theatre has built up a worldwide reputation for its plays. Not surprisingly, Chichester is known as a "City of Culture".

The countryside, dominated by the South Downs, with its old market towns of Midhurst and Petworth and small villages is an Area of Outstanding Natural Beauty. Within the countryside are to be found several stately homes, set in glorious parkland, including Goodwood, Petworth, Cowdray ruins, Uppark and Stansted Park.

The scenic, unspoilt coastline and picturesque harbour are only a short journey from Chichester. The Chichester Harbour which covers fifty miles of shoreline is a natural habitat for a wide variety of flora and fauna and a pleasureable way of viewing the harbour is by water tour from West Itchenor. Many harbour villages are steeped in history with their ancient churches, such as Bosham, where it is said King Canute tried to turn back the tide, which comes across the Shore Road up to the walls of the houses.

The areas has a wide range of accommodation, especially bed and breakfast establishments and quality hotels, who provide a warm welcome to visitors.

For information (including free visitors' guide) please contact:
Tourtist Information Centre,
29A South Street,
Chichester,
West Sussex
PO19 1AH.
Tel: 01243 775888
Fax: 01243 539449
www.chichester.gov.uk

277

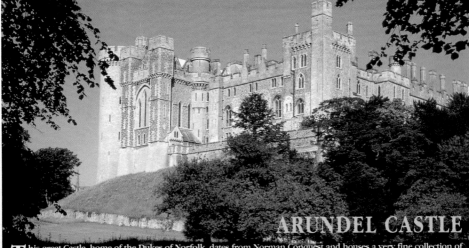

English Heritage

Canterbury, Dover, Hastings, Winchester; the historical associations of these cities and towns are legendary. Discover their stories with a visit to one of the many English Heritage sites in the South East of England.

Visit St Augustine's Abbey, part of the World Heritage Site in Canterbury. This great shrine was founded by St. Augustine in 597, the year he arrived in England from Rome. The site marks the re-birth of Christianity in this country. The museum with its artefacts uncovered on site, computer graphics and the interactive audio tour tells the remarkable story of the site.

October 14h 1066 is arguably the most important date in England's history. Today you can stand on the very spot where Harold was slain as you take the audio tour of the battlefield at Battle Abbey in East Sussex. The events leading up to the Battle of Hastings are explained through exhibitions and displays, whilst characters from the past come alive on the audio tour to help the visitor relive this fateful day.

In the beautiful Cathedral city of Winchester a visit to Wolvesey Castle, one of the greatest medieval buildings in England is a must. These atmospheric ruins were once home to the powerful Bishops of Winchester and were where Queen Mary I met Philip I of Spain for her wedding breakfast.

At Dover Castle there are a full 2000 years of history to discover, from the Anglo Saxon Church, the Roman Lighthouse and King Henry II's towering Keep to the Secret Wartime Tunnels deep within the White Cliffs – where Sir Winston Churchill and Admiral Ramsey masterminded the evacuation of Dunkirk.

At Osborne House on the Isle of Wight you can take an intriguing glimpse into both the public and private life of Britain's longest reigning monarch – Queen Victoria – as you see both the magnificent state rooms and the private family rooms. Highlight of the visit include the horse and carriage ride to the charming Swiss Cottage, where the Royal children played, and a visit to the newly restored walled garden.

Walmer Castle and Gardens in Kent remains a royal residence in use, as it is one of the favourite castles of HM the Queen Mother, who stays here in her capacity as Lord Warden of the Cinq Ports. The garden newly created to celebrate her 95th birthday is a delight not to be missed. The Duke of Wellington is another famous figure who resided at Walmer and visitors can see the room in which he died and of course the famous Wellington Boot!

Throughout the year sites are bought alive with re-enactments, firework displays and concerts. For free details on places, events or how you can benefit from English Heritage membership, please telephone 01793 414910 or visit us at www.english-heritage.org.uk.

Address
English Heritage
3 High Street
Tonbridge
Kent TN9 1SG
Tel: 01732 77800
Fax: 01732 778001
Membership: 01793 414910
www.english-heritage.org.uk

Sussex Country

Picture the ideal English country scene of gently rolling hills, medieval cottages, glorious gardens, old villages and fairytale castles. You'll find it in Sussex Country, an area of southern England which can legitimately claim to have shaped the nation we live in.

There is Pevensey, the probable landing point of William the Conqueror's invading army in 1066, and Lewes, where a medieval battle saw the barons defeat the King, thus beginning our system of Government.

There are coastal strongholds such as Seaford, steeped in smuggler's lore, where wrecking was once commonplace. The Ashdown Forest and River Ouse Valley are but two inspirational haunts of some of England's greatest writers and artists.

For historic houses, look at Firle Place and Glynde Place, little more than 3 miles apart yet steeped in family histories that would divide them during the English Civil War.

For fairytale castles with moats and towers we offer Herstmonceaux; and for beautiful gardens to enjoy there is Sheffield Park.

As you would expect on a coast faced with threats of invasion, there are many defensive buildings, including a Martello Tower and Newhaven Fort. The beaches at Seaford, Birling Gap and Pevensey all fly the Seaside Award flag for clean bathing waters. Sussex Country has several Country Parks and other delightful areas to explore with marvellous names like 'The Meanders' and 'High and Over'. There are rural walks and cycle paths, particularly in the Cuckmere Valley where the Cuckoo Trail has been developed, and for steam train enthusiasts there are the Bluebell Railway and the Lavender Line. You'll find farm attractions to visit, and local farmers and fishermen offering the freshest produce including English wines, cheeses and seafood. There are truly unusual shops including the best in contemporary art and crafts, stylish bars and restaurants. Lewes is antique hunter's heaven with furniture, bookshops and bargain stalls to rummage around. And for unique holiday photographs there are some amazing features not to miss, including the Long Man of Wilmington and The Seven Sisters cliffs. Whenever you visit there are festivals, country fairs, exhibitions and events to enjoy whether at local village level or on the grand scale of Glyndebourne International Opera – and 3 tourist information centres to assist with planning your stay.

Free holiday guide and further information available from:
www.sussex-country-tourism.co.uk

Sussex Country TIC
01323 442667

Lewes TIC
01273 483448

Seaford TIC
01323 897426

Royal Pavilion

Universally acclaimed as one of the most dazzling and exotically beautiful buildings in the British Isles, the Royal Pavilion is the spectacular fantasy palace of King George IV. An important symbol of the Regency period, the Pavilion dramatically reflects the tastes and personality of George IV, one of the greatest royal builders of British history. The famous seaside residence was also used as a summer family home by both King William IV and Queen Victoria.

Decorated in the Chinese taste with an Indian exterior, this Regency Palace is quite breath-taking. Originally a simple farmhouse, in 1787 architect Henry Holland created a neo-classical villa on the site. It was later transformed into its current Indian style by John Nash between 1815 and 1822.

Magnificent decorations and fantastic furnishings have been re-created in the recent extensive restoration programme. From the opulence of the main State Rooms to the charm of the first floor bedroom suites, the Royal Pavilion is filled with astonishing colours and superb craftsmanship.

Witness the magnificence of the Music Room with its domed ceiling of over 26,000 gilded scalloped-shaped shells and hand-knotted carpet, and promenade through the pink and blue bamboo grove of the Long Gallery. Visit the Great Kitchen, adorned with cast iron palm trees, where lavish menus were created and then served in the dramatic setting of the Banqueting Room, lit by a huge crystal chandelier held by a silvered dragon.

The Royal Pavilion is surrounded by picturesque Regency gardens, recently replanted to John Nash's original 1826 design, a truly fitting setting for this magical palace. Light lunches and refreshments can be enjoyed in the Queen Adelaide tearooms, while the Pavilion shop offers many gifts and souvenirs exclusive to the Palace.

Address
The Royal Pavilion
Brighton
East Sussex BN1 1EE
Tel: 01273 290900
www.royalpavilion.brighton.co.uk

Opening Times
Open – Daily Oct-May 10am-5pm, June-Sept 10am-6pm (except 25 & 26 December)

Admission
Adult £4.90*
Child £3.00*
*Prices valid until 31.3.2001

Location
Brighton Town Centre – 49 minutes by train from London

Facilities
Public guided tours daily at 11.30am and 2.30pm
Gift Shop, Tea room & Gardens

BRICKWALL
HOUSE & GARDENS
Northiam, Nr. Rye, East Sussex TN31 6NL

Home of the Frewen family since 1666.
17th century Drawing Room, superb plaster ceilings and family portraits. The grounds contain formal walled garden, topiary and arboretum.
Tours by family member.
Location: 7 miles NW of Rye on B2088.
Open by appointment only for groups
of 10 upwards. Also licensed for weddings.
Admission to house and garden £3.
Contact Bursar, Mr Peter Mould.
Phone 01797 253388 or Fax 01797 252567
The Frewen Educational Trust

Set amid 33 acres of woodland and gardens Beauport Park is everything a quintessentially English Country House Hotel should be. Built in 1719 it was later remodelled by Gen. Sir James Munray who became Governor of Quebec.

The elegantly furnished bedrooms each enjoy remote control colour television, electric trouser press, hair dryer, auto dial telephone, radio and tea and coffee making facilities. All have private bathrooms and shower en-suite.

Situate just 3 miles from both Battle and Hastings and in the Heart of 1066 Country you could not be more perfectly placed for exploring East Sussex, an area rich in history and beauty. For further information please telephone or write quoting 'Essence of England'.

THE BEAUPORT PARK HOTEL
Battle Road • Hastings • East Sussex TN38 8EA
Tel: 01424 851222 Fax: 01424 852465

NETHERFIELD PLACE
Battle, East Sussex TN33 9PP
Telephone: 01424 774455 Fax: 01424 774024
e-mail: reservations@netherfieldplace.demon.co.uk
website: netherfieldplace-demon.co.uk
14 Rooms (13 en suite), 1 Four Poster.
AA ☆☆☆ Red, RAC ☆☆☆ Blue Ribbon, Egon Ronay, Michelin.
Award winning Country House set in 30 acres of Parkland. A haven for those who enjoy peace and tranquility in a grand setting, whilst touring the South East's castles and gardens. For the sportsman, two all weather tennis courts, golf and croquet.

RS Ⓒ ☐ P ⑂ V ◐ ⌒ ✿ 🏨 SPECIAL 1 2 3 4

FLACKLEY ASH HOTEL
Peasmarsh, Rye, East Sussex TN31 6YH
Telephone: 01797 230651 Fax: 01797 230510
42 Rooms (all en suite), 3 Four Posters.
AA/RAC ☆☆☆, ETC ☆☆☆
Georgian Country House set in beautiful gardens with croquet and putting. Indoor swimming pool and Leisure centre with gym, saunas, whirlpool spa, steam room. Aromatherapy and beauty treatments. Warm, friendly atmosphere, fine wines and good food. Visit castles, gardens and the Ancient Cinque Port of Rye.

RS Ⓒ ☐ 🍽 P ⑂ V GF SP ⌒ ⟿ ✿ 🏨 🏨 SPECIAL
1 2 3 4 B

ROYAL VICTORIA HOTEL
Marina, St. Leonards, Hastings, E. Sussex
Telephone: 01424 445544 Fax: 01424 721995
Email: reception@royal-vic-hotel.demon.co.uk
Website: www.uk-travelguide.co.uk/royal-vic-hotel
AA/RAC/ETC ☆☆☆, Egon Ronay.
50 Rooms (all en suite).
Standing on St. Leonards sea front, under one mile from historic Hastings. Tastefully and comfortably furnished, the hotel has been host to many European heads of state and nobility, including Queen Victoria in her childhood. Renowned sea terrace restaurant and piano bar with excellent views across the English Channel.

RS Ⓒ ⊘ Ⓒ ☐ 🍽 P ⑂ V ⬍ 🏨 🏨 SPECIAL 1 2 3
4 5 C

Great Dixter House & Gardens

Great Dixter – birthplace and home of gardening writer Christopher Lloyd was built in the middle of the 15th century. Sir Edwin Lutyens was commissioned in 1910 to restore the main part of the house to its original medieval splendour and to build the domestic quarters necessary to accommodate an Edwardian household. A hall house dating from around 1500 was also added. Having been originally located in nearby Benenden, it was dismantled piece by piece and re-erected at Great Dixter.

The Great Hall, constructed of oak culled from the Wealden forest, is one of the largest surviving timber-framed halls in the country and is unique with its combination of both tie and hammer beams, whilst the furniture, tapestries and needlework on display (many of which are the creations of the Lloyd family themselves) offer the visitor a rare insight not only into the way a home has developed over five centuries, but how it continues developing to the present day.

Christopher has devoted his lifetime to creating one of the most experimental and constantly changing gardens of our time. Incorporating many medieval buildings, the gardens encompass the house, each complementing the other and providing stimulation for the senses throughout the seasons.

With the variety of clipped topiary, carpets of wild meadow flowers, the ever changing tapestry of mixed borders (including the famous Long Border), dreamy ponds and a startling exuberant Exotic Garden, Great Dixter will both captivate and astonish at every turn and continues to do so throughout every season as Christopher experiments endlessly. The picture changes with the years and with the seasons, providing different experiences, inspirations and surprises at each successive visit.

Many of the plants seen in the gardens can be purchased at our plant nursery. A mail order catalogue is available. We are known as clematis specialists. A range of gifts that are unique to Great Dixter can also be bought in our gift shop.

Great Dixter House & Gardens, Northiam, Nr Rye, East Sussex TN31 6PH
Tel: 01797 252878
Fax: 01797 252879
Email: greatdixter@compuserve.com

Contact
Elaine Francis,
Business Manager

Open
April-Oct, Tues-Sun & Bank Holiday Mons, 2pm-5pm (last admission)

2000 Admission Prices
Adult: house & garden £6.00, garden only £4.50.
Child: house & garden £1.50, garden only £1.00.

CALEDONIAN HOTEL
Osborne Road, Jesmond, Newcastle upon Tyne
Telephone: 0191 281 7881 Fax: 0191 281 6241
89 Rooms (all en suite), 1 Four Poster
AA ☆☆☆, RAC ☆☆☆, ETB 👑👑👑👑👑
Located in the heart of one of Newcastle's most prestigious residential areas, all of the rooms have colour television with Sky Movies, News & Sport, radio, direct dial delephone, trouser press, hair dryer and tea and coffee making facilities. Including four luxurious suites, including The Roslyn with a Four Poster Bed.

RS 🌀🚫🕐🛏🅰🍵 P 🍴 V GF ⬆ ✂ SPECIAL 1 2 3 4 C

Newcastle upon Tyne

Newcastle is the capital city of Northumbria in the North East of England. A Weissman Travel Reports survey voted Newcastle the eighth best party city in the world in 1995. It is the fastest growing destination in the country for overseas visitors and one of Britain's favourite City-Break destinations. It's a stylish, thriving and exciting City with a rich heritage and cultural life, many and varied attractions with a reputation for hospitality and a friendly welcome second to none.

The City lies on the East Coast railway which connects London, York and Durham to Edinburgh, so it is an easy place to visit and is used as a base to tour York, Durham, the Scottish Borders and the capital by many European visitors who appreciate the uncongested natural beauty and history of this unspoilt region of Britain.

Newcastle has an ancient history reaching back to the days of Romans when Newcastle was the outpost of Empire with legions stationed on Hadrian's Wall, now a World Heritage Site.

Using the railway to visit Newcastle is appropriate, for it is here that George Stephenson invented the locomotive and developed modern railways.

The City's 12th century Castle Keep still watches over the River Tyne and its bridges, as its Roman and Norman predecessors did, protecting the river crossings and port. The great bridges dominate the skyline of Quayside's historic waterfront and the great arc of the new Tyne Bridge most prominent. The historic timber-framed buildings in this old maritime quarter now contain shops, restaurants, pubs and nightclubs which form a thriving nightlife scene.

Newcastle's commercial heart lies on a plateau above the Quayside. It's elegant 19th century classical architecture built at the height of Newcastle's pre-eminence in the early days of Queen Victoria's reign. The magnificent set piece is Grey Street, a street which has a subtle descending curve and richly decorated buildings and is dominated by an imposing column dedicated to Earl Grey, who lent his name to one of the world's favourite blends of tea.

You'll enjoy Newcastle, make it a definite place to visit.

A comprehensive free information pack of Newcastle is available from the City and Tourist Information Centre, City Library, Princess Square, Newcastle upon Tyne NE99 1DX Tel: 0191 261 0610 Fax: 0191 221 0115

Rugby Art Gallery Museum & Library

Little Elborow Street, Rugby CV21 3B2
Tel: 01788 533201 Fax: 01788 533204
Email: rugbyartgallery&museum@rugby.gov.uk
www.rugbygalleryandmuseum.org.uk

The museum offers the opportunity to learn about the discoveries of the remarkable Tripontium Collection of Roman artefacts and explore more recent developments in Rugby at work, at home and in the community. The purpose-built Art Gallery is 400 square metres of gallery space which offers views over the town. Here visitors can see a series of changing temporary exhibitions, including Rugby's Collection of Modern Art which includes work by nationally known artists such as Stanley Spencer and L S Lowry. When the Rugby Collection is not on display, visitors and researchers can view by appointment. A programme of talks and workshops take place throughout the year. There is provision for school parties and families.

Opening Hours

Tuesday and Thursday 10am-8pm
Wednesday and Friday 10am-5pm
Saturday 10am-4pm
Sundays and Bank Holidays 1-5pm
Mondays Closed

THE ARDENCOTE MANOR HOTEL & COUNTRY CLUB

Lye Green Road, Claverdon, near Warwick CV35 8LS
Telephone: 01926 843111 Fax: 01926 842646
Website: www.ardencote.com
75 Rooms (all en suite)
AA ☆☆☆, ETB 👑 👑 👑 👑.
This historic former gentleman's residence set in 42 acres of landscaped grounds, is the perfect venue for business or pleasure. Along with luxurious en suite accommodation, conference rooms and two excellent restaurants, there is a superb Sports & Leisure Complex, 3 acre trout fishing lake, 9 hole golf course, a suite of Beauty Rooms and hair Salon for ultimate pampering.

RS 🕾 📞 🗂 ☕ P 🍴 V GF 🏊 🕐 ⚘ ➳ ✈ 🐾 🚗 SPECIAL 1 2 3 4 B

THE LEAMINGTON HOTEL AND BISTRO

64 Upper Holly Walk, Leamington Spa, Warwickshire CV32 4JL
Telephone: 01926 883777 Fax: 01926 330467
30 Rooms (all en suite). AA ☆☆☆ ❀, RAC ☆☆☆, ETB 👑 👑 👑 👑 Commended, Egon Ronay Listed.
A stylishly appointed Town House Hotel recently refurbished, 2 minutes walk from town centre. Elegant Bistro restaurant, cocktail bar, guest lounge and function room. All 30 bedrooms have en suite bathrooms, with luxury beds. **Purpose-built Executive Disabled Bedroom.** All public areas fully fitted for disabled use. Convenient for touring Shakespeare country, Cotswolds, Oxford. Close to NEC and Birmingham airport.

RS 🚭 📞 🗂 ⚘ ☕ P 🍴 V GF ⚘ ➳ ✈ 🚗 SPECIAL 1 2 3 C

THE WARWICK ARMS HOTEL

17 High Street, Warwick CU34 4AT
Telephone: 01926 492759 Fax: 01926 410587
35 Rooms (all en suite).
RAC ☆☆☆.
The Warwick Arms is an early 18th century Coaching Inn, tastefully refurbished to modern standards, without loosing its old fashioned grace and charm. The hotel offers an á la carte restaurant, lounge bar and coffee shop. It is situated in the town centre very close to warwick castle.

RS 🕾 📞 🗂 ☕ P 🍴 V ⚘ 🚗 🐾 SPECIAL 1 2 3 4 C

THE LORD LEYCESTER HOTEL

Jury Street, Warwick CV34 4EJ
Telephone: 01926 491481 Fax: 01926 491561
51 Rooms (all en suite), 1 Four Poster. ETB 👑 👑 👑 👑
In the centre of England, Georgian period hotel, 50 bedrooms with old world charm. In city centre opposite Warwick Castle. Close to Stratford upon Avon and Royal Leamington Spa. Excellent cuisine. So much history to explore. Superb road links (London 1hr 20min, Oxford 1hr). Please telephone or fax for details. Under new management.

RS 🕾 📞 🗂 ⚘ ☕ P 🍴 V ➳ ⚘ 🚗 🐾 SPECIAL 1 2 3 4 C

Warwick Castle

Experience a thousand years of history.

Over a thousand years of secrets hide in the shadows of Warwick Castle. Murder, mystery, intrigue and scandal: the Castle has witnessed it all, and now reveals the secret life of England as you have never seen it before.

From the days of William the Conqueror to the reign of Queen Victoria, the Castle has provided a backdrop for many turbulent times.

Here you can join a mediaeval household in our Kingmaker attraction, watching them prepare for the final battle of the Earl of Warwick. Enter the eerie Ghost Tower, where it is said that the unquiet spirit of Sir Fulke Greville, murdered most foully by a manservant, still roams.

Descend into the gloomy depths of the Dungeon and Torture Chamber, then step forward in time and marvel at the grandeur of the State Rooms. The 14th century Great Hall lies at the heart of the Castle and here you can see the death mask of Oliver Cromwell and Bonnie Prince Charlie's shield.

Witness the perfect manners and hidden indiscretions of Daisy, Countess of Warwick and her friends at the Royal Weekend Party 1898 or stroll through the 60 acres of grounds and gardens, landscaped by Capability Brown, which surround the Castle today.

Warwick Castle
Warwick
Warwickshire
CV34 4QU
Tel: 01926 406600
www.warwick-castle.co.uk

Opening times
Open every day (except Christmas Day) from 10am-6pm (5pm from Nov to March). Last admission is half an hour before closing.

Location
2 miles from junction 15 of the M40

MALLORY COURT

Harbury Lane, Bishops Tachbrook,
Leamington Spa, Warwickshire CV33 9QB
Tel: 01926 330214 Fax: 01926 451714
Email: mallorycourt@mallory.co.uk

 AA ★★★ (Red)

Surrounded by ten acres of attractive gardens, Mallory Court affords a stunning vista across the beautiful Warwickshire countryside. Offering every home comfort, arriving guests are enveloped by the welcoming ambience and peace and quiet of a private house rather than a hotel. The public rooms are bedecked with floral arrangements and during the winter season one can relax by the burning log fires. The sun lounge is at its most inviting throughout the summer months when it opens onto the terrace. The luxurious bedrooms are individually furnished and enhanced by soft fabrics, thick carpets and en-suite facilities. Cuisine is an important criterion and the dishes served in the elegant oak panelled restaurant are a fushion of classical and modern British flavours.

HIPSLEY FARM COTTAGES

**Hipsley Lane, Hurley, Atherstone
Warwickshire, CV9 2LR
Tel/Fax: 01827 872437 Mrs A Prosser
email: am@hipsley.co.uk**
6 Self Catering cottages, ETC ☆☆☆☆

Hipsley farm is situated in beautiful, rolling countryside. The old barns and cowsheds have been carefully converted into warm, comfortable and attractive cottages. Each one individually furnished to the highest standards. All cottages fully equipped including gas central heating, colour t.v., all bed linen and towels. Excellent laundry facilities. Large garden. Enjoy the putting green, barbeque and lovely farm walks. Within easy reach of theatres, castles, cathedrals and museums in Stratford, Warwick, Lichfield and Birmingham.

📞 P GF ⌁ 🏠 SPECIAL Dogs and Disabled

WARWICKSHIRE FARM HOLIDAYS

STAY ON A FARM IN WARWICKSHIRE

Farming families offering value for money, good food and a warm welcome in quality bed & breakfast and self-catering accommodation. All farms are Farm Holiday Bureau members and Heart of England Tourist Board inspected. **TEL: 01295 770652 FAX: 01295 770632.**
e-mail: crandonhouse@talk21.com

NAILCOTE HALL HOTEL
Nailcote Lane, Berkswell, Warwickshire CV7 7DE
Telephone: 024 76466174 Fax: 024 76470720
38 Rooms (all en suite).
AA ☆☆☆☆ ❀❀. ETB highly commended.
A 17th century country house hotel, set in 15 acres of parkland, ideally located in the heart of England. Enjoy the traditional style of the award winning Oak Room Restaurant or Mediterranean atmosphere of Rick's bar, combine with 38 delightful rooms, superb leisure complex, 9-hole championship golf course to make Nailcote " A venue for all reasons".

RS 📞 🏢 P ⏏ V GF ♿ SP ⏰ ⌁ 🚣 🎣
❀ 🏠 🏠 1 2 3 4 A B

CHARLECOTE PARK
Warwick CV35 9ER
Tel: 01789 470277 Fax: 01789 470544
Email: charlecote@smtp.ntrust.org.uk
www.ntrustsevern.org.uk

Built in the 1550s the mellow brickwork and great chimneys represent the best of English Tudor craftsmanship. Elizabeth I spent two nights here in 1572 and Shakespeare was allegedly caught poaching the deer park.
The rich interiors are furnished in 'Romantic' style and contain important objects from William Beckford's Fonthill Abbey. The River Avon flows through the attractive park landscaped by 'Capability Brown' and also contains Red and Fallow Deer and Jacob Sheep which have been at Charlecote since 1756.

🌿 THE NATIONAL TRUST

Five beautifully preserved Tudor houses all associated with William Shakespeare and his family.

In Town:
Shakespeare's Birthplace, *Henley Street* Nash's House & New Place, *Chapel Street,* Hall's Croft, Old Town.

Out of Town:
Anne Hathaway's Cottage, *Shottery* Mary Arden's House & The Shakespeare Countryside Museum, *Wilmcote.*

Shakespeare's Birthplace
Step into the house where William Shakespeare was born in 1564 and re-enter the Tudor World. Newly refurbished, the birthplace of the Man of the Millennium now offers visitors a fascinating insight into life as it was when Shakespeare was a child.

Nash's House & New Place, *Chapel Street*
Nash's House was owned by Thomas Nash, first husband of Shakespeare's grand-daughter, Elizabeth. Houses an exceptional collection of 17th century oak furniture and tapestries, also has displays on the history of Stratford. Shakespeare spent his last years in New Place, next door to Nash's House.

Hall's Croft, *Old Town*
Hall's Croft is one of the finest half timbered, gabled houses in Stratford-upon-Avon. It is named after Dr John Hall who married Shakespeare's daughter Susanna. John ran a successful medical practice treating many patients rich and poor, in the town and district.

Anne Hathaway's Cottage, *Shottery*
Retrace the steps William Shakespeare must have taken when courting Anne Hathaway before they married in 1582. This thatched farmhouse in the village of Shottery, just on the edge of Stratford, continued to be home to the descendants of the Hathaway family until the 19th century.

Mary Arden's House and the Shakespeare Countryside Museum, *Wilmcote*
Mary Arden's House was the home of Shakespeare's mother, Mary Arden, before she married John Shakespeare and moved to Stratford. This fine Tudor farmhouse with its many old outbuildings and fascinating displays, brings to life the work and traditions of the countryside from Shakespeare's time to the 20th century. Mary Arden's house, the Shakespeare Countryside Museum and the adjacent Glebe farm all offer something for everyone to enjoy, making an excellent day out.

Address
The Shakespeare Houses
The Shakespeare Birthplace Trust
Henley Street
Stratford-Upon-Avon
Warwickshire CV37 6QW

For further information
Tel: 01789 204016
Fax: 01789 296083
www.shakespeare.org.uk
info@shakespeare.org.uk

Opening Times
Open daily all year round.
Except 23, 24, 25, 26 Dec

Admission
Inclusive tickets available to three in-town, or all five houses.

The Shakespeare Birthplace Trust is a Registered Charity, No. 209302

Glebe Farm House

Loxley, Warwick CV35 9JW
Telephone: 01789 842501
Fax: 01789 841194
Email: scorpiolimited@msn.com
www.glebefarmhouse.com

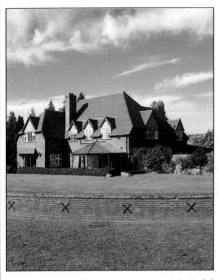

The pleasure of staying at this delightful country house is that of visiting a private home. Just three miles from historic Stratford-upon-Avon and eight miles from Warwick, Glebe Farm is surrounded by a superb expanse of secluded lawned garden which opens onto 30 acres of beautiful farmland where one can ramble and enjoy the sounds and sights of local wildlife.

Owner Kate McGovern is an accomplished cook and her dinners, served in the attractive surroundings of a conservatory overlooking the gardens, will tempt every palate. Whenever possible fresh produce from the kitchen garden are used. Kate is a talented water colour artist and many of her paintings adorn the walls throughout the house which is furnished and decorated with immaculate taste.

THE BIRMINGHAM BOTANICAL GARDENS & GLASSHOUSES

Westbourne Road, Edgbaston, Birmingham B15 3TR
Tel: 0121 454 1860 Fax: 0121 454 7835
Email: admin@bham-bot-gdns.demon.co.uk
www.bham-bot-gdns.demon.co.uk

Two miles from city centre. Home to the widest range of plants in the Midlands, including the National Bonsai Collection.
Inside: glasshouses take visitors from the Tropical Rainforest to the Arid Desert. Outside: 15 acres of beautiful landscaped and themed gardens. Lots for children: exotic birds, insect-eating plants, giant 'cacti', adventure playground and walkabout trails. Disabled access, ample seating. Bands on summer Sunday and Bank Holiday afternoons. Special events – please telephone for details.

OPEN DAILY

SOLIHULL TOURIST INFORMATION CENTRE

Central Library, Homer Road, Solihull B91 3RG
Tel: 0121 704 6130 Fax: 0121 704 8224
Email: tourism@solihull.gov.uk   www.solihull.gov.uk

Our Friendly, knowledgeable staff will be happy to assist you with all your Tourist related enquiries including accommodation, travel and places to visit, both locally and nationally.

We're here to help!

HIMLEY HALL

Himley Park,
Himley, Dudley
West Midlands DY3 4DF
Telephone: 01902 326665
Facsimile: 01902 894163

Set amongst 180 acres of 'Capability' Brown landscaped parkland, this Grade II* listed building was once home to the Earls of Dudley.
The Hall is open to the public during the spring and summer months, with an exciting temporary exhibitions programme.
Admission to the Hall is free!

Arbury Hall

Built on the site of, and from the masonry of an Augustinian Priory which was founded in the 12th century, Arbury Hall has been the seat of the Viscount Daventry and the Newdigate family since 1586.

Rightly deserving its title, "The Gothic Gem of the Midlands", Arbury hall proudly sits in the centre of a large wooded estate, (a deer park until the beginning of this century), amidst spectacular gardens and surrounded by lakes and canals.

The Hall was 'gothicised' by the 5th Baronet, Sir Roger Newdigate, in the 18th century. A gifted amateur draughtsman and architect, he designed much of the spectacular plasterwork for which the house is renowned himself, copying unashamedly from his favourite medieval buildings, Westminster Abbey in particular. He carefully conserved the original Tudor/Elizabethan house in such a way as to make Arbury a unique stately home.

The plasterwork is of such splendour that it has been immortalised by the famous English authoress, George Eliot (who was born on the estate and knew the house well). Her descriptions of the Saloon and Dining Room ceilings in her book, "Scenes of Clerical Life", are as true today as when the book was written.

Apart from the magnificent plasterwork, the house contains a notable collection of paintings (including family portraits and those of royalty), furniture and other works of art, such as a complete set of Jacobean drinking glasses, accumulated down the centuries by successive generations of the family; and here and there are reminders of the connection the estate had with the lives of three English Queens and its relationship with the Shakespeare story.

Words cannot adequately describe the splendour of Arbury and its magnificent gardens with rolling lawns and serpentine paths bordered by rhododendrons and other colourful shrubs and flowers, including a giant wisteria.

An ideal location for Corporate Hospitality Events, Photo shoots, Product Launches and Activity Days. Corporate lunches and dinners catered for.

Arbury Hall, Nuneaton, Warwickshire
CV10 7PT
Tel: 024 76382804
Fax: 024 76641147

Open all year, on Tues, Weds & Thurs only, for Corporate Events. Pre-booked visits to the Hall and Gardens for parties/groups of 25 or over on Tues, Weds & Thurs only, from Easter to end of September. Hall & Gardens open 2pm-5pm on Bank Holiday weekends only (Sun & Mon) Easter to September.

Admission
Hall and Gardens
Adult £5.00 Child £3.00
Family Ticket £12.00

Location
2 miles SW of Nuneaton off B4102

Facilities
Gift/Craft Shop,
Tea room

West Wiltshire
The Heart of Wessex

Wessex is more than a location. Enigmatic images of Stonehenge, magnificent ancestral homes, sleepy villages and hill carvings celebrating victorious battles are conjured up.

West Wiltshire is the Heart of Wessex. The area's timeless charm has inspired endless lines of prose and has fascinated countless visitors. There are enchanted Italianate style gardens at Iford, and ancient manor houses at Great Chalfield and Westwood. Extensive country parks include 80 acres of broadleaf woodland at The Woodland Park and Barton Farm Country Park, nr Bradford on Avon, contains a magnificent 14th century tithe barn (one of Englands largest).

No tour of the area is complete without a visit to Longleat the pride of the 7th Marquess of Bath. Longleat House is a magnificent 16th century stately home set in breathtaking rolling parkland, and offers a host of visitor attractions for all the family.

The district is fortunate in possessing a number of superb local museums, telling the story of the area's history, including Trowbridge Museum which depicts the growth of the West of England woollen industry over the centuries.

One of West Wiltshire's finest attractions is its countryside. Over half of the district has been designated as an Area of Outstanding Natural Beauty.

The five historic market towns of West Wiltshire are a delight to visit. From the ancient and picturesque town of Bradford on Avon with its steep hills and quaint weavers cottages, to the army garrison town of Warminster which dates back to Saxon times.

Trowbridge, Melksham and Westbury are also attractive woollen towns steeped in history with fine architectural examples of the woollen industry remaining. East of Westbury visitors will find the famous Westbury White Horse, originally cut in 1778, which affords magnificent views over the region.

West Wiltshire is a wonderful place to stay with a wide variety of accommodation from elegant country house hotels to picturesque village guest houses and an excellent base from which to explore the attractions of the South West, including the historic sites of Stonehenge, Avebury, Stourhead, Lacock and the cities of Bath, Salisbury, Wells and many more.

For a free brochure on the area contact Tourism Dep't (EE) WWDC, Trinity House Bryer Ash Business Park Trowbridge Wiltshire BA14 8HE www.westwiltshire.gov.uk

Bradford on Avon TIC
34 Silver Street
Tel: 01225 865797

Melksham TIC
Church Street
Tel: 01225 707424

Trowbridge TIC
St Stephen's Place
Tel: 01225 777054

Warminster TIC
Central Car Park
Tel: 01985 218548

Westbury TIC
Edward Street
Tel: 01373 827158

The Heart of Wiltshire

Discover The Heart of Wiltshire, a landscape steeped in prehistory, at the centre of which stands Avebury World Heritage Site, just eighteen miles north of Stonehenge and within easy reach of the historic City of Bath..

King Charles II was recommended by John Aubrey to visit Avebury because "...it does as much exceed in greatness the renowned Stonehenge as a cathedral does a parish church". Today Avebury attracts visitors from around the world who come to marvel at the largest stone circle in Europe, which dates back to 2000BC. One of the most impressive ceremonial landscapes in Britain, Avebury offers the visitor an opportunity to explore the site and learn of the history that shaped the landscape. The countryside includes many other important monuments including causewayed camps, hedges and barrows. The chalk downlands and grasslands of the Marlborough Downs and Vale of Pewsey have supported communities from the earliest times . Follow the footsteps of ancient civilisations and explore the rural landscape which reveals much of its past.

The Kennet and Avon Canal passes through the countryside, much of which is designated an Area Of Outstanding Natural Beauty. Discover the romantic charms of a cruise along the canal visiting the many historical and architectural attractions along its banks.Visit the Caen Hill flight of 29 locks at Devizes, a magnificent feat of engineering which carries the canal up a rise of 234'.

The historic market town of Marlborough has one of the most impressive high streets in Europe, flanked by splendid Georgian and Tudor buildings among which you will find many excellent inns and hotels. Marlborough College dominates one end of the high street. Founded in 1843 as a public school and originally intended for sons of the clergy, past pupils have included Sir John Betjeman and William Morris.

Free Visitor guide and other holiday information from:

Marlborough Tourist Information Centre.
George Lane Car Park
Marlborough SN8 1EE
Tel: 01672 513989
(24 hours)

Hotels, Inns, Bed & Breakfast
Historic Houses, Castles & Gardens,
Antiques & Curios,
Arts & Crafts, Books & Tours

Welcome to Heritage Britain, a brand new website with more than 2000 years of history and culture. Whatever your interest in Britain, we aim to help you find out more within these pages.

Visit the definitive heritage site and discover the history behind Britain and Ireland's long and colourful past.

Stay in a splendid country house hotel or a medieval inn and savour the delights of the British countryside or a historic British town.

Travel back in time by visiting the myriad of historic houses, castles and gardens or museums and galleries that adorn this Sceptred Isle

Scour the local shops or fairs for arts and crafts, antiques, collectables, curios or objets d'art.

You can even contact a genealogist to help you trace your family tree.

Heritage Britain - the essential website for domestic travellers and overseas visitors to Britain and Ireland.

www.heritagebritain.com
mail@heritagebritain.com

Bowood House & Gardens
Calne, Wiltshire SN11 0LZ.
Tel. Calne (01249) 812102
Website:www.bowood-estate.co.uk

Bowood is the magnificent family home of the Marquis and Marchioness of Lansdowne designed by Robert Adam in the 18th century.
It stands in glorious parkland with sloping lawns stretching away from the house to the lake beyond. Splendours within the park include the Cascade, Doric Temple and terraced rose gardens. The interior of the house contains a remarkable collection of family heirlooms and works of art.
There is a massive Adventure Playground for children 12 years and under.
Bowood is open daily from 11.00am to 6.00pm from 18th April to 28th October 2001.

CORSHAM COURT
HOME OF THE METHUEN FAMILY

Corsham Court is one of England's finest Stately Homes. It was a Royal Manor in the days of the Saxon Kings and the present building is based upon an Elizabethan Manor dating from 1582. Magnificent Georgian State Rooms were added in 1760.

It houses one of the oldest and most distinguished collections of Old Masters and furniture in the country, and with the 'Capability' Brown gardens and arboretum, and architecture by John Nash and Thomas Bellamy, Corsham Court provides the visitor with a wonderful opportunity to enjoy the many delights of this historic and beautiful Stately Home.

Open throughout the year by appointment to groups of 15 or more persons.

Open 20th March to 30th September daily except Mondays (but including Bank Holidays) from 2.00pm until 5.30pm. From 1st October to 19th March open weekends from 2.00pm to 4.30pm. Closed December. Last entry 30 minutes before close.

CORSHAM COURT, Wiltshire SN13 0BZ
Tel/Fax: (01249) 701610

North Wiltshire

North Wiltshire, where the Cotswolds meet the Wiltshire Downs, is an area of rich countryside in a peaceful and visibly ancient landscape.

Over half the district is in an Area of Outsanding Natural Beauty with wooded river valleys and picturesque villages of mellow stone cottages portraying the idyllic English scene.

Among them are the film locations of Castle Combe and the National Trust village of Lacock which provided the romantic setting for Jane Austin's *Pride and Prejudice* and *Emma* and where within the abbey photography itself was pioneered.

Discover Malmesbury, England's oldest borough with the remains of its impressive Norman Abbey. View Cherhill White Horse carved into the rolling downs near Calne, the former home town of Joseph Prestly who discovered oxygen.

Trace the architectural heritage endowed by wealthy "wool" merchants in imposing town houses and manors and the Flemish Weavers Cottages' at Corsham.

Seek out the wealth of beautiful churches and imposing stately homes of Bowood and Corsham Court set in landscaped parks and the glorious gardens of Luckington Court and Abbey House, Malmesbury.

Historic towns of Chippenham and Wootton Bassett offer a choice of shopping and leisure activities and colourful street markets create an atmosphere reminiscent of another era.

Get away by exploring the miles of cycleways, bridleways and footpaths that cross the district. Take part in many exciting water sports at Cotswold Water Park or indulge in being a racing driver at Castle Combe Racing Circuit.

Easy access from the M4 and regular Intercity Rail Services, just one hour from London, makes North Wiltshire an ideal base from which to explore the nearby areas of Bath, Stonehenge and the glorious Cotswolds.

Throughout the year North Wiltshire hosts many major events including Chippenham Folk Festival, the North Wiltshire Classic Car Discovery Tour and Corsham Dickens Festival.

Friendly country pubs offer traditional Wiltshire fare and quality inspected accommodation from homely B&B's and town centre coaching inns to luxurious country house hotels ensures a memorable stay at any time of year.

For further information on places to visit, where to stay, outdoor activities and events please contact:

North Wiltshire District Council (Dept EE20)
Chippenham Tourist Information Centre
The Citadel
Bath Road
Chippenham
Wiltshire

Tel: 01249 706333
Fax: 01249 460776
Email:
tourism@northwilts.gov.uk

Salisbury and South Wiltshire

You haven't been to Britain until you've been to Salisbury and South Wiltshire – just two hours from Central London and with 6,000 years of history, the region really does offer the ultimate heritage holiday experience.

Stonehenge, a World Heritage Site whose true past still remains a mystery, stands impressively as a prehistoric monument of unique importance and is surrounded by the remains of ceremonial areas – some older than the monument itself.

The massive Iron Age hillfort of Old Sarum is the site of the original City of Salisbury. The fort was used by the Romans, Saxons and Normans and grew into one of the most flourishing settlements in medieval England. Infighting and a lack of water led to the City being relocated to the Salisbury that we know today and it was here that the world famous Cathedral was built between 1220 and 1258.

Salisbury Cathedral is the only Cathedral in England to have been built throughout in the same Early English style and possesses the tallest spire in England, the world's oldest working clock and one of the four surviving copies of the Magna Carta, the basis of the American Constitution.

To help you find out more about the region's rich and varied past, there are many excellent museums, stately homes and gardens and even the ruins of an ancient castle for you to explore.

The area is not just about the past, for Salisbury and South Wiltshire still has its feet firmly in the present. Salisbury is a vibrant, living City with an excellent range of entertainment, restaurants, places to stay, leisure facilities and is also a mecca for shoppers.

Much of South Wiltshire is designated an Area of Outstanding Natural Beauty and is increasingly accessible to those who enjoy countryside pursuits. Walkers, cyclists and horse riders are all spoilt for choice with a network of minor roads and bridleways, allowing exploration of the small towns, unspoilt villages, glorious chalk downlands and peaceful valleys, each with its own unique history and story to tell.

For your FREE copy of the Official Guide to Salisbury and South Wiltshire contact Salisbury Tourist Information Centre, Dept HHC00
Fish Row
Salisbury
Wiltshire SP1 1EJ
England
Tel: (0) 1722 334956
Fax: (0) 1722 422059
Email:
visitorinfo@salisbury.gov.uk
www.salisbury.gov.uk/tourism

Villiers Inn

AA ☆☆☆ ETB ☆☆☆

Villiers Inn is a warm hearted, full-service hotel with personality! In the 1800's it was a farmhouse and has now been converted to include 33 first class en-suite bedrooms. The "Pig on the Wall" Restaurant & Bar is a popular & informal environment offering a menu ranging from traditional fayre to contemporary dishes. Alternatively the Bopeeptree Rooms offers a slightly more informal ambience. The Ridgeway Hall is a purpose-built, self-contained conference centre with natural lighting throughout, designed for both business and pleasure for up to 90 guests.

**Moormead Road, Wroughton, Swindon,
Wiltshire SN4 9BY
Telephone: 01793 814744 Facsimile: 01793 814119
e-mail: hotels@villiersinn.co.uk**

The Pear Tree
(at Purton)

**Church End, Purton,
Swindon, Wiltshire SN5 9ED
Tel: 01793 772100
Fax: 01793 772369**

Francis and Anne Young's elegant cotswold stone hotel was once Purton vicarage. It is set in 7.5 acres of gardens on the outskirts of the saxon village of Purton in rural Wiltshire. With its stylish individually decorated bedrooms, named after characters from the village and its award winning conservatory restaurant, The Pear Tree is the ideal base to explore the countryside and heritage of Wessex. Oxford, Stonehenge, the Cotswolds and Bath are all of within an hours drive.

EXPLORE THE HISTORY OF WESSEX

OLD WARDOUR CASTLE
Tel: 01747 870487.
Wiltshire, Off A30 South West of Tisbury. Picturesque garden setting for 14th century castle, damaged during the Civil War.

OLD SARUM
Tel: 01722 335398.
Wiltshire, Off A345 North of Salisbury. 4000 years of fascinating history. Castle, Royal Palace & Cathedral Site.

PORTLAND CASTLE
Tel: 01305 820539.
Dorset, Overlooking Portland Harbour. One of the best preserved of Henry VIII's coastal forts. Breathtaking views of the harbour.

ENGLISH HERITAGE

Antrobus Arms Hotel
**Church Street, Amesbury, Wiltshire
Tel: 01980 623163 Fax: 01980 622112**

Attractive town hotel with spectacular walled garden and stunning Victorian fountain at the rear. Situated two miles from Stonehenge, six miles from Salisbury. All Bedrooms have central heating, TV, tea/coffee making facilities, direct dial telephones and all are en-suite. The Antrobus is many things to many people and several things to individuals – feature breaks, corporate gatherings, tailor-made special events. Just call for details.

Swindon

Take time to discover Swindon – where the West Country meets the Cotswolds. This vibrant, growing town has a warm welcome for visitors from all over the world.

Swindon is probably the fastest growing town in Europe and is now home to many national and international companies. However, the origins of Swindon's success originate from the development of Isambard Kingdom Brunel's Great Western Railway Works in 1840. The Works were to become one of the largest industrial enterprises in Europe and the driving force of the Victorian world. The GWR produced some of the finest locomotives and carriages ever seen.

Museum of the Great Western Railway

Today, the fascinating history of Brunel's railway is brought alive at STEAM - Museum of the Great Western Railway which celebrates the lives of the many hundreds of thousands of people who were employed in the Great Western Works and chronicles a time when steam was the powerhouse of the world!

The refurbished buildings of the Great Western Historic area are now home to the Great Western Designer Outlet Village, English Heritage and the National Monuments Record Centre, which holds England's entire heritage under one roof! A selection of the 7 million photographs are exhibited in The Gallery, and the Public Search Room allows visitors to look up English towns and villages and see what the archive holds.

As well as having its own appeal, Swindon is surrounded by some beautiful and exciting countryside. A short drive to the south will take you into the heart of the magnificent Wiltshire Downs, with picturesque market towns, the world famous White Horses and the impressive prehistoric sites of Avebury and Stonehenge. To the north, past the upper reaches of the River Thames, are many charming Cotswold villages, including Lechlade and Bourton on the Water.

Call Swindon Information Centre for your copy of the Swindon Short Breaks Brochure, or visit www.wiltshiretourism.co.uk

Swindon Tourist
Information Centre
37 Regent Street
Swindon
SN1 1JL

Tel: 01793 530328
or 466454
Fax: 01793 434031
Email: econdev@swindon.gov.uk
www.wiltshiretourism.co.uk

The Cottage in the Wood
HOTEL AND RESTAURANT
Holywell Road, Malvern Wells, Worcs. WR14 4LG
Telephone: 01684 575859 Fax: 01684 560662

Perhaps the most stunning setting for any hotel in England, perched high on the Malvern Hills, looking 30 miles across the Severn Vale. Owned and run by the Pattin family for 13 years, it's a relaxing and peaceful base from which to tour this area of outstanding natural beauty. The widely known restaurant provides exceptional food backed by a choice of 600 wines. En suite rooms from £95 to £145 B&B or two nights or more bargain breaks from £62 to £96 D.B.B. p.p.p.n. depending on season. AA/ETC ☆☆☆, Two AA Restaurant Rosettes.

The Malvern Hills Hotel at British Camp
Wynds Point, Malvern, Worcestershire WR13 6DW
Tel: 01684 540690 Fax: 01684 540327
e-mail: malhilhotl@aol.com www.malvernhillshotel.com

The hotel straddles the Herefordshire/Worcestershire hilltop border at British Camp, the ancient Iron Age hillfort also known as the Herefordshire Beacon. The panoramic view far over Worcestershire and Herefordshire from the summit of British Camp, pronounced by the celebrated 17th century diarist John Evelyn to be "one of the goodliest vistas in England", remains as spectacular today as it was some four centuries ago. In addition to walks with breathtaking views, the hotel offers excellent bar food, real ales, an elegant restaurant and extensive wine list, all in the traditions of a hostelry with a heritage of more than half a millennium.

English Tourism Council

★★ HOTEL

AA/RAC ★★

HOLDFAST COTTAGE HOTEL
Marlbank Road, Little Malvern WR13 6NA
Tel: 01684 310288 Fax: 01684 311117
www.holdfast-cottage.co.uk

A wonderfully warm and relaxing Country house Hotel set in two acres of gardens tucked into the foot of the Malvern Hills. Personal care and service is reflected in everything from the Award Winning Restaurant Menu which includes home made Rolls, Ice Creams, Sorbets and Chocolates to the personal touches in the individual pretty en-suite bedrooms. The Hotel is family owned and run by the proprietors Stephen and Jane Knowles offering true hospitality and an ideal centre to discover Elgar's heartland. Away Breaks available all week, all year. Children and Pets welcome.
ETB Silver Quality Award
AA Two Food Rosettes

THE COLWALL PARK HOTEL
Walwyn Road, Colwall, Malvern, Worcestershire WR13 6QG
Telephone: 01684 540206 Fax: 01684 540847
24 Rooms (all en suite).
AA ☆☆☆ ❀❀ 78%. RAC ☆☆☆. ETB 👑👑👑👑 highly commended.
An impressive, turn of the century, mock Tudor country house hotel. Set in the idyllic location of the village of Colwall. Fully refurbished facilities are available, including our two AA rosette restaurant and well appointed bedrooms with views of the hills and gardens. Ideally situated for touring, the three counties.

RS 🍸🚭💿🖥🍵☕ P 🍴 V 🍽 🦢❀🚗🛏
SPECIAL 1 2 3 4 C

THE MILL AT HARVINGTON
Anchor Lane, Harvington, Evesham, Worcs WR11 5NR
Telephone: 01386 870688 Fax: 01386 870688
21 Rooms (all en suite). AA ☆☆ 80%, RAC 2 Merits HCR, ETB 👑👑👑👑 Highly Commended, Good Food Guide (7 yrs), Good Hotel Guide (7 yrs), Which Hotel Guide (7 yrs), Egon Ronay, Michelin.
Owner-run hotel and restaurant, beautifully converted from former Georgian house and bakery. Situated in 8 acres of parkland with a 600 feet frontage onto the River Avon by Harvington Lock. Relaxed, friendly atmosphere and genuine hospitality from an interested staff add ambience to the restaurant, where local produce is a speciality.

RS 💿🖥🍺☕ P 🍴 V GF SP 🕐🍽 🦢❀🚗🛏
SPECIAL 1 2 3 4 C

Malvern Hills

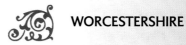

You can still find many areas of rural charm and beauty in England, but the Malverns district is unique. Nowhere else can equal its combination of old-fashioned English landscape and spectacular geography with cultural activities of real quality.

Dramatic hills

At the heart of the district are the Malvern Hills, a ridge of ancient granite that rises dramatically from the valley of the River Severn. Ideal for walking, you can enjoy immense views, eastward to the Cotswolds and westward to the Wye Valley and the Welsh mountains. From the riverside town of Upton Upon Severn to the little known Teme Valley and the areas around the historic towns of Ledbury and Bromyard.

A cultural tradition

The spa town of Great Malvern clings to the steep slopes of these hills, made famous by the purity of their water. With its refreshing air and elegant Victorian environment Malvern has appealed to generations of artists, indeed it was Malvern scenery that inspired Sir Edward Elgar, the most eminent Malvernian and Britain's favourite composer. His presence attracted writers like George Bernard Shaw and John Masefield and did much to establish the Malvern tradition in music and the theatre. Today the Malverns are the home of the internationally famous English String and Symphony Orchestras, Malvern Festival, of excellent theatre, of folk and jazz festivals and many other cultural activities.

Untouched countryside

Yet the Malverns district is agricultural as well as cultural, well known for its hops and its world famous Herefordshire cattle. Malvern is the home of the huge Three Counties Show ground, venue for one of Britain's most popular flower shows, as well as numerous events throughout the year from antiques to craft fairs. And all around the hills are miles of countryside scarcely touched by the modern world, with woodland, quiet footpaths, small roads ideal for cycling, cider orchards, hop yards, traditional black and white timber buildings, ancient churches and attractive country inns.

A warm welcome

The Malverns welcome visitors warmly, with top quality accommodation ranging from hotels to camping sites, and with excellent places where you can eat and drink, either simply or with great sophistication.

To find the real England, still at its best, visit the Malverns. It is a district unique for culture and for country living.

For further information contact:
Malvern Tourist
Information Centre
21 Church Street
Malvern
Worcs WR14 2AA
Tel: 01684 892289
Fax: 01684 892872
For free accommodation guide and events list.

WHITE LION HOTEL
21 High Street, Upton-upon-Severn,
Worcestershire WR8 0HJ
Telephone: 01684 592551 Fax: 01684 593333
Email: Reservations@Whitelionhotel.demon.co.uk
Internet: www.whitelionhotel.demon.co.uk
10 Rooms (all en suite).
AA ☆☆☆ ❀, RAC ☆☆☆.
The Inn of Henry Fieldings 'The History of Tom Jones'. Uptons Premier Eating House. Come and discover where the locals go to treat themselves. Where we use only the freshest ingredients to create dishes with imagination and flair. Sample our homemade bread with your lunchtime snacks or full Brasserie menu served lunch and dinner. Why not stay the night or enjoy a short break in one of our individually decorated en suite rooms. Call in and enjoy our secret in the friendliest place around.

RS 🅒 🖴 ☕ P 🍴 V 🥄 ➤ 🚗 🏠 SPECIAL 1 2 3 C D

MOUNT PLEASANT HOTEL
Belle Vue Terrace, Great Malvern, Worcs
Telephone: 01684 561837 Fax: 01684 569968
15 Rooms (all en suite).
AA ☆☆, RAC ☆☆, ETB 👑👑👑 Commended
An attractive early Georgian building and orangery set in over an acre of mature terraced gardens with exceptional views. Close to the theatre and shops yet with direct access to Malvern Hills from the garden. An informal hotel with good food and all the facilities of a larger establishment.

RS 🅒 🖴 ☕ P 🍴 V ✿❀ 🏠 SPECIAL 1 2 3 4 C

The Commandery
Civil War Centre

The first view of the Commandery is a deceptive one, for behind the small timber-framed entrance is a stunning complex of buildings, medieval to Georgian in period, holding interests rich and varied for the visitor.

Used as the Royalist headquarters at the Battle of Worcester in 1651, the Commandery today offers a glimpse through its period rooms at the stunning architecture of Tudor and Stuart times whilst acting as home to the country's only museum devoted to telling the story of England's Civil War.

As this dramatic story unfolds, take your place at the trial of King Charles I, visit a Royalist Encampment on the eve of the battle and enjoy the video re-enactment of the last battle of the war narrated by Charles II and Oliver Cromwell.

As well as permanent displays, the Commandery has a wealth of events throughout the year for you to enjoy. With a history spanning the centuries, our regular time travelling events bring back characters from the Commandery's past to entertain and educate, using our own costumed staff or with the help of re-enactment societies such as Worcester Militia.

The Commandery is an excellent venue for an evening visit. We can arrange catering and specialist entertainment should you wish it, or you can choose from one of our popular evening packages: Commandery Chronicle, Lady Alice's Ghostly Tour or Roundhead and Royalist Revel. Alternatively you can rent the magnificent Great Hall itself for an event of your own.

The Commandery has delightful gardens, a well stocked gift shop and a tea-room offering light lunches and afternoon teas all for you to enjoy.

The Commandery – Where History awaits you.

Finding us is simple, with excellent road links from the M5 at junction 7 the Commandery is right in the heart of Worcester, just 3 minutes walk from the Cathedral.

For further information contact us at:
The Commandery
Sidbury
Worcester WR1 2HU

Tel: 01905 361821
Fax: 01905 361822

We are open daily throughout the year, except Christmas, Boxing and New Years Day.
Mon-Sat 10am-5pm
Sun from 1.30am-5pm

ST ANDREW'S HOUSE HOTEL
St Andrew's Drive, Worcester Road, Droitwich Spa,
Worcs WR9 8AL
Telephone: 01905 779677 Fax: 01905 779752
29 Rooms (29 all en suite).
ETB 🏵🏵🏵 Commended.
The St Andrew's House was built in the 1820's as the home
of the Town Clerk of Droitwich Spa, it was converted in the
early 1900's and substantially extended in the 1930's. The
house has been fully modernised to provide all the comforts
expected by today's clientele where one can relax in the
comfort this beautiful Grade II listed building and its
surrounding gardens.

THE ABBEY
Abbey Road, Great Malvern, Worcestershire WR14 3ET
Telephone: 01684 892332 Fax: 01684 892662
105 Rooms (all en suite). 6 Four Posters.
AA ☆☆☆, ETB 🏵🏵🏵.
The Abbey Hotel, 150 years old in 1999, has benefited from
a £1 million upgrade programme in 1998. Relax in our
lounge bar overlooking the Benedictine Priory, or join us for
dinner in the Priory View restaurant. While visiting take
advantage of the complimentary entrance to The Malvern
Splash leisure centre.

THE STAR HOTEL
High Street, Upton-upon-Severn, Worcestershire
WR8 0HQ
Telephone: 01684 592300 Fax: 01684 592929
15 Rooms (all en suite). AA ☆☆, RAC ☆☆
ETB 🏵🏵🏵 Commended
Riverside, 15 bedroom 17th century coaching house offers the
best in traditional hospitality and character. The Star is ideally
located to M5 and M50. All bedrooms have private bath or
shower, direct-dial telephone, colour television, hair dryer,
trouser press and tea and coffee-making facilities. A beer
garden overlooking the river. The Star has limited car parking.

THE MILL AT HARVINGTON
Anchor Lane, Harvington, Evesham, Worcs WR11 5NR
Telephone: 01386 870688 Fax: 01386 870688
21 Rooms (all en suite). AA ☆☆ 80%, RAC 2 Merits HCR,
ETB ☆☆ Silver Award, Good Food Guide (8 yrs), Good Hotel
Guide (8 yrs), Which Hotel Guide (8 yrs), Egon Ronay,
Michelin.
Owner-run hotel and restaurant, beautifully converted from
former Georgian house and bakery. Situated in 8 acres of
parkland with a 600 feet frontage onto the River Avon by
Harvington Lock. Relaxed, friendly atmosphere and genuine
hospitality from an interested staff add ambience to the
restaurant, where local produce is a speciality.

H. W. KEIL LTD

Telephone:
01386 852408
Fax: *01386 852069*

TUDOR HOUSE
BROADWAY
WORCESTERSHIRE
WR12 7DP

*Member of the
British Antique
Dealers' Association*

17th & 18th Century Furniture – Works of Art

*One of our many interesting rooms where we show
an extensive stock of fine quality furniture from
the Gothic times to the end of the 18th century.*

Discover Bromsgrove – The Gateway to Rural Worcestershire

Many people who visit Bromsgrove for the first time are surprised by the range of attractions to be found in this busy Worcestershire market town.

Here you will find Georgian buildings and timber framed and gabled houses, the parish church of St John, which stands on the hill where its Saxon predecessor once stood, Bromsgrove School which dates back to the 1500's and still retains part of its 17th Century structure and the 18th Century Perry Hall Hotel, the former home of AE Housman, author of "A Shropshire Lad".

In the centre of the town is Bromsgrove Museum which gives an insight into local history with displays of past crafts and industry such as nail, glass, lead, button and salt making. The Bromsgrove Guild (a unique organization of specialist craftsmen founded in 1894 and famous in the English speaking world for its skills) is also featured. In the early 1900's the Guild was commissioned to design and produce the gates and railings to Buckingham Palace. The museum also incorporates a street scene of Victorian/Edwardian shops, including toys, costume, haberdashery, wireless, ladies hairdressing, shoes, millinery, gramophones, cameras, chemist, stationers, newsagent, jewellers and cobblers.

A short distance out of town is Avoncroft Museum of Buildings, where the visitor can see over 600 years of buildings all in an afternoon. Each building provides a fascinating snap-shot of life in its particular period.

Bromsgrove is surrounded by some beautiful countryside, undulating farmland rising in the north to the Clent and Lickey Hills, outstandingly attractive with exceptional views. Add to this a wide range of pleasantly situated shops, superb hotel accommodation, pubs and restaurants, you have the ideal place to visit.

Address
Bromsgrove District Council
Leisure Services
The Council House
Burcot Lane
Bromsgrove
Worcestershire
B60 1AA

Tel: 01527 881379
for a free visitors brochure
Fax: 01527 881217
e-mail: dpts@bromsgrove.
gov.uk

Burton Constable Hall
The Treasure House of Holderness

Burton Constable Hall was built during the reign of Queen Elizabeth I and is the ancestral home of the Constable family. Visitors are able to visit nearly 30 rooms, including the Great Hall, Long Gallery, Dining Room, Chapel and Bedrooms, filled with fine furniture, paintings and sculpture, whilst back-stairs there is still evidence of the domestic army who once ran the house.
Opening times: Easter Sunday 31st Oct, open daily (closed Fridays), Grounds and Tea Room 12 noon to 5pm, Hall 1pm-5pm.

Burton Constable Hall
near Hull, East Yorkshire HU11 4LN
Tel: 01964 562400

CANNON HALL
CAWTHORNE · BARNSLEY · S75 4AT

Cannon Hall is an eighteenth century country house set in 70 acres of parkland.
Displays of pottery, paintings, furniture, glassware. 13th/18th Royal Hussars Museum. Ground floor of museum, formal gardens, cafe and toilets are accessible by wheelchair Education service; Events; Wedding facilities.

Opening times 1 Apr to 31 Oct:
Tuesday-Saturday, 10.30 am - 5.00 pm
Sunday, 12.00noon - 5.00 pm
Last admission at 4.15pm
Victorian Kitchen Cafe: Open Sat/Sun, 10.30 am - 4.30 pm
Winter opening: weekends only.

Admission:
Adults £1.00, Children/Concessions £0.50p
FAMILY AND SEASON TICKETS AVAILABLE
Telephone: 01226 790270

 BARNSLEY
Metropolitan Borough Council

Visit
The Yorkshire Wold's Premier Country House
SLEDMERE HOUSE
Nr Driffield, East Yorkshire
The Home of Sir Tatton Sykes

Sledmere House is renown for some of the finest plasterwork in Yorkshire, the work of Joseph Rose. The famous pipe organ is played for visitors on Wed, Fri and Sunday from 2 to 4pm. Enjoy a stroll in the delightful Capability Brown Park or the tranquility of the 18th century walled Rose Gardens. You may have lunch or tea in the flower decked terrace or cafe, and browse in our excellent gift shop. Sledmere House is open Easter weekend and from the beginning of May to end September (closed Saturday and Monday). 11.30am to 4.30pm. Open all Bank Hols. For further details or a free leaflet please contact:

The Secretary
Tel: 01377 236637 Fax: 01377 236500

Brodsworth Hall & Gardens
Brodsworth, Nr. Doncaster, South Yorkshire DN5 7XJ
Telephone: 01302 722598
www.english-heritage.org.uk

Savour the poignant atmosphere of the most complete example of a Victorian country house in England. Thirty rooms on view ranging from the faded grandeur of the reception rooms to the cluttered remains of the servants' wing with its great kitchen from the age of Mrs Beeton. The house is set within enchanting period gardens. Open daily except Mondays Apr-Oct. Gardens open noon, house opens 1pm. Adults £5, Concessions £3.80, Child £2.50. English Heritage members free.

ENGLISH HERITAGE

Burton Agnes Hall

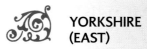

Burton Agnes Hall is a magnificent example of Elizabethan architecture built in 1598 by Sir Henry Griffith. It is still lived in by descendants of the same family though it has passed through the female line a number of times. The Hall is filled with treasures collected and commissioned by the family over the centuries. The original Elizabethan carving and plasterwork still decorates many rooms while there are some lovely examples of Georgian furniture and porcelain and, collected this century, a marvellous collection of modern French and English paintings of the Impressionist Schools. These look particularly impressive in the Long Gallery at the top of the house where you also get a panoramic view of the countryside with the sea in the distance.

The original family still keep an eye on the house in the form of the ghost of one of Sir Henry Griffith's three daughters who was set on by robbers when she was out riding. She was brought back to the Hall dying and very upset to think that she was not going to see the building completed and made her sisters promise that her skull would be kept in the house. They buried her in the churchyard and she haunted the house until they remembered and brought it back to the house. She is still seen occasionally just seeing that all is well.

Beside the present Hall is the old Norman Manor house, now encased in brick, but you can still see the lower chamber with its massive priers and groined and vaulted roof and the Great Hall above.

Over a hundred yew topiary bushes and lawns surround the house while the old walled garden is filled with collections of roses, clematis, pinks, herbs and many other unusual plants. They are contained in borders, a potager of herbs and vegetables, a maze, a jungle garden and coloured gardens divided by trelliswork and each containing a paved area and a giant game. In the courtyard you can see how the herbs and flowers are preserved and used.

Address
Burton Agnes Hall
Burton Agnes
Driffield
East Yorkshire
YO25 0ND
Tel: 01262 490324

Opening Times
Easter/1st April-31st
October 11am-5pm

Hall Admission
Adults £4.50, OAPs £4.25,
Children £2 25

Location
On the A166/A614 York
to Bridlington road about
35 mile

Facilities
Gift shop, Licensed Cafe,
Icecream parlour, Plant sales,
Children's Corner, Herb and
flower workroom/shop.

MOUNT ROYALE

The Mount, York YO2 2DA
Telephone: 01904 628856 Fax: 01904 611171
Email: reservations@mountroyale.co.uk
www.mountroyale.co.uk

The Mount Royale is a tasteful blending of two elegant William IV residences which befits its status as York's leading privately owned hotel. Personally run by the Oxtoby family who take pride in providing their guests with the best of British standards. A peaceful haven near York City Centre with a beautiful large old English garden, heated outdoor pool and excellent restaurant.

23 Rooms (all en suite), 3 Four Posters.
AA ✩✩✩, ETB ♥♥♥♥ Highly Commended, Les Routiers.

FAIRFAX HOUSE

Castlegate, York YO1 9RN
Tel: (01904) 655543 Fax: (01904) 652262
website: www.fairfaxhouse.co.uk

Fairfax House in York is without doubt one of the finest mid-18th century townhouses in England, filled with an outstanding collection of Georgian furniture.

Regular set-piece exhibitions bring the House to life in a very tangible way.

Special for 2001: *1st March-3rd June* 'Cutting Edge - The Evolution of Eating'. *1st Sept-4th Nov* 'Obsession - An Insight into the Mind of the Modern Collector'.

Each winter our unique Keeping of Christmas exhibition (*3rd December-6th January*) re-creates the 18th century festive tradition in superb detail.

Open every day, 26th February-6th January

THE WORSLEY ARMS HOTEL
Hovingham, York, North Yorkshire YO6 4LA
Telephone: 01653 628234 Fax: 01653 628130
18 Rooms (all en suite).
AA ✩✩✩ ❀❀, RAC ✩✩✩, ETB ♥♥♥♥ Highly Commended, HCR Merit Awards RAC, Good Hotel Guide, Egon Ronay.
Boasting a number of delightful private rooms, the decor and log fires create an atmosphere of peace and tranquility. With local produce in abundance, the food remains truly British and is presented with flair and imagination. There is plenty to see and do nearby, including Castle Howard, only 5 miles away.

DEAN COURT HOTEL
Duncombe Place, York YO1 2EF
Telephone: 01904 625082 Fax: 01904 620305
39 Rooms (all en suite) inc 4-poster and other "de luxe" rooms.
AA ✩✩✩❀, RAC ✩✩✩, Connoisseur Hotel (Best Western).
In its idyllic situation, in the very shadow of majestic York Minster, the hotel commands an unrivalled position in this wonderful city. Beautiful rooms, superb food and an efficient and immensely friendly staff make the hotel an obvious choice. Other facilities include the ever popular Terry's Cafe – Conservatory, Chapter Bar and comfortable lounges. Own car park and free valet parking.

KNAVESMIRE MANOR HOTEL
302 Tadcaster Road, York, YO2 2HE
Telephone: 01904 702941 Fax: 01904 709274
21 Rooms (all en suite), 1 Four Posters.
AA ✩✩, RAC ✩✩
THE CIRCLE Selected Individual Hotels.
Once a Rowntree family home this fine Georgian House overlooks York racecourse, close to the historic city centre. A choice of comfortable hotel or motel rooms with all facilities and excellent cusisine from Arnold's Restaurant. Magnificent tropical indoor pool, sauna and spa in sunny corner of walled gardens. Large car park.

NUNMILL HOUSE
85 Bishopthorpe Road, N. Yorks YO23 1NX
Telephone: 01904 634047 Fax: 01904 655879
8 Rooms (7 en suite), 3 Four Posters.
Email: b&b@nunmill.co.uk
Internet: www.nunmill.co.uk
AA ◆◆◆◆ Selected, ETB ◆◆◆◆. Member: Worldwide Best Bed & Breakfast.
A splendid Victorian house, lovingly restored to enhance all original features. Each bedroom (some with four poster bed) is individually furnished and smoke-free, ideal for those who are looking for comfortable yet affordable en suite accommodation. Easy walk to York's historic attractions. Please send s.a.e. for colour brochure.

THE YORKE ARMS
**Ramsgill, Pateley Bridge, Harrogate,
North Yorkshire HG3 5RL**
Telephone: 01423 755243 Fax: 01423 755330
14 Rooms (all en suite).
AA ✩✩, ETB ✩✩.
Situated in the picturesque village of Ramsgill and at the head of the Gouthwaite reservoir. All rooms offer comfortable en-suite accommodation. An extensive à la carte menu of modern British cuisine and traditional dishes is offered in the elegant dining room or the Brasserie every day except Sunday evening (hotel residents only). Acclaimed by the Which? Good Food Guide (1999) as one of the Top 50 Restaurants in the UK.

York Tourism

There are few cities in Britain that have the magical beauty of York. Where visitors can enjoy outstanding archaeology and a history that dips back nearly 2,000 years combined with bustling shopping streets and numerous award-winning attractions.

The city itself protected by the historic city walls is a web of ancient timbered houses and narrow winding streets just waiting to be explored. The whole city exudes an atmosphere of history with the numerous historic attractions representing the many ages that York has weathered.

The Jorvik Viking Centre is an exciting concept where visitors are whisked back 1,000 years to a reconstructed Viking village complete with authentic sounds and smells of the time.

The National Railway Museum tells the continuing story of British railways up to the present day and is the largest museum of its kind in Europe.

The world famous Castle Museum has an array of fascinating shops in cobbled streets for you to explore.

The Yorkshire Museum which is set in ten acres of botanical gardens displays some of the finest Roman, Anglo-saxon, Viking and Medieval treasures discovered in Britain.

York Minster, the pride of the city is one of the largest Gothic cathedrals north of the Alps and is a joy to anyone who visits.

The Merchant Adventurers' hall, built in the 1350s is one of the finest Medieval guild halls surviving in Europe. It was here that merchants transacted business and held feasts, as their successors still do today.

Fairfax House, a classical masterpiece of its age is without doubt one of the finest town houses in England, obtaining one of the best collections of mid-18th century English furniture and clocks.

Eating out is a delight in York. Its numerous restaurants range from contemporary English cuisine; roast beef and Yorkshire pudding; Italian; French; Mexican; Chinese specialities and even Creole!

York Tourism Bureau
20 George Hudson Street,
York YO1 6WR

Tel: 01904 554455

Fax: 01904 554460

Email: yt@york-tourism.co.uk

315

Castle Howard

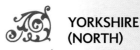

Castle Howard, home of the Howard Family, was designed by Sir John Vanbrugh for Charles Howard, 3rd Earl of Carlisle in 1699.

It was remarkable that the Earl of Carlisle chose a celebrated playwright and soldier to design his palace and Castle Howard was the first building attempted by Vanbrugh.

The piece de resistance of Castle Howard is the magnificent gilded dome which was the first in England ever to adorn a private home.

Castle Howard has been open to the public since the day it was built and contains magnificent collections of furniture, paintings, porcelain and statuary, most of which has been collected by succeeding generations of the Howard Family. Furniture by Chippendale and Sheraton, paintings by Gainsborough, Holbein, Reynolds and Rubens, ancient Greek and Roman statuary and exquisite porcelain and china are all on view inside the House.

Surrounding the House are over 1,000 acres of breathtaking parkland, lawns, woodland gardens, lakes, fountains and magnificent Rose Gardens with collections of old and modern roses. The woodland garden, Ray Wood, has a unique collection of rare trees, shrubs, rhododendrons, magnolias and azaleas.

The Temple of the Four Winds, also designed by Sir John Vanbrugh and the Mausoleum which is internationally regarded as Nicholas Hawksmoor's finest work can also be seen in the Grounds. Castle Howard is frequently used as a setting for major television dramas. 'Brideshead Revisited' Evelyn Waugh's classic novel, was filmed here in the 1980's and in 1994 Castle Howard was the principal location for the dramatisation of Edith Wharton's 'The Buccaneers'.

Outdoor classical concerts are held at Castle Howard during the Summer Season and attract in excess of 20,000 visitors on each occasion.

Castle Howard welcomes visitors from all over the world and the inclusive ticket covers entry to the House, Grounds and Gardens, Adventure Playgrounds, Exhibition Wing, Gift Shops, Plant Centre and Cafeterias.'

Optional extra is the Victorian Style motor launch which operates on the Great Lake during the Summer months weather permitting.

Address
Castle Howard
York
North Yorkshire
YO6 7DA
Tel: 01653 648444
Fax: 01653 648462

Opening Times
Open Daily
mid March to late October

Location
15 miles North of York off the A64

Facilities
Private Tours, Gift Shops, Cafeterias

Harrogate District

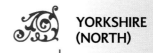

The Harrogate District – over 500 square miles of beautiful countryside, delightful dales, magnificent moorland, floral splendour, historic haunts, family attractions, bustling towns and quaint villages.

Harrogate evolved as a Victorian spa resort and the heritage can be appreciated today in the Royal Baths Assembly Rooms where the Turkish Baths are still open seven days a week; while visitors can 'take the waters' at the Royal Pump Room Museum. Now a renowned international conference and exhibition centre, the town is a cosmopolitan delight with a selection of award winning parks and gardens. A high quality selection of hotels, restaurants, shops and entertainment complete the picture.

Knaresborough

Four miles from Harrogate, the charming, historic town of Knaresborough nestles on the cliffs above the River Nidd and surrounds the cobbled medieval market square. Major attractions include Mother Shipton's Cave and the Petrifying Well, the Old Court House Museum and the Castle overlooking the famous viaduct view. An eleven mile drive north will bring the visitor to the Cathedral City of Ripon. Dating back over 1100 years, the city is rich in history with its Cathedral, Wakeman's House and a Prison and Police Museum. The Ripon Hornblower 'sets the watch' every evening at 9 o'clock in the Market Place.

Only a few miles from Ripon, in beautiful Studley Royal Park, stands the splendid structure of Fountains Abbey - an important historic monument founded in 1132 and today protected by the National Trust and also designated a World Heritage Site.

Also within a few miles of Ripon is Lightwater Valley - an action packed leisure park for the whole family with exciting attractions including the World's longest rollercoaster.

Garden and history lovers should visit the notable stately homes of Ripley Castle and Newby Hall, Nr Ripon.

North west of Harrogate is picturesque Pateley Bridge, a delightful Dales town which makes an excellent base for exploring the surrounding Nidderdale countryside. Itineraries could include the Nidderdale Museum, Gouthwaite Reservoir - a well known bird sanctuary, How Stean Gorge, Stump Cross Caverns, Brimham Rocks, and Masham - home of two breweries.

To the northeast are the settlements of Aldborough and Boroughbridge - Aldborough being within the walls of the Roman City Isurium Brigantum.

Free Brochure &
Accommodation List from
Dept. EE.
Harrogate T.I.C.
Royal Baths
Assembly Rooms
Crescent Rd,
HG1 2RR
Tel: 01423 537357

Knaresborough T.I.C.
Tel: 01423 866886

Boroughbridge T.I.C.
Tel: 01423 323373

Pateley Bridge T.I.C.
Tel: 01423 711147

Ripon T.I.C.
Tel: 01765 604625

Devonshire Arms
COUNTRY HOUSE HOTEL
Bolton Abbey, Skipton, North Yorkshire, BD23 6AJ
Tel: 01756 710441 Fax: 01756 710564

The Devonshire Arms Country House Hotel lies in magnificent scenery at the southern end of the Yorkshire Dales National Park. The Hotel is in park-like surroundings on the river Wharfe with heather moorland a mile or so away.

Owned by the Duke and Duchess of Devonshire, most of the hotel is furnished with antiques from their family home, Chatsworth. The interior design is the work of the Duchess.

The Burlington Restaurant, named after the ancestor who brought this estate to the family, is now a very popular venue for all sorts of celebrations. Recently the hotel has added "The Devonshire Club" with its heated swimming pool, tennis court and the very latest in heath, beauty and fitness facilities (for hotel guests).

LOCATION – The Devonshire is on the B6160 to Bolton Abbey 250 yards north from its roundabout junction with the A59 Skipton to Harrogate Road. The M1 and M62 are reached via Leeds – 23 miles away.

The Buck Inn
BUCKDEN, UPPER WHARFEDALE,
Nr. SKIPTON, YORKSHIRE DALES BD23 5JA.
Tel: 01756 760228 Fax: 01756 760227
www.thebuckinn.yorks.net email: thebuckinn@yorks.net

An Inn for All Seasons. Discover "The Buck" and enjoy the Dales. The Buck Inn at Buckden is a traditional old Georgian coaching inn with an enviable reputation, lots of olde worlde charm and character. The Buck offers the visitor the highest standards of comfort, 14 beautifully furnished en-suite bedrooms, comprising of 7 double, 4 twins, 1 single, 1 four poster and the beautiful Wharfedale suite, all with colour TV, direct dial telephone, tea and coffee making facilities. Extensive menus include fresh Dalesbred meats, fresh fish and locally grown vegetables. The cosy bar has hand pulled real ales including the Theakston range, Black sheep and also a guest beer which is changed on a regular basis. An interesting residents restaurant has been created in the courtyard wherein olden days local wool auctions were held.

THE
DEVONSH RF
FELL

Having recently undergone a dramatic and creative refurbishment with each bedroom individually designed, by Lady Hartington, daughter-in-law of the Duke and Duchess Devonshire.

The Hotel was acquired as a sister property to the renowned Devonshire Arms only 6 miles away in Bolton Abbey. With spectacular views across the dales and the river Wharfe and the stunningly different modern interiors including fish tanks in the cisterns of the ladies loo, a hotel as startlingly different from the original Fell Hotel as indeed from anything else in the Dales.

The hotel's Bistro is renowned for its fish board, which often lists treats such as lobster, scallops and seabass. Game is also available in season.

The Devonshire Fell Hotel & Bistro
Burnsall, Skipton
North Yorkshire BD23 6BT
Tel: 01756 729009
Reservations: 01756 718111

THE
WHITE HOUSE
10 Park Parade, Harrogate, N. Yorks HG1 5AH.
Tel: 01423 501388 Fax: 01423 527973

What a delightful surprise! This graceful Hotel overlooks the famous stray and is proudly owned by Jennie Forster, who is not only a charming host but also the Head Chef, providing excellent dinners from the imaginative menus rewarded with 2 AA Rosettes for the last 5 years. The cherished antique furniture evokes a more leisurely pace of life and everywhere you are surrounded by thoughtful comforts, whether in the lounge or library and our luxurious bedrooms are stylishly furnished and thoughtfully equipped, in keeping with the hotel's Victorian character.

10 en-suite (bath/shower) rooms. Single £75-£95, Double £90-£145.

Bolton Abbey

Bolton Abbey is a Heritage Estate and lies within the Yorkshire Dales National Park.

For over a hundred years visitors have flocked to Bolton Abbey in Wharfedale as the ideal beauty spot for a day out, with the historic and romantic associations of Bolton Priory and Barden Tower, and the geological phenomenon of the Strid, as well as the beautiful landscape of moorland and farmland, which forms the Bolton Abbey Estate and provides a habitat for a wide range of wildlife and interesting flora and fauna.

This part of Wharfedale is owned, and has been cared for, by successive generations of Dukes of Devonshire and their forebears going back to medieval times, when the Augustinian canons settled here and built Bolton Priory, most of which is now a graceful ruin but the nave is still used as the Parish Church.

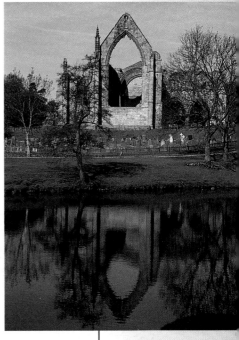

The Estate provides extensive access and visitors can walk along the riverside or footpaths that lead through woodland to over 13500 acres of moorland. There are three Estate car parks strategically placed along the river valley and the Estate has provided places of refreshment to meet all tastes. The Devonshire Arms Hotel has world renowned hospitality and a brasserie serves light meals. The Tea Cottage in the village is part of a former medieval barn and food is all home-made. The Cavendish Pavilion is situated on the riverside and was totally refurbished in 1993 and now boasts an excellent restaurant as well as self-service cafeteria. Barden tea-room is in a former medieval Priest's House and has recently been awarded membership of the Tea Council Guild of Tea Shops and more recently the Devonshire Fell at Burnsall provides a refreshing change to more traditional Dales hospitality.

Strid Wood – 1 mile from Bolton Abbey – is worthy of a visit not only for its sylvan theme, but it abounds in bird-life and is rich in fauna and flora. The woodland has been dedicated a Site of Special Scientific Interest, admission is free. There are nature trails, together with many fine views, an educational trail for children at the northern end and information available from the shops at each entrance.

Information on Bolton Abbey, Strid Wood and walks can be obtained from the Estate Office, Bolton Abbey, Skipton BD23 6EX, telephone 01756 710533. Electric wheelchairs (giving access to Strid Wood and the Priory) are available free of charge for elderly and disabled persons and can be booked in advance by telephoning.

A car park charge of £3.50 per vehicle covers admission to the Estate and tickets are transferable to all Estate Car Parks.

Address
Bolton Abbey Estate
Estate Office
Bolton Abbey
Skipton BD23 6EX
Tel: 01756 710533
www.boltonabbey.com

Open
Daily all year.

Admission (2001)
Free.
Car park charge £3.50 per vehicle.

Facilities
Hotel, licensed restaurant, cafeteria, shop, picnic sites, nature trails, tea rooms, riverside walks.

Location
B6160 off A59 betwixt Skipton and Harrogate.

Ripley Castle

Ripley Castle has been home to the Ingilby family for twenty-six generations, and reflects each generation with its rich history. The original tower contains memorabilia from the battle of Marston Moor after which Oliver Cromwell stayed and this combines with the elegance of the Georgian era with fine chandeliers, family portraits and furniture collected over the Centuries. Visitors will enjoy the guided tours which bring history to life with amusing anecdotes of the Ingilby family. The Castle overlooks the deer park and lakes designed by Capability Brown, and the magnificent gardens are a kaleidoscope of colour through every season with walled kitchen gardens and hot houses. Ripley is an original Estate village and visitors will enjoy the individual gift shops and a fine delicatessen in the Courtyard.

THE BOAR'S HEAD HOTEL

The Boar's Head, at the heart of the Ripley Castle Estate, is one of the Great Inns of Britain. This is an Inn with high-quality accommodation, a bar for locals, as well as for visitors to have a pint in, and dining facilities where you don't have to wear a tie or talk in hushed whispers over a sculpture on a plate! We believe that staying with us is an experience, with the emphasis on quality, fun, individuality and informality!

Each bedroom is individually decorated and king-sized beds enable you to lose your partner in the night. Catamarans have been thoughtfully provided in the bathroom so that you can push the boat out during your stay, and satellite TV and mini-bar provide world-wide entertainment and spiritual consolation. This is a great destination from which to explore the best of Yorkshire.

Address
Ripley Castle
Ripley, Harrogate
North Yorkshire HG3 3AY
Tel: 01423 770152
Fax: 01423 771745
www.ripleycastle.co.uk

Opening Times
Gardens: 10.00-17.00
Castle & Gardens:
Winter: Jan-Mar and Nov-Dec
Tues, Wed, Thurs, Sat and Sun
10.30-12.30
Summer: Apr, May, June, Sept,
Oct & Bank Holidays
Thurs-Sun. July & Aug open
Daily 10.30-15.00
Groups of 15 or more can
visit Ripley Castle & Gardens
by arrangement any day of the
year (exc. Christmas Day),
10.30-18.30.

Location
3 miles north of Harrogate
(A61) and only 40 minutes
from York and Leeds

The Boar's Head Hotel
Ripley Castle Estate
Harrogate
North Yorkshire HG3 3AY
Tel: 01423 771888
Fax: 01423 771509
www.boarsheadripley.co.uk

Golden Fleece Hotel

Market Place, Thirsk, Yorkshire YO7 1LL
Tel: 01845 523108 Fax: 01845 523996

The Golden Fleece Hotel is one of Yorkshire's most famous 17th century Coaching Inns. Situated in the cobbled market place known as 'Darrowby' in James Herriot's novels, it offers a warm and friendly atmosphere together with traditional and à la carte meals, draught ales and fine wines.
The Hotel is ideally placed with Yorkshire's beautiful Dales and Moors National Parks only a short drive away.

ETC ★★ Silver Award   AA ★★ 69%

RS ⊘ 🖥 🍵 P 🎀 V ⟋ 🏨 SPECIAL 1 2 3 4 C

Solberge Hall Hotel

Newby Wiske, Northallerton, Yorks DL7 9ER
Tel: 01609 779191 Fax: 01609 780472
AA ★★★ ❀

This charming country house, parts of which date back to the 18th century, sits in 16 acres of woodland and gardens.
The bedrooms are spacious and well equipped with a number of Four Poster and superior rooms.
The Garden Room Restaurant has daily changing and à la carte menus in and an extensive wine list.
On the edge of the Dales National Park and within easy reach of York and the Yorkshire Moors.

RS ⊘ 🖥 🍵 P 🎀 V GF ⟋ 🐦 🏨 SPECIAL 1 2 3 4 C

Skipton Castle

One December day in 1645, a column of soldiers, weary and tattered but with colours flying and trumpets sounding, marched out of the Castle gate and away down the wide High Street, surrendering (with honour) after a three-year siege. Skipton Castle had been the King's last stronghold in the North of England. For five centuries the Lords and Castle of Skipton had played major roles on the stage of English history : now Cromwell decreed that the Castle should be destroyed. But it was saved by the determination of its owner, Lady Anne Clifford (the last of her line); today it stands, fully roofed, guarding still the busy market town beneath its walls.

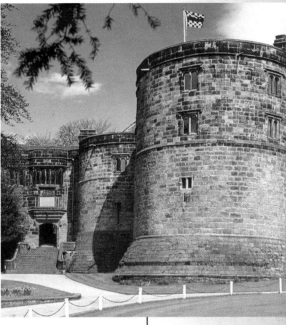

Explore the Castle from dungeon to Watch Tower : see how each age left its mark. Look out through the Norman arrow-slits which 'covered' the main entrance; visit the 'lost' 13th century chapel – fully revealed only recently – used as stabling for centuries; pause in the beautiful Conduit Court, with its apartments built in Henry VII's time by the 10th Lord; his father and grandfather had died in the brutal civil 'Wars of the Roses'. Here is one of the most complete medieval castles to survive in England.

Savour Skipton's peaceful environment, the smooth lawns, the fine views; in the Tea Room, sample traditional fare; browse in the Shop, with its noted books section and wide range of other gifts for all ages.

In the Parish Church, close to the Castle walls, the tombs of several Lords of Skipton can be seen; that of George Clifford is especially splendid; he was the 15th Lord, the 3rd Earl of Cumberland, 'Queen's Champion' to Elizabeth I, and an Admiral against the Armada.

In the bustling High Street nearby, expect to see market stalls – Skipton has four market days each week – and in and around the town can be found a wide variety of shops, restaurants and accommodation. The Leeds & Liverpool Canal, busy with leisure boaters, gives access to delightful countryside; and the famous 'Settle & Carlisle' railway line provides one of England's most dramatic journeys.

Skipton's position at the southern gateway to the Yorkshire Dales (which was the strategic reason for the Castle's existence in the Middle Ages) today draws many visitors intent on exploring the National Park – a region of unspoilt stone-built villages and farms, clear rivers, spacious uplands and wooded valleys.

Town, countryside, Castle – how much there is to enjoy at Skipton!

Address
Skipton Castle,
Skipton,
North Yorkshire
BD23 1AQ
Enquiries:
Telephone 01756 792442
or see our web site
www.skiptoncastle.co.uk

Opening Times
Open every day
(except Christmas Day)
10 am (Sundays 12 noon)

Admission
Adults £4.40
Senior Citizens £3.80
Under-18s £2.20
Family (2 adults,
3 under-18s) £11.90

GEORGE & DRAGON HOTEL
17 Market Place, Kirkbymoorside, North Yorkshire YO6 6AA
Telephone: 01751 433334 Fax: 01751 433334
19 Rooms (all en suite).
AA ☆☆ ❀ (70%).
This 17th century coaching inn lies in the centre of the town and has been developed into a hotel of character, with staff who offer friendly and efficient service. The pub, with its blazing fire and cricketing theme, has a great atmosphere and a reputation for its food. All home-cooked, soups, pates, hearty pies and casseroles, plus quality meats and seafood in season, can be enjoyed there or in the dining room. Quietly located in two buildings to the rear, the comfortable bedrooms are all individual.

WHITFIELD HOUSE HOTEL
Darnholm, Goathland, North Yorkshire YO22 5LA
Telephone: 01947 896215 Fax: 01947 896043
9 Rooms (all en suite).
AA ☆, ETC ☆☆.
Situated in the heart of the North York Moors National Park, Whitfield House Hotel offers a warm friendly atmosphere and superb country cooking.
An ideal location for touring, walking or just relaxing in 'Heartbeat Country'.
Local attractions include the North York Moors Railway and Whitby just 9 miles away.

North Yorkshire Moors National Park

The North York Moors is one of our most treasured landscapes. Rolling heather moorlands, picturesque dales and a rugged coast make it an ideal place to escape from the pressures of modern life. But with so many visitors flooding here each year, it is important that we protect this landscape which we enjoy so much.

The North York Moors is a National Park, one of just 8 such protected landscapes in England. The National Park's job is to conserve the special features of the area and to help people enjoy and understand them.

Few places have such a variety of things to see and do. The open moors offer a freedom and solitude that is rare in today's crowded planet. Descending into the sheltered dales is like entering another world of winding streams and deep woodlands. The coast too has many special qualities: high, windswept cliffs, secluded fishing villages, sea birds roaming effortlessly on the wind…

History and wildlife add flesh to this landscape. Bronze age barrows, mediaeval castles and later industry including coal pits and ironstone mines remind us of people who lived here long before us. The haunting ruins of Rievaulx and Byland Abbeys are a fitting testament to hundreds of monks who once tamed the land.

Look out too for the wild animals and plants that have made their homes in the area. Explore carefully and you could well stumble on some of nature's greatest treasures, from tiny insects to mighty oak trees. With hundreds of miles of public rights of way, quiet activities such as rambling and pony trekking are the best ways to enjoy the area's natural beauty.

We can all do our bit to protect the North York Moors. Keeping to footpaths and not dropping litter are obvious to any country lover. But if you are planning to come here on holiday, why not leave your car at home?

Cars can be a real environmental menace, and no-one wants to see the Moors overrun with traffic. Public transport is an easy alternative that is kinder to the environment. Trains and buses can take you to many sites in the Park, and during the busiest times of the year the National Park runs its own Moorsbus service. Once you are here, the best way to discover the countryside is on foot, bike or horseback. So why not enjoy a trouble free holiday without your car?

To find out more about the North York Moors and how best to explore it, or to get the latest Moorsbus and Moors Connections timetables, contact the National Park Authority.
Tel: 01439 770657

BAGDEN HALL HOTEL & GOLF COURSE
Wakefield Road, Scissett, Huddersfield HD8 9LE
Telephone: 01484 865330 Fax: 01484 861001
www.bagdenhall.demon.co.uk
17 Rooms (all en suite). 1 Four Poster.
AA ☆☆☆. RAC ☆☆☆. ETB ♛♛♛♛ Highly commended.

Bagden Hall became a hotel in 1992, carefully and lovingly converted to preserve the original character of the building, combining the comforts and luxuries of a high quality hotel with the warmth and hospitality of a true country home. At Bagden Hall you will find that good quality and value go hand in hand.

HEALDS HALL HOTEL
Leeds Road, Liversedge, West Yorkshire
Telephone: 01924 409112 Fax: 01924 401895
24 Rooms (all en suite).
AA ☆☆ ❀, RAC ☆☆, ETB Commended,
RAC Silver Award for Restaurant and Hospitality, AA ❀ for food.

With associations with the Bronte family, this capacious Victorian house has been sympathetically and stylishly modernised by Tom and Nora Harrington, who purchased the property in 1978. Guests are assured of the highest standards of accommodation in all en suite bedrooms which have full facilities. Particularly worthy of note are the interesting and reasonably priced à la carte and new Bistro menus. In tranquil and mature gardens, this hospitable hotel is conveniently placed just 3 miles from the M62 and 4 miles from the M1, further reasons for its popularity as a centre for conferences and business functions.

THE HOTEL METROPOLE
King Street, Leeds LS1 2HQ
Telephone: 0113 245 0841 Fax: 0113 242 5156
118 Rooms (all en suite).
AA ☆☆☆☆, RAC ☆☆☆☆, ETB ♛♛♛♛ Highly Commended.

At the heart of the city, The Hotel Metropole's distinctive Victorian facade is one of the most striking in the city, and the style and splendour continue throughout the hotel. Free car parking onsite, Leeds train station 2 mins walk.

MERRION HOTEL
Wade Lane, Leeds LS2 8NH
Telephone: 0113 2439191 Fax: 0113 2423527
109 Rooms (all en suite). AA ☆☆☆, ETB ♛♛♛♛
The modern, recently refurbished hotel is well placed in the centre of the city, adjacent to two modern shopping centres. Easy access to the historic city of York, the North Yorkshire Moors and coast makes it the ideal base for touring. The M62, M1 and the railway station are just minutes' away.

Leeds
Museums & Galleries

Temple Newsam House

The magnificent Tudor-Jacobean house, "the Hampton Court of the North" contains over 30 fine rooms open to the public with Old Master paintings, furniture, silver and ceramics. The 1,000 acre 'Capability' Brown park contains the Home Farm, a rare breeds collection and magnificent flower gardens.

Location: OS ref SE358 321. 5m E of city centre, off A63 Selby Road. **Opening times:** 1 Apr-31 Oct, Tues-Sat 10am-5pm, Sun 1-5pm; 1 Nov-31 Dec & Mar, Tues-Sat 10am-4pm, Sun 12 noon-4pm. Closed Jan & Feb. **Admission:** Adults £2, Child 50p, Concessions £1. Groups (10+): Adult £1, Child 50p.

Abbey House Museum

Once gateway to the celebrated Kirkstall Abbey, Abbey House is now home to Leeds Museums & Galleries' exciting collections of social history. Following a major refurbishment (funded by the Heritage Lottery Fund) visitors can now experience new galleries displaying toys and games of yesteryear, the history of the Abbey itself and three streets of shops and houses showing just how life was lived in the 1880s. The museum also boasts a grand new shop and cafe. It is the perfect day out for all the family, a historic window shopping experience no one can afford to miss.

Abbey House Museum re-opens Saturday 20th January 2001.

For opening times and further information please contact Abbey House Museum.

Lotherton Hall

Modest late Victorian and Edwardian country house of great charm and character, formerly the home of the Gascoigne family. Fine collections of furniture, silver, pottery and porcelain, paintings, sculpture and costume, including many family heirlooms. Famous period gardens with a deer park and bird garden.

Location: OS02 Ref. SE450 360. 1m E of A1 at Aberford on Towton road (B1217). **Opening times:** 1 Apr-31 Oct, Tue-Sat 10am-5pm; 1 Nov-31 Dec & Mar, Tue-Sat 10am-4pm; Sun 12 noon-4pm. Closed Jan & Feb. **Admission:** Adults £2, Child 50p, OAP/Student £1, Groups £1. Car parking charges apply.

Temple Newsam House
Leeds LS15 OAE
Tel: 0113 264 7321
Fax: 0113 260 2285

Abbey House Museum
Abbey Walk,
Kirkstall,
Leeds LS5 3EH
Tel: 0113 230 5492
Fax: 0113 230 5499

Lotherton Hall
Aberford LS25 3EB
Tel: 0113 281 3259
Fax: 0113 281 2100

Harewood House

Harewood is a magnificent Historic House set within beautiful landscaped grounds shaped by "Capability" Brown, and has been the Lascelles' family home for over 200 years.

Currently lived in by the Queen's cousin, the Earl of Harewood, and the former home of his mother HRH Princess Mary, the Princess Royal, daughter of King George V, much of her Royal memorabilia is displayed throughout the State Rooms.

The House, an architectural masterpiece, was designed by John Carr of York and built over 13 years between 1759 and 1772, with splendid interiors by Robert Adam.

In the rooms hang paintings by Reynolds, Gainsborough, Romney and Hoppner, with the Gallery housing renaissance masterpieces by Bellini, El Greco, Tintoretto, Titian and Veronese. Within the two Watercolour Rooms are collections of watercolours by Turner, Girtin and Varley. In contrast, Lord Harewood's Sitting Room is home to an extensive 20th century collection of artworks by Picasso, Piper, Sickert and Sir Sidney Nolan.

Collections throughout the House include Sèvres porcelain, Crown Derby china and Chippendale furniture. Harewood was Chippendale's largest house commission and every room contains exquisite samples of his work, including the newly restored 'Chippendale State Bed' – the most lavish of his creations and unseen for 150 years! The year 2001 concentrates on portraiture with historical and contemporary exhibitions in addition to Harewood's own outstanding collections.

Winner of Yorkshire in Bloom 2000, Harewood's magnificent Grounds contain superb collections of Rhododendron from April to June and Sir Charles Barry's Parterre Terrace, offering splendid views of the rolling landscape beyond.

The popular Lakeside Bird Garden, set up by Lady Harewood in 1970, is internationally renowned for its programme of conservation and breeding of rare and endangered species, including penguins, flamingos, owls, parrots and emus among many other exotic species.

Throughout the year are changing art exhibitions within Harewood's contemporary Terrace Gallery and within the Grounds, there are an extensive range of special events from car rallies and craft festivals to open air concerts and theatre performances.

With the Adventure Playgrounds for younger visitors and woodland walks or boat trips on the Lake, there is something for everyone at Harwood for a wonderful day out in a spectacular historical setting.

Harewood House Trust,
Moor House,
Harewood,
Leeds LS17 9LQ

Tel: 0113 218 1010
Fax: 0113 218 1002
Email:
business@harewood.org
www.harewood.org

Open
March 14-Nov 4 2001

Admission
Adults £7.50, OAP £6.75, Child £5 (2001 prices) includes admission to the House, Grounds and Gardens, Bird Garden and Terrace Gallery.

Facilities
Gift Shop, Café/Restaurant, Free Parking, Disabled Facilities.

Location
7 miles from Leeds and Harrogate on A61, 5 miles from the A1 and half an hour from York.

This section will give you information regarding some of the Islands surrounding Britain. - The Channels Islands and the Isle of Man.

THE CHANNEL ISLANDS

The Channel Islands are situated between the south coast of England and France and consist of the Bailiwick of Guernsey (including Alderney, Heme, Sark, Jethou, Brechou and Lihou) and Jersey.

GUERNSEY

75 miles from Weymouth in Dorset and 25 miles from the French coastline. Alderney, Sark and Herme are 21, 8 and 3 miles respectively from Guernsey.

Guernsey Tourist Board
Tel: 01481 723552

JERSEY

100 miles south of England, 14 miles from France and 28 miles from Guernsey.

Jersey Tourism
Tel: 01534 500800

THE ISLE OF MAN

The Isle of Man is almost equidistant between England, Scotland, Wales and Ireland.

Isle of Man Tourism
Tel: 01624 686766

Duke of Richmond Hotel

Cambridge Park, St. Peter Port
Guernsey, Channel Islanes
Tel: 01481 726221 Fax: 01481 728945
Email: duke@guernsey.net   www.dukeofrichmond.co.uk

The Duke of Richmond is one of Guernsey's leading international Hotels. Situated between Cambridge Park and Candie Gardens – in walking distance of the Beau Sejour Leisure Centre and the High Street shops – its luxury suites overlook the town and harbour of St. Peter Port.

The Hotel is open all year and is a favourite meeting place for people in Guernsey. In summer refreshments are served on the sun terrace or around our exclusive swimming pool. Children are welcome. Whether you like informal meals at lunchtime or dinner in the candle-lit restaurant, you will enjoy superb cuisine, fine wines, friendly service and good company. Please write for tariff and brochure.

LE FRIQUET COUNTRY HOTEL
Rue du Friquet, Castel, Guernsey, Channel Islands
Telephone: 01481 256509 Fax: 01481 253573
26 Rooms (all en suite). TB ❦ ❦ ❦ ❦ Highly commended 83%.
This beautiful old Guernsey Farmhouse, set in approximately six acres of mature gardens (with sun terrace and swimming pool), is in an ideal setting for a relaxing break. The rooms have all the comforts of home and the restaurant is one of the most popular on the island. When Booking mention the Heritage Handbook Company and take an 8% Discount off your room rate.

RS 🌲 🕐 🛏 🍷 🍽 P 🍴 V SP ⚘ SPECIAL
2 **3** C D

OLD COURT HOUSE HOTEL
Gorey Village, Grouville, Jersey JE3 9FS
Telephone: 01534 854444 Fax: 01534 853587
Email: ochhotel@itl.net
Web site: http://www.jersey.co.uk/hotels/ochhotel/
58 Rooms (all en suite). AA/RAC ☆☆☆, Jsy 3 Suns.
The Old Court House Hotel is situated in its own grounds opposite the 3 mile beach, Royal Bay of Grouville. Our Restaurant offers table d'hote and à la carte menus. Many rooms have private balconies. We can arrange flights from regional airports. Free car hire based on 2 persons for 4 nights or more.

RS 🌲 🕐 🛏 🍷 P 🍴 V GF 🚼 SP ⚘ 🏠 **1** **2** **3** **4**
B/C

Peel Castle, Isle of Man
Courtesy of Isle of Man Tourism

THE ISLANDS of Britain are surely amongst the most unique in the world. Whilst their languages and commercial interests are dominated by the mainland, they have managed to retain customs and a way of life that is deliciously different

The islands of Britain are surely amongst the most unique in the world. Whilst their languages and commercial interests are dominated by the mainland, they have managed to retain customs and a way of life that is deliciously different.

We concentrate in this section on three of the largest and most important - Jersey, Guernsey in the south and the ruggedly beautiful Isle of man in the north.

The Isle of man lies like a jewel in the Irish Sea almost equidistant between England, Ireland, Scotland and Wales and indeed on a clear day the 'Calf of Man' affords a view to all five kingdoms. Long and thin in shape the Isle of Man is self governed, enjoys lower taxes than the rest of the UK and is rich in both natural and man made heritage with particularly strong evidence of marauding vikings remaining.

St Aubin's harbour, Jersey - Courtesy of Jersey Tourism

Le Trepied Tomb, Guernsey - Courtesy of Guernsey Tourism

In contrast the two largest channel Islands, Guernsey and Jersey, benefit from the softer climate that the Northern French coast offers. French influence is very strong and this provides a truly continental feel. Jersey and Guernsey are also self governing and again therefore enjoy tax haven status. Heritage abounds here too as one would expect form outposts in such a strong strategic position and they were of course the only parts of the UK to suffer from German occupation during World war two. Attractions concerned with these events are particularly fascinating and are well worth a visit.

The Island of Guernsey

The history of the Bailiwick is fascinating and explains to some extent its unique character. From ancient neolithic tombs and menhirs, Gallo-Roman wrecks and artefacts, through to fortifications constructed during Napoleonic times and the Second World War, man has left evidence of his presence everywhere. Brought to the British Crown in 1066 by William the Conqueror, the Bailiwick has remained loyal to it virtually ever since. Today, it still retains its independence, with its own government and currency - though British money is also in circulation - and even its status in regard to the European Union is special.

Visit Guernsey's arts and crafts centres and discover how candles, pottery and jewellery are made. There are also galleries and a host of other attractions, including museums and the former house of Victor Hugo, the French novelist and poet who lived in exile on Guernsey for 15 years where he completed 'Les Miserables'.

St. Peter Port must be one of the world's most beautiful harbour capitals and retains much of its original charm as a traditional fishing village. The town is a collection of narrow streets leading uphill from the sea to a skyline of church steeples and steep-roofed granite houses.

The attractive cobbled High Street is flanked with traffic-free arcades and is lined with modern shops and boutiques, offering all manner of value for money merchandise.

Dining out is one of the great delights of a holiday in Guernsey. Whether you are looking for sophisticated gourmet fare or simple home cooking, the Island's vast range of restaurants and cafes will satisfy your appetite as well as your pocket. A varied programme of night-time entertainment also ensures that holiday fun continues well after the sun has set. From cinemas showing the latest film releases, to theatre, concerts and fireworks displays, there is always something to keep you entertained.

Any holiday to Guernsey would be incomplete without a day trip to one or more of the neighbouring islands, all of which are easily reached. Frequent boat services operate to Herm and Sark, whilst Jersey and Alderney are easily accessible by air or sea. Herm has dazzling beaches, whilst Sark lives in a rural time warp without traffic. Alderney's cobbled streets, pretty cottages and Victorian forts are another world again. But one thing all the islands have in common is their ease of access, relaxing atmosphere and unassuming friendliness.

Address
Guernsey Tourist Board,
P.O. Box 23,
St. Peter Port,
Guernsey, GY1 3AN.
Tel: +44 (0)1481 723552
Fax: +44 (0)1481 721246

The Moorings Hotel and Restaurant

Gorey Pier, Gorey JE3 6EW
Tel: 01534 853633 Fax: 01534 857618
e-mail: Casino@itl.net

15 bedroom hotel with modern facilities situated beneath the 13th century Mont Orgueil Castle overlooking the quaint Gorey Harbour. Gourmet Restaurant famous for Seafood. Open all year. Off-season breaks and Christmas programme.

B&B rates from £36.00.
AA/RAC ☆☆☆ TB 3 Suns, Ashley Courtney, Good Food Guide, RAC highly recommended.

MILLBROOK HOUSE
Rue de Trachy, Millbrook, St Helier, Jersey JE2 3JN
Tel: 01534 733036 Fax: 01534 724317

Come where the air is clear for peace and quiet and character to an elegant 18th century country house, secluded in 10 acres of garden and parkland yet close to transport and the amenities of St Helier. Comfortably furnished rooms, good food, wines and service. Make a stay at Millbrook House a pleasurable and memorable experience.

27 Rooms (all en suite), 2 Suns, AA ◆◆◆, RAC Highly Acclaimed, Les Routiers.

THE DOLPHIN
Hotel & Restaurant

Gorey Pier, Jersey JE3 6EW
Tel: 01534 853370 Fax: 01534 855343
Email: casino@itl.net

Well-appointed 17 bedroom Hotel and Restaurant overlooking the picturesque Gorey Harbour and sandy beach. Bar, Grill Bar, excellent cuisine, well-known for sea specialities. Winter Breaks from £199 including flight and car hire. Open all year round. Rates from £29 B&B.

AA/RAC 2 Suns

CHATEAU LA CHAIRE HOTEL
Rozel Bay, St Martin, Jersey
Telephone: 01534 863354 Fax: 01534 865137
Email: res@chateau-la-chaire.co.uk
Internet: www.chateau-la-chaire.co.uk
14 Rooms (all en suite), 1 Four Poster.
AA ☆☆☆ (Red), RAC ☆☆☆ Gold Ribbon, Jersey Tourist Board 4 Suns, Jersey Tourism Gold Merit Award.
A finer setting for a hotel is hard to imagine. Nestled above the picturesque Rozel Bay, surrounded by terraced gardens within a wooded valley. Superb cuisine, fine wines and personal, friendly service creating an atmosphere we are sure you will come to appreciate as a guest at Chateau La Chaire.

LA HAULE MANOR HOTEL & RESTAURANT
Dept. H.H. St Aubin Bay, Jersey JE3 8BS
Telephone: 01534 741426 Fax: 01534 745501
14 Rooms (all en suite), 1 Four Poster.
Three Suns.
Standing in its own grounds slightly elevated with wonderful sea views over St Aubins Bay. La Haule Manor, dating back to the 15th century, is now a first class hotel with excellent accommodation, fine cuisine, friendly but inobtrusive service and is also conveniently situated for shopping and sightseeing. A totally relaxing experience.

The Island of Jersey

In search of a truly spectacular, yet little known, holiday destination? The Island of Jersey, just 14 miles off the coast of France and 100 miles south of the English coast, has been a favourite of British and European travellers for decades. Its abundant summertime pleasures include sunny, mild weather, some of the cleanest beaches in Europe, dozens of guided nature walks and bike excursions along "green lanes" and more things to see than you would expect in an island which measures just 9 miles by 5 miles.

It is a comfortable destination for American travellers as it is part of the British Isles and English is the language spoken on the Island.

The Island is astonishingly rich in heritage. Its museums interpret in modern, interactive ways the Island's 8,000 year recorded history. Jersey and the other Channel Islands were the only part of Britain occupied by the Germans during the Second World War. Today's visitors can find out more about this time by visiting the German Underground Hospital or in the Occupation Tapestry Gallery, where a 72-foot long tapestry tells the story of the years between 1940 and 1945. It was made by the islanders to mark the fiftieth anniversary of the Liberation and was unveiled by HRH the Prince of Wales in 1995.

Reminders of times past can be found at medieval Mont Orgueil Castle which overlooks the small harbour of Gorey. The castle dominates the east coast and from its turrets there are views across to the coast of France. It has protected the Island from invasion since the early 13th century and has played an important part in the Island's history.

From the main town of St. Helier there are views across the water to Elizabeth Castle which is set on its own islet in St. Aubin's Bay. Named by Sir Walter Raleigh when he was Governor of Jersey in 1600, after Queen Elizabeth I.

St. Helier has at its centre, Royal Square where the Battle of Jersey was fought in 1781 and where the Island's government buildings are to be found. Its pedestrianised streets are a magnet for shoppers and the Victorian Central Market, with its displays of food and flowers, is not be be missed.

In the countryside Hamptonne Country Life Museum recreates the country life of years gone by, with farmhouses and outbuildings dating back six centuries which have been restored using traditional crafts.

Jersey's home grown produce features on most menus, together with freshly caught fish and seafood. There are more restaurants per square mile than in most major cities.

The abundance of flowers is another of Jersey's attractions and it is often referred to as "The Floral Island". Flowers even feature in Jersey's best known event – the Battle of Flowers – which takes place on the second Thursday of August each year. It was first held in 1902 to celebrate the coronation of King Edward VII and Queen Alexandra. The Battle is a carnival parade featuring floats decorated in hundreds of thousands of fresh flowers accompanied by bands and dancers and brings thousands of people to the Island each year.

Lastly a value-added note for visitors – the Island of Jersey has no VAT so vacationers get full value for every dollar whether it's on their plates, in their gas tanks, or in their accommodation.

Jersey Tourism
Jersey Tourism, USA
(Toll free)
Tel: +212 861 4031
Fax: +212 861 4070
New York only
888 454 5543
outside New York

Jersey Tourism, Canada
Tel: +416 485 8724
Fax: +416 485 8256

Jersey Tourism
Liberation Square, St. Helier,
Jersey JE1 1BB
Tel: 01534 500800
(Brochure enquiries)
Tel: 01534 500777
(Visitor information)
Fax: 01534 500808
www.jersey.com

MAN
OF YOUR DREAMS

For a short break or a longer holiday the Isle of Man has something for everyone. Call for your free brochure or visit our website at **www.gov.im/tourism**
Alternatively tel **08457 686868**

HH1

Ireland consists of the following counties:-

IRELAND
Carlow
Cavan
Clare
Cork
Donegal
Dublin
Galway
Kerry
Kildare
Kilkenny
Laois
Leitrim
Limerick
Longford
Louth
Mayo
Meath
Monaghan
Offaly
Roscommon
Sligo
Tipperary
Waterford
Westmeath
Wexford
Wicklow

Irish Tourist Board
Baggerot Street Bridge
Dublin 2
00353 1 602 4000

London Office
150 New Bond Street
London W1Y 0AQ
Tel: 0207 518 0800

Northern Ireland consists of the following counties:-

NORTHERN IRELAND
Antrim
Armagh
Down
Fermanagh
Londonderry
Tyrone

Northern Ireland T.B.
59 North Street
Belfast, BT1 1NB
Tel: 02890 23 1221

London Office
24 Haymarket
London, W1Y 4DG
Tel: 0207 766 9920

Co. Clare Coastline
Courtesy of Graham Waite Photo Library

IRELAND

I n recent years IRELAND has busied itself getting the attractions that visitors want and need just right. All of this investment has enhanced the things Ireland already has in abundance – beautiful scenery and the friendliest people you'll find anywhere. The traditional magic of Ireland – the incomparable scenery, the wonderful fresh food, the fun – remains unchanged. Now everything that was always appealing is just that much better and more satisfying to discover than ever.

The beauty of Ireland is legendary. From the green pastures to the deep moody lakes and the wild rolling hills, Ireland is among the world's great travel experiences. For a relatively small island, Ireland offers an astonishing variety of countryside and coastline.

This scenic symphony is accompanied by the everchanging moods of the weather to give a heady mist that is unforgettable. Nowhere will you find air and water more crystal clear or vast stretches of countryside barely touched by the hand of man.

Touring around Ireland is a return to the halcyon days when the pace was slower and the countryside was there to be savoured around the next unfolding bend of the road. And after the day's exploration, anticipation of civilised comforts amid the gentle curiosity of friendly, welcoming people.

Entertaining and being entertained is a

central part of the Ireland experience. Over the centuries the Irish have evolved ways of amusing each other and visitors that few can match. Most notably the Irish way with words resulted in a tradition of play-writing and story-telling, which gave the world literary giants like Swift, Sheridan, Wilde, Joyce and O'Casey. They say that every drinker in a Dublin pub has a novel at home waiting to be finished. Everywhere you go you will find festivals, summer schools, seminars and

Kilmalkedar Church, Dingle Peninsula
Courtesy of Graham Waite Photo Library

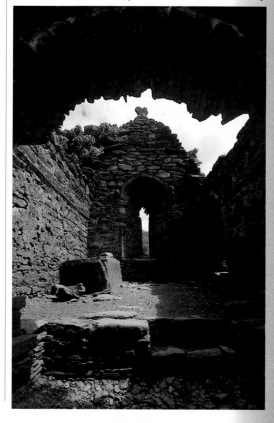

Above: Blarney Castle, Co. Cork
Below: Birr Castle, Co Offaly

symposia dedicated to the urban and rural literary traditions of the island.

In recent times Ireland has enjoyed a real renaissance in the arts. Its young population seeking to express itself has produced a flowering in music, and film-making especially, that has attracted world attention. Savour this heady atmosphere and strut with the best of them along the fashionable side streets of Dublin's Temple Bar or snatch a glimpse of the mega famous as they flit to their next noncultural rendezvous. Throughout the country you will find music played in some pubs most nights. Don't forget this is a participatory activity so don't be afraid to join in – you'll be very welcome.

CULTURE & HISTORY - Few places on the planet are as crammed with history as Ireland. Everywhere you look lie the

Right: Outskirts of Dingle, Co. Kerry
Below: Rugged Coastline at Slea Head, Co Kerry
Courtesy of Graham Waite Photo Library

Recent times have witnessed a transformation in turning these into the finest cuisine to be seen anywhere, as the Irish have learned to work their Celtic wizardry in the kitchen. The raw materials that hoof or swim around the landscape soon find their way onto the plates of diners in the fine restaurants that now abound. No evening in Ireland is complete without a quik nip into the "local" for a swift half of the world famous "black stuff" or a warming glass of the amber water of life, *uisce beatha*, or whiskey to you. Either way you'll soon be joining in with the singing. The singing, laughter, talk and music are summed up in one word by the Irish, the *craic*. It's short-hand for great times.

PLACES TO STAY - The phrase "spoilt for choice" recurs in any account of Ireland's many and varied places to stay. The country truly caters for every taste and budget. At one end of the spectrum there are castles and fine country mansions to cosset the discerning taste, while those seeking comfort without castellations can be sure of the quality and service to be had in the many fine hotels dotted around the country. Ireland's farmhouses and town and country houses bring the visitor close to the Irish people themselves. Here you will enjoy the warmth of the ordinary home plus the calorific bonus of the traditional Irish breakfast. Those of a more independent spirit will enjoy renting an Irish cottage or indeed staying under the heavens in a caravan or camping establishment. Whatever the choice, none will disappoint in the

ruins of ancient monuments and castles, some older even than the pyramids. Successive influences on the culture we find in Ireland today are there in abundance from the standing stones of prehistoric occupiers to the Round Towers and High Crosses of the mediaeval monks. Yet the complexity of Ireland's past is easy to understand and appreciate. The accessibility of our museums and interpretative centres makes the exploration of this rich past both rewarding and diverting. In Ireland the past is not a strange country but part of the everyday consciousness and creativity of its people.

EATING & DRINKING - Ireland enjoys the distinction of producing some of the finest food and drink in the world.

high standard of service and comfort provided.

CAPITAL, COAST & COUNTRY - No-one ever visits Dublin once. This enchanting Georgian city will draw you back again and again. Small enough to walk around (follow the sign-posted Trail); beautiful enough to make you walk very slowly; friendly enough to captivate you. In Dublin, you'll realise what it means to be in a young country, where half the population is under 25 years old.

You'll find two classic cathedrals, universities, a castle, and one of the most beautiful 2,000 acre city-centre parks anywhere, The Phoenix Park. Stroll around Merrion Square – one of the finest Georgian squares in Europe – or St. Stephen's Green, the favourite haunt of James Joyce. There are museums of art and archaeology, of writing, even one devoted to Irish whiskey. Theatres like the Abbey and the Gate will remind you that this is the town of Shaw and Synge, Beckett and Behan, Joyce and Yeats.

In the rich farmland to the north of Dublin are some of our most important historic sites. In the picturesque Boyne valley, you will find the ruins of great monasteries and the 5,000 year old Newgrange burial chamber – one of Europe's most impressive remains of Neolithic civilisation.

To the west are the flat plains of County Kildare, the main centre for the

breeding, training and racing of some of the world's finest horses and home to the Irish Derby at the Curragh.

Head south and you climb into the Wicklow mountains – as green and uncrowded as anywhere in the world. Here you will find the magnificent gardens of the Powerscourt Estate and the remains of the great monastery at Glendalough.

Go east and, in just twenty minutes, you can be swimming or sailing in the wide

Lismore Castle, Co. Waterford

holiday, as many different areas are within reach.

SOUTHERN RIVER VALLEYS - Ireland's south-east corner is a gentle land of golden sandy beaches and rolling countryside. To the west lie the Slieve Bloom mountains with their gentle rounded hills and pretty streams, ideal for exploring on foot to discover some of the best-kept secrets of Ireland's scenery.

Wexford is a country of seaside resorts and wonderful beaches – a favourite holiday place for visitors arriving by ferry from nearby Rosslare. Wexford town was founded by the Vikings and today has a famous Festival Opera. Here too, you will find a Heritage Park, bringing Irish history to life.

Kilkenny is a superb mediaeval castle town – having many beautiful buildings to explore, including the school of Swift and Congreve. In Waterford you can visit the famous crystal glass factory and bring home treasured souvenirs. In Middleton, the home of Irish Whiskey, you can tour the old distillery and soak up the atmosphere of a very special place.

Outside the main towns, you will find unspoilt villages, welcoming riverside pubs and magnificent caves at Dunmore.

For a gentle introduction to some of the beauties of Ireland, you will not find a prettier or sunnier region than the south-east.

expanse of beautiful waters that stretch from Dun Laoghaire to Bray and on down to Arklow.

If the Shannon is for boats, then the Irish Lakelands are for rods and lines. It is a region filled with fish that holds a powerful attraction for fishermen. Bream, Rudd, Tench, Pike, Roach, Perch and Dace provide the coarse fisherman with wonderful sport. Many of the lakes also provide opportunities for boating and windsurfing, and beside them are some challenging golf courses. This region is ideal for a touring based

Muckross House, Killarney, Co. Kerry

SOUTH COAST & KINGDOM

Here amidst mountains and peninsulas you will find some of our most breathtaking scenery. Hazy mountain panoramas shimmering in the pearly ocean light, rattling streams of sparkling clear water tumbling down wooded slopes. You can spend days just watching and wondering at the splendour of the views as you take the 21-kilometre scenic route over the twisting Moll's Gap road to Killarney, or the 112-kilometre winding lanes to the Ring of Kerry of the 130-kilometre tour of the Dingle Peninsula.

Thanks to the warmth of the Gulf Stream, the weather here is mild and even-tempered all year around. You'll find palm trees and many exotic plants growing, while puffins and seals play on the rocks.

Visit Cork, Ireland's second city, home and host to the world famous Jazz Festival. Nearby is the Blarney Stone at Blarney Castle (kiss the Blarney stone and you'll never be at a loss for words). While Cobh, Cork's own natural harbour, is now fast emerging as a major tourist centre focusing on it's long maritime past.

NORTHERN & ATLANTIC

Limerick and Galway are the main cities of Ireland's West Coast. The latter famed for its annual Race Meeting and Oyster Festival. The former as guardian of the mighty River Shannon. Galway nestles at the neck of Galway Bay and is reputed to have been Columbus' final point of departure on his epoch-making voyage of discovery.

In early Connemara you will find the

world famous marble, as green and beautiful and enduring as Ireland itself. You can buy marble jewellery and gifts and even furniture from the quarry itself.

Connemara is one of the most beautiful areas of Ireland; a land of rock and mountain, criss-crossed with streams and marshes. This is one of the best places to hear traditional Irish music in the pubs and to see the classic long low thatched cottages with the fragrant peat smoke rising from the chimneys.In the Burren you will discover the 'mountains of the moon', wild and rocky and rich in prehistoric monuments.

Look closely at the cracks in the rugged limestone and you will discover many rare and delicate flowers and plants that have made this inhospitable land their home. Such rugged country is ideal for pony-trekking expeditions, and golfers will find some of our most dramatic links courses. The region is an angler's paradise, with trout and salmon thronging some of the clearest waters in Europe.

Courtesy of Graham Waite Photo Library

Bunratty Castle (Shannon Heritage), Co Clare

Donegal and the North Coast is one of the least polluted places in Europe, with splendid golf courses like Royal Portruth to tempt the discerning player.

Further along the coast the mighty Giants Causeway attracts many thousands of visitors to its lunar like landscape. Belfast to the east of Lough Neagh is the largest city in the area with a host of attractions for the short break holidaymaker.

To the south is Sligo, Yeats Country – with the name places of its towns and beauty spots echoing in his plays and poems. Yeats is buried in Drumcliff churchyard at the foot of his beloved Benbulbe Mountain. The Yeats School in Sligo attracts students from all over the world, as does Lough Gill and its beautiful Isle of Innisfree.

In Lough Derg, pilgrims who are prepared to fast for three days seek out the Station Island where St. Patrick fasted for rather longer. Less serious visitors may look for the disappearing lake at Lough Nasool or one of Ireland's prettiest towns, Glenties.

Antrim Coastline between Portrush and Dunluce Castle
Courtesy of The Northern Ireland Tourist Board

People who have never been to Northern Ireland think it is somehow different from the rest of the island. In some way that is true, but in most ways it is as "Irish" as anywhere else. People are genuinely friendly to visitors as they don't see too many of them – and appreciative of anyone who wants to see the "real" Northern Ireland for themselves. Service levels are high, whether you choose a four star hotel' a bed-and-breakfast or farmhouse' or one of the restored cottages once lived in by farm workers or fishermen.

Lough Erne is one of the most beautiful waterways in Europe' but there are so few boats on it that you can cruise for hours without seeing another craft. Lower Lough Erne is a large lake stretching for 26 miles with numerous small islands' while upper Lough Erne is more like a river winding through a maze of islands. The town of Enniskillen stands on an isthmus between Lower and Upper, with green hills forming a dramatic backdrop.

Castle Coole, Fermanagh - Courtesy of The Northern Ireland Tourist Board

By hiring a cruiser for a few days you can explore at leisure' but make a point of visiting Devenish Island with its 12th Century tower' Boa Island with its early Christian carvings, and the village of Belleck for its world-famous pottery and good "craic" in the pubs at night. You can stop off at hotels or other villages close to the lake, and a personal favourite is Bellanaleck on Lower Lough Erne where you can enjoy real Irish cooking in a thatched cottage restaurant' the Sheelin.

The Guidhall at Londonderry
Courtesy of The Northern Ireland Tourist Board

Northern Ireland has dramatic seascapes as well as lakes and mountains' and the drive north from the port of Larne to Ballycastle is unforgettable. While in Ballycastle you can visit remote Rathlin Island' and you can sail to Ballycastle directly on the summer only ferry from Campbeltown on the Mull of Kintyre. West of Ballycastle you will find some of Northern Ireland's top attractions, and if you have gone easy on the poteen then sway along Carrick-a-Rede rope bridge made to help fishermen reach their boats. Little villages including Ballintoy and Portballintrae are worth discovering, but the sight you must not miss is the Giant's Causeway.

Formed of 40,000 basalt columns stretching out into the sea, this natural wonder is steeped in mythology. The giant Finn McCool is said to have built the causeway to bring his lover from the Hebrides, and while fighting with a Scottish giant he flung a huge piece of earth across the sea. The hole it left is now Lough Neagh, but the missile fell short and now forms the Isle of Man. Close to the Giant's Causeway you can also tour the distillery at Bushmills – where the produce is legal! – see the clifftop ruins of Dunluce Castle' and enjoy the seaside resorts of Portrush and Portstewart' famed for their wide' white sands. One of Ireland's top golf courses, Royal Portrush, is nearby.

One of the great things about

Stranlough - Courtesy of The National Trust (Northern Ireland)

Northern Ireland is that everywhere is within easy reach' as it is only the same size as Yorkshire. You could base yourself in Belfast to enjoy city attractions' and make day trips to the Causeway Coast' the mountains of Mourne, historic Armagh and scenic Ards peninsula.

Belfast has come alive over the last few years, and the nightlife is particularly good along the "Golden Mile" from the Grand Opera House to historic Queen's University. You can take a guided walking tour to Belfast pubs' and one "must" is the Crown Bar with beautifully preserved Victorian decor. Old and new come together in Belfast, with the turn-of-the-century City Hall contrasting with the Waterfront Hall, opened in 1997 to give northern Ireland a world-class concert venue.

Many people think of Belfast for all the wrong reasons, and indeed some visitors want to hear more about the recent unhappy history of Northern Ireland. This is something the people do not shirk from, and in Belfast you can take a citybus tour called living History which visits many areas

Mussenden Temple, Londonderry - Courtesy of The Northern Ireland Tourist Board

familiar from newsreels. The tour is conducted with such understanding and respect for all points of few that you cannot but be moved.Derry, 120 miles from Belfast and 70 miles from the Giant's Causeway, is a historic jewel which is the only intact walled town in Ireland. You can walk all around the 17th Century walls in 20 – 30 minutes, learning how they where constructed to defend the English and Scottish settles. The walls alone make Derry worth visiting, but if you step inside the award-winning Tower Museum you will discover all about the history of Northern Ireland from the Siege of Derry (1688/89) to the present day.

The city enjoys a beautiful settling beside the River Foyle, which becomes Lough Foyle all the open sea. Nearby hills and a beautiful coastline beckon you, and within a few minutes you can be on the Inishowen peninsula in Donegal.

Then, of course, you will be in the Irish Republic, crossing the border easily as thousands do every day. It is one island, after all – but Northern Ireland is a little different' and proud of it.

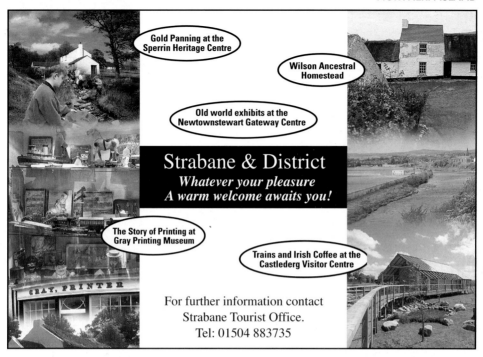

Gold Panning at the
Sperrin Heritage Centre

Wilson Ancestral
Homestead

Old world exhibits at the
Newtownstewart Gateway Centre

Strabane & District
Whatever your pleasure
A warm welcome awaits you!

The Story of Printing at
Gray Printing Museum

Trains and Irish Coffee at the
Castlederg Visitor Centre

For further information contact
Strabane Tourist Office.
Tel: 01504 883735

GALGORM MANOR
136 Fenaghy Road, Ballymena Co. Antrim,
Northern Ireland BT42 1EA
Telephone: 01266 881001 Fax: 01266 880080
23 Rooms (all en suite), 2 Four Posters.
AA ☆☆☆☆, RAC ☆☆☆☆, NITB ☆☆☆☆
A 19th century converted gentlemen's residence set in 86 acres. Its 23 bedrooms offer stunning river views as well as 6 self catering mews cottages. The dining room has an enviable reputation for fresh produce cooked to perfection. We also offer 18 stables, clay pigeon shooting, ballooning, archery and of course fishing.

SPECIAL **1 2 3 4** B B/C

THE OLD INN
15 Main Street, Crawfordsburn, Co. Down BT19 1JH
Telephone: 01247 853255 Fax: 01247 852775
33 Rooms (all en suite), 4 Four Posters
AA ☆☆☆, RAC ☆☆☆, NITB ☆☆☆, Egon Ronay,
Johansens Taste of Ulster, Ackermans, Ashley Courtenay.
Charming Thatched Country Inn dating to 1614. 20 minutes from Belfast. 32 individually designed bedrooms, garden cottage in award-winning gardens. Highly acclaimed restaurant 1614, renowned for excellent cuisine and extensive wine list. The Parlour Bar offers an all-day menu. Churn Bistro is open in the evening for casual dining.

1 2 3 4 C

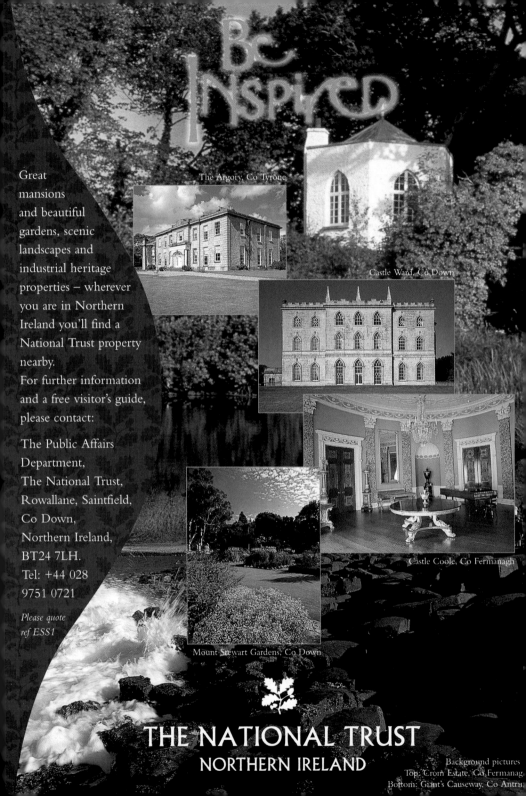

BE INSPIRED

The Argory, Co Tyrone

Castle Ward, Co Down

Castle Coole, Co Fermanagh

Mount Stewart Gardens, Co Down

Great mansions and beautiful gardens, scenic landscapes and industrial heritage properties – wherever you are in Northern Ireland you'll find a National Trust property nearby.

For further information and a free visitor's guide, please contact:

The Public Affairs Department,
The National Trust,
Rowallane, Saintfield,
Co Down,
Northern Ireland,
BT24 7LH.
Tel: +44 028 9751 0721

Please quote ref ESS1

THE NATIONAL TRUST
NORTHERN IRELAND

Background pictures
Top: Crom Estate, Co Fermanagh
Bottom: Giant's Causeway, Co Antrim

Northern Ireland

Northern Ireland is different. In an area which covers only one-sixth of the island of Ireland, the six counties of Ulster combine to present a wealth of unspoilt beauty, breathtaking coastlines, some of the best fishing in Ireland and a welcome that is second to none.

In addition, each county spreads its own tapestry of historical and scenic beauty. On uncongested roads the visitor can explore a varied landscape that changes from county to county. From the famous Giant's Causeway in Co. Antrim, to Benone Strand, the longest beach in Ireland, in Co. Londonderry, and the lakeland landscape of Co. Fermanagh to "Where the mountains Sweep Down to the Sea" in Co. Down. A walker's paradise awaits in the Sperrin Mountains of Co. Tyrone while Co. Armagh's Planetarium and Eartharium are an ideal opportunity to take a 'quantum leap' into the future.

Past, present and future rub shoulders in an area where the myths and legends of pre-history play an important role in the present-day tourist attractions while a turbulent history lends itself to the people's intense interest in and knowledge of their historical heritage.

From stone-age tombs to seventeenth-century castles, Northern Ireland's historic monuments have a special charm because they can be found in some delightful places; the corner of a field or someone's front garden, making history as accessible as the stunning scenic beauty on all sides.

The nature of the landscape not only provides the visitor with a feast of beauty but a superb environment for such activities as golf, fishing, walking, water sports, horse-riding and hire-cruising. For those whose interests lie in more leisurely pursuits, a varied cultural life is easily accessible by the way of established theatres, museums, visitor and interpretative centres.

Recent history may have obscured the essential character of Northern Ireland but nothing can eliminate the inherent friendliness of the people and unique beauty of the surroundings.

Network Tourist Information Centres

Belfast
(02890) 246609

Belfast City Airport
(02890) 457745

Belfast International Airport
(02894) 422888

Ballycastle
(028 207) 62024

Carrickfergus
(01960) 366455

Giant's Causeway
(028 207) 31855

Larne
(02828) 260088

Lisburn
(02892) 660038

Armagh
(02837) 527808

Banbridge
(028 406) 23322

Bangor
(02891) 270069

Downpatrick
(02844) 612233

Kilkeel
(028 417) 62525

Newcastle
(028437) 22222

Newtownards
(01247) 826846

Portaferry
(01247) 729882

Enniskillen
(02866) 323110

Coleraine
(028 703) 44723

Limavady
(028 777) 22226

Londonderry
(02871) 267284

Tyrone
(028 867) 66727

Killymaddy
(01868) 767259/725311

Omagh
(02882) 247831/247832

Sea View House Hotel
Ballylickey, Bantry, Co. Cork IRL
Tel: 353 27 50073/50462
Fax: 353 27 51555
Email: seaviewhousehotel@eircom.net
www.cmvhotels.com

This delightful Country House Hotel stands on private grounds close by Ballylickey Bridge, over the Ouvane River, 70 yards off the main road, 3 miles from Bantry and 8 miles from Glengarriff. From the main rooms it commands views of the famous Bantry Bay and the mountains in the distance.

Peace, quiet, unique beauty – all these are yours on holiday or business visits to Seaview House. Locally and abroad it is renowned for its comfort and cuisine. Owned and personally run by Miss Kathleen O'Sullivan, you can be confident of a most friendly welcome and interest in the enjoyment of your holiday.

Courtmacsherry Hotel
Courtmacsherry, Co. Cork
Tel: 023 46198 Fax: 023 46137
13 Rooms (10 en suite). AA ☆☆ ❀

This friendly, family-owned hotel, situated on 10 acres of garden and woodland, overlooking Courtmacsherry Bay, was formerly the summer residence of the Earls of Shannon. The Cork Tree Restaurant offers superb cuisine and the choice of 100 wines. Horse riding and tuition from our own renowned stables. Golf, tennis, river and sea angling can be arranged. The beautiful West Cork coastline and the mountains of Kerry are within easy reach by car. Self-catering cottages are also available all year. Open Easter to end of September.

BANTRY BAY HOTEL
Wolfe Tone Square, Bantry, West Cork, Ireland
Telephone: (027) 50062/(027) 50289 Fax: (027) 50261
Email: bantrybay@eircom.net
www.bantrybayhotel.com
14 Rooms (all en suite).
Bórd Fáilte (Irish Tourist Board) ☆☆☆.
The Bantry Hotel Hotel overlooking magnificent Wolfe Tone Square in the centre of historic Bantry, combines fine drinks and the freshest of local produce (much of it caught in breathtaking Bantry Bay – former HQ of the Royal Navy's Atlantic Fleet) with engaging conversation in beautiful surroundings. A visit is an absolute must.

RS ⊘ ▭ ⌀ 🍽 P ⑪ ✦ 🐾 🔭 SPECIAL 1 2 3 4 C

MARYBOROUGH HOUSE HOTEL
Maryborough Hill, Douglas, Cork
Telephone: 021 436 5555 Fax: 021 436 5662
79 Rooms (all en suite). TB ☆☆☆☆.
Distinctive, delightful and different – the Maryborough is set on 24 acres of listed gardens and woodland and located only 10 minutes from Cork City. This charming 18th century house with its creatively designed extension features exquisite conference, banqueting and leisure facilities. There are 57 spacious bedrooms and some with balconies overlook the magnificent gardens and orchards. Zings restaurant offers a contemporary relaxed design with an exciting mixture of modern flavours and styles.

RS ⌢ ⊘ ⊘ ▭ ⌀ 🍽 P ⑪ V GF ⬆ 🔭 ⊘ ✦ ↦ 🐾 ❀ 📷 🏠 SPECIAL 1 2 3 4

Bantry House

Bantry House, overlooking Bantry Bay in Co. Cork, has one of the most beautiful settings anywhere in the British isles. Owned by the White family since 1739, it was the seat of the 4 Earls of Bantry (1816-1891) and in 1945 was the first house in Ireland to be opened to the public on a full-time basis.

Bantry House contains furniture, paintings and other objets d'art collected mainly by Richard White, 2nd Earl of Bantry, on his extensive travels in Europe in the 19th century. He was also responsible for laying out formal gardens. Now being restored, these were once rightly described as 'the Second Earl's first love'. With its Tea Room and Craft Shop, Bantry House is open March to October. Admission to house and grounds is free to residents.

Both East and West Wings of Bantry House provide guest accommodation. In the East Wing are 4 double and 2 twin rooms, all with bathrooms en suite and direct-dial telephones.

The West Wing has 2 room suite on the top floor: a further two twin rooms with a shared bathroom on the 1st floor are especially convenient for families with older children.

Facilities for residents include a sitting room, a billiard room and a balcony TV room overlooking the Italian Garden with its fountain, parterres and "stairway to the sky".

Bantry House,
Bantry,
Co. Cork.
Tel: 027 50047
Fax: 027 50795

Opening times
& rates upon
application

Cork City Gaol

CORK is an historic city with a very rich historical and archeological heritage – much of it still in evidence today. Part of this heritage, Cork City Gaol is located two kilometres from the city's main thoroughfare and while the magnificent castle-like building is now a major and unique visitor attraction, this prison once housed 19th century prisoners, often in wretched conditions.

The main Gaol building is contained within an oval enclosure; the very high walls ensuring no escape but also denying law abiding citizens the opportunity to see one of the finest examples of Ireland's architectural heritage. A listed building, the Gaol was constructed by Sir Thomas Deane to designs of Robertson, and boasts that its drawings were copied by John Hogan – Ireland's most celebrated neo-classical sculptor.

Apart from those who ended up in Gaol for political ideals, most prisoners were incarcerated for offenses which we would now not consider serious. Visitors having first presented themselves to the Governor, follow in the footsteps of amazingly life-like characters through furnished cells and, with fascinating sound effects and exhibitions, can experience day to day life for prisoners and Gaoler.

Wandering through the wings of Cork City Gaol the atmosphere suggests you are accompanied by the shuffling feet of inmates, each representing their particular period in Irish history from pre-famine times to the foundation of the state. Original graffiti on cell walls tell the innermost feelings of some inmates, while a very spectacular sound and image presentation tells the social history and contrasting lifestyles of 19th century Cork and why some people turned to crime.

The Radio Museum Experience – the story of Radio, incorporating the RTE Museum Collection is now open. IN 1927 Cork's first Radio Station, 6CK was located in the Gaol. Today on an unforgettable journey down the wavelengths of time you can meet Marconi, the Italian genius, whose name is synonymous with radio itself, view some remarkable equipment from the RTE museum collection and visit the restored 6CK Studio.

Cork City Gaol
Sunday's Well, Cork.
Tel: 021 305022
Fax: 021 307230

Opening Hours
Open 7 Days a Week
Mar-Oct 9.30am to 6pm
Nov-Feb 10.00am to 5.00pm
(Last Admission 1 hour
before closing)

Admission Charged
Separate Admission to Gaol &
"Radio Museum Experience".

Facilities
Gaol Tours in English, Irish,
German, French, Spanish,
Japanese, Dutch and Italian.
Refreshment area and well
stocked souvenir shop and
parking.

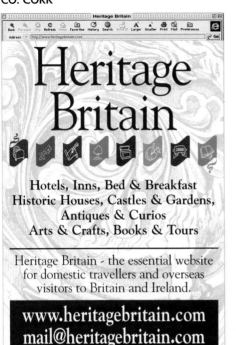

Riverstown House

Georgian House dating from 1602. Remodelled in the 1730's by Dr Jemmett Browne, Bishop of Cork who engaged the Italian stuccodores Paul & Filippo La Francini to adorn the ceiling of the dining room with allegorical figures and also its walls with classical figures and exuberant Rococco flowers and foliage.

Situated 6 km from Cork City on the old Cork-Dublin Road, 1 mile from Glanmire village, turn right at Riverstowl Cross.

Open May-Sept, Wed-Sat 2pm-6pm.
Other times by appointment 021 4821205

ANNES GROVE GARDENS
Castletownroche, Co. Cork
Tel/Fax: 00 353 22 26145

Extensive, supremely romantic Robinsonian woodland and riverside gardens with notable plant collection, surround an 18th century house and intimate, compartmented walled garden.
Open 17 March-30 September, Mon-Sat 10am-5pm; Sun 1pm-6pm. Reductions and guided tours for pre-booked groups. Nursery sales. Self-catering accommodation also available. 1m north of Castletownroche, between Mallow and Fermoy on N72 (Killarney-Rosslare road).

INNISHANNON HOUSE HOTEL
Innishannon, Co. Cork, Ireland.
Telephone: 021 775121 Fax: 021 775609.
14 Rooms (all en suite), 2 Four Posters. 1 suite (for up to 6 guests).
AA ☆☆☆ ❀❀ 1993/94/95/96/97/98, ITB ☆☆☆, RAC Hospitality, Comfort, Service and Restaurant 94/95/96/97/98, Michelin Guide, Egon Ronay, Charming Small Hotels of Britain and Ireland. "The most romantic hotel in Ireland" was built in 1720 on the banks of the Bandon River as the home of a prosperous farmer. Today, totally refurbished in country house style, it is a haven for the gourmet traveller. Salmon and trout fishing from the lawn, boating from our pier. Member Manor House Hotels.

ACTONS HOTEL
Pier Road, Kinsale, Co. Cork
Telephone: +353 214 772135 Fax: +353 214 772231
75 Rooms (all en suite).
AA ☆☆☆ ❀. TB ☆☆☆
Actons Hotel, splendidly located in landscaped gardens overlooking Kinsale's beautiful harbour. Its award winning restaurant, a member of the renowned Kinsale Good Food Circle is noted for its cuisine. Many of its 75 guestrooms enjoy spectacular sea views. Health and Fitness Centre. Kinsale - idyllic location for gourmet dining, golf and scenic walks.

LONGUEVILLE HOUSE
Mallow, Co. Cork, Ireland
Telephone: 00 353 22 47156 Fax: 00 353 22 47459
20 Rooms (all en suite).
AA ☆☆☆ ❀❀❀, RAC Blue Ribbon, ITB ☆☆☆☆, Bridgestone Food Guide ☆☆.
Longueville House, situated in the heart of a 500 acre wooded estate, working farm and gardens, overlooks the Blackwater River Valley, famous for its salmon and brown trout fishing. The house, a listed Heritage Georgian Manor (1720), is owned and managed by the O'Callaghan family, your hosts.

LISS ARD LAKE LODGE
Skibbereen, Co. Cork, Ireland
Telephone: 00353 28 40000 Fax: 00353 28 40001
16 Rooms (all en suite).
Bridgestone Guide, Egon Ronay, Michelin.
Liss Ard Lake Lodge located in the south west of Ireland, is set in the magnificent Liss Ard Gardens and overlooks Lake Abisdealy. Guests can leave behind the stresses of everyday life and relax in luxurious natural surroundings. The Lake Lodge Restaurant serves a light, creative cuisine using organic meat, vegetables and local fish.

The Queenstown Story

By the time of Queen Victoria's visit in 1849, when Cove was renamed Queenstown, the village had grown to a busy town. It became a hive of naval and commercial activity as Cork harbour's important strategic position in the North Atlantic was recognised. Tall ships called to transport convicts to Australia and to carry Irish emigrants to North America. Later the early transatlantic steamers and finally the great ocean liners continued the task of carrying the Irish to new lives in new lands.

From 1848-1950 over 6 million adults and children emigrated from Ireland – about 2.5 million left Cobh, making it the single most important port of emigration.

Now Cobh's unique origins, it's history and legacy are dramatically recalled at The Queenstown Story – a multi-media exhibition at Cobh's Victorian Railway Station. It demonstrates the conditions on board the early emigrant vessels, including the dreaded "coffin ship", an "Irish Wake" – the special farewell for emigrating sons and daughters – many of whom never returned to Ireland, the life aboard a convict ship leaving Cove for Australia in 1801, and the development of ocean travel, from tall ships to the majesty and splendour of the great ocean liners of the 20th century.

Also demonstrated are Cobh's special connections with the ill-fated Titanic which sank on her maiden voyage in 1912, the horror of World War I and the sinking of the Lusitania off Cork Harbour with the loss of 1,198 lives, the famous personalities and dignitaries who arrive at and depart from Cobh aboard the great ocean liners.

Cobh Heritage Centre,
Cobh, Co. Cork
Tel: 021 4813591
Fax: 021 4813595
Email: cobhher@indigo.ie

Open 10am to 6pm
(last admission 5pm)
7 days a week

Admission
Adults £3.95
OAP's/Students £3.20
Children £2.00,
Family £12.00

Facilities
Self service cafe serving home made produce made locally, Christy's Irish Stores, Parking & Toilets.

Ireland's Premier Showcave

- *Take a Detour* •
- *An experience not to be missed* •
- *Let us make it a day you will remember* •

OPEN EVERY DAY
FROM 10.00 MID-MARCH to NOVEMBER
LAST TOUR: 18.30 JULY & AUGUST
17.30 OTHER MONTHS
WINTER OPENING: 3 TOURS DAILY

SPECIAL RATES: FAMILIES AND GROUPS

**TEL: 065 7077036 FAX: 065 7077107
BALLYVAUGHAN, CO. CLARE**

Tinarana House
Killaloe, Co. Clare
…A Haven of Peace & Tranquillity…

**Killaloe, Co. Clare
Tel: 061 376966 Fax: 061 375369
E-mail: info@tinarana.com
Website: www.tinarana.com**

KINCORA HALL HOTEL

The Ancient Capital of Ireland. On entering one has an immediate sense of warmth with beautifully crafted woodwork and a magnificent open hearth.
A cuisine delight in the Thomond Room Restaurant where attention and creativity are the hallmarks of the Chefs work. Before retiring to one of the deluxe bedrooms, a nightcap will end a blissfully relaxing day in the Tobermurragh Bar. Kincora Hall Hotel also boasts its own private marina.

Kincora Hall Hotel
Killaloe, Co Clare
Tel: 061-376000 Fax: 061-376665

DROMOLAND CASTLE
Newmarket-on-Fergus, Co. Clare, Ireland
Telephone: 061 368144 Fax: 061 363355
75 Rooms (all en suite).
AA ☆☆☆☆☆. RAC ☆☆☆☆☆. ITB ☆☆☆☆☆
Dromoland Castle, one of Irelands most famous Baronial Castles, is now one of Europe's leading resort Hotels. The 375 acre estate offers championship golf, lake and river fishing, a health and leisure centre, scenic walks and a 17th century rose garden. Two award winning restaurants offer a choice of gourmet and traditional cuisine. The Castle is located 8 miles from Shannon Airport and 6 miles from the town of Ennis in Co. Clare.

RS 🎣🕐📠☎️ P ♨️ V GF ⌕ ⫛ ⇥ ⇤ ❀ ⛳🏨
SPECIAL 1 2 3 4

HYLANDS HOTEL
Ballyvaughan, County Clare
Telephone: 065 77037/77015 Fax: 065 77131
30 Rooms (all en suite).
RAC ☆☆☆, TB ☆☆☆, Bridgestone 100 Best Hotels in Ireland, Egon Ronay for 95/96/97.
A family owned and operated 3 star hotel dating back to the early 18th Century. Has a tradition of good food and takes every care in selecting locally grown produce, offering an array of the finest seafood. Situated in the picturesque village of Ballyvaughan which nestles at the foot of the Burren hills, it is ideally located for easy access to the Aran Islands, Kerry and Connemara. Entertainment in high season. Village Inns Hotels member.

RS 🚭🕐📠☎️ ☕ P ♨️ V GF ⇤ 🏨 SPECIAL 1
2 3 4 C

Shannon Heritage

The Shannon Heritage portfolio of products has continuously developed since the first Mediaeval Banquet was held at the restored Bunratty Castle in 1963. Today, the portfolio consists of 4 exciting day visitor attractions and 5 evening dinner entertainments.

Bunratty Castle and Folk Park, Co. Clare, is open daily all year round. Visitors can see an authentically restored 15th century castle with the Folk Park, which consists of a recreation of a village street and rural life in 19th century Ireland.

World famous **Mediaeval Banquets** are held in the Castle throughout the year. A traditional Irish night is held from May-Oct at the Great Barn in the Folk Park.

Lough Gur stone centre, situated 26 km from Limerick city is one of Ireland's most important pre-historic sites (open May-Sept).

At **Craggaunowen**, the Living Past, situated in Co. Clare, visitors can view a recreation of some of the homesteads and artefacts seen in Ireland over a thousand years ago (open April-Oct).

The **Killaloe Heritage Centre**, Co. Clare (May-Sept) explores the monastic history of the region and the use of the river Shannon.

The interpretative centre at **King John's Castle**, Limerick City (open daily April-Oct) contains a new, exciting exhibition. The Castle itself dates back to the 13th century.

Medieval themed wedding receptions are held in the castle from October to April. The Castle also houses an apartment which is available for rental.

Knappogue Castle (near Quin, Co. Clare) was built in 1467 and from May to October is open to visitors and offers Medieval Banquets – subject to demand.

The Cliffs of Moher Visitors Centre & O'Brien's Tower, situated on the coast of Co. Clare offers spectacular cliff scenery and views of the Atlantic Ocean (open all year round).

Dunguaire Castle, Co. Galway is a 16th century Castle and from May-Oct is open to visitors and offers Mediaeval Banquets – subject to demand.

Address
Shannon Heritage,
Bunratty Castle and
Folk Park, Bunratty,
County Clare

Tel: 061 360788
Fax: 061 361020

Email:
reservations@shannon-dev.ie
Website:
www.shannonheritage.com

The National Library of Ireland

The National Library traces its origins from the Library of the Royal Dublin Society, founded in 1731. In 1877 a substantial portion of the Royal Dublin Society Library was purchased by the State and the new National Library was established.

The Library's current collection of some six million items constitutes probably the most outstanding collection of Irish documentary material in the world, offering an invaluable representation of Irish history and heritage.

The main Library building in Kildare Street opened in 1890. Other Library premises on Kildare Street include 2-3 Kildare Street which houses the Office of the Chief Herald, the Heraldic Museum and the Department of Manuscripts.

Housing a collection of some three hundred thousand photographs, the National Photographic Archive, in the Temple Bar area of Dublin, is the newest Library building. The programme of exhibitions at the Archive features selected images from the photographic collections.

Facilities: Exhibitions, Genealogy Advisory Service and Shop.

Open: Mon-Wed 10.00-21.00, Thurs-Fri 10.00-17.00, Sat 10.00-13.00. Closed: Sundays, Bank Holidays, 23 Dec-2 Jan and Good Friday.
Admission Free

National Library of Ireland, Kildare Street, Dublin 2.
Telephone: +353 1 6030200
Fax: +353 1 6766690
email: info@nli.ie
www.nli.ie

RIVERHOUSE HOTEL
23-24 Eustace St., Temple Bar,
Dublin 2, Ireland
Telephone: 01 670 7655 Fax: 01 670 7650

29-bedroom hotel with the emphasis on personal service and friendly welcome. Located in the heart of Dublin's colourful and exciting Temple Bar area. All bedrooms are en suite and with tea/coffee making facilities, TV, radio, direct dial phone and hairdryer. Facilities include Bar and Night Club. Public multi storey car park nearby. All rooms (all en suite).

THE DUN LAOGHAIRE Kingston
HOTEL BARS & RESTAURANT

The Kingston Hotel is a family-run hotel in the centre of Dun Laoghaire, overlooking Dublin Bay. We are situated within walking distance of the Dublin/Holyhead Ferryport and only minutes from the City Centre by DART. All 38 bedrooms are en suite, many with panoramic views over the bay. Rich in maritime history and scenic beauty, Dun Laoghaire is Dublin's premier resort town. Enjoy a leisurely stroll along the promenade after dining on the Kingston Hotel's excellent cuisine.

THE DUN LAOGHAIRE KINGSTON
Adelaide Street, Dun Laoghaire, Co. Dublin
Tel: 280 1810 Fax: 280 1237

TWO CENTURIES APART... FIFTEEN MINUTES AWAY

NEWBRIDGE HOUSE

Donabate, Co. Dublin
Tel: +353 1 843 6534 Fax:+353 1 872 7530

Delightful 18th Century manor set on 350 acres of parkland boasting one of the finest Georgian interiors in Ireland. Each room has its own style of antique and original furniture - indeed the house appears more or less as it did 150 years ago. The grounds contain a twenty-nine acre traditional farm, complete with farmyard animals.

SKERRIES MILLS

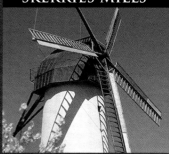

Skerries, Co Dublin
Tel: +353 1 849 5208 Fax: +353 1 849 5213

Winner of the 1999 Tidy Towns Heritage Award.
The history of the mills can be traced to the early 16th Century and a bakery was established on the site by 1840. All three mills have now been restored to working order. Guided and self-guided tours available.

ARDGILLAN CASTLE

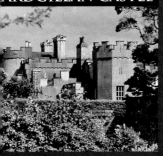

Balbriggan, Co Dublin
Tel: +353 1 849 2212 Fax: +353 1 849 2786

The castle was built in 1738 by Robert Taylor and set on 194 acres of rolling pasture land, mixed woodland and gardens. Now beautifully restored and furnished in Victorian style, the principal rooms and kitchen are open to the public.

Opening times available from the above telephone numbers.
For further information contact Dublin Tourism on +353 1 605 7755
Properties managed & operated by Fingal County Council

Detail from Breton Girl (1902) by Roderic O'Connor in The Merrion art collection.

Detail from Rococo ceiling in The Merrion Hotel.

The walls of The Merrion are known for their great art, and even our doors are collectors' items.

Since we opened our handsome Georgian doors in 1997, The Merrion has been recognised as Ireland's finest five star hotel.

The Merrion was created from four listed Georgian townhouses and boasts an exemplary collection of unique Irish art.

The MERRION

DUBLIN'S FINEST HOTEL

A member of *The Leading Hotels of the World*

Upper Merrion Street, Dublin 2, Ireland. Tel: 353 1 6030600 Fax: 353 1 6030700
email: info@merrionhotel.com http://www.merrionhotel.com

DEER PARK HOTEL & GOLF COURSES

14km from Dublin City/Airport on a quiet hillside overlooking the bay. Deer Park is an elegant 3 Star Hotel set in the tranquil surroundings of Howth Castle Demesne.
Featuring Ireland's largest golf complex 5 courses range from a 9 hole par 35 to an 18 hole 6,174 metre par 72.
All 78 rooms ensuite with TV and tea/coffee making facilities.
Luxury swimming pool, sauna and steam room.

**Deer Park Hotel and Golf Courses
Howth, Co. Dublin
Tel: 01 8322624 Fax: 01 8392405
Email: sales@deerpark.iol.ie
www.deerpark-hotel.ie**

THE COURT HOTEL
Killiney Bay, Co. Dublin, Ireland
Telephone: 353 1 2851622 Fax: 353 1 2852085
Email: book@killineycourt.ie
Website: http://www.killineycourt.ie
86 Rooms (all en suite).
AA ☆☆☆, RAC ☆☆☆, TB ☆☆☆, Egon Ronay Cuisine Award, Adrian & Golden Bell International Marketing Award for our Website.
Victorian Mansion situated overlooking the breathtaking Killiney Bay, with own DART rail commuter station to city centre, main train stations, and Dun Laoghaire Ferryport. Excellent standards of accommodation and Cuisine. The Court Hotel's International Conference Centre achieves standards reflecting those within the EU. Close to Leopardstown Racecourse and Woodbrook Championship golf course.

TUDOR HOUSE
Dalkey, County Dublin, Ireland
Telephone: 01 2851528 Fax: 01 2848133
6 Rooms (all en suite). RAC. TB ☆☆☆☆
Tudor House is an elegant listed manor house in secluded grounds offering period ambience and personal friendly service. The en-suite bedrooms are individually decorated and enjoy views of Dublin Bay. It is in the heart of Dalkey, a charming heritage town with Norman Castles and quaint harbours, excellent restaurants and pubs, yet offering rapid access to Dublin City.

DRINK IN THE VIEW

A VISIT TO THE HOME OF GUINNESS IS THE HIGH POINT OF ANY TRIP TO DUBLIN

THE NEW **GUINNESS** EXPERIENCE OPENS IN DECEMBER 2000. AT THE **GUINNESS STOREHOUSE** YOU'LL DISCOVER ALL THERE IS TO KNOW ABOUT THE WORLD FAMOUS BEER. IT'S A DRAMATIC STORY THAT BEGINS OVER 250 YEARS AGO AND ENDS IN GRAVITY, THE SKY BAR, WITH A COMPLIMENTARY PINT OF **GUINNESS** AND AN ASTONISHING VIEW OF DUBLIN CITY!

A VISIT INCLUDES: BREWING/ADVERTISING/THE ARTHUR GUINNESS STORY/TRANSPORT **GUINNESS** AROUND THE WORLD/BARS/GALLERY/STORE

GUINNESS STOREHOUSE – THE HOME OF **GUINNESS**

St. James's Gate Dublin 8 Ireland	WINTER OPENING HOURS	SUMMER OPENING HOURS
For further information:	1st October to 31st March	1st April to 30th September
00 353 (0)1 408 4800	Monday – Sunday	Monday – Sunday
Website: www.guinness.com	9.30am to 5.00pm (last admission)	9.30am to 7.00pm (last admission)

ADAMS TRINITY HOTEL
...may you never want for anything!

What better location in Dublin than the Adams Trinity Hotel. Located mid-way between Dublin Castle, Grafton Street, and Trinity College; it faces the vibrant Temple Bar area. Traditional style bedrooms have a perfect balance of opulence and modern comfort and are finished to an exceptionally luxurious standard. The Hotel features the 'Black and White' award winning Mercantile Bar and Restaurant, which is a favourite for Dublin's society lunches or drinks in the evening. This enormous three-floor venue with its magnificent decor, sweeping staircases and intricate design brings you back to the time of the Greek Gods. The Adams Trinity Hotel is small enough to offer all guests that same personal attention and warmth; it has that little something special.

Adams Trinity Hotel, 28 Dame Lane, Dublin 2
Tel: 01670 7100 Fax: 01670 7171

HARRINGTON HALL
70 Harcourt Street, Dublin 2, Ireland
Tel: 353 1 475 3497 Fax: 353 1 475 4544

Open for business 20th March 1998, awaiting classification. Harrington Hall, with its private parking in the heart of Georgian Dublin, provides the perfect location for holiday and business visitors alike to enjoy the surrounding galleries, museums, cathedrals, theatres, fashionable shopping streets, restaurants and pubs. Privately owned, meticulously refurbished to retain old world Georgian splendour while equipped to today's exacting standards. All rooms fully en-suite, direct-dial telephones, hospitality trays and internet facilities. Multi-channel; TV. All floors served by elevator.

30 Rooms (all en suite). ITB ☆☆☆☆

NUMBER 31
31 Leeson Close, Dublin 2
Tel: 00353 1 676 5011 Fax: 00353 1 676 2929

An award winning four star guest house right in the heart of Georgian Dublin. The former home of Ireland's leading architect, Sam Stephenson. Just a few minutes walk from St. Stephen's Green. An oasis of greenery tranquility, where guests are encouraged to come back to relax and feel at home at any time of the day. Vast breakfasts in the dining room or in a sunny plant filled conservatory. Recommended by the Good Hotel Guide, Bridgestone 100 Best Place, Fodors.

LONGFIELDS HOTEL
9/10 Fitzwilliam Street, Dublin, Ireland
Telephone: 01676 1367 Fax: 01676 1542
26 Rooms (all en suite).
AA ☆☆☆ ❀❀, RAC ☆☆☆, ITB ☆☆☆, RAC HC&R Awards, Egon Ronay Award for Fish Meat and Cheese.
Located in the Heart of Dublin's Georgian quarter, just off Stephens Green, Longfields is regarded as one of Dublin's finest small hotels. A quiet haven for the discerning visitor, Longfields makes an ideal base for forays into the capital's prime fashionable shopping areas. It is imperative to book in advance if you wish to dine in its renowned No. 10 Restaurant.

JACKSON COURT HOTEL
29/30 Harcourt Street, Dublin 2
Telephone: 01 4758777 Fax: 01 4758793
25 Rooms (all en suite).
ITB ☆☆ Superior.
Jackson Court Hotel is one of Dublin's newest hotels situated in the heart of the city, only a few minutes walk from Stephens Green. All rooms are en suite. The hotel has a lovely restaurant, busy bar and Dublin's No. 1 nightclub. The combination of local Dubliners and visitors from abroad lends the hotel a lively, cosmopolitan atmosphere.

Here's an invitation to visit some of Ireland's finest gardens.

Ardgillan Victorian Garden

ARDGILLAN DEMESNE,
BALBRIGGAN, Co. DUBLIN
TEL: + 353 1 849 2324 (Gardens)
TEL: + 353 1 849 2212 (House)

Fragrant Rose Gardens.
Restored Walled Garden
of herbs and vegetables
featuring an unusual fruit
alcove wall.
Period House furnished
in Victorian style.
Tea Rooms and Walks.

Garden open all year 10:00 - 17:00
Guided tour each Thursday at
15:30 during June, July & August.

Talbot Botanic Gardens

MALAHIDE CASTLE DEMESNE,
MALAHIDE, Co. DUBLIN
TEL: + 353 1 846 2456 (Gardens)
TEL: + 353 1 846 2184 (Castle)

22 acre Botanic Gardens
including a walled garden and
a fine collection of southern
hemisphere plants.
Magnificent Medieval Castle -
beautiful furniture & paintings,
Restaurant and Playground.
Fry Model Railway.

Garden open 1st May - 30th
September 14:00 - 17:00 daily.
Guided tour each Wednesday at
14:00 or by appointment.

Newbridge Demesne

DONABATE, Co. DUBLIN
TEL: + 353 1 843 6064 (Demesne)
TEL: + 353 1 843 6534 (House)

Walled Orchard Garden.
Delightful Georgian Manor -
fine interiors, original
furniture and Museum.
Traditional Farm with
farmyard animals.
Tea Rooms, Picnic area,
Walks & extensive Playground.

Demesne open all year.

For further information contact:
Dublin Tourism Enterprises on + 353 1 605 7754
Gardens managed & operated by Fingal County Council

Ardgillan Castle

Ardgillan Castle is one of Ireland's major East Coast visitor attractions, located 20km north of Dublin Airport. The Castle is set in 194 acres of rolling pastureland, woodland and gardens, overlooking the Bay of Drogheda.

Although referred to as a Castle, the residence at Ardgillan is a large country-style house with castellated embellishments. Originally named 'Prospect', the central section was built in 1738 by the Rev. Robert Taylor, with the west and east wings added in the late 1700's. Ardgillan remained the family home of the Taylors until 1961.

Open to the public as a Heritage House since 1992, visitors to Ardgillan are taken on a conducted tour of the groundfloor rooms of the house which are furnished and decorated in the Victorian style. The basement kitchen area is now also part of the guided tour and reflects the Edwardian years of the early part of this century. Upstairs in Ardgillan is reserved as an Exhibition space and offers a regular and varied programme of events. Amenities within the Castle also include Tea-Rooms, open in conjunction with the Castle and offer light snacks.

Ardgillan is also a joy for gardening enthusiasts. The formal gardens comprise a Rose-Garden and Victorian Conservatory originally constructed by the Scottish firm of McKenzie and Moncur in the 1880's for one of the Jameson properties. The Walled Garden is 2 acres in size, divided into five sections for plants, shrubs, fruit trees, vegetables and herbs. The woodland adjoining the walled garden is being developed after the style of William Robinson. Guided tours of the Gardens are available during the months of June/July/August on Thursday afternoons at 3.30pm.

Ardgillan Castle
Balbriggan, Co Dublin
Tel: (01) 849 2212
Fax: (01) 849 2786

Opening Times 1999
1st April to 30th Sept
Open Tues to Sun and Public Holidays 11am to 6pm.
Open 7 days for months of July and August.
1st Oct to 31st March
Open Tues to Sun and and Public Holidays 11am to 4.30pm.
Closed 23rd Dec to 1st Jan inclusive.

Admission
Conducted Tour of the Castle: £3 Adults
Also available Senior Citizen/Group/Family rates

Facilities
2 Carparks, Coachpark, Several picnic areas, toilets in the grounds & in the Castle, Tearooms in Castle, Coffee Shop in park (open June/July/August), Disabled access to Castle

Kylemore Abbey

Kylemore Abbey, home of the Benedictine Nuns is situated in the Kylemore Pass in Connemara. The house was originally built in 1868 by Mitchell Henry as a gift for his wife Margaret. The design is neo-gothic and the house displays all of the decorative features of the period.

The Benedictine Nuns bought the house in 1920 having fled their convent in Ypres, Belgium in 1917. They immediately set about re-establishing their international boarding school for girls (they had run a very successful school in Belgium for 300 years) which is still very much alive today.

Kylemore Abbey is open to visitors. Visitor facilities include a visitor centre, an exhibition housed in the main reception rooms of the house and a video which takes the visitor through the varied history of the house and the people who have lived here.

Visitors may relax in the restaurant or browse in one of best craft shops in the West of Ireland or one can stroll by the lake to the Gothic Church which is a miniature cathedral. The church which was built by Mitchell Henry in 1870 is considered a building of national importance and has undergone extensive restoration work which took over three years to complete.

At a seperate entrance is the recently restored Victorian walled garden. 6 acres enclosing a kitchen flower garden which has been carved out of a mountain and bog. It is truly spectacular to see. This has been the latest successful restoration project for the Benedictine Nuns at Kylemore Abbey.

OPEN ALL YEAR
(or on request)

VISITOR CENTRE
9.30 - 6.00

EXHIBITION/GOTHIC
CHURCH .
9.30 - 6.00

CRAFT SHOP
9.00 - 6.00

RESTAURANT
9.30 - 5.30

(The above times may vary slightly during the Spring and Autumn months.)
Reservations/Information:
Phone: 09541146
Fax: 095 41145

Ross Lake House Hotel

Rosscahill, Oughterard, Co. Galway, Ireland
Tel: 091 550109 Fax: 091 550184
email: rosslake@iol.ie www.rosslakehotel.com

Rosslake House is a wonderful Georgian house set in the magnificent wilderness of Connemara. Six acres of mature gardens surround the house creating an air of peace and tranquility. Hosts Henry and Elaine Reid have beautifully restored this manor house to its former glory. A high quality Irish menu is prepared daily featuring a tempting variety of fresh produce from nearby Connemara Hills, Streams and Lakes as well as fish straight from the Atlantic.

MOUNT FALCON CASTLE
Ballina, Co. Mayo, Ireland
Telephone: 096 70811 Fax: 096 71517
10 Rooms (8 en suite). ITB ☆☆☆ Guest house. Galtee Breakfast Award, Regional Winner 1994, Member of Blue Book and recommended by Egon Ronay.
Mount Falcon – a pleasantly different holiday, whether you wish to relax in the quiet comfort of a log fire or catch your first salmon on the famous River Moy. Mount Falcon prides itself on the friendly atmosphere, superb cuisine and the individual attention paid to all guests.

TRAVELLERS FRIEND HOTEL & THEATRE
Old Westport Road, Castlebar, Co. Mayo
Telephone: 094 23111/094 21919 Fax: 094 21919
15 Rooms (all en suite).
ITB ☆☆☆, Tourism Endeavour Award 1996.
Luxurious, family run, 3 Star hotel. Open log fires welcome you. We enjoy an enviable reputation for excellent cuisine, service, entertainment and theatre shows, executive style bedrooms all en-suite, with d/d phone, 12 channel TV and radio and hair dryer. Master suites and connecting family rooms available. Conference and banqueting facilities. Private car park.

SWEENEY'S OUGHTERARD HOUSE
Oughterard, Co. Galway, Ireland
Telephone: 091 552207/552142 Fax: 091 552161
20 Rooms (all en suite), 4 Four Posters. TB ☆☆☆
Sweeney's, a comfortable family-run country house managed by the third generation of the Sweeney Higgins family. 20 bedrooms, some with four posters, mature garden and beech trees. Ideal base for touring Conamara and Galway City. Fishing and golf nearby. Restaurant featuring seafood, lobster, oysters and local lamb. Cellar with 300 wines. Cosy bar and lounges. Dogs welcome

SKEFFINGTON ARMS HOTEL
Eyre Square, Galway
Telephone: 091 563173 Fax: 091 561679
23 Rooms (all en suite). TB ☆☆☆
The newly refurbished Skeffington Arms Hotel has been caring for guests for over one hundred years. The Hotel is overlooking Eyre Square within walking distance of rail and bus terminal. Our very popular bars and restaurant are justifiably renowned for their fine food and friendly service.

IMPERIAL HOTEL
Eyre Square, Galway, Ireland
Telephone: 091 563033 Fax: 091 568410
84 Rooms (all en suite).
RAC ☆☆☆, ITB ☆☆☆.
A three star hotel located in Galway city centre, adjacent to main shopping area, pubs and speciality restaurants. Hotel incorporates Times Restaurant and Blakes Bar. Friendly staff with an Irish welcome.

FLANNERY'S BEST WESTERN MOTOR HOTEL
(EEI) Dublin Road, Galway, Ireland
Telephone: (091) 755111 Fax: (091) 753078
136 Rooms (all en suite). TB ☆☆☆
Situated 2kms from the city centre, we provide the perfect vantage point for exploring Galway's cultural and historic wonders. We also provide a gateway to the pure, natural beauty of Connemara. Each of our rooms are comfortably furnished for all your needs, while our friendly staff wait to greet you with a true Irish welcome.

Royal Tara China

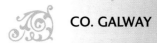

Tara Hall, home of Royal Tara China, was formerly the seat of the Joyces, one of the 14 tribes of Galway. The last occupant Colonel Pierce Joyce was an associate and intimate friend of the legendary Lawrence of Arabia and took part with him in the famous Desert Campaigns.

In 1953 it was the enterprise and initiative of yet another resident of Tara Hall which led to the establishment of this valuable industry at Mervue. Kerry O Sullivan founded Royal Tara China in the picturesque and historic surroundings of Tara Hall only minutes from Galway City centre.

Today the five showrooms are located in what were once the library and drawing rooms, and feature original fireplaces, one of which is made of Connemara marble and dates back to 1750. Fine plaster-work and original cornices and mouldings can also be seen throughout the house. Visitors may relax in the Georgian tearooms or weather permitting take tea outdoors overlooking the 3 acres of beautifully landscaped grounds.

The 300 year old art of china flourishes today at Tara Hall, where every item is handmade in the original methods by our craftspeople. The entire process takes 10 days to complete and each piece is handled 30 times over this period.

At our 17th century mansion new skills have been added to the delicate art of producing fine bone china and include an even wider offering which includes cold cast bronzes, crystal cast cottages and hand-painted cold cast porcelain figures, all of which adds a new exciting dimension to an already unique guided factory tour.

Royal Tara China
Visitor Centre
Tara hall
Galway
Ireland

Visitor Centre
Open 7 days all year
Jun - Oct 7 days
9am - 6pm, July/Aug/Sept
7 days 9am - 8pm, December
7 days 9am - 9pm

Tour Times
Free of charge
Mon - Fri All year
9.30, 10.30, 11.30,
12.30, 1.30, 2.30, 3.30

Groups welcome

Tel: 00 353 91 751301
Fax: 00353 91 757574

SHEEN FALLS LODGE
Kenmare, Co. Kerry, Ireland
Telephone: 00353 64 41600 Fax: 00353 64 41386
Email: info@sheenfallslodge.ie
61 Rooms (all en suite). AA ☆☆☆☆ (Red) ❀, RAC Blue Ribbon, TB ☆☆☆☆☆, Relais & Chateaux.
A haven set within 300 acres of magical woodlands and crystal cascading waterfalls. With its luxurious rooms, its reserves of ageing ports and its rare books, the lodge retains the warm, welcoming atmosphere of a country manor house. Outstanding cuisine and excellence in service combine to create an unforgettable experience.

PARK HOTEL KENMARE
Kenmare, Co. Kerry
Telephone: 064 41200 Fax: 064 41402
Email: phkenmare@iol.ie
50 Rooms (all en suite), 7 Four Posters.
AA ☆☆☆☆ (Red), ITB ☆☆☆☆☆, Egon Ronay Hotel of Year in UK and Ireland 1988, Michelin Star.
Deluxe Chateau style country house hotel beside the town of Kenmare and overlooking the estuary. Built in 1897 the hotel has won many awards for its Irish professional standards. Open Easter-Christmas and New Year. On Ring of Kerry and set in Ireland's Lake District. 1-800-964470 (UK), 1-800-525-4800 (USA).

KILLARNEY PARK HOTEL
Kenmare Place, Killarney, Co. Kerry, Ireland
Telephone: 064 35555 Fax: 064 35266
E-mail: info@killarneyparkhotel.ie
Website: www.killarneyparkhotel.ie
76 Rooms (all en suite).
AA, RAC ☆☆☆☆, TB ☆☆☆☆☆, AA Hotel of the Year 97/98.
This five star hotel is superbly located in the centre of Killarney town, literally a stone's throw from all Killarney has to offer, yet with the quietness, intimacy and privacy associated with times past. Guests can relax and enjoy the Grecian styled leisure facilities, the hotel's library, drawing room, billiard room, superb cuisine and first class hospitality. Conference facilities.

CARAGH LODGE
Caragh Lake, Killorglin, Co. Kerry
Telephone: 353 66 9769115 Fax: 353 66 9769316
Email: caraghl@iol.ie
Website: www.caraghlodge.com
15 Rooms (all en suite).
AA, RAC, TB ☆☆☆☆, RAC Best Small Hotel 1996, RAC Gold Ribbon 1999, Johansens Country House & Small Hotel Award 1999, RAC Gold Ribbon 1999.
Caragh Lodge sits on the shore of Caragh Lake, looking towards the breathtaking heights of the McGillicuddy Reeks. Surrounded by award-winning gardens. The en suite rooms are sumptuously decorated with period furnishings and antiques, whilst the dining room features only the finest Irish cuisine. The ideal base for golf, fishing or touring holidays.

Muckross House
Gardens & Traditional Farms

A visit to Killarney, or indeed Co. Kerry, is not complete without a visit to the world renowned Muckross House And Gardens. Situated on the shores of Muckross Lake, second largest of Killarney's three famed lakes, and set amid the splendid and spectacular landscapes of the Killarney National Park, Muckross House is a 'must' for every visitor to the area.

The House, a magnificent Victorian mansion, was built in 1843. The architect was Mr. William Burn who built many houses for the nobility in England including Knowsley for the Earl Of Derby. The elegantly furnished rooms portray the lifestyles of the landed gentry, while downstairs in the basement one can experience the working conditions of the servants employed in the House.

Skilled craftworkers at Muckross House use Traditional methods to produce high quality items of Weaving, Bookbinding and Pottery.

The gardens at Muckross House are famed for their beauty worldwide. In particular they are noted for their fine collection of Rhododendrons and Azaleas, extensive water garden, and an outstanding rock garden hewn out of natural limestone.

Using Muckross House as a base the visitor can explore and enjoy the surrounding national Park, which is Ireland's oldest National Park.

The latest development at Muckross House is an exciting outdoor representation of the lifestyles and farming traditions of a rural community in the 1930's. Three separate working farms, complete with animals, poultry and traditional farm machinery will help you relive the past. 'Muckross Traditional Farms' will take the visitor for a stroll down memory lane, to a time before the advent of electricity when all work was carried out using traditional methods. Meet and chat with the farmers and their wives as they go about their daily work in the houses, on the land, and with the animals. This is not a museum - but a real life working community carrying our their daily tasks as their forebears had done. Enjoy a trip on the Muckrose Vintage coach, complimentary to farms visitors.

KILLARNEY NATIONAL PARK holds much of interest, including, Muckross Abbey, a Franciscan Friary founded in 1448; unique Yew Woods and Oak Woods. The only native herd of red deer in Ireland, Dinis Cottage, the meeting of the waters, and other beauty spots, free exhibition and audio visual show.

Muckross House
& Gardens,
National Park,
Killarney,
Co. Kerry.
Tel: 064 31440
Fax: 064 33926

Kerry County Museum

Where History Comes Alive!

Kerry County Museum at the Ashe Memorial Hall is the ideal starting point for tours of County Kerry. It consists of 3 superb attractions which tell the story of Kerry and Ireland over 8,000 years:

Kerry in Colour - a panoramic multi-image audio-visual tour of County Kerry featuring scenery, historic sites, people and traditions.

Kerry County Museum - A museum with a difference ! Kerry County museum tells the story of Kerry and Ireland from the earliest evidence for man (c. 8,000 B.C.) to the present day, using the most modern interpretative techniques and display media. The fully air conditioned gallery is divided into 11 sections covering the recognised periods of archaeology and history, where the major technological, social and political changes of the period are discussed in simple terms. Each section contains lifesize reconstructions of daily life or important events, scale models, visual presentations, illustrated textpanels and priceless archaeological treasures and memorabilia which help to inform and entertain the visitor in a visually challenging and exciting environment. The museum also hosts major temporary exhibitions and an exhibition on Sport in Ireland over the last 100 years is planned for millennium year.

Geraldine Tralee - The Geraldine experience recreates medieval Tralee on a market day in the year 1450, and travelling there brings you into the world of the Middle Ages. The gateman grumbles about tolls and taxes as you pass under the portcullis of Tralee's town gate. The town merchants display their wares on shelves before their shop windows and a worman sets down a basket of fish which she hopes to sell from the street. Step into your time car and travel back in time through the reconstructed streets, houses, port, abbey and castle of medieval Tralee (on board commentary available in 7 languages). The sights, sounds and smells of market day in an Irish medieval town are faithfully reproduced, creating the unique experience that makes Geraldine Tralee a "must see" for visitors.

Opening Hours
10.00 - 18.00 hrs (17.00 Nov 1st - Dec 31st)
March 17 - December 31.
Closed Dec. 24-26, Jan. 1 - March 16.

Group Bookings
Kerry County Museum,
Ashe Memorial Hall,
Denny Street, Tralee, Co. Kerry, Ireland.
Telephone: **066 7127777**
Facsimile: **066 7127444**
E-mail:kcmuseum@indigo.ie

The Skellig Experience

The Skellig Experience Heritage Centre retraces the history of The Skellig Islands. The Skellig Islands off the Kerry Coast are renowned for their scenery, sea bird colonies, long lived lighthouse service, their Early Christian monastic architecture and rich underwater life. In any era of the past 1400 years, the name of Skellig has travelled to the ends of the known world.

The two Skellig Islands – Skellig Michael and Small Skellig stand like fairytale castles in the Atlantic Ocean, 8 miles south west of Valentia, County Kerry.

The Skellig Islands have been silent witnesses to many aspects of Irish maritime history. Irish mythology records an early reference to a shipwreck here nearly 3400 years ago. The King of the World is reputed to have visited the Skelligs in the year 200AD.

The Skellig Experience is a purpose build visitor centre opened in April 1992. The centre concentrates on four themes: The history and archaeology of Skellig Michaels Early Christian monastery; the sea birds, their habitat and world wide travels; the lighthouses which have given 161 years of service to mariners; and the underwater Skellig which has the colour and magic equal to any sea in the world.

Among the facilities at the centre is an 80-seater auditorium where a 16 minute audio visual takes visitors on a tour of the islands.

Cafe and retail area also available.

The Skellig Experience Heritage Centre,
Valentia Islands,
Ring of Kerry, Ireland
For further details
Telephone: 066 76306 or
064 31633
Fax: 064 34506
E-mail: cobhher@indigo.ie

Opening Hours
Apr, May, June & Sept (7 days)
10am, last admission 6pm; July & Aug (7 days) 9.30am, last admission 6pm; Oct (Sun through Thurs) 10am, last admission 5.30pm.

Admission Prices
Exhibition: Adults £3.00, Children £1.50, Senior Citizens/Students £2.70, Family £7 (2 adults and up to 4 children under 12).

Exhibition & Cruise: Adults £15.00, Children £7.50, Senior Citizens/Students £13.50, Family £40.00 (2 adults and up to 2 children under 12, £5 extra per additional child).

LANGTON HOUSE HOTEL
69 John Street, Kilkenny
Tel: 056 65133 Fax: 056 63693

This famous Kilkenny hostelry could justly be regarded as a national treasure. It has won Pub of the Year awards in 1986, 1987, 1988 and 1990. Its restaurant has won the National Restaurant Award in 1986, 1988 and 1989. Now open is a wonderful new hotel extension with the same standards of excellence that have made Langtons famous, complete with Executive rooms and two penthouses. The new Langton House completes the award-winning picture.

SLANEY MANOR
FERRYCARRIG, WEXFORD
Tel: 053 20051 Fax: 053 20510

Slaney Manor was built by the Percival family in the 1820s and it later became the home of Admiral Beatty of Jutland. It has retained all the characteristics of 19th century affluent country living. The Manor House occupies an elevated site of 30 hectares with magnificent views of the Slaney valley. The hotel is conveniently located for Wexford Town, Johnstown Castle & Gardens, Irish National Heritage Park and the John F. Kennedy Park and Arboretum.

Berkeley House
DeLuxe Guest Accommodation
5 Lower Patrick St.,
Kilkenny, Ireland
Tel: 056 64848 Fax: 056 64829

At Berkeley House we strive to be leaders in our field and spare no effort to provide friendly, clean, efficient and comfortable accommodation for our guests. All rooms are en-suite with television, telephone and tea/coffee facilities. Parking is provided to the rear of the building.

IN THE VERY **OF THE CITY**

HOTEL KILKENNY
College Road, Kilkenny
Telephone: 056 62000 Fax: 056 65984
103 Rooms (all en suite).
Hotel Kilkenny is situated in award winning landscaped gardens, just 5 minutes walk from medieval Kilkenny. The hotel has completed a major development project to include a new 5 star health and fitness club with a 20m pool, the refurbishment of all of the bedrooms, and the bar and lobby areas, and new stone conservatory to the front of the original Rosehill House. The all new Hotel Kilkenny. Why resort to less?

THE RISING SUN
Mullinavat, Co. Kilkenny, Ireland
Telephone: 051-898173 Fax: 051 898435
10 Rooms (all en suite).
A family run guesthouse, 8 miles from Waterford City on the main Waterford - Dublin road. It has 10 luxurious bedrooms all en-suite with D/O telephone and TV. The Rising Sun Guesthouse is the ideal base for sports enthusiasts, surrounded by some beautiful golf courses within 15 - 30 mins drive. The old world charm of stone and timberwork sets the tone of comfort and relaxation in the bar and lounge. Traditional home cooked lunches and bar food served daily.

BRANNIGANS GLENDINE INN
Castlecomer Road, Kilkenny, Ireland
Telephone:056 21069 Fax: 056 65897
7 Rooms (all en suite).
TB ☆☆.
Fully licensed tavern for over 200 years with 7 bedrooms, all en-suite. Located 200m from Kilkenny Golf Club and only 0.5km from the historic city of Kilkenny. We assure you of a friendly welcome.

Kilkenny Castle

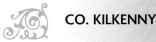

Kilkenny Castle has been standing for over eight hundred years, dominating Kilkenny city and the south-east of Ireland. It was originally built as the symbol and reality of Norman control in the area, and it has continued throughout the many different periods of Irish history to symbolise the fortunes of one of the most powerful Irish families, The Butlers of Ormonde.

The Butler Family – Dukes, Marquesses and Earls of Ormonde, bought the Castle in 1391 and it was to be their principal seat until 1935. They were a remarkable family, resilient, politically astute and faithful to the Crown and to Ireland after their fashion. When the Butlers prospered, Kilkenny Castle was rebuilt and redecorated; when they fell from grace, it became run-down and dilapidated.

Today, it is in state care and set in extensive parkland. Two wings of the Castle have been restored to their nineteenth century splendour. The final phase of restoration is now complete and includes the medieval South Tower and a conference centre. The river wing also houses the Butler Gallery – a modern art gallery.

Address
Kilkenny Castle
Kilkenny,
Ireland
Tel: 056 21450
Fax: 056 63488

Opening Times
Apr to May
10.30-17.00 every day
June to Sept
10.00-19.00 every day
Oct to Mar
Tues to Sun 10.30-12.45
& 14.00-17.00
(Closed Mon from October 1st
to March 31st). Closed over
Christmas and on Good Friday
Last admission 1 hour before
closing. Access by guided
tour only. Group Bookings
must be made in advance.

Facilities
Film presentation (English),
Bookshop, Tea-room (May-
Sept) and Gardens.

389

Rothe House

As a centre of civilisation and culture for more than a millennium, Kilkenny offers a unique selection of historic sites and buildings from the seventh century A.D. onwards. These reflect the city's status and heritage as 'Ireland's Medieval Capital'.

Rothe House is an example of a typical middle class house of the Tudor period. It was built by a rich merchant, John Rothe and his wife Rose Archer during the years 1594-1610. Rothe placed his arms and those of his wife over the main gate, where they may still be seen. In his 'great stone mansion' he and his wife had twelve children.

In a detailed will made one year before his death in 1620, Rothe gives us a clear picture of his family, his house and his property. The family lived here in some splendour and there is much evidence of music and literature. There were two sunny courtyards for recreation and leisure. In the second courtyard may be seen the only source of water, the well, with its well-house of 1604. Also in this courtyard there is a reconstructed megalithic tomb moved here for preservation.

The newly restored building contains the great common kitchen, the bakery and the brewhouse. Kilkenny Archaeological Society bought the property in 1960. The building contains an interesting collection of pictures and artefacts relating to Kilkenny's past. The reception room has some fine oak furniture and charming pictures. There is a fascinating museum collection which includes an extensive collection of costumes.

Family history research assistance is provided by Kilkenny archaeological society, at Rothe House, in tracing ancestors whose roots lie in the Kilkenny area.

Rothe House
Parliament Street,
Kilkenny
Tel: 056 22893

2000 Admission charges
Adult IR£2.00, Seniors and
Students IR£1.50,
Children IR£1.00.

Castle Oaks House Hotel
Holiday Village & Country Club

Ireland's "Shannon Region" proudly presents "A Little Piece of Heaven". This unique Georgian mansion is situated in the small picturesque village of Castelconnell, just 6 miles from Limerick City, off the main Dublin Road (N7). Sitting on 25 acres of mature and landscaped gardens and grounds, the Castle Oaks House Hotel and Holiday Village commands a spectacular view of the surrounding River Shannon, on the banks of the famous Castleconnell Fishery and boasts miles of beautiful riverside and wooded walks. All the luxurious appointed 20 bedrooms are furnished to compliment their unique style. Enjoy a pre-dinner drink in our "Island Bar" before sampling our Chef's delights in the "President's Room" of the Acorn Restaurant. Guests can enjoy the Country Club facilities which include a heated indoor swimming pool, sauna, steam room and jacuzzi, fully equipped gymnasium and 2 outdoor floodlit tennis courts. Located on the grounds you will find our 24, 3 bedroom, Self Catering Holiday Village houses, the perfect alternative to hotel accommodation, which also carries a 3 star rating from Board Failte.

Castle Oaks House Hotel
Holiday Village & Country Club
Castleconnell, Co. Limerick, Ireland.
Tel: 061 377666 Fax: 061-377717

Email: info@castle-oaks.com   Website: www.castle-oaks.com

WOODFIELD HOUSE HOTEL
Ennis Road, Limerick, Ireland
Telephone: 061 453022 Fax: 061 326755
26 Rooms (all en suite).
ITB ☆☆☆.
Woodfield House Hotel is a charming old world hotel. The hotel is small and intimate and consists of 26 bedrooms with en-suite facilities. Ground floor accommodation available for disabled guests. The hotel has its own private car park and is situated on the main road to Shannon and the west of Ireland.

HANRATTY'S HOTEL
5 Glentworth Street, Limerick
Telephone: 061 410999 Fax: 061 411077.
22 Rooms (all en suite). ITB ☆☆
Hanratty's Hotel, founded in 1796, is Limerick's oldest hotel, steeped in folklore and history. Situated in the centre of Limerick's lively, cultural and social life, within walking distance of the year-round Link Theatre, the Cinema complex, and within a few minutes' drive of the prestigious concert hall at the University of Limerick. Nightlife action flourishes around Hanratty's. In Limerick Hanratty's Hotel is central to every facility and service. This strategic location at the centre of the city which has made Hanratty's the choice hotel for more than 200 years, which has enhanced with growth and development of Limerick.

Glin Castle
The home of the Knight of Glin

Glin Castle is a member of Ireland's Blue Book

The 29th Knight of Glin and Madam FitzGerald welcome you to their home.

Glin Castle. stands proudly in the middle of its 500 acre wooded demesne on the banks of the river Shannon. The toy-fortress like quality is echoed by its three sets of battlemented Gothic folly lodges, one of which is a tea and craft shop.

The present Glin Castle which succeeds the medieval ruin in the village of Glin was built in the late 18th century with entertaining in mind. The entrance hall with a screen of Corinthian pillars has a superb neoclassical plaster ceiling and the enfilade of reception rooms are filled with a unique collection of Irish 18th century mahogany furniture. Family portraits and Irish pictures line the walls and the library bookcase has a secret door leading to the hall and the very rare flying staircase.

After a stroll in the well-kept pleasure grounds and walled garden, or the woodland walk to the grotto, the Sitting room with a crackling wood fire makes an ideal cosy gathering place for drinks before dinner.

The Diningroom windows catch the setting sun reflected in the river in the evenings. This room is filled with baronial oak furniture and a gallery of former Knights inclucling a number of notable eccentrics such as "the Knight of the Women" and "the Big Knight".

Across the hall, the Drawingroom has an Adam period ceiling, a beautiful Bossi chimneypiece and six long windows which overlook the croquet lawn. After-dinner coffee and conversation frequently takes place here.

Upstairs there are individual sets of bedrooms, bathrooms and dressing rooms. Wall-to-wall carpets are scattered with rugs, and chaises longues stand at the end of comfortable, plump, chintz-covered beds. Pictures and blue and white porcelain plates adorn the walls. The bedrooms at the back of the castle overlook the garden, while those at the front have a view of the river.

For Accomodation Rates Contact.

Glin Castle
Glin, Co Limerick
Ireland

Tel: 068 34112
Fax: 068 34364
Email: knight@iol.ie

Discover the true Essence of Irish Heritage

TOWNS AND VILLAGES IN IRELAND HAVE BEEN DESIGNATED HERITAGE TOWNS BECAUSE OF THEIR UNIQUE CHARACTER PROVIDED BY A COMBINATION OF ARCHITECTURE STYLES, OFTEN SPANNING MANY CENTURIES: WHICH GIVES THEM - AND THEIR VISITORS - A SPECIAL FEELING FOR THE PAST. WHY NOT VISIT THE HERITAGE CENTRE IN MANY OF THE TOWNS OF IRELAND.

Architecture

See original town walls, cathedrals, round towers medieval buildings and traditional shop pub fronts.

Saints and Religion

Discover the history of pagan Ireland, early Christianity, the missionary spirit of Abbeyleix and see the legacy today of their buildings. These towns were the early centre of learning in a land of Saints and Scholars.

Emigration and Famine

A visit to Cobh and many others towns will tell the story of thousands of Irish who left their native land - some never reach their destiny - some never to return.

Building a Nation

Learn about the High Kings in Cashel, Ballina/Killaloe. The invasion and conquest from the Vikings to fortifications, the Anglo Irish contributed to Ireland's Heritage. From our scientific and georgian heritage of Birr, to planned towns, Westport, Abbeyleix and Lismore, there are many many stories to be experienced in our Towns.

Making a Living

The maritime heritage from Wexford, Dalkey, Youghal, the wine port of Kinsale, the seaside town of Kilrush to Clew Bay Westport.

HERITAGE TOWNS
of Ireland

For further Information and a detailed listings of towns and what's on contact:
Central Reservations, City Hall, Cashel, Co. Tipperary,
Tel: (00 353 62) 62511 Fax: (00 353 62) 62068
OR PICK UP A BROCHURE AT ANY TOURIST OFFICE.

The Hunt Museum

One of Europe's greatest private collections of works of art from antiquity to the 20th Century is on view in the Hunt Museum, Limerick.

The Hunt Museum houses a unique collection of some 2,000 original works of Art and Antiquity collected by John and Gertrude Hunt over their lifetimes. The wide ranging and fascinating collection reflects the interests and expertise of the collectors – the Hung Collection is particularly well known for its religious works of art, but there is a wealth of material from the ancient civilisations of Egypt, Greece and Rome. Among the many important works of Art in the Collection are the personal seal of Charles I, King of England, the Mary Queen of Scots Cross, a coin revered since the middle ages as being one of the 30 pieces of silver and a bronze horse by Leonardo da Vinci. There are also paintings by Renoir, Picasso, O'Conor and Yeats.

During your visit to the museum you will explore the Collection and the lives of the collectors through an interactive display and interpretation of the Collection. While chronological and thematic groupings are presented, often the objects are mixed together, because they look good. This was how they resided during their life as a private collection in the Hunt family home, giving the museum a comfortable and domestic feel, which has proved popular with our visitors. A significant feature is the use of drawers in the display cabinets, which allows the visitor to explore the objects. Open one drawer to discover a Picasso, a neighbouring drawer to find Neolithic axes. Guided tours and informal tours are available on a daily basis.

The museum is housed in the old Custom House, one of Limerick's finest Georgian Buildings on the banks of the River Shannon. It has been sensitively restored and renovated. Designed by Davis Dukart in 1765, and completed in 1769, the building occupies one of the best city riverside locations in Ireland. Our garden opens onto the Custom House Quay and Park and the adjacent Potato Market can be accessed by a footbridge across the Abbey River. Views from the museum galleries of the River Shannon's Curragour Falls are magnificent.

Facilities of the museum are second to none, the museum gift shop stocks unique gifts inspired by the Hunt Collection and quality Irish crafted goods and our restaurant is renowned for its food and friendly atmosphere.

Address
The Hunt Museum
The Custom House
Rutland Street
Limerick

Tel: +353 61 312833
Fax: +353 61 312834
Email:
info@huntmuseum.com

Open all year round:
Mon to Sat 10am-5pm
Sun 2pm-5pm

Admission
Adult IR £4.20
Child IR£2.00
Family IR £10

Birr Castle Demesne
Voyage of Discovery

Birr Castle Demesne hosts the largest gardens in the country, with Formal Garden, thousands of rare trees and plants, rivers, lake and waterfalls.

In the grounds, the Great Telescope (1840s), the largest in the world for 70 years.

The new Ireland's Historic Science Centre features the many pioneering achievements of the Parsons family and of other great Irish scientists in the fields of astronomy, photography, engineering and horticulture.

Birr, Co. Offaly, Ireland

www.birrcastle.com

BROSNA LODGE HOTEL
Banagher on the Shannon, Co. Offaly, Ireland
Telephone: 0509 51350 Fax: 0509 51521
14 Rooms (all en suite).
TB ☆☆. Best new Inn. McGabnann's Bar.
Our country house hotel close to the banks of the River Shannon, welcomes guests with superb hospitality and relaxed elegance. 14 recently refurbished bedrooms, all en-suite, compliments the exquisite food and service in Snipes Restaurant. Serene mature gardens surround the hotel. With unique peat bogs, mountains, the River Shannon and Clonmacroise you will delight in this gentle and little known part of Ireland. Fishing, golf, pony trekking, nature and historical tours can be arranged locally. Brosna Lodge Hotel in Banagher. A beautiful place to stay.

KNOCKLOFTY COUNTRY HOUSE HOTEL
Knocklofty, Clonmel, Co. Tipperary, Ireland
Telephone: (052) 38222/38353 Fax: (052) 38300
17 Rooms (16 en suite). ITB ☆☆☆, Egon Ronay.
Formerly the residence of the Earls of Donoughmore, Knocklofty House dates back to the 16th century. Magnificent views of surrounding countryside and River Suir, of which guests can enjoy 1 mile stretch of private fishing. Oak-panelled dining room with excellent cuisine by award winning chefs. Ideal wedding and conference venue. Very relaxed homely atmosphere.

CASHEL PALACE HOTEL
Cashel, Co. Tipperary
Telephone: 062 62707 Fax: 062 61521

Located in the centre of the heritage town of Cashel, this lovingly restored Queen Anne style house, built in 1730, has become a charming internationally acclaimed hotel. Each room is individually decorated with fine paintings, genuine antiques and numerous personal touches. Surrounded by history, you'll savour the experience that will form a lasting impression.

13 Rooms (all en suite). 1 Four Poster. TB ☆☆☆

Castle Leake is a 15th century Norman Castle overlooking the River Suir two miles (4km) from Cashel off the main Tipperary/Limerick Road. The house is not grand but exudes a personal warmth together with convenience and hospitality. It is ideally located for fishing, golfing, hunting/horse riding, walking or doing nothing.

Dining tends to be communal with bedrooms, spacious and en-suite. Come to Castle Leake and experience the best of Irish Country Life.

Castle Leake
Cashel, Co Tipperary.
Tel: 062 61233

Tipperary Crystal

Tipperary Crystal was founded in 1988 by a group of ex-Waterford Crystal Master Craftsmen, whose desire it was to use their skills and expertise in the continuation of the art of crystal making, as traditionally practised by Irish craftsmen for hundreds of years.

Each piece of Tipperary Crystal is hand-crafted here on the premises and is of excellent design, superb quality and good value, all achieved with the same tools of the trade employed by master craftsmen of Ireland for over 200 years.

In 1990 Tipperary Crystal became the first Irish Crystal Company to be awarded the Quality Association of Ireland's 'Q' mark and the international Quality Standards ISO 9002 mark for its quality control system.

1991 began with the launch of Tipperary at Tiffany's in New York. This exclusive range of Crystal was designed by the renowned Irish Designer Sybil Connolly. Her inspiration came from the wooden trellis work on the exterior of the 'Swiss Cottage' in Cahir, Co. Tipperary, which was built for the earl of Glengall in the early 19th century.

Tipperary distributes its Crystal worldwide and has a warehouse distribution facility in New Jersey and accounts at Tiffany's and many other premium US retail outlets. Tipperary Crystal has also begun to attract large amounts of interest from the Far East, Asian and Australian retailers. For the past two years Tipperary Crystal has sponsored the Trophies for the Volvo Masters and matchplay events in Asia.

The Thatched Cottage home of Tipperary Crystal, in the scenic valley of The Slievenamon Mountains on the south east coast of Ireland, has become synonymous with the production of Fine Irish Crystal.

The design and layout of the factory and showrooms make Tipperary Cyrstal an ideal tourist attraction. Guided Tours provide the visitor with a window to the world of the skilled artisans of Tipperary as they produce breathtakingly beautiful Crystal items that can only be described as masterful works of art.

Tipperary Crystal has no hesitation in claiming that it's Crystal can be compared to any of the world's top crystal manufacturing companies, and are always working on ideas for new product ranges to add to their existing extensive range. And, if someday you find yourself in the County of Tipperary, we invite you to come by and watch us ply our craft.

Tipperary Crystal
Barrynoran,
Carrick-on-Suir,
Co. Tipperary, Ireland
Tel: 051 641188
Fax: 051 641190
Email: tippcrys@iol.ie

We are open all year round (opening times are included on our leaflet).

Admission Free

Guided tours run Apr-Oct.

Bureau de change and restaurant facilities.

Curraghmore
Portlaw, Co. Waterford
Tel: 051-387102 Fax: 051-387481

Magnificent home of The Marquis of Waterford and his ancestors since 1170. Outstanding Arboretum. Interior of house contains exceptionally fine plasterwork. Grounds include bridge built in 1205 for King John to cross River Clodagh and unique shell grotto built and personally decorated by Catherine Poer, Countess of Tyrone in 1754.

Location 14 miles from Waterford, 8 miles from Kilmacthomas, 5 miles from Carrick-on-Suir, 2 miles from Portlaw.

House may be viewed 9am-1pm Monday to Friday, January, May and June. Admission £4. Also to groups by prior appointment Monday to Friday year round.

The grounds and Shell House are open every Thursday and Bank Holiday between Easter and mid October between the hours of 2 – 5pm. Admission £3.

RICHMOND HOUSE
Cappoquin, Co. Waterford, Ireland
Telephone: 058 54278 Fax: 058 54988
Internet: http://www.amireland.com.richmond
9 Luxurious Rooms (all en suite).
Bórd Failte ☆☆☆☆, AA ☆☆☆☆, RAC Highly Acclaimed. Richmond House was built in 1704 and still retains an aura of old world elegance. This charming country house, managed by the Deevy family, provides luxurious accommodation and superb cuisine. Beautifully restored and renovated to the highest standards demanded by todays discerning traveller. A first class establishment, offering peace and tranquility. Richmond House is well worth a visit.

🎧🛏🍺 P 🍴 V ☑️ ⚓ ❀ 🚗🚘 SPECIAL 2 3 4 C

ROUND TOWER HOTEL
College Road, Ardmore, County Waterford
Telephone: 024 94494 Fax: 024 94254
10 Rooms (all en suite).
AA ☆ 63%, TB ☆, Member Waterford Tourism Ltd, Member West Waterford Good Food Tree.
Situated within walking distance of Ardmore's award winning beach, the Round Tower Hotel offers 10 well appointed en suite bedrooms. Fresh local produce feature prominently on both the bar and restaurant menus. The ancient monastic settlement, cathedral and round tower are situated behind the hotel.

RS 🎧🛏🍷 P 🍴 V ☑️ ⚓ ❀ 🚗🚘 SPECIAL 2 3 D

BALLYRAFTER HOUSE HOTEL
Lismore, County Waterford, Ireland
Telephone: 058 54002 Fax: 058 53050
10 Rooms (all en suite). 1 Four Poster
AA ☆☆ ❀❀, RAC ☆☆, TB ☆☆, Good Food Tree.☆☆
Ballyrafter House is an unusually attractive country residence built in the 1800's. The refurbishment of the house and individual style has retained its old world charm and character for today's visitor to savour. Established by the Willoughby family in 1966, whom continue to provide comfortable en-suite accommodation with traditional Irish and European cuisine. Ballyrafter House Hotel makes an ideal base for day trips to Blarney, Kilkenny, The Rock of Cashel, Killarney and the Waterford Crystal Factory.

🎧🛏🍺 P 🍴 V ⚓ ❀ 🚗🚘 1 2 3 4 C

DOOLEY'S HOTEL
The Quay, Waterford, Ireland
Telephone: +353-51-873531/2 Fax: +353-51-870262
e-mail: hotel@iol.ie www.dooleys-hotel.ie
113 Rooms (all en suite). AA ☆☆☆, RAC ☆☆, ITB ☆☆☆.
City Centre 3 star family run hotel. In Viking city of Waterford. Elegant restaurant and friendly welcoming staff. Comfortable 'Dry Dock Bar' with live musical entertainment nightly in season. Wednesday night is traditional Irish music night. Bar menu available all day. Visit Waterford Crystal show rooms. Hotel adjoining Waterford's Heritage Centre – a visit is a must. Land and water based activities available, ideal location for golfers. Latest addition: New Conference Centre.

RS 🎧🚭🎧🛏🍷🍴 V 🍽🚘 SPECIAL 1 2 3 4 C

Lismore Castle

Situated in the beautiful Blackwater Valley commanding a superb position overlooking the River Blackwater. This is one of the most delightful parts of Ireland.

Lismore Castle was originally built by King John who later handed it over to the Church. It remained as a Bishops residence until 1589 when it was acquired by Sir Walter Raleigh and then sold on to Richard Boyle, Earl of Cork in 1602.

It has been the Irish home of the Dukes of Devonshire since 1753 (when the 4th Duke married the daughter of the 4th Earl of Cork).

Much of the Castle dates back to the early 17th century but there are parts which date back as far as 1127.

The most recent rehabilitation of the Castle was undertaken by the 6th Duke in 1840.

ACCOMMODATION – The Castle is ideal for holiday parties or small business conferences of up to 16 people. The accommodation includes drawing room, sitting room, dining room, billiards room and banqueting hall for larger receptions. There are five double bedrooms, two twin bedrooms and two single bedrooms with eight bathrooms. The Castle is fully staffed including a butler and cook who uses the finest local ingredients in her excellent dishes.

RECREATION – Lismore Castle has its own Salmon, Sea Trout and Brown Trout fishing in the River Blackwater. The famous Careysville Salmon Fishery is also part of the Estate.

Deep sea and big game fishing can be arranged from Dungarvan, Youghal and Kinsale.

There is a nine hole Golf Course on the Estate and several other 18 hole courses in the area.

There are race courses within easy reach of Lismore. Hunting and riding can also be arranged.

There is a hard tennis court in the garden for the use of guests.

Not forgetting the wonderful walks along the river or on the Knockmealdown Mountains which are only about 10 minutes drive from Lismore.

The city of Cork is under an hour away by car where there is an opera house and theatre.

GARDENS – The gardens extending to over 7 acres are open to the public and are divided into two parts by the main drive. The distinctive feature of the lower garden is the peat soil which was brought three miles down from the Knockmealdown mountains to give the correct growing conditions for the magnificent specimen Camellias, Rhododendrons and Magnolias. Of particular interest is the Yew Walk planted in 1707.

The upper garden was laid out in 1626 and provides spectacular views of the Castle.

Lismore Castle
Lismore,
Co. Waterford
Tel: 058 54424
Fax: 058 54896

The Castle can be rented by private groups of up to 16 people when the Duke is not staying.

Rates (1999)IR£169 per person (IR£159 per person for groups over 12).
Min charge IR£1,200 per night. Charges are for half board plus afternoon tea. Lunches can be arranged if required.

LISMORE CASTLE GARDENS
Open daily from Mid April to Mid Sept, 1.45pm-4.45pm.

Admission Charges(1999)
Adults £2.50
Children (under 16) £1.50
Reduced rates for parties over 20.

MARLFIELD HOUSE

Gorey, County Wexford
Telephone: 055 21124 Fax: 055 21572
Email: info@marlfieldhouse.ie
Website: www.marlfieldhouse.com

Formerly the residence of the Earls of Courtown Marlfield was renovated by the Bowe Family in 1978. It is a regency period house filled with antiques and set amidst 35 hectares of woodland walks and gardens. Kitchen garden provides fresh produce for award winning restaurant. Five minutes to 18 hole golf course and sandy beaches. Wicklow 30 minutes, Kilkenny 1.5 hours.
20 Rooms (all en suite). 6 Four Posters. AA ☆☆☆ (Red), RAC Gold Ribbon award, Johansen's Country Hotel of the Year 1997. Good Hotel Guide, Cesar award 1996.

The Irish National Heritage Park

Stroll through this magnificent park with its homesteads, places of ritual, burial modes and long forgotten remains. Your senses come alive with the sights and sounds stretching back almost 9000 years. Discover how the Celts, Vikings and Normans came together, intermarried and formed Irish Society as it is today.

Opening Times:
March 1st – November 5th 9.30am – 6.30pm.
Times subject to seasonal change.
Last admissions 5.00pm. Open seven days.

The Irish National Heritage Park
Ferrycarrig, Co. Wexford, Ireland
Tel: 053 20733 Fax: 053 20911
Email: info@inhp.com Website: www.inhp.com

Danby Lodge Hotel

Killinick, Co. Wexford
Tel/Fax: 053 58191

Nestling in the heart of South County Wexford, Danby Lodge has rightfully earned for itself a reputation for excellence in cuisine and accommodation. Once the home of the painter Francis Danby, this 3 star guesthouse bears all the hallmarks of a charming country residence.

Conveniently located on the main Rosslare to Wexford road, Danby Lodge offers the visitor a quiet country getaway yet just minutes drive from the port of Rosslare and the town of Wexford.

Proprietors Raymond and Margaret Parle wish to make their home your home away from home.

AA & RAC Recommended

Powerscourt House & Gardens

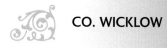

One of the World's Great Gardens situated 12 miles south of Dublin in the foothills of the Wicklow Mountains. The name Powerscourt drives from 'de la Poer' which was the name of the Norman family who built a castle here around 1300. In 1603 King James I of England granted the lands and castle to one of his generals, Sir Richard Wingfield, along with the title of Viscount Powerscourt.

The Wingfield family lived at Powerscourt for the next three centuries and built the present house and created the world famous gardens which stretch out over 45 acres. They are a sublime blend of formal gardens, sweeping terraces, statuary and ornamental lakes together with secret hollows, rambling walks, walled gardens and over 200 variations of trees and shrubs. Special features of the Gardens are the Japanese Garden, the Pepperpot Tower Folly, the Herbaceous border and the extensive range of roses.

A fire gutted the 18th century Palladian House in 1974 and it lay derelict for over 20 years. It re-opened in 1997 with an innovative new use for the shell of this great mansion, encorporating a terrace cafe, speciality shops and an exhibition on the history of the House and Gardens.

5km from the formal Gardens is Ireland's Highest Waterfall which has been a favourite family picnic spot for years. It was here that Lord Powerscourt introduced the first Japanese Sika deer to Ireland. Their descendants can often still be seen at dusk or early in the morning around the Waterfall area.

Powerscourt Estate,
Enniskerry,
Co. Wicklow
Tel: 01 204 6000
Fax: 01 286 3561

Opening Times
House & Gardens daily:
1st March-31st Oct
9.30am-5.30pm,
1st Nov-29th Feb
9.30am till dusk
Closed 25th & 26th Dec

Admission
Adults £6.00, Students/seniors £5.00, Children £3.00 (under 5's Free), Special rates for groups (20+) available, (separate charge for Waterfall)

Facilities
Terrace Cafe, Speciality Shops, Garden Pavilion, Interior's Gallery, House Exhibition

THE OLD RECTORY HOTEL AND RESTAURANT
Rosbercon, New Ross, Co. Wexford
Telephone: 051 421719 Fax: 051 422974
12 Rooms (all en suite)
AA ☆☆, ITB ☆☆, Member of Irish Family Hotels.
Centrally located in the sunny south east, set in mature gardens, overlooking the river Barrow and New Ross. Very comfortable bedrooms. Relax by the fire in our bar and enjoy an excellent meal in our cosy restaurant. James and Geraldine look forward to welcoming you to the warmth of a family run hotel. Open all year round. Live music every weekend.

BRANDON HOUSE HOTEL & LEISURE CENTRE
New Ross, Co. Wexford
Telephone: 051 421703 Fax: 051 421567
e-mail: brandonhouse@tinet.ie
60 Rooms (all en suite). AA ☆☆, TB ☆☆☆
A comfortable country manor hotel set in landscaped grounds overlooking the River Barrow. Dine in the AA award winning Gallery Restaurant or relax in the Library Bar. Leisure Centre with 20m swimming pool incorporating kiddies pool and fully equipped gymnasium and treatment rooms. Ideal base for touring counties Wexford, Waterford, Kilkenny and Wicklow.

FERRYCARRIG HOTEL
Ferrycarrig Bridge, Wexford
Telephone: 053 20999 Fax: 053 20982
103 Rooms (all en suite). AA ☆☆☆☆, ❀❀, RAC ☆☆☆☆, TB ☆☆☆☆. Tides Gourmet Restaurant.
Ferrycarrig Hotel boasts one of the most inspiring locations of any hotel in Ireland with sweeping views across the river Slaney estuary. Facilities include 103 bedrooms and suites, a 5 star health & fitness club with 20m pool, and 2 award-winning waterfront restaurants. The hotel is part owner of St Helen's Bay Golf Club. Ferrycarrig Hotel, the peace of Ireland you've been dreaming of.

GORMANSTOWN MANOR
Farm Guest House, Near Wicklow Town and Brittas Bay, Co. Wicklow
Telephone: 0404 69432 Fax: 0404 61832
Email: gormanstownmanor@tinet.ie
10 Rooms (all en suite), AA QQQ, Bordfáite approved, Tourist Quality Services Approved.
A warm welcome awaits you at this charming family-run guest house with Irish hospitality at its best in Wickow, "The Garden of Ireland". Peaceful, relaxed atmosphere and wonderful surroundings including gardens, nature walks and superb personal services. Enjoy golf, gardens, heritage, sandy beaches, picturesque mountains, valleys, rivers and breathtaking scenery. We have T.V's and direct dial telephones in bedrooms. Golf driving range on farm and close to 20 golf courses. Early booking essential. Open all year round.

Avondale House

Avondale House is set in an estate of 500 acres of forest and parkland along the west bank of the Avonmore River. Built in 1779 by Samuel Hayes, a barrister, who represented Wicklow in the Irish House of Commons, Avondale passed to the Parnell family in 1795, and it was at Avondale on 27th June 1846 that one of the greatest political leaders of modern Irish history, Charles Stewart Parnell, was born. Avondale House is now a museum to his memory, and a major refurbishment programme has restored much of the House to its decor of 1850. Parnell spent much of his time at Avondale until his death in October 1891.

Avondale House is synonymous with the birth of Irish Forestry. The state purchased Avondale in 1904 and it was at Avondale that the first silvicultural experiment plots were laid out; along the lines of a continental forest garden. These plots generally one acre in extent can be seen today, flanking the magnificent Great Ride, which provides probably the most beautiful of Avondale's many walks.

Avondale too is rich in wildlife and as you stroll through the woods of Avondale watch out for many of the creatures which live there, the squirrel, the badger, the hare and the rabbit. Along the river walk one might spot the otter playing away on the muddy banks. The calls and songs from the trees above are no doubt coming from some of the ninety different bird species which have been spotted in Avondale.

Avondale House is open mid March to October 31st daily. Visitors are introduced to Avondale by way of a specially commissioned video, which describes the life of "Parnell of Avondale".

Avondale also offers a unique venue for business meetings, conferences and corporate functions and entertainment.

Only one hour from Dublin, Avondale has to be the most peaceful and tranquil setting for business or pleasure – where history and beauty blend for the perfect day out.

Avondale House, Rathdrum, Co. Wicklow
Tel: 0404 46111
Fax: 0404 46111
www@coillte.ie

Opening times
17th Mar-31st Oct
Daily 11am-6pm
Last admission 5pm.

Admission
Adults £3.25
Seniors/Students £3.00
Family (2 Adults +
2 Children) £8.75
Group rates available –
booking necessary.

Facilities
Restaurant (wine licence)
serving morning coffee,
light lunches, afternoon teas,
gift shops, picnic areas, car
parking, tree trails.

Scotland consists of the following regions:-

SCOTLAND
Aberdeenshire
Angus
Argyll & Bute
Clackmannanshire
Dumfires & Galloway
Dundee
East Ayrshire
East Dunbartonshire
East Lothian
East Renfrewshire
Edinburgh
Falkirk
Fife
Glasgow
Highland
Inverclyde
Mid Lothian
Moray
North Ayrshire
North Lanarkshire
Orkney Islands
Perth and Kinross
Renfrewshire
Scottish Borders
Shetland Islands
South Ayrshire
South Lanarkshire
Stirling
West Dunbartonshire
West Lothian
Western Isles

Scottish Tourist Board
23 Ravelston Terrace
Edinburgh, EH4 3EU
Tel: 0131 332 2433

London Office
19 Cockspur Street
London SW1Y 5BL
Tel: 0207 930 8661

TOURIST BOARD RATINGS

At the point of going to press many of our advertisers had not been advised of their new tourist board ratings which are now commended in stars rather than crowns.

Therefore, some of the establishments will be showing their new ratings in stars whilst others will be showing the old crown ratings.

All the hotels should now know their ratings and will be happy to let you know upon request.

The same applies to the various symbols for Bed and Breakfast, Guest House and Self Catering accommodation

For a detailed account of all ratings please contact :

British Tourist Authority
Thames Tower
Blacks Road
Hammersmith
London, W6 9EL
TEL: 020 8846 9000

SCOTLAND

Scotland's greatest attraction is, perhaps, it's magnificent scenery- sparkling blue lochs, majestic, craggy mountains, extensive heather covered moors, rolling hills and dense forests. It's a land of space and peace where nature-lovers will find species such as the red squirrel, red deer, wild cat, osprey, eagle, extinct elsewhere in the British Isles.

It's vast stretches of land and water also make Scotland a sportsmans' paradise. The angler can fish in the clear waters of loch, river or sea for trout or salmon, with a fair chance of a good and hearty catch. The golfer, too, will not want for somewhere to exercise his skills. Troon, Turnberry, St Andrews and Gleneagles regularly test the world's finest Golfers. There are 400 courses, many in beautiful coastal settings. The walker has an extensive choice

Crathes Castle, Banchory, Kincardineshire - Courtesy of the National trust for Scotland

Dunvegan Castle, Isle of Skye

of hills to climb and views to admire, while the avid mountaineer can aim for a multitude of snow capped peaks over 3000 feet, known in Scotland as riding "Munros". There is nowhere better in Britain to view weather changes as they move in spectacularly to engulf you. Pony-trekking is popular particularly in the South, and those with a keen eye can take a shot at grouse or deer (in season and under the watchful eye of the game-keeper, of course). Visitors who do not wish to participate in such sports can watch the Highland Games at different locations throughout the summer. They will see such specialities as tossing the Caber, highland dancing and massed pipe bands.

Most of the population lives in the south. Edinburgh (Scotland's capital city), Glasgow, Dundee, Aberdeen, Inverness and Perth are all fine cities with excellent museums, good art collections and exciting architecture. Many smaller towns and fishing villages are very quaint, frequently set against a backdrop of hillside, loch, glen, or harbour.

Ruined abbeys and castles, battlefields and stately homes provide a wealth of material for history and heritage lovers. Some areas have special connections with famous Scots - Bonny Prince Charlie, Rob Roy, Sir Walter Scott, William Wallace, Robert Burns and Robert the Bruce. Anyone with Scottish ancestry will instantly feel attracted to his or her clan, there may even be a family castle and certainly many family tales to relate.

A Whiskey Trail through the glens of the north enables the discriminating visitor to whet their palate on Scotlands' most famous and celebrated drink, or those addicted to bagpipes, the kilt or haggis will have no difficulty in finding them in this dramatic region of Scotland.

The Scottish Borders is one of the finest introductions to the nature and character of a country. The open space of green hills and rich farming plains with their network of well established fishing rivers indicate a land blessed with good architecture and unpolluted water.

The picturesque ruins of several

Blair Castle, Pitlochry, Perthsire

Above:
Neidpath Castle, Peebles, Scotland, film location of 'The Bruce'.
Below: Hawick Museum, Borders

abbeys bear witness to the turbulence of centuries of Border wars and religious strife focusing attention on a tapestry of history, heritage, culture and recreation, and this is a region inundated with fine houses, castles and museums to visit. Floors Castle in Kelso and home of the Duke and Duchess of Roxburghe is perhaps the largest inhabited castle in Scotland.

Abbotsford, near Mekrose, was built and lived in by Sir Walter Scott where the library holds over 9,000 rare volumes.

Lauder in Berwickshire is the home of Thirlestane Castle one of Scotland's oldest and most splendid castles whilst Mellerstain House, the home of the Earl and Countess of Haddington, is famous for it's exquisite plaster ceilings and wonderful art collection.

If you want to see where the English were defeated three times in one day then visit Neidpath Castle which towers over the River Tweed near Peebles. - Mary Stuart and Oliver Cromwell stayed there. Neidpath is one of many Scottish historic houses used as a film location. 'The Bruce' was a filmed at Neidpath, Duart Castle on the Isle of Mull was the location for 'Entrapment' and Floors Castle in Kelso was the home of Tarzan the Earl of Greystoke in 'Greystoke'.

Glamis Castle, Glamis, Angus

Traquair House is Scotland's oldest inhabited house and was originally a hunting lodge for the kings of Scotland. It has strong associations with Mary Queen of Scots.

Small towns like Kelso and Peebles, unspoiled in their rural setting, unveil to the visitor the timeless appeal of Scotland – breathing space, charming locations and friendly people, spirited and generous. All this is evident at the colourful festivals of the Border Ridings hosted in many towns.

To round off your historic journey through The Borders visit the Hawick and Jedburgh Museums - Drumlanrig's Tower, a 15th century stronghold of the Black Douglas, The Scott Gallery and Jedburgh Castle Jail and Museum offers an insight into law and prison sentences in the 19th century.

Turn north to Scotland's capital, Edinburgh, a stunningly beautiful city. Here nature's gift of volcanic rock as a site for castle and a medieval town, enhanced by enlightened municipal planning of

The Isle of Skye

magnificent gardens and Georgian architecture, has created visual splendour which has escaped the ravages of time. There is no finer stage for the world's biggest festival of arts and music. Take time to visit Lauriston Castle or take a walk in the Royal Botanic Garden, renowned for its plant collection, rock garden and with a Chinese garden in the making. There are gardens of all varieties throughout Scotland.

Edinburgh is beside the River Forth, close to small towns and villages which hug the coastline to the North Sea. Seaside means golf courses, all challenging and most open to visitors at reasonable cost.

Hisotric Houses in this region include Lennoxlove House in Haddington which dates back to 1400 and is situated on 600 acres to the south east of Edinburgh and Hopetoun, a magnificent House dated back to the end of 17th century and standing proudly in one hundred acres of glorious parkland.

St Andrews, across the Forth, has several courses to test the enthusiast. The Home of Golf, it is attractive and is home also to Scotland's oldest

Sunset over the bay of Oban, Argyll and the distant Isle of Mull

medieval university. The Fife coast has a ribbon of former fishing villages (the East Neuk) which are delightful and charming places to relax.

The pastoral landscape is marked in neighbouring Perthshire which gives a first glimpse of the Highlands. Perthshire, labelled "All of Scotland", really is a beautiful country with a fabulous selection of accommodation available ranging from hotels that number amongst the best in Britain to small and personalised B&B's. It is also noted for its "Rob Roy" connections as highlighted in the recent Hollywood Blockbuster starring Liam Neeson. Historic monuments in Perthshire include Blair Castle, where, twice a day, bagpipes can be heard echoing through the corridors of this 13th

Urquhart Castle, Lochness, Highlands

century stronghold. The last siege of a castle in Britain took place at Blair around 250 years ago - the year after Bonnie Price Charlie had stayed on his way south. The Castle stands on 130,000 acres which a includes a 70,000 acre deer forest.

Further on towards the north east and Royal Deeside you will surely wish to visit - the private home of the Queen and the Royal Family at Balmoral Castle, with the gardens open to the public in summer.

Balmoral in Ballater was purchased by Queen Victoria in 1848 whilst Braemar, a fortress situated in the Cairngorms on Royal Deeside, Duff House and Ballindalloch Castle in Banffshire and Delgattie which dates back to 1030 are all worth going out of your way for a visit.

Nearby, at the eastern end of the Cairngorm Mountains, the village of Braemar, venue for the Braemar Gathering, the best known of the Highland games.

Culzean Castle, Ayrshire

Scone Castle, Perthshire

Sixty miles along Deeside to Aberdeen, the award winning 'Britain in Bloom' city, endowed with public gardens and parks, granite architecture and wedding its ancient culture of fishing and farming to the modern oil industry. From the overnight trip to the Shetland Isles is an ideal introduction to Scotland's network of passenger and vehicle ferries most of which operate on the west coast. They reveal a unique world of mystical, timeless experience in the Western Isles. Lewis, Harris, Uist, Skye and Mull are but a few of these magical islands.

Orkney too is well worth a visit, famed for its Norse culture and pictish standing stones. Although it is easy to reach by sea and air these islands really are on the edge of British civilisation.

Aberdeen is also a base to embark on the only Malt Whiskey Trail in the world through the glens of the Livet and the Spey and their many famous distilleries. You can follow the signposts with their distinct 'pagoda

Ballindalloch Castle, Banffshire

roof' symbol and taste some of Scotland's finest whisky. The distlilleries include Glenlivet, Cardhu, Glen Grant, Glenfiddich Starthisla and Glenfarclas. It might be best to leave the car at home.

The next step of journey could take you to Aviemore, premier winter sport resort, one of five in Scotland, and then Inverness, the Highland capital. The most Northern city in Britain, Inverness has also enjoyed its fair share of historic moments through the ages, none more important to Scotland as the Battle of Culloden, which celebrated its 250th anniversary in 1996. This is one of the most beautiful areas of Scotland with the snow capped Cairngorm Mountains (the highest in Britain), Loch Ness with its mysterious Monster 'Nessie', and perhaps surprisingly some fine sandy beaches. The most remarkable geological feature is the Great Glen, a vast rift valley which splits Scotland in two: its three deep lochs are connected by the Caledonian Canal. The grouse on the heather covered moor and the red deer on the forested hillside provide game for the sportsman The landscape is littered with relics of Iron Age forts and

Torosay Castle, Isle of Mull

Bronze Age burial grounds such as the impressive stone cairns at Clava, ringed with a group of standing stones, Inverness also offers the same access to the Isle of Skye that the dejected Bonnie Prince Charlie chose in the aftermath of defeat. To the north the moors and hills of Ross-shire and Sutherland, to the west, Loch Ness with its famous inhabitant. Continue down the Caledonian Canal to Fort William and Britain's highest mountain Ben Nevis. The Region of Fort William and Lochaber must rank as one of the most sparsely populated areas in Britain and is blessed with spectacular scenery, a joy at any time of year.

The Western Isles, with a sea warmed gently by the Gulf Stream, and Argyll are also particularly recommended for the abundance of architectural, natural and living heritage and their accessibility to Glasgow. Loch Lomond is a must on any itinerary as is the whole of this central region that offers beauty, mystery and intrigue at almost every corner.

The tour includes the Pass of Glencoe on route to Glasgow.

Drumlanrig Castle, Thornhill, Dumfies-shire

Glencoe is a climbing and ski centre and notorious in clan history for the massacre of the Macdonalds.

Strathclyde, although dominated by Glasgow, is a softer more verdant region and Lanarkshire in particular is a delight. Visit the award winning New Lanark Mills or the fascinating Wanlockhead Mining Museum just outside Biggar. Glasgow itself has impressive art galleries and museums and a vibrant music and theatre lifestyle. Fashion is a major keynote in its extensive shopping facilities.

Above: Mount Stuart, Isle of Bute
Below: Duart Castle, Isle of Mull

Head for the Borders again through Ayrshire, home of the national poet Robert Burns who died in 1796. Ayrshire is also the reputed birthplace of Robert the Bruce, the future King of Scotland and hero to the nation and dotted throughout visitors can find relics and landmarks which make claim on the Warrior king Many respected his Immortal Memory on the bicentenary commemoration at his mausoleum in St Michael's Kirkyard.

Dumfries & Galloway is a vast region where the small indigenous population finds itself greatly outnumbered by sheep. Bordering England, Galloway has seen turbulence and cross border raids and, until quite relatively recent times, was deemed quite lawless. Things have changed now, of course, and the various American connections include the birthplace of John Paul Jones at Arbigland, where the coastal waters of the Solway Firth no doubt inspired the founder of the US Navy.

Despite the historic houses, castles, gardens, distilleries, despite the museums, galleries, lcohs and glens, perhaps the greatest attraction of all though are the people of Scotland whose warm welcome and charm is legend throughout the world.

Melrose Abbey, Roxburghshire, Borders

Baxters

VISITORS CENTRE
SPEYSIDE

Unique Shops and Restaurants

Culinary Theatre and Demonstrations

Old Museum Shop

The Baxters Experience & The Baxters Story

A Unique Scottish Experience

OPEN 7 DAYS A WEEK
9am-6pm April-October, 10am-5pm November-March
FREE ADMISSION

Free car and coach parking with facilities for the disabled.

W. A. Baxter & Sons Ltd. Fochabers, Scotland IV32 7LD

Tel: 01343 820666 Fax: 01343 821790

Why not visit us on the web at: www.baxters.com

Top:
Cawdor Castle, Nairn, Highlands

Middle:
Glasgow Art Gallery & Museum

Bottom:
Floors Castle, Roxburghshire, Borders

SCOTTISH
TOURIST BOARD
23 Ravelston Terrace
Edinburgh, EH4 3EU
Tel: 0131 332 2433

London Office
19 Cockspur Street
London SW1Y 5BL
Tel: 0207 930 8661

Kildrummy Castle Hotel

*Set in the heart of rural Aberdeenshire, 35 miles West of
Aberdeen, a 3 hour's drive North if Edinburgh, Kildrummy
Castle offers a rare opportunity to enjoy the style and
elegance of a by-gone era combined with all the comfort and
service of a modern first class hotel. The hotel overlooks the
ruins of the original 13th century castle and is adjacent to the
renowned Kildrummy Castle Gardens.
Our award-winning restaurant specialises in the use of fresh
local produce, fish and shell-fish from the Moray Firth and
North Sea, game from local estates and of course
Aberdeen Angus Beef*

KILDRUMMY, BY ALFORD,
ABERDEENSHIRE, AB32 8RA, SCOTLAND.
Tel: 019755 71288 U.S. Toll Free 800-325-5463
Email: bookings@kildrummycastlehotel.co.uk
www.kildrummycastlehotel.co.uk
STB ★★★★

Banchory Lodge Hotel

Banchory, Kincardineshire, Scotland
Tel No: 01330 822625
Fax No: 01330 825019

Banchory Lodge hotel is an historic building in the
picturesque setting which makes Royal Deeside a lovely place
to visit. The main dining room not only overlooks the river,
which runs through the grounds, but is also supplied with
fresh salmon by it. There are two dining rooms, the main
restaurant and a smaller room. The cocktail bar, with its open
fire, intricately carved oak panelling and original oil
paintings, provides a pleasant setting for aperitifs and for
choosing from the traditional menu. [B]

KILDRUMMY CASTLE HOTEL
Kildrummy, Alford, Aberdeenshire AB33 8RA
Telephone: 019755 71288 Fax: 019755 71345
Email: bookings@kildrummycastlehotel.co.uk
www.kildrummycastlehotel.co.uk
16 Rooms (all en suite), 2 Four Posters.
RAC ☆☆☆, STB ☆☆☆☆.
In the heart of the Grampian Highlands, 3 hours drive north
of Edinburgh, Kildrummy Castle offers the ideal base from
which to explore Balmoral and Royal Deeside, The Malt
Whisky Traill. Scotland's only Castle Traill, the Granite City
of Aberdeen, the Spey valley and Inverness.

[RS][icons...][SPECIAL] [1][2][3][B]

BALGONIE COUNTRY HOUSE
Braemar Place, Ballater AB35 5NQ
Telephone: 013397 55482 Fax: 013397 55482
9 Rooms (all en suite). AA ☆☆ (Red), STB ☆☆☆☆,
'Johansens Country House Hotel Award for Excellence 1997'.
AA Inspectors' Hotel of the Year, Scotland, 1994.
Set in its own 3-acre gardens, Balgonie is a lovely Edwardian
house offering high standards of hospitality, fine cuisine and
service. Balgonie makes an ideal base from which to explore
the rich heritage of Scotland's north-east with castles,
distilleries, gardens and areas of outstanding beauty all
within easy reach.

[icons...][SPECIAL][1][2][3][C]

UDNY ARMS HOTEL
Newburgh, AB51 0BL
Telephone: 01358 789444 Fax: 01358 798012
26 Rooms, AA ☆☆☆ ✿. STB ☆☆☆, Michelin.
The Udny Arms on the Ythan estuary is renowned for its
friendly welcome and award-winning food. Golfers have
three championship courses within 10 minutes' drive.
Nature lovers and anglers can enjoy the estuary and the
nearby nature reserve, while the whisky and castle trails are
also within easy reach.

[RS][icons...][SPECIAL] [1][2][3][4][C]

MELDRUM HOUSE
Old Meldrum, Aberdeenshire AB51 0AE
Telephone: 01651 872294 Fax: 01651 872464
Email: dpmeldrum@aol.com
www.meldrumhouse.com
9 Rooms (all en suite), 2 Four Posters, Private 18 Hole Golf
Course.
Meldrum House dates from the 13th century and stands in
15 acres of breathtaking countryside. This exquisite baronial
house, steeped in Scottish history, extends a warm welcome
to guests and offers traditional Scottish hospitality and
relaxation in the magnificent surroundings which are
complemented with many antiques, objets d'art and
ancestral portraits.

[RS][icons...] [SPECIAL][2][3]

Balmoral Castle

In 1842 Queen Victoria and her consort Prince Albert visited Scotland for the first time and so began a love affair with the country that has been passed down to successive monarchs ever since. The couple were particularly taken with the Highlands and received glowing accounts of Sir Robert Gordons small deeside castle at Balmoral. Not only was the scenery beautiful but the air was said to be unusually pure.

In 1847 Sir Robert died and encouraged by her physician Sir James Clark they seized the opportunity to negotiate for the property. In September 1848 they arrived to take possession of a property which they had never seen and they were not disappointed. Over the next few years the Royal Family were able to spend six weeks at Balmoral each Autumn and they were of course, by now, certain that the perfect holiday retreat had been found.

Many improvements were planned and then inspected each year that they returned. In 1852 it became obvious that Sir Robert Gordons 'very small house' could no longer accommodate the large household in attendance and the growing demands of hospitality. The City Architect of Aberdeen, William Smith, was selected to build a new castle 100 yards to the North West and on the 28th of September 1853 Queen Victoria laid the foundation stone. For two seasons the family stayed in the old house and the new Balmoral was ready for them in 1855.

'The whole house has a very fine effect' the Queen noted and Prince Albert was no less delighted. 'The way in which the building and grounds come out gives me much pleasure and surpasses my fondest expectations'. When the time approached for them to leave for the south, the Queen confided to her diary 'every year I seem to become fonder of this dear place, still more so, now that great and excellent taste has been stamped everywhere'.

After the death of Prince Albert in 1861 the Queen spent more and more time at the estate. Her ministers were less than happy that their sovereign chose to spend a third of the year 500 miles from London but the Queen found the solitude which she needed so much at Balmoral, so full of her happiest memories. Each of her successors has also become attached to Balmoral - the castle, the grounds, the stunning surrounding countryside and the warm affection of the local people.

Contact Details
Balmoral Castle
The Estates Office
Balmoral Estates, Ballater
Aberdeenshire AB35 5TB
Tel: 013397 42334 or 42335
Fax: 013397 42034
Email:
info@balmoralcastle.com
www.balmoralcastle.com

Opening Dates
Open daily from Thurs 12th
April until Tues 31st July 2001.

Admission
Adults £4.50
Seniors £3.50
Children (5-16) £1.00

Location
Off the A93 between
Ballater and Braemar

Facilities
Exhibitions, Gardens, Self-Service Cafeteria and Gift Shops. Also pony trekking and pony cart rides (when ponies are available).

The Marcliffe at Pitfodels

North Deeside Road, Aberdeen AB15 9YA
Telephone: 01224 861000 Fax: 01224 868860
Email: reservations@marcliffe.com
Web site: http://www.nettrak.co.uk/marcliffe/

Situated in 8 acres of wooded grounds and ideally positioned for visiting Scotland's scenic North East, is the new luxury Marcliffe at Pitfodels, owned by Stewart Spence and family.

Many of the beautifully appointed rooms have antique furniture and paintings; all have satellite TV and direct-dial telephones. There are two restaurants: The Conservatory serving breakfast, lunch (outside in Summer) and dinner; The Invery Room serves dinner only. Our chefs specialise in Grampian produce – Aberdeen Angus beef, game with fish and shellfish from local rivers and ports. The wine cellar holds over 400 wines and the Drawing Room bar is stocked with more than 100 malt whiskies.

Golf at Royal Aberdeen and Cruden Bay can be arranged, as well as salmon fishing, stalking and grouse or pheasant shooting.

Please write or phone for details.

THE CASTLE HOTEL
Huntly, Aberdeenshire, Scotland
Telephone: 01466 792696 Fax: 01466 792641
email: castlehot@enterprise.net
www.castlehotel.uk.com
18 Rooms (all en suite), 3 Four Posters.
AA ☆☆☆, STB ☆☆☆.
A magnificent eighteenth century building, former home of the Dukes of Gordon, standing in its own grounds, above the ruins of Huntly Castle, amidst tranquil surroundings. We offer good, comfortable accommodation in a relaxed atmosphere. Ideally situated for touring the whisky and castle trails for which the area is famous.

WATERSIDE INN
Fraserburgh Road, Peterhead,
Aberdeenshire AB42 7BN
Telephone: 01779 471121 Fax: 01779 470670
109 Rooms (all en suite)
AA ☆☆☆ ❀, RAC ☆☆☆, STB ☆☆☆☆, Egon Ronay.
Waterside Inn on the Ugie estuary is renowned for its hospitality and friendliness. This is complemented by its award-winning team of chefs. An over-indulgence can be worked off in the swimming pool. Golf tickets for three days plus Lighthouse Museum, Macduff Aquarium, Duff House and Maritime Heritage Centre to visit.

TOR-na-COILLE HOTEL
BANCHORY • ROYAL DEESIDE

Follow the Victorian Heritage Trail and find one of Deeside's best kept secrets

Once a Victorian House, the Tor-na-Coille Hotel is now a privately owned and managed Country House Hotel set in magnificent woodland on the outskirts of picturesque Banchory.

Heart of the Whisky and Castle Trail.

Award-winning Chef, formal and informal dining. Renowned for its native fare and hospitality.

Inchmarlo Road, Banchory, Aberdeenshire AB31 4AB
Tel: 01330 822242 Fax: 01330 824012
E-mail: tornacoille@btinternet.com

INVESTOR IN PEOPLE

SCOTLAND   AA 3 Star   4 Star S.T.B.

Pittodrie House Hotel

Dating back to 1480. Pittodrie House is the ancestral home of owner Theo Smith. Family paintings and antiques grace public room and bedrooms. In the gracious Drawing Room and Library log fires burn. Individual in decor all bedrooms preserve the atmosphere of a fine country house. 'Taste of Scotland' dishes predominate on daily changed menus. Within the 3,000 acre estate sportsmen are well catered for and facilities include, Squash, Tennis, Snooker, Table Tennis and Clay Shooting. A mere half hours drive from Dyce Airport, Pittodrie also has its own Helipad Grid Ref. 697239.

OPEN: All year NO. ROOMS: 27 all en-suite
ROOM TELEPHONES: Yes TV IN ROOMS: Yes
PETS: Yes CHILDREN: Yes DISABLED: Unsuitable
LOCATION: Off A96 two miles north of Inverurie –
take turn to Chapel of Garioch
SWIMMING POOL/HEALTH CLUB: No
CONFERENCE FACILITIES: Yes

Chapel of Garioch, by Inverurie, Aberdeenshire AB51 9HS
Tel: 01467 681444 Fax: 01467 681648

Braemar Castle

ABERDEENSHIRE

Situated amongst the magnificent splendour of the Cairngorms on Royal Deeside the strategic importance of placing a castle at Braemar was recognised very early in Scottish history.

The main outstanding years for Braemar Castle are in 1628 when the building of the Castle commenced by John Erksine, Earl of Mar, as a bulwark against the rising power of the Farquharsons. In 1689 during the short-lived Jacobite rising, the Castle was burned out by the Black Colonel, John Farquharson of Inverey and finally in 1748 it was restored as a garrison post by the Hanoverian Government to dominate the turbulent province of Mar. Within the framework of these dates history has swung a full circle: in turn a centre of Jacobite resistance and a seat of Hanoverian authority, the Castle that was built to overawe the Farquharsons of Invercauld is now in their ownership and was lived in by them for many years.

The L-plan Castle of fairytale proportions with its remarkable star shaped defensive curtain wall, also has a central round tower with a spiral staircase, barrel vaulted ceilings, a massive iron "yett" and an underground prison.

The rooms that are open to the public include the Dining Room which has many interesting features including a fine suite of Hepplewhite chairs and a sideboard of Adam design. The Drawing room, which is delicately decorated in pink has a fine carved fireplace and the relics of former Government troops who carved their names on the shutters. The Four-poster bedroom on the third floor is most attractive with its two semi-circular closets and it is said "The Green Lady" likes to leave her outline on the bedspread!

The Castle has many pieces of valuable furniture, paintings and interesting curios including the largest Cairngorm ever found.

The Castle grounds were the original venue for the Braemar Gathering up until 1906 when it became too small for the amount of visitors attending the Games.

Address
Braemar Castle
Braemar
Aberdeenshire
AB35 5XR
Tel/Fax: 013397 41219

Opening Times
Open 1st April to end of
October, Saturday to Thursday.
Friday opening in July
& August.

Admission
Adults £3.00 OAP's/Parties
£2.50 Children £1.00

Location
1/2 mile north-east of Braemar
on the A93

Facilities
Shops and grounds with
picnic benches/toilets

429

Raemoir
Royal Deeside

Tel: 01330 824884
Fax: 01330 822171
AA 76% 🏵🏵 for Food
RAC Restaurant Comfort Hospitality
Awards, Michelin

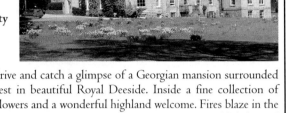

'Raemoir is an enchanted place'.

Wind your way up a long tree-lined drive and catch a glimpse of a Georgian mansion surrounded by 3,500 acres of Parkland and Forest in beautiful Royal Deeside. Inside a fine collection of antiques and paintings, profusion of flowers and a wonderful highland welcome. Fires blaze in the elegant reception rooms on cooler days and an air of timelessness and reassuring old-fashioned traditions are maintained.

The food served in the beautiful candlelit oval dining room is acknowledged by all the guides as the finest in the area.

The bedrooms are lovely and have all been interior designed by our in-house design team.

Surrounded by romantic castles such as Crathes and Dunnotter and the whole area is a treat for the imagination. Do come and visit us.

Caledonian Specialist Locations
Lower Courthill, By Tain, Ross-shire
Scotland IV19 1NE
Tel/Fax: 01862 892361
Email: andrew.ramsay@hemscott.net

For all your vacation needs contact us for a no-obligation quote. All types of vacations at very competitive rates. Packages are tailor-made. Individuals, couples, families or groups. See and stay in castles. Visit islands with 25-mile long beaches, traditional farming and fishing and stone-age sites. Visit seabird colonies. Golf, famous courses, beautiful cities etc. Prices are very competitive. High season from $1800 per 14 days including air, accommodation, car hire.

Atholl Hotel
54 King's Gate Aberdeen AB15 4YN
Tel: 01224 323505 Fax: 01224 321555

The Atholl Hotel situated in Aberdeen's residential West End has retained with its loyal clientele a relaxed and friendly atmosphere.

All 35 bedrooms have private bathrooms and have recently been extensively refurbished to provide the highest standard of comfort.

The stylish Oakhill and Beechgrove Suites cater for all types of functions and conferences up to 60 guests.

The Hotel has a reputation for fine cuisine and excellent friendly service, and the personal ownership with an eye for detail and high standards, ensures your stay is one to remember.

Scottish Tourist Board ☆☆☆

Duff House

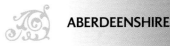

The north-east corner of Scotland, incorporating Banffshire and part of Aberdeenshire, is unknown to many but contains treasures awaiting discovery by the discriminating traveller.

One of the treasures is Duff House adjacent to the ancient and royal burgh of Banff and its near neighbour the burgh of Macduff. The House stands within wooded parkland near the spot where the River Deveron flows into the Moray Firth. With the sea on the north and the tree-clad Deveron Valley on the south Duff House has a dramatic and varied setting.

Duff House was commissioned in 1735 by the wealthy landowner William Duff of Braco, 1st earl Fife. His architect was William Adam who produced a sumptuous baroque design consisting of a four-storey central block flanked by curving wings which terminated with substantial pavilions. Sadly the complete design was never constructed as client and architect disputed building costs. This resulted in a court case which the client lost. By 1739 only the central block had been erected but was not completed internally.

The 2nd Earl Fife furnished the interior and thereafter the House was used by succeeding generations of the Duff family as one of their several residences. The 6th Earl Fife married Princess Louise, the eldest daughter of the future King Edward VII in 1889, and ten years later he was created Duke of Fife.

In 1906 the Duke presented Duff House to the burghs of Banff and McDuff for their mutual benefit. Initially the House was leased as a hotel and part of the surrounding parkland was laid out as a golf course. This is still used by the Duff House Royal Golf Club. Between 1913 and 1923 Duff House became a sanitorium specialising in the treatment of diabetes. With the outbreak of the Second World War the House was requisitioned by the government and adapted as a prisoner of war camp. Part of the House was bombed in July 1940 resulting in the death of several German prisoners. Thereafter it stopped being a prison and was occupied by Norwegian and Polish troops.

Duff House stood derelict for several years after the War until 1952 when a scheme of repair and maintenance was undertaken. By 1985 there was limited public access to unfurnished rooms. Under the combined partnership of Historic Scotland, the National Galleries of Scotland and the local authorities Duff House was completely refurbished and opened in 1995 as a Country House Gallery. The visitor can now see period furnishings and a collection of paintings, many by renowned Scottish and foreign artists. Special exhibitions, outdoor events, lectures and musical recitals are held at advertised times throughout the year.

Address
Duff House
Banff AB45 3SX
Tel: 01261 818181
Fax: 01261 818900

Opening Times
April-October
Daily from 11am-5pm
November-March
Thursday to Sunday from
11am-4pm
2000 – Same times.

Admission
Adults £3.50
Concession £2.50
Family £8.50
Group prices available

Location
45 miles north of Aberdeen.

Facilities
Tearoom, shop, woodland walks, childrens' play area, car park.
Entry is free to all facilities.
Disabled access throughout the House.

Heritage Britain

**Hotels, Inns, Bed & Breakfast
Historic Houses, Castles & Gardens,
Antiques & Curios,
Arts & Crafts, Books & Tours**

Welcome to Heritage Britain, a brand new website with more than 2000 years of history and culture. Whatever your interest in Britain, we aim to help you find out more within these pages.

Visit the definitive heritage site and discover the history behind Britain and Ireland's long and colourful past.

Stay in a splendid country house hotel or a medieval inn and savour the delights of the British countryside or a historic British town.

Travel back in time by visiting the myriad of historic houses, castles and gardens or museums and galleries that adorn this Sceptred Isle

Scour the local shops or fairs for arts and crafts, antiques, collectables, curios or objets d'art.

You can even contact a genealogist to help you trace your family tree.

Heritage Britain - the essential website for domestic travellers and overseas visitors to Britain and Ireland.

**www.heritagebritain.com
mail@heritagebritain.com**

WATERSIDE INN
Fraserburgh Road, Peterhead,
Aberdeenshire AB42 7BN
Telephone: 01779 471121 Fax: 01779 470670
109 Rooms (all en suite)
AA ☆☆☆ ❀, RAC ☆☆☆, STB ☆☆☆☆, Egon Ronay.
Waterside Inn on the Ugie estuary is renowned for its hospitality and friendliness. This is complemented by its award-winning team of chefs. An over-indulgence can be worked off in the swimming pool. Golf tickets for three days plus Lighthouse Museum, Macduff Aquarium, Duff House and Maritime Heritage Centre to visit.

RS 🚭 📵 🛏 ⚲ ☕ P ⑾ V GF SP ⤳ ↦ ❀
SPECIAL 2 3 C

MARYCULTER HOUSE HOTEL
South Deeside Road, Maryculter, Aberdeen
Telephone 01224 732124 Fax: 01224 733510
23 Rooms (all en suite).
AA ☆☆☆, RAC ☆☆☆, STB ♛♛♛, AA Rosette for Food.
13th century country house hotel in 5 acres of woodland grounds on the banks of the River Dee. Award winning cuisine complemented by an extensive wine list and malt whisky collection. Individual bedrooms many with river views. Beautiful Royal Deeside and vibrant Aberdeen on the doorstep.

RS 🚭 📵 🛏 ⚲ ☕ P ⑾ V GF ⤳ 🚗 🏠 SPECIAL
1 2 3 4 C

Delgatie Castle

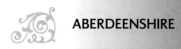

Dating from about 1030 the Castle's rich heritage is intertwined with Scotland's history.

The home of the late Capt. Hay of Delgatie, Fuedal Baron, the Castle has largely been in the Hay family most of the last 650 years since it was taken from the Earl of Buchan in 1314 after the Battle of Bannockburn, when Robert the Bruce routed the invading English army.

The original painted ceilings dating from 1592 and 1597 are considered some of the finest in Scotland. Strange animals are depicted, some with human heads, thought to represent the actual inhabitants of the time.

The turnpike stair of 97 treads is reputed to be one of the widest in Scotland, measuring over five foot and is unuaual for being built within the thickness of the wall.

Capt. Hay, having returned from service in the Indian Army, bought the castlt two years after architects deemed it was too far gone to save and he embarked on the mammoth task of restoration. Even after forty years of planning and painstaking effort, improvement and refurbishing continues.

Delgatie Castle
Delgatie Turriff
Aberdeenshire
Tel/Fax: 01888 563479

Opening times
2 April to 24 Oct,
10am-5pm daily

Admission
Adults £3.00
Concessions £2.00
Children under 5 free

Facilities
Tearoom, shop, woodland
and lochside walks, car park
and picnic area.

Location
2 miles north of Turriff on
A947 Delgaty Road.

THE LINKS

**Mid Links, Montrose,
Angus DD10 8RL
Scotland
Tel: 01674 671000
Fax: 01674 672698
www.linkshotel.com**
AA ☆☆☆, S.T.B. ☆☆☆☆

The Links Hotel, Montrose, is situated in a Scenic Coastal Town, on the A92 Tourist Trail Aberdeen - Dundee and is ideally located for anglers, general touring around the historic Scottish Glens and Highlands and is in the heart of Scotland's Golfing Country.

The Hotel is a former Edwardian Townhouse with distinctive architecture and has recently undergone extensive renovation and refurbishment to restore it to its former glory. There is a friendly, relaxed atmosphere where the accent is on the informal.

LETHAM GRANGE RESORT

**Colliston,
by Arbroath,
Angus DD11 4RL
Tel: 01241 890373**

The wonderful sporting County House Hotel lies at the heart of "Carnoustie Country" and is surrounded by its own two championship golf courses and a very attractive estate. For the sporting enthusiast there are 60 golf courses within 60 minutes from the resort, the hotel also boasts its own ice rink and can also arrange falconry, fieldsports, fishing and much more. However you may prefer to simply luxuriate in the Victorian grandeur and spoil yourself with scrumptious dinners cooked by award-winning chefs. To find out more about Leisure Breaks, Golf Breaks, Company Seminars, Team Building or simply to book a game of golf on the Augusta of Scotland telephone 01241 890373.

DUNDEE HILTON

**Earl Grey Place, Dundee DD1 4DE
Tel: 01382 229271 Fax: 01382 200072**

The Hilton Dundee is the perfect location to discover this wonderful city. Ideally located in the city centre and overlooking the River Tay. The hotel has 129 bedrooms, Unicorn Restaurant, bar, leisure facilities including a swimming pool and free car parking.

Termed the "City of Discovery", Dundee is the home of Captain Scott's Ship, RSS Discovery. Guests may also wish to explore Glamis Castle, shop in the city centre or visit one of the nearby golf courses such as Carnoustie and St. Andrews.

"We take time to make the difference, you'll discover it all at Hilton Dundee".

Glamis Castle

Glamis Castle, situated near Forfar on the A94 between Perth and Aberdeen, has been the family home of the Earls of Strathmore and Kinghorne since 1372 when Sir John Lyon was created Thane of Glamis and given the Castle by King Robert II of Scotland. Four years later Sir John married Princess Joanna, the king's daughter.

Glamis Castle has been lived in and visited by many members of the Scottish and British Royal Families. It was the childhood home of Her Majesty Queen Elizabeth The Queen Mother, and the birthplace of Her Royal Highness Princess Margaret. The Castle is also the legendary setting of Shakespeare's famous play 'Macbeth". Above all it remains a family home, lived in and loved by the Strathmore family.

The Castle, a five-storey L-shaped tower block, was originally a royal hunting lodge. It was remodelled in the seventeenth century and is built of pink sandstone. It contains the Great Hall with its magnificent plasterwork ceiling dated 1621, a beautiful family Chapel constructed inside the Castle in 1688, an eighteenth century Billiard Room housing what is left of the extensive library once at Glamis, a nineteenth century Dining Room containing family portraits, and the Royal Apartments used by Her Majesty Queen Elizabeth and His late Majesty King George.

The Castle stands in an extensive park landscaped towards the end of the eighteenth century which contains the beautiful Italian Garden – two acres enclosed within high yew hedges, and a Nature Trail amongst magnificent Douglas Firs and hardwood trees.

Glamis Castle provides a magnificent setting for corporate hospitality. Seated around the family table in the Dining Room, up to thirty-six guests can dine in the grand style or, alternatively, up to ninety can be accommodated at smaller tables.

Private receptions, cocktail parties or product launches can be held in either the Dining Room or the Great Hall, while the sixteenth century Kitchens of the Castle provide an atmospheric venue for buffet lunches, receptions or small dinner parties.

Glamis Castle is open to visitors from April to the end of October and for functions and special events throughout the year.

With a spacious Restaurant serving a wide range of refreshments and a variety of Gift Shops offering quality souvenirs, Glamis Castle has plenty to ensure a memorable visit.

Address
Glamis Castle
Glamis
Angus DD8 1RJ

Opening Times
31 March-28 Oct daily
10.30am-5.30pm
(July/Aug 10am-5.30pm).
Last admission 4.45pm

**Admission for entry
to Castle & Grounds**
Adults £6.20
Children (5-16) £3.10
Senior Citizens £4.70
Students £4.70
Family Ticket £17.00

Facilities
Gift Shops, Restaurant,
Italian Garden, Nature Trail,
Pinetum, Children's Play Park
and Parking Facilities

Inveraray Castle

The present Inveraray Castle and Town of Inveraray date from the middle of the 18th century. The 3rd Duke of Argyll succeeded to the title in 1743 and embarked on the complete rebuilding of the Castle – the old 15th century Castle was situated some 100 metres to the North – and the moving and reconstruction of the new Town of Inveraray as part of his 'grand conception'. The Royal Burgh of Inveraray is one of the earliest and best preserved planned towns in Scotland.

Inveraray is situated about 60 miles North-West of Glasgow on the A83 Trunk Road and is one of the most important tourist centres in the West of Scotland. It makes an ideal base for exploring the whole of the South Western and Mid Western Highlands and close by there are interesting and varied visitor attractions including Inveraray Jail, Ardkinglas and Crarae Gardens, Auchindrain, Wildlife Park and Cruachan Hydro-Electric Power Station.

Inveraray Castle was designed by Roger Morris and is amongst the earliest examples of Gothic revival architecture in Britain.

Built of local greenish blue chloritic schist stone, it is a most impressive ediface complementing the grandeur of the surrounding country.

The superintending architect of the early work, which began in 1745, was William Adam who was succeeded in 1748 by his son John. The elaborate decoration of the State Rooms was designed by Robert Mylne and executed between 1772 and 1789. The pitched and conical roofs were added after a fire in 1877 to the design of A. Salvin in the time of the 8th Duke of Argyll.

The visitor to the Castle may see a fine collection of family pictures and superb French tapestries set in painted rooms of outstanding beauty. The Armoury Hall alone contains some 1300 pieces. Scottish and Continental furniture, English and Continental china and family artefacts form part of a unique collection spanning the generations which are identified by a magnificent genealogical display in the Clan Room.

Inveraray Castle is above all the family home of the Duke and Duchess of Argyll.

Address
Inveraray Castle
Argyll Estates Office,
Cherry Park,
Inveraray, Argyll
PA32 8XE
Tel: 01499 302203
Fax: 01499 302421
Email: enquiries@inveraray-castle.com
www.inveraray-castle.com

Admission
Adults £5.50, Senior Citizens £4.50, Students (on production of student card £4.50, Children under 16 £3.50, Family Ticket (2 adults & 2+ children) £14.00. Special arrangements for school parties. Details on application to the address above. A 20% discount is allowed on groups of 20 or more persons.

Opening Times
1st Sat in April to 2nd Sun in Oct, Mon-Thurs and Sat 10am-1pm & 2pm-5.45pm. Closed Fridays. Sun 1pm-5.45. July & August ONLY OPEN FRIDAYS.
Mon-Sat 10am-5.45pm. Last admissions 12.30 & 5.0pm.

Facilities
Craft Shop, Self Service Tearoom.

Mount Stuart - Isle of Bute

Award winning *Mount Stuart*, one of Britain's most spectacular High Victorian Gothic houses, is the magnificent architectural fantasy of the 3rd Marquess of Bute (1847-1900) and the Scottish architect Robert Rowand Anderson.

It is situated on the Island of Bute in the Firth of Clyde and can be easily reached by frequent ferry service from Wemyss Bay, Renfrewshire (60 mins from Glasgow Airport), or Colintraive in Argyll. Frequent bus services from Rothersay pier (meeting every ferry) to Mount Stuart.

The scale and ambition of Mount Stuart is equalled only by Bute's collaboration with William Burgess to restore Cardiff Castle and Castle Coch. The profusion of astrological designs, stained glass and marble is breathtaking, and all combine to envelop the visitor in the mystique and history of the house. Fabulous interiors and architectural detail. The fine collection of full-length family portraits illustrate several centuries of Bute family history.

The house sits in 300 acres of designed landscape and 18th century woodlands established by the 2nd Earl of Bute and further developed by the 3rd Earl (1713-1792), who advised on the foundation of Kew Gardens.

Four circular walks have been waymarked in the grounds to help visitors find their way around. *The Pinetum Walk*, has an interesting collection of specimen conifers. *The Garden Walk*, takes in all the significant features of the designed landscape including the Kitchen Garden, the Rock Garden, the Wee Garden and some six acres and the Calvary Pond. *The Shore Walk* is the best route to take to see the resident wildlife. *The Kerry Trail* is the longest walk and takes in some of the outlying features of the gardens and grounds.

In order to enjoy the many different aspects of Mount Stuart as well as the rest of this magical Island, plan to spend at least two or three days here.

Address
Mount Stuart House
& Gardens
Isle of Bute PA20 9LR
Tel: 01700 503877
Fax: 01700 505313
website:
www.mountstuart.com

Opening Times
Open 2 May to 30 Sept daily except Tuesdays and Thursdays from 10am (house 11am) till 6pm. Please call for detailed opening times.

Admission
2000 prices: Adult £6.00, Child £2.50, Family £15.00 Season £15.00 Senior Citizen/Students/Group concessions given.

Facilities
Free car parking, courtesy transportation between houses and visitors reception, countryside ranger service. Guided house or garden tours, picnic areas, Restaurant, Tearoom, Gift Shop, Audio Visual Room, Guide Dogs only.

Torosay Castle – Isle of Mull

Torosay Castle was completed in 1858 by the eminent architect David Bryce in the Scottish Baronial style. It is one of the finer examples of his work and possibly one of the few still used as a family home and open to the public. Bryce's clever architecture results in the Castle combining elegance and informality, grandeur and homeliness.

Inside Torosay Castle visitors are welcome to wander round the principle rooms which all contain a wide range of family portraits, memorabilia and antique furniture set in a relaxed and welcoming atmosphere.

In the archive rooms visitors can learn all about David Guthrie James' adventurous life which includes sailing in one of the last Windjammers, successful escape from P.O.W. camp and polar exploration. Visitors are welcome to browse through all the material and books on show.

Torosay is surrounded by 12 acres of spectacular gardens including formal terraces (attributed to Sir Robert Lorimar) which are covered with roses, other climbers and underplanted with perennials, an impressive statue walk which consists of 19 limestone figures were sculpted by Antonio Bonazza and brought to Torosay in about 1900, this remains one of the most significant collections of such statuery in Britain. Torosay gardens provide an interesting and unusual contrast of formal and woodland gardens, and the dramatic and wild scenery makes the setting all the more special.

Mull Miniature Railway

This unique island 101/4" gauge railway runs from Craignure to Torosay and operates steam and diesel hauled trains. The journey is one of great beauty with panoramic views of Ben Nevis, the Glencoe Hills, the Island of Lismore, Ben Cruachan and Duart Castle. Interesting wildlife can be seen in the woodland section of the journey as the train climbs gradients as steep as 1 in 52, and in spring and summer the primroses and the rhododendrons make the journey a particular delight. A variety of tickets are available and trains can be chartered by prior arrangement.

A visit to Mull Rail and Torosay Castle and Gardens set on the magnificent island of Mull is an experience not to be missed, and is fun to visit, and visit again, in all seasons and all weather.

Address
Torosay Castle & Gardens
Craignure
Isle of Mull

Tel: 01680 812 421
Rail Tel: 01680 812494

Opening Times
Garden open all year 9am-7pm (until dusk in winter).
Castle open Easter-mid October 10.30am-5pm.

Admission
(1998 prices)
£4.50 Adults
£1.50 Child
£3.50 Concessions
£10.00 Family

Location
11/2 miles South of Craignure

Facilities
Tearoom, Craft/Gift Shop, Free Parking

KILLIECHRONAN HOUSE
Loch Na Keal, Isle of Mull, Argyll
Telephone: 01680 300403 Fax: 01680 300463
6 Rooms (all en suite).
AA ❀, STB ☆☆☆☆

Killiechronan House tastefully provides good food, comfortable accommodation and a personal welcome emulating its imposing situation at the head of Loch na Keal. The Estate of over 5000 acres offers fishing, ponytrekking, hill walking as well as active farming and forestry enterprises, being situated centrally on the Isle of Mull. The House was refurbished during the winter of 1994.

MANOR HOUSE
Gallanach Road, Oban, Argyll
Telephone: 01631 562087 Fax: 01631 563053
11 Rooms (all en suite).
AA ❀, STB ☆☆☆☆

The Manor House, situated in its own grounds on the foreshore of Oban Bay, offers the unique location for touring the Highlands and Islands. The Isle of Mull is just 40 minutes away. Coll and Tiree are a day's cruise up the Sound of Mull and many more places are just waiting for your visit. Always a 'welcome back' where we try to do everything to make your stay most pleasurable. Specialities are local Hebridean fish and crustaceans, also lamb and venison from our own estate.

Isle of Eriska Hotel
Ledaig by Oban, Argyll PA37 1SD
Tel: 01631 720371 Fax: 01631 720531
Email: office@eriska-hotel.co.uk
www.eriska-hotel.co.uk

There's always a touch of magic about a private island. Eriska is reached over a bridge, tiny admittedly, but the Atlantic does flow beneath. And once over it, the feeling of privacy and seclusion makes the Isle of Eriska seem much more remote than a mere two hour's drive from Glasgow or Edinburgh. The 300 acres is dedicated solely to the wellbeing of the 30 guests and the Buchanan-Smith family have, for 30 years, strived to combine the highest standards of service with warmth and hospitality to match.

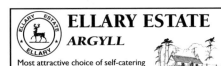

Duart Castle - Isle of Mull

The Isle of Mull is one of the most beautiful and varied islands on the west coast of Scotland, part of the kingdom of the Lords of the Isles, it later became a stronghold of the clan Maclean.

As you sail on the ferry from Oban you can see Duart Castle perched on a rocky cliff, dominating the Sound of Mull.

It was in the 13th century that the Macleans realised the importance of this position and built the first part of the castle. These walls form part of the courtyard you see today. From that time until the 17th century the Macleans lived at Duart, controlling the sea lanes around Mull, fighting among themselves, the Macdonalds and finally the Campbells.

Lachlan Cattanache, the 11th Chief, is best remembered as the Chief who left his wife, Margaret, on the Lady's Rock, hoping she would drown, as she had failed to produce an heir. However she was rescued by a kinsman and returned to her brother, the Duke of Argyll. Lachlan himself was murdered in Edinburgh in 1527, by one of Margaret's cousins.

The Macleans were staunchly loyal to the Jacobite cause and fought with the Old Pretender in 1715, and Bonnie Prince Charlie in 1745, which cost them dearly in almost all respects. The castle was garrisoned by government forces after the '45 and burnt in 1756 when the garrison left.

Duart remained a ruin until it was bought back in 1911, by the 26th Chief, Sir Fitzroy Maclean. Sir Fitzroy, who had fought in the Crimea War, was over 70 when he restored the castle.

When you visit Duart today you can see the prisoners from the Spanish Galleon, blown up by the Macleans in 1588, coughing in the dungeons. There is an exhibition of the "Swan", a small man-of-war, sent by Cromwell to capture the 10-year-old Chief that sank directly below the castle.

The castle is full of stories of the Maclean family who have lived there for so many centuries. And, for those prepared to climb the ancient worn steps, the turnpike stairs takes you to the top of the 13th century keep and a walkway round the battlements where you can see the spectacular views over the Sound of Mull.

Duart is home to the 28th Chief, Sir Lachlan Maclean and his family.

Address
Duart Castle
Isle of Mull
Tel: 01680 812309

Opening Times
Daily from 1st May to
mid October
10.30-6.00pm

Admission
Adults £3.50 (1999)
Concessions £3.00

Location
Duart is 3 miles from
Craignure off A849 on
the way to Iona

Facilities
Car parking and grounds
are free of charge. There is
a tea room and a shop.

Blairquhan Castle & Gardens

The Hunter Blairs are descended from the Hunters of Hunterston, who have lived at Hunterston in North Ayrshire since 1110. In the mid 18th century a younger son of our branch of the family, Hunter of Abbothill, near Ayr, went to Edinburgh where he became Lord Provost and MP for the City and was created a Baronet. He married Jean Blair, the heiress of Dunskey in Wigtownshire and added her name to his. (Robert Burns wrote an Elegy on his early death - very inspiring - but, luckily, the poet said at the time, the verse was indifferent but the grief was sincere').

Blairquhan was bought for his second son, Sir David, the 3rd Baronet, in 1798. (He was related, on his mother's side, to the Kennedys who were the original owners of Blairquhan).

Sir David found both the Estate and Castle in a bad way. He decided, eventually, to abandon the old Castle and make a new house on a site slightly to the North. William Burn was the chosen architect - later to become the most successful country house architect in Great Britain - and between 1821 and 1824 the house was built, preserving some of the stones from the old castle in the kitchen courtyard. John Tweedie designed the gardens and Sir David himself, who was an enthusiastic amateur landscape architect, laid out the grounds. Fittings and furniture were sent for from Ayr, Edinburgh and London - and they still remain - even including the blankets on the four poster beds with the date "1824" woven into them.

Blairquhan can be yours alone for whatever period you like - for a few hours, a night, a week or even longer. It has not been altered at all since it was built - partly for that reason it is extraordinarily well laid out for every sort of entertaining as well as for conferences and for house parties.

In recent years the house has been discreetly modernised to provide comfortable living. There are ten double bedrooms (four of these have Four Poster beds, one has a Two Poster and the remainder have twin beds), each with its own bathroom adjoining. There are five single bedrooms.

Address

Blairquhan Estate Office
Maybole
Ayrshire KA19 7LZ
Tel: 01655 770239
Fax: 01655 770278

Opening Times

15th July to 13th August inclusive (not Mondays), 1.30pm. Last entry to house 4.15pm.

Admission

Adult £5.00
Children £3.00
O.A.P. £4.00

Open at other times by appointment. The Castle is available for parties, conferences and corporate entertainment.

Other accomodation on the Estate:
Milton (sleeping 21)
7 holiday cottages sleeping 5 - 8.

Salmon and trout fishing on River Girvan and trout fishing on two stocked lochs.

Brodick Castle - Isle of Arran

Situated on the lovely Isle of Arran and backed by the majestic Goatfell mountain range, Brodick Castle dates from the 13th Century and is the ancestral home and hunting lodge of Scotland's premier family, the Dukes of Hamilton.

The castle contents are extraordinary. Representing the family passions for sport, and in particular racing, many of the paintings and silver trophies demonst-rating the extravagant lifestyle of a bygone era. Brodick is also home to the single most significant collection of fine art, porcelain, furniture and objet d'art which was acquired in the 19th century by William Beckford.

The story of this bizarrely eccentric and rich man is a fascinating insight into Victorian morals and social history. Around the Castle there are 80 acres of woodland garden that holds one of Europe's finest collections of rhododendrons. With a mild frost-free climate due to the Gulf Stream, many sub tropical plants grow very well. Rhododendrons, azaleas and camellias bloom in profusion from February through to summer and the walled garden and herbaceous beds continue to give splendid shows of colour until the autumn. Plants are available for sale.

There are 12 miles of Country Park trails with a Ranger Information Service. Children enjoy the adventure playground and there is a full summer guided walks and events programme. Self service licensed tearoom/restaurant with 'Taste of Scotland' award. Gift/Book shop.

Address
Brodick Castle &
Country Park
Isle of Arran
KA27 8HY
Tel: 01770 302202

Opening Times
Open 1 April to 31st Oct,
daily 11am to 4.30pm (last
admission 4pm).

Garden & Country Park open
all year daily 9.30am to sunset.

Reception Centre & Shop
(dates as Castle) open
10am to 5pm.

Award-winning
'Taste of Scotland' licensed
self-service restaurant
11am - 5pm.

Free entry for all National
Trust and National Trust
for Scotland members.
Parties, please pre-book.

Hawick Museum

A warm welcome awaits you at a quartet of museums and galleries in scenic Roxburghshire.

Located in Hawick, one hours drive equidistant from Carlisle and Edinburgh on the A7, there are treasures in store! Enjoy a day exploring Hawick, renowned for its world-famous quality knitwear and luxurious cashmere. Conveniently set on the High Street is Hawick's newest and most exciting visitor attraction – Drumlanrig's Tower. A former stronghold of the Black Douglas, dating from the 15th century, this beautifully restored town house offers an insight into Borders history. Up to the minute displays feature touch screen audio visuals, costumed figures, period rooms and a wonderful shop with tourist information point.

A pleasant walk away lies Wilton Lodge Park – 107 acres of award winning gardens. This splendid location features Hawick Museum & The Scott Gallery – providing visitors with a wealth of local history displays including knitwear, natural sciences, a Victorian schoolroom plus a changing exhibition programme of contemporary art.

Two museums in the Royal Burgh of Jedburgh, located between Edinburgh and Newcastle on the A68, offer visitors the chance to discover both the rich history of the area and the story of Mary Queen of Scots.

Jedburgh's award-winning visitor centre set in beautiful gardens is dedicated to the memory of Mary Stuart. Her tragic yet romantic life story is movingly portrayed in a wonderful 16th century fortified bastle house, known as Mary Queen of Scots' House, where she stayed during recuperation from illness in 1566.

At the top of the Castle Gate in the centre of Jedburgh stands a most imposing building. Built in 1824, Jedburgh Castle Jail and Museum offers visitors the chance to discover what life was like in a Howard Reform Prison during the 19th century! The Castle Jail has recently re-opened following extensive renovations and has new displays installed throughout including two large cell blocks with reconstructed period cells, costumed figures and equipment from the original prison. The Jailer's House now acts as a museum on the history of Jedburgh and environs, and has a wealth of displays including an audio visual room. There are excellent parking facilities for cars and coaches to the rear of the building.

Museum and Gallery Service
Hawick Museum
Wilton Lodge Park
Hawick TD9 7JL

Tel: 01450 373457
Fax: 01450 378506

Jedburgh Castle Jail & Museum

Built in the 1820's to a design by Archibald Elliot following prison reform priciples of John Howard, Jedburgh Castle Jail & Museum offers an insight into what prison life was like during the 19th century. Here visitors may trace the history of law and order and discover the harsh sentences, including transportation, imposed upon children and adults.

The imposing structure stands on the site of the former Castle of Jedburgh, which was razed to the ground in 1409, and enjoys commanding views from the top of the Castlegate over the scenic town of Jedburgh. The building is a scheduled monument of importance - rated category A and enjoying an unique architectural status in the Scottish Borders. It offers a fascinating chronicle of the 19th century for both architecture historians and visitors seeking something different for a day out.

Nowadays the Jailer's House acts as a museum for the Royal Burgh of Jedburgh, with traditional displays, costumed figures and audio visuals bringing history to life. Discover fascinating facts on the links Jedburgh has with leading figures in scientific discovery. The kaleidoscope was invented by Sir David Brewster - a native of Jedburgh. Mary Somerville, an eminent scientist of her day hailed from Jedburgh. She has an Oxford College named in her honour. James Hutton, the father of modern geology, studied formations of sandstone cliffs in Jedburgh and formulated revolutionary theories which challenged theological beliefs of his day concerning the creation of the earth.

Displays on crime & punishment and the Prison Reform movement, are set within the magnificent castellated cell blocks. Here the stories of inmates, prison staff and infamous sons and daughters of Jedburgh are recounted against the background of law and order in Scotland.

There are extensive grounds, facilities for picnics, parking to the rear of the building and a souvenir shop with refreshments on site.

Address
Jedburgh Castle
Castle Gate
Jedburgh TD8 6BD

Admission
£1.25/75p concessions.

Opening Times
Open from Late March to
31 October.
10 - 4.30 Monday to Saturday,
1 - 4 Sundays.
Group bookings or school
trips are welcome.
Evening visits are by
arrangement with the Curator.
Tel/Fax: 01835 864750
or 01450 373457

Floors Castle

Floors Castle, home of the Duke and Duchess of Roxburghe, is in a beautiful setting overlooking the River Tweed and the Cheviot Hills.

It is reputedly the largest inhabited castle in Scotland. Designed by William Adam, who was both master-builder and architect for the first Duke of Roxburghe, the building of Floors started in 1721.

It was the present Duke's great, great grandfather, James the 6th Duke, who called in W H Playfair, a prominent architect in Scotland, to embellish the plain Adam features of the building. In about 1894 Playfair, letting his imagination and talent run riot, transformed the Castle creating a multitude of spires and domes. Sir Walter Scott commented "The modern mansion of Fleurs with its terrace, its woods and its extensive lawn, forms altogether a Kingdom for Oberon or Titania to dwell in".

Externally, the Castle has not been altered since the 6th Duke's time but internally, several of the rooms, including the Dining Room and Ballroom were remodelled at the turn of the century. This was to accommodate the magnificent tapestries which the present Duke's grandmother Duchess May brought from her family's Long Island mansion. These apartments now display the outstanding collection of French 17th and 18th century furniture, the Chinese and European porcelain and some very fine works of art. Many of the treasures in the Castle today were collected by Duchess May who was devoted to Floors.

The Castle has been seen on cinema screens worldwide in the film 'Greystoke' as the home of Tarzan the Earl of Greystoke.

The extensive parkland and gardens overlooking the Tweed provides a variety of wooded walks. The Walled Garden contains splendid herbaceous borders and in the outer walled garden a summerhouse built for Queen Victoria's visit in 1867 can still be seen.

Address
Floors Castle
Kelso
Roxburghshire
TD5 7ST

Opening Times
Daily from

Easter to October 31

10.00am to 4.30pm

Admission
£5.00

Facilities
Gift shop, Restaurant
Coffee Shop
Garden Centre
Car parking
Facilities for disabled

TRAQUAIR ARMS

AA ◆◆◆, STB ☆☆.

Traditional Scottish inn 40 mins south of Edinburgh, the Johnston's run it with genuine concern for the comforts of the guests. 10 Rooms (all en suite). Imaginative menus utilise the best local produce. Local real ales. Egon Ronay guide says 'Bed & Breakfast is recommended particularly the handsome Scottish breakfast.' 'Taste of Scotland' recommended.

(€) ☐ 🍺 P ⑪ V ～ 🛏 🏠 SPECIAL 1 2 3 C

TRAQUAIR ARMS HOTEL
Traquair Road, Innerleithen, Peeblesshire EH44 6PD
Telephone: 01896 830229 Fax: 01896 830260
e-mail: traquair.arms@scottishborders.com

TRAQUAIR
House

Scotland's oldest continually inhabited House spanning over 1000 years of Scottish history. Originally a hunting lodge for the kings of Scotland it has been visited by 27 Scottish monarchs. Strong associations with Mary Queen of Scots and the Jacobites. Fascinating collection of embroideries and books and there is a secret stairway used by Catholic priests. 18th century brewery that brews the world famous Traquair Ales and there is also a maze, craftworkshops, gift and cashmere shops, 1745 Cottage Restaurant and extensive woodland walks.

TRAQUAIR HOUSE
Innerleithen, Peeblesshire, Scotland EH44 6PW
Tel: 01896 830323/831370 Fax: 01896 830639
e-mail: traquair.house@scotborders.co.uk

Neidpath Castle

From about 1200 the Lords were a family of Frasers, of whom the last, a compatriot of William Wallace, defeated the English Armies three times in one day at Roslin, 15 miles north of Neidpath. The English took Sir Simon in 1307 and he suffered the same fate as Wallace. The Lordship went, with his daughter Mary to the Hay Family in 1312.

The Hays built the castle as it appears today and held it for nearly 380 years. During that period Mary Stuart and later her son James VI visited Neidpath. Different visitors were the troops of Oliver Cromwell who lay siege to Neidpath in 1650. After this the castle was converted to a tower house, a rare example of 17th Century comfort within a medieval tower.

In 1686 the Douglas's took possession of the castle by purchase. The last Douglas of Neidpath, the 3rd Earl of March and 4th Duke of Queensberry was castigated by William Wordsworth in a sonnet, for having the trees around Neidpath cut down in 1795. On the death of "Old Q" in 1810 the castle and estate passed to Earl of Wemyss, the present owners.

The castle stands high above the River Tweed in a wooded gorge, to the west of Peebles town. The views from the parapets repay the climb up the turnpike stairs. Of interest is the water draw well cut from living rock, the gloomy pit prison, with inhabitant! The Laigh Hall contains artifacts and displays of local interest including a large Tartan collection. Worth the visit alone are the stunningly beautiful batik wall hangings displayed in the Great Hall, by Monica Hannasch, they depict the life and times of Mary Queen of Scots.

The surrounding area of tree clad hills provide scenic walks. There is ample parking and a picnic area for visitors. The castle and grounds appear in the recently made films "The Bruce", "King Lear" and "Merlin – The Magic Begins", Joan of Arc (documentary), "Steel Tempest" and "Hamlet".

Address
Neidpath Castle –
Scottish Borders
Tel/Fax: 01721720333

Open Times
Easter Week, May & Spring Bank Holidays, then 29 June until 9 September 2001.

Admission
Adults £3.00
Concessions £2.50
Child £1.00
Family £7.50

Location
Neidpath is 1 mile west of Peebles on the A72 road

Facilities
Car Park, Coach Park and Grounds, included in entry ticket charge

455

Discover Dumfries

Take a look at Dumfries and the beautiful valley of the Nith from the Camera Obscura at Dumfries Museum.

This historic astronomical instrument occupies the topmost floor of the old windmill tower at Dumfries Museum, overlooking the town and the surrounding countryside. It was installed in 1836 when the building was converted into an Observatory. Today it is the oldest working camera obscura in the world.

The mechanism itself is relatively simple. A mirror is raised and lowered, reflecting an image downward through a lens, onto a plaster topped table about twelve feet below in the hushed atmosphere of a darkened room. As the astonished spectators stand around this table top screen, they see a moving, panoramic view. On a clear day the range is almost 50 miles!

Dumfries Museum itself is a treasure house of the heritage of south west Scotland. Its exhibitions tell the story of human life and endeavour in Dumfries and Galloway set against the ever changing natural environment of the area.

The Robert Burns Centre, an award-winning visitor centre to Scotland's national poet, is situated close by in an eighteenth century watermill on the banks of the River Nith. It tells of Robert Burns and his life in the busy streets and lively atmosphere of Dumfries in the 1790s.

A short walk away on the opposite bank of the River Nith is the simple sandstone dwelling in which Robert Burns spent the last three years of his brilliant life. Burns House retains its eighteenth century character and contains many evocative items connected with the poet.

Further down the valley, close to the Nith's estuary with the Solway Firth is John Paul Jones' Cottage, the birthplace of the American naval hero. The cottage has been painstakingly restored and furnished in the style of the early 1700s. In the reconstruction of the cabin of Jones' most famous ship, the Bonhomme Richard, there is an exciting audio visual re-enactment of the Battle of Flamborough Head in which he defeated the HMS Serapis in 1779. The cottage has an attractive rural picnic area offering marvellous views of the Solway Firth and the Lake District beyond.

Address
Dumfries Museum
The Observatory
Dumfries
DG2 7SW

Telephone: 01387 253374
www.dumfriesmuseum.
demon.co.uk

for information on
• Dumfries Museum and
  Camera Obscura
• Robert Burns Centre
• Burns House
• John Paul Jones' Cottage

Shambellie House
Museum of Costume

Shambellie House is situated on the outskirts of the historic village of New Abbey, seven miles south of Dumfries. Set in old wooded grounds dating from 1780's, Shambellie is not visible from the road. However, a two minute walk up the original driveway through the gardens, provides the first glimpse of this impressive Scottish Baronial home. On entering, the visitor is invited to step back in time and experience the grace, elegance and refinement of a bygone era.

In 1844, William Stewart inherited Shambellie Estate from his father and in 1845 he married Katherine, daughter of John Hardie of Leith. 10 years later, with a growing family and modest funds, William Stewart decided to build a house which would incorporate the latest ideas of family comfort and convenience.

The celebrated Scottish architect, David Bryce, usually designed houses on a grander scale than Mr Stewart envisaged and the first design had to be rejected on the grounds of cost. The next design was more manageable in financial terms, costing just under £3000.

The house commands spectacular views of some well known local landmarks. From the master bedroom the mountain of Criffel can be seen in the background and Monument Hill in the foreground. The tower on the top of the hill was built to commemorate the Battle of Waterloo in 1815. To the south, the remains of Sweetheart Abbey can be seen nestling in the village below.

In 1977, Charles Stewart, the great-grandson of the original owner, gave the house and its unique costume collection to the National Museums of Scotland.

Charles Stewart always had an intense interest in what people wore. Driven by what he referred to as "holy greed", he began collecting clothes before the Second World War, finding many pieces at market stalls, in friends' attics and forgotten trunks.

"Although my pretext for collecting costumes was still that I needed it to draw for book illustrations, the real reason was that insensibly I had become that obsessed and demented being, a Collector."

Each room with its costumed figures shows a different social event at Shambellie House between the period of 1860 and 1930. Step back in time and enjoy the splendour of this unique Victorian country house.

Address
Shambellie House Museum of Costume
New Abbey
Dumfries DG2 8HQ
Tel: (01387) 850375
Fax: (01387) 850461

Opening Times
Open 1 April to
31 October

Admission
Adults £2.50
Concession £1.50
Children Free

Facilities
• Gift Shop
• Tearoom
• Picnic Area
• Parking
• Toilets

Culcreuch Castle Hotel & Country Park

**Fintry, Loch Lomond, Stirling &
Trossachs, Stirlingshire G63 0LW
Tel: 01360 860555 Fax: 01360 860556
Email: Info@culcreuch.com
www.culcreuch.com**

Once the ancestral home of the Clan Galbraith, 700 year-old Culcreuch Castle, the oldest inhabited Castle in central Scotland, now warmly welcomes friends from all over the world to stay in arguably one of the most romantic and historic hotels in the principality. Set in 1600 acres of parkland grounds, encapsulated by spectacular highland scenery, the warmth of the welcome after each exhilarating day in the country is legendary – the glow of our log fires, the smell of peaty smoke, the fine malts, the fellowship recounting the day's events in the Dungeon Bar. And afterwards, relaxing with new friends over an award-winning Candlelit Dinner in the panelled Dining Room. Traditional Scottish fayre prepared from locally-produced ingredients complemented by a well-stocked wine cellar.

Just heaven AND centrally located for ALL the major attractions AND 45 Golf Courses within 45 minutes drive! Colour brochure on request.

THE STIRLING HIGHLAND HOTEL
Spittal Street, Stirling FK8 1DU
Telephone: 01786 475444 Fax: 01786 462929

76 Rooms (all en suite). AA/RAC ☆☆☆☆,
STB ✦✦✦✦✦ Highly Commended. ❀❀.
Imaginatively converted from the old High School, retaining many original characteristics, this unique hotel is set around a quadrangle, above the town, close to the castle. Stylish public areas feature wood panelling and vaulted ceilings. Dine in Rizzio's, our cheery trattoria or enjoy fine dining in Scholars, awarded 2 Red Rosettes.

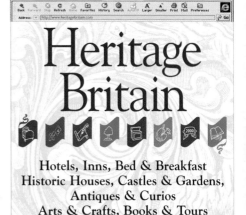

Falkirk & Callendar House

Falkirk district is an area truly steeped in tradition; where many of the most influential characters in the history of Scotland left their mark. William Wallace, Edward I, John Knox, Mary Queen of Scots, Oliver Cromwell, the Young Pretender, James Watt and many others, had course to take the road to Falkirk.

This district was many things to many people – the ancient seat of the Livingstons of Callendar, the location of the famous "Speckled Kirk", the "Tryst" for the cattle drovers who walked from as far as Lewis or Ireland, or the place where dreams of glory were resurrected or finally laid to rest on a bloody battlefield.

Almost 2,000 years ago, the Roman Army mounted a series of campaigns over Scottish soil. The most enduring memorial to their presence here is the Antonine Wall, built around 142 AD. It took its name from the then Emperor of Rome, Antoninus Pius, who ordered its construction as a defence against the northern tribes.

It stretched from Old Kirkpatrick on the Clyde, to Carriden on the Forth, and, despite the passage of time, substantial lengths of this remarkable monument can still be seen today in the district.

It was in the mid-eighteenth century that the fate of Falkirk District became bonded with that of the nation. Industry was poised on the brink of a fantastic revolution, and this area had a major part to play. In 1760 a red glow appeared in the sky above Carron, heralding the arrival of Carron Company's iron foundry, the first in Scotland.

The completion of the Forth & Clyde and Union Canals had a great influence on the development of further industry in the district. Sawmills, timber yards, foundries, coal pits, chemical works, brick works, and small shipyards hugged their banks. And in 1803 the world's first practical steamship, "The Charlotte Dundas", was launched into the waters of the Forth and Clyde by William Symington.

Today, you can visit Falkirk's shopping malls at Callendar Square and the Howgate, and dine in the areas' many hotels and restaurants, explore the canals, visit the Bo'ness and Kinneil Steam Railway, and go underground at the Birkhill Clay Mine.

Easy to get to in Central Scotland, the area is served by two motorways (M9, M80). Falkirk itself is well served by public transport and has two railway stations.

Address
Callendar House
Callendar Park
Falkirk FX1 1YR
Tel: 01324 503770
Fax: 01324 503771

Opening Times
Open all year round

Hall Admission
Adults £3.00
Children: £1.00

Facilities
Georgian Teashop at
the Stables
Gift Shop
Parking
Disabled Access
Education Services
to Schools

Looking for a special place to stay?

Then look no further...

Balbirnie House is a quite unique multi-award-winning hotel which combines understated luxury with superb service and outstanding value. Located in the heart of Fife, only half hour equidistant from Edinburgh, St. Andrews, Perth and Dundee. Many distinctive feature breaks are available year round. Choose from the "Pampered Weekend Break", "Champagne Break" or "The Golfing Enthusiasts Stay". Fully inclusive prices start from only £89.50 per person per night.

Full information, including our latest newsletter is available from our website, alternatively contact directly:

Nicholas Russell, Hotel Manager,
Balbirnie House, Balbirnie Park,
Markinch by Glenrothes, Fife KY7 6NE.
Tel: 01592 610066 Fax: 01592 610529
Email: balbirnie@breathemail.net
www.balbirnie.co.uk

THE PEAT INN
by Cupar, Fife KY15 5LY
Tel: 01334 840206 Fax: 01334 840530
Email: reception@thepeatinn.co.uk

Situated just 6 miles from St. Andrews in the village named after the inn, David Wilson's cooking has earned an International reputation using Scotland's finest natural produce with great creativity.
The restaurant is in the original inn (18th century), stylish and comfortable with an open log fire in the reception lounge.
The Residence has 8 luxurious suites each with bedroom, sitting room and marble bathroom with bath and shower. It is a haven of peace where one can relax after the delights of the table and the award-winning wine list with consumer friendly prices.

ABBOT HOUSE
HERITAGE CENTRE

Come and visit Abbot House, Dunfermline's Heritage Centre for the Ancient Capital of Scotland. See 1000 years of history revealed in this award winning journey from the birth of a nation to the present day.

Admission to the ground floor is free and includes Cafe, Gift Shop, Garden with access to Abbey Grounds. We regret access to upper floors is not possible for wheelchair users.
Open 10am-5pm every day except Christmas Day and New Years Day.
Admission: Adults £3, Senior Citizens/Unwaged £2, Accompanied Children under 14 Free. Reductions for parties of 20 or more.
Please phone for details.

ABBOT HOUSE
Maygate, Dunfermline, Fife KY12 7NE
Tel: 01383 733266 Fax: 01383 624908
Email: dht@abbothouse.fsnet.co.uk
www.abbothouse.co.uk

Kingdom of Fife

The ancient Kingdom of Fife lies just north of Edinburgh beyond the Firth of Forth and is easily reached by road and rail. It is a land steeped in tradition with an outstanding heritage. For long before Edinburgh, the Kingdom was the centre of secular and religious power in Scotland. Dunfermline was the stronghold of Celtic Kings and in the grounds of its Abbey – the splendid "Westminster of the North" – lie buried twenty-two kings, queens, princes and princesses. Robert the Bruce himself lies directly beneath the carved oak pulpit. Here you may visit the shrine of St Margaret or the birthplace of the richest man in the world, Andrew Carnegie. Dunfermline is also a town of peaceful parks and gardens. Pittencrieff Park alone is set in 76 acres of woodland, lawns and formal gardens and is a sanctuary to many species of birds.

Further north St Andrews, now better known as the home of golf, was, before the Reformation, the ecclesiastical capital of Scotland. It took builders more than 150 years to complete the construction of the cathedral, the largest ever to be built in Scotland and now, more than 7 centuries later visitors still marvel at its splendour. Close by is the castle which was built as the bishop's palace. Steep cliffs protected it to the north while rock-cut ditches once defended the landward approaches. As the main residence of Scotland's leading churchmen, the castle was the setting for many important events throughout the Middle Ages. But it was during the turmoil leading to the Reformation of 1560 that some of the most murderous acts were perpetrated within or before its walls. More than 400 years have elapsed since the Reformation and today the ruined castle can now be enjoyed in peace by visitors.

Along the coast the delightful fishing villages of the East Neuk and 17th century Culross are separated by stretches of fine golden sand. Inland the countryside is a haven for birdwatchers, ramblers and those who just wish to escape to a land of peace for a while.

There are historic houses all over the Kingdom, including the Royal Palace at Falkland, which was once the principal hunting lodge of the Stewart Dynasty. Today it is in the care of the National Trust for Scotland and is open to the public from April to October.

The Kingdom of Fife has a fine tradition of arts and crafts. Examples of craft work from golf clubs to jewellery, from ceramics to knitwear can be found throughout Fife. For art lovers, the Crawford Art Centre in St Andrews provides exciting exhibitions of visual arts from sculpture and painting to photography, design and architecture. In Kirkcaldy the Art Gallery houses an outstanding collection of work by the Scottish Colourists including S J Peploe and William McTaggart, and in Dunfermline the Small Gallery hosts changing exhibitions of local artists throughout the year.

The Kingdom of Fife is a magical land of contrasts, studded with historic towns and pretty coastal villages.

The Kingdom of Fife – once discovered, never forgotten.

If you would like more information, please write to:
Kingdom of Fife Tourist Board
70 Market Street
St Andrews
Fife KY16 9NU.
Tel: 01334 472021
Fax: 01334 478422

The National Trust for Scotland

Nobody can doubt the extraordinary variety and richness of Scotland's heritage and nowhere is it better shown than in the properties owned and cared for by Scotland's leading conservation charity, The National Trust for Scotland.

Culzean Castle and Country Park, Ayrshire

The Trust was established in 1931 to act as a guardian of Scotland's magnificent heritage of architectural, scenic and historic treasures, and encourage public access to them. In its care are over 100 varied properties embracing castles and mansion houses, glorious gardens, historic sites and battlefields such as Bannockburn and Culloden, islands, countryside, waterfalls, coastline, birthplaces of famous Scots and fascinating industrial heritage sites including two water mills and a printing works!

Each year the properties open for visitors to enjoy the huge variety in them – from plant collections in gardens to the paintings, silver, furniture and porcelain contained within the castles and great houses.

Most properties hold special events throughout the year and these range from craft fairs and concerts to guided walks led by countryside rangers and expert gardeners. A free 'What's On' guide is available from the address below. Many properties also have shops, with a wide range of high-quality items, tearooms and restaurants, offering the best of Scottish fare, and other facilities like adventure playgrounds, making them an ideal day out for all the family.

As a charity, The National Trust for Scotland depends on the subscriptions of its members, donations and legacies to keep its properties open and to continue its conservation work. Amongst its benefits, membership allows free access to properties for one year – ideal if you are touring Scotland this summer.

For further information about the Trust's properties, events and membership benefits, please contact their Public Affairs Department, 28 Charlotte Square, Edinburgh EH2 4EG or visit their web site at www.nts.org.uk

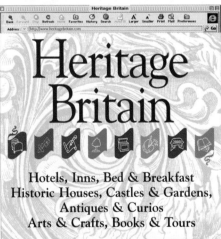

Glasgow Museums

fun friendly

...and they're **FREE**

ART GALLERY AND MUSEUM, KELVINGROVE

THE BURRELL COLLECTION

PEOPLE'S PALACE

GALLERY OF MODERN ART

MUSEUM OF TRANSPORT

FOSSIL GROVE

ST MUNGO MUSEUM

SCOTLAND STREET SCHOOL MUSEUM

OPEN 7 DAYS
For information ☎ **0141 287 4350**

Glasgow

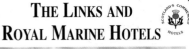

468

Cawdor Castle

This splendid romantic castle dating from the late 14th century was built as a private fortress by the Thanes of Cawdor, and remains the home of The Dowager Countess Cawdor to this day. The ancient medieval tower was built around the legendary holly-tree.

Although the house has evolved over 600 years, later additions mainly of the 17th century were all built in the Scottish vernacular style with slated roofs over walls and crow-stepped gables of mellow local stone. This style gives Cawdor a strong sense of unity, and the massive, severe exterior belies an intimate interior that gives the place a surprisingly personal, friendly atmosphere.

Good furniture, fine portraits and pictures, interesting objects and outstanding tapestries are arranged to please the family rather than to echo fashion or impress. Memories of Shakespeare's Macbeth give Cawdor an elusive, evocative quality that delights visitors.

The Flower Garden has again a family feel to it, where plants are chosen out of affection rather than affectation. This is a lovely spot between spring and late summer. The Wild Garden beside its stream leads into beautiful trails through a spectacular mature mixed woodland, through which paths are helpfully marked and colour-coded.

The walled garden has been restored over the last twenty years by Lord and Lady Cawdor, to recreate a 16th century atmosphere, the date of the garden walls. It comprises a holly maze, paradise garden, knot garden and orchard.

For the keen shopper there is a Gift Shop: items include cashmere, china, leather goods, children's toys, sweets and a wide selection of products made in Scotland, many exclusively for Cawdor Castle. The Book Shop sells a wide and unusual selection of books, prints, stationery and cards. The Wool Shop: the best of Scottish cashmere, capes, ponchos and a large collection of sweaters, scarves and stoles.

The licensed restaurant serves good country cooking and delicious home baking.

For the amateur golfer there is an interesting, but not too taxing, 9-hole golf course, definitely worth trying.

Address

Cawdor Castle
Nairn
Scotland IV12 5RD
Tel: 01667 404615
Fax 01667 404674
E-mail:
info@cawdorcastle.com
www.cawdorcastle.com

Opening Times

Open May - October daily
from 10,00am to 5.00pm

Location

Situated between Inverness
and Nairn on the B9090
off the A96

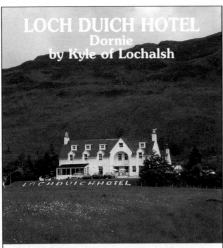

Eilean Donan Castle

Eilean Donan Castle is built in a small island where three lochs converge – Loch Alsh, Loch Long, and Loch Duich. Because there is a fresh water well on the island it has been inhabited from earliest times. There is evidence of a Pictish fort from vitrified rock which has been found near the Castle, and in the 7th century St. Donan lived on the island as a religious hermit.

The first fortified stronghold was built about 1260 by Alexander 2nd. In 1263 Alexander 3rd gave the Castle to Colin Fitzgerald who was the progenitor of the Mackenzies.

The MacRaes formed the bodyguard to the Earls of Seaforth, and became known as Mackenzie's Coat of Mail. They often served as constables of the Castle and were involved in many raids and seiges.

In 1719 the Castle had a garrison of 48 Spaniards sent over to help the Old Pretender regain his throne. The English sent three frigates up the loch to take the Castle, but it was only after they gained access and set fire to the Spaniard's arsenal that the Castle was blown up and became a ruin for the next 200 years.

Colonel MacRae-Gilstrap bought the ruined Castle in 1912, and with the help of Farquhar MacRae rebuilt the castle between 1912 and 1932. Farquhar MacRae had seen a vision of the ruined stronghold restored to its former glory. Later, plans of Eilean Donan were found in Edinburgh Castle, and every detail was found to be true of Farquhar's vision.

The countryside surrounding Eilean Donan is of exceptional beauty and grandeur, with breathtaking mountain, loch and forest scenery. For nature lovers there are Otters and Seals, Wild Goats, Red and Roe Deer to be seen, whilst overhead one may see Ravens, Buzzards, and if lucky, the occasional Golden Eagle. The impressive Falls of Glomach, near Dornie, are well worth the long hard climb up to them. One of the highest in Britain, the water thunders down 300ft.

Nearby is the famous Isle of Skye, with its magnificent range of mountains, the Cuillins, and many places of interest to visit.

Sixteen miles South of Eilean Donan are the imposing remains of three Pictish Brochs, which were once to be seen all over the North of Scotland.

Address
Eilean Donan Castle
Nairnside
Inverness IV1 2BT
Tel: 01463 790229

Opening Times
Open daily from Easter until end of October
10am-5.30pm

Admission (2000)
Admission £3.75
Concessions and parties £2.75
Children under 12 free

Facilities
Visitors can see the Billeting Room, Banqueting Hall and Bedrooms also a 1930's kitchen. There is a Gift Shop and Coffee Shop attached to the Castle and plenty of free parking places

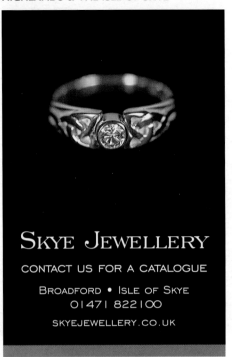

FLODIGARRY COUNTRY HOUSE HOTEL
Staffin, Isle of Skye, Scotland IV51 9HZ
Telephone: 01470 552203 Fax: 01470 552301
19 Rooms (all en suite). 2 Four Posters.
STB ☆☆☆☆ Highly Commended, Country House Hotel of the Year, Taste of Scotland, Macallan Award, Talisker Awards, Best Service, Best Accommodation.
This fine mansion house is steeped in history with Jacobite associations. Built in 1895 by Alexander MacDonald adjacent to where his legendary ancestor Flora once lived, its originality has been carefully preserved. Unspoilt, a sheltered haven set in five acres of gardens and woodland amidst the dramatic scenery of northern Skye. Excellent cuisine.

GLEN MHOR HOTEL & RESTAURANT
9-12 Ness Bank, Inverness, Scotland IV2 4SG
Telephone: 01463 234308 Fax: 01463 713170
30 Rooms (all en suite), 1 Four Poster.
STB 1999/2000 ☆☆☆.
Beautiful, quiet central location. Privately owned and directed traditional style hotel with modern en suite. Standard and Executive rooms, car parking. Enjoys long-standing reputation for friendly attentive service and marvellous Scottish food. Choice of restaurants. Ideal base for great golf, fishing, touring, theatre and many other leisure pursuits.

TIGH AN EILEAN HOTEL
Shieldaig, Ross-shire, IV54 8XN
Telephone: 01520 755251 Fax: 01520 755321
11 Rooms (11 en suite).
AA ☆ ❀ 74%, RAC ☆ + Dining Award STB ☆☆☆☆, Good Hotel Guide, Which? Hotel Guide.
On the edge of the sea, glorious views over Loch Shieldaig are enjoyed from most rooms. Award winning cuisine is offered from this Commended Hotel. The surroundings are rustic but this belies the contemporary comforts within, the excellent facilities available and the beautiful furnishings.

DUNDONNELL HOTEL
Dundonnell, Little Loch Broom,
Nr Ullapool, Ross-shire
Telephone: 01854 633204 Fax: 01854 633366
E-Mail: selbie@dundonnellhotel.co.uk
Web: http://www.sol.co.uk/d/dundonnellhotel
28 Rooms (all en suite).
AA ☆☆☆ ❀❀ 75%, RAC ☆☆☆, STB ☆☆☆☆, Member Scotlands Hotels of Distinction.
An 'oasis' in the West, this long established family run hotel offers high standards in food and accommodation in a stunning lochside location, midway between Ullapool and Gairloch, making it an ideal centre for exploring the area where walking and wild life are in abundance. Close to An Teallach and many other Munros and Inverewe Gardens.

Dunvegan Castle
The Jewel in the Crown of the Isle of Skye

Any visit to this enchanted isle must be deemed incomplete without savouring the wealth of history offered by Dunvegan Castle. The North of Scotland's oldest inhabited Castle, having been the seat and home of the MacLeod Chiefs for 800 years. Dunvegan Castle is a fortress stronghold in an idyllic lochside setting, surrounded by dramatic scenery, where seals play and eagles soar. On display are many fine oil paintings, great Clan treasures; "The Fairy Flag" - the sacred banner of the Clan which is said to possess "miraculous powers" for the MacLeod clan., the Dunvegan Cup - a unique mazer of the middle ages and the Speckled Bagpipes - famous throughout the piping world. Also on view are many items in the Bonnie Prince Charlie exhibition.

There is so much to see and do at Dunvegan Castle. Take a walk around the recently opened Walled Garden with it's own Standing Stone Pyramid or visit the Pedigree Highland Cattle Fold. Dunvegan Castle is also famous for its magnificent Water Gardens and Woodland Walks. You can visit the seal colony - a favourite with children and adults alike - and take a fascinating and exhilarating boat trip through Loch Dunvegan to observe, at close quarters, these playful sea mammals - take your camera, you will get some wonderful photos.

There are two Castle craft and souvenir shops. In addition there is The St Kilda Connection, an exceptional woollen shop which boasts an extensive selection of extremely high quality knitwear and the Macleod of Dunvegan, offering high quality ladies', gents' and children's clothing, kilts, accessories and country-wear. The Castle Restaurant has an all day table licence and provides good Scottish Fayre and home baking.

Dunvegan Castle is the showpiece of the Hebrides - it occupies a truly stunning position on the shore of Loch Dunvegan - it is Skye's most famous landmark and one of the most visited attractions in Scotland, with over 145,000 visitors per annum.

Details
Dunvegan Castle
Tel: 01470 521206
Fax: 01470 521205
e-mail:
info@dunvegancastle.com
Website:
www.dunvegancastle.com

Opening Times
Mid March -End Oct
Mon-Sun: 10am-5.30pm
Nov-Mar Castles & Gardens only
11am-4pm
Last admissions 1/2hr
before closing

Admission
Castle & Gardens
Adults £5.50
Children £3.00
OAP & Students £4.80
Parties £5.00
Gardens only
Adults £3.80
Children £2.00

Location
1 mile north of Dunvegan
Village, 23 miles west of
Portree, on the
Isle of Skye

Dunrobin Castle

Dunrobin is the most northerly of Scotland's great houses, being 50 miles north of Inverness on the A9. The nearest airport is Inverness and the castle has its own railway station.

The Earldom of Sutherland, which was created in 1235, is one of the seven ancient earldoms of Scotland. Dunrobin is mentioned for the first time as a stronghold of the family in 1401 and its name may mean "Robin's Castle" after Robert, the 6th Earl of Sutherland. The castle was transformed in 1845 by Sir Charles Barry from a traditional Scottish castle into a vast palace in Franco-Scots style and subsequently redesigned by Sir Robert Lorimer after a fire in 1915.

The Castle contains an opulent and fascinating collection of furniture, pictures, objets d'art and family memorabilia displayed in many cases in their original setting. All State rooms are open to the public and decorated with flowers from the garden.

The Victorian formal gardens were designed in the grand French style to echo the architecture of Dunrobin Castle, which rises above them and looks out over the Moray Firth. The gardens were laid out by the architect Charles Barry in 1850. Descending the stone terraces, one can see the round garden, grove, parterre and herbaceous borders laid out beneath. The round ponds, all with fountains, are a particular feature, together with the wrought iron Westminster gates. Roses have been replaced with hardy geraniums, antirrhinums and Potentilla fruticosa "Abbotswood". In the policies, there are a number of woodland walks.

An eighteenth century summerhouse which was converted into a museum in the nineteenth century is now also open to the public. It contains a unique and eccentric collection which reflects the family's wide interests through the centuries. They cover ornithology, archaeology, local history, big game hunting, ethnography, beach-combing, Egyptology and geology.

Falconry Display.

Address

Dunrobin Castle
Golspie
Sutherland
KW10 6SF

Tel: 01408 633177
Fax: 01408 634081
Email:
dunrobin.est@btinternet.com

Opening Times

April, May and Oct: Mon-Sat 10.30am-4.30pm. Sun 1pm-4.30pm. Last entry 4.00pm.

June-Sept: Mon-Sat 10.30am-5.30pm. Sun 12.30-5.30pm. Last entry 5.00pm.

Admission

Adults £6.00, OAPs £4.50,
Children £4.50,
Family ticket £17.00.
Group Rate: Adults £5.50,
OAPs £4.50, Children £4.50.

Eilean Donan Castle, Highlands

Strathaven Hotel

Hamilton Road, Strathaven Lanarkshire ML10 6SZ
Telephone: 01357 521778 • Fax 01357 520789
e-mail: sthotel@globalnet.co.uk
www.strathavenhotel.com

The Strathaven Hotel is a picturesque Country House Hotel set in two acres of mature gardens – the perfect setting for business or pleasure. A family run hotel boasting 22 en-suite bedrooms. Bar Lunches and Suppers served in the East Lounge with both Table d'Hote and Grill Menu available in the award-winning Avon Restaurant for the more discerning diners.

A premier venue for Weddings, Anniversaries, Christenings and Birthdays – the Strathaven Suite accommodates up to 180.

A warm welcome awaits you.

SUMMERLEE HERITAGE PARK

Winner of 'Best Working Attraction' Award

Summerlee Heritage Park is an STB Commended visitor attraction covering 22 acres on the site of the former Summerlee Ironworks.

It has both indoor and outdoor facilities including an exhibition hall with working machinery, Scotland's only working electric tramway and a recreated mine with a miners' row.

Cafeteria • Play Area • Shop • Free Parking

Opening hours: 10am to 5pm, seven days.
(Winter hours: 10am to 4pm)

**Summerlee Heritage Park
Heritage Way, Coatbridge
Telephone: 01236 431261**

ADMISSION FREE

NORTH LANARKSHIRE COUNCIL

Unique Heritage properties in beautiful countryside close to Edinburgh and Glasgow these stone cottages are over 200 years old yet fully modernised. We have no new buildings on our 2,000 acre country estate so time appears to stand still. Robie Burns used to visit, come and see why!
For brochure contact Richard or Patricia Carmichael, Carmichael Country Cottages, Carmichael Estate, Biggar ML12 6PG.
Tel: 01899 308336 Fax: 01899 308481
www.carmichael.co.uk/cottages   E-mail: chiefcarm@aol.com

SHIELDHILL HOTEL
Quothquan by Biggar ML12 6NA
Telephone: 01899 220035 Fax: 01899 221092
11 Rooms (all en suite), 4 Four Posters.
AA ☆☆☆ ❀❀, RAC ☆☆☆, ETB ♛♛♛ Highly Commended, RAC Merit Award for Food, Egon Ronay, Good Hotel Guide.
Almost equidistant from Edinburgh, Glasgow and Carlisle, Shieldhill has stood amidst the rolling hills of the Upper Clyde Valley for 700 years. Shieldhill lends itself to exclusive use either for business conferences or private functions, but most of all is the perfect place to relax and enjoy the warm hospitality.

RS 🚫 📶 🗂 P 🍴 V ✂ 🔥 🏨 🏠 SPECIAL 1 2 3 4 C

New Lanark - Conservation Trust

The village of New Lanark is unique. It was built in 1785 by David Dale, a Scottish industrialist, to take advantage of the water power of the Falls of Clyde, to spin cotton. Within 14 years he had built four huge mills and housing for 1,500 workers, making New Lanark one of the most successful spinning complexes in Britain.

In 1800, Robert Owen, a young Welshman, married Dale's daughter and took over ownership of the mills. Owen had radical ideas about the formation of man's character and spent 25 years in New Lanark putting these into practice. He abolished child labour in the mills, in favour of free education. By shortening the working day he increased production, and used his profits to benefit the workers. The Village Store was operated on Co-operative principles, profits being used to pay the teachers at Owen's School for Children. Owen provided opportunities for learning and recreation for all his workers, and New Lanark soon became known as a "model" village of its time.

Robert Owen left New Lanark for America in 1825, but New Lanark carried on production of cotton products until 1968, when the mills closed down. The village fell into decay and wholesale demolition seemed a real possibility, until the New Lanark Conservation Trust was formed in 1974, to bring the village back to life. Today, New Lanark is one of Scotland's top visitor attractions, as well as a living community and a thriving business centre. The village has been nominated as a World Heritage Site and has won countless awards, both for tourism and conservation.

The Visitor Centre interprets the history of the village in a series of exhibitions such as the Millworkers' House, the Village Store, Robert Owen's House and "The Annie McLeod Experience", a dramatic dark ride in which a ten year old mill girl gives you a glimpse of her daily life. The Centre has a variety of specialist shopping, including "Owen's Warehouse", which maintains the traditions and heritage Robert Owen created. Its huge themed area specialises in the best of quality Scottish Tartan, gifts and countrywear, with a dedication to service and value of which Robert Owen himself would be proud.

The spectacular setting, in beautiful countryside by the Falls of Clyde, makes New Lanark an ideal place for those who wish to capture the essence of Scotland's heritage while enjoying a relaxing day out.

In May 1998 the New Lanark Mill Hotel, a 38 bedroom conversion of the original Mill One, opened to the public offering the opportunity to stay in the beautiful conservation village. In addition, 8 self-catering cottages known as the Waterhouses have been added to given an experience to remember.

Address

New Lanark Mill Hotel and the Waterhouses, New Lanark ML11 9DB. Tel: 01555 667200 Fax: 01555 667222 website: www.newlanark.org e-mail: visit@newlanark.org New Lanark Conservation Trust, New Lanark Mills, Lanark ML11 9DB. Tel: 01555 661345 Fax: 01555 665738

Opening Times

Visitor Centre: Open Daily 11am-5pm throughout the year. Closed 25 Dec and 1-2 Jan. The village itself is a living community and open at all times.

Admission

Admission prices to 31 Mar 1999: Adults: £3.75 Concesions: £2.25 Family: £9.95 (2 adults/ 2 children) or £12.50 (2 adults/4 children)

Facilities

Ample free parking. Large Gift and Coffee Shops. Owen's Warehouse – themed mill shop. Visitor Centre is wheelchair friendly

Dalhousie Castle

Bonnyrigg, Edinburgh EH19 3JB, Scotland
Tel: 01875 820153 Fax: 01875 821936
E-mail: res@dalhousiecastle.co.uk Website: www.dalhousiecastle.co.uk

Just 7 miles from Edinburgh city centre and 14 miles from Edinburgh Airport, 13th Dalhousie Castle is now a prestigious hotel and restaurant.

Ten of the twenty-nine Castle bedrooms are historically themed with sumptuous fabrics and furnishings giving the rooms an exclusive feel. Five additional bedrooms are available in the 100 year old Lodge, just two minutes walk from the Castle and furnished in a relaxing country house style.

The vaulted Dungeon Restaurant provides a delightful setting to enjoy the traditional Scottish and classical French 'Castle Cuisine'.

☆☆☆, Johansens and Taste of Scotland approved, AA ☆☆☆ approved.

Jane Welsh Carlyle Museum
at Lodge Street, Haddington, East Lothian

Jane Baillie Welsh was the only child of a 19th century Haddington medical practitioner. In 1821 she met and later married Thomas Carlyle, the historian, writer and philosopher.

The enchanting home and gardens of her youth have been restored to reflect the Regency style of the period.

The rooms and gardens are open to the public from April-September, Wednesday, Thursday, Friday and Saturday, 2-5pm.

Admission £1.50, Concession £1

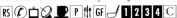

BAYSWELL HOTEL
Bayswell Park, Dunbar, East Lothian EH42 1AE
Telephone: 01368 862225 Fax: 01368 862225
13 Rooms (all en suite).
AA ☆☆, RAC ☆☆, STB ♔ ♔ ♔ ♔ commended.
Situated on a clifftop with unrivalled views across the Firth of Forth, the hotel offers spacious rooms with en-suite facilities, direct-dial telephone, trouser press, colour television with satellite channels and tea/coffee tray. Family-owned and managed, we have two restaurants and two well-stocked bars. 18 Golf courses within easy reach. Just off the A1.

RS 🔆 📺 ☕ 🍵 🅿 ⑪ GF ⌇ 1 2 3 4 C

GREYWALLS
Muirfield, Gullane, East Lothian EH31 2EG
Telephone: 01620 842144 Fax: 01620 842241
email: hotel@greywalls.co.uk
www.greywalls.co.uk
23 Rooms (all en suite).
AA ☆☆☆ (Red) ❀❀, STB ☆☆☆☆
Greywalls began its life as an hotel in the 1940s and is still owned and run by the same family. A Lutyens house set in a Jekyll garden, Greywalls is surrounded by golf courses, close to beautiful sandy beaches and just 30 minutes from Edinburgh. Something for everyone!

RS ☏ 🔆 🅿 ⑪ GF ⌚ ⌇ 🚗 🚘 1 2 3 4 A

BRAID HILLS HOTEL
134 Braid Road, Edinburgh EH10 6JD
Telephone: 0131 447 8888 Fax: 0131 452 8477
68 Rooms (all en suite), 2 Four Posters.
AA/RAC ☆☆☆, STB ☆☆☆☆, Egon Ronay.
The Braid Hills Hotel is magnificently situated with panoramic views across Edinburgh and beyond to the Firth of Forth and the hills of Fife. Although only two miles from the city centre, it boasts a secluded setting far from the traffic and congestion of the city centre itself.

RS ☏ 🚫 🔆 📺 ☕ 🍵 🅿 ⑪ V GF ⌇ ❀ 🚗 🚘
SPECIAL 1 2 3 4 C

TWEEDDALE ARMS HOTEL
Gifford, East Lothian EH41 4QU
Proprietors: Christopher and Wilda Crook
Tel: 01620 810240 Fax: 01620 810488

Built circa 1685 and still traditionally Black & White, the Tweeddale Arms looks out through lime trees to the Green and the River. Located in Gifford, a sweetly-lying, tidy village at the foot of the Lammremuir Hills, within easy reach of 17 of Scotland's finest golf courses including Muirfield, and yet visitors can also enjoy the experience of Scotland's Capital, Edinburgh with its historic Castle, visitor attractions and finest shopping – only 30 minutes from Gifford. Indeed, enjoy the Edinburgh experience from the country.

STB ♔ ♔ ♔ ♔ Commended

Lennoxlove House

Lennoxlove, originally named Lethington, has been the home of the Dukes of Hamilton since 1947. The house, dating from before 1400, is situated in 600 acres, just 20 miles south east of Edinburgh and 1 mile south of the historic town of Haddington, set in the beautiful countryside of East Lothian.

The house was owned by the Maitlands, one of whom, William, was Secretary of State during the time of Mary Queen of Scots. The house was renamed Lennoxlove after the Duchess of Richmond and Lennox bequeathed money to her nephew, Lord Blantyre, to enable him to buy it on condition that it was called 'Lennox's Love to Blantyre'. The Duchess, known as La Belle Stewart and model for Britannia, was a favourite of King Charles II and two of his gifts to her, a Flemish tortoiseshell cabinet and a Boulle pewter and ebony worktable, are on display at Lennoxlove.

Also on display in the house is the silver casket which contained forged letters implicating Mary Queen of Scots in the murder of her husband Lord Darnley, a sapphire ring given to Lord John Hamilton just prior to her execution and a death mask said to be hers.

The house is now home to the former Hamilton Palace collection of furniture, paintings and porcelain, brought together over many years by the Hamiltons and in particular the 10th Duke and his father-in-law William Beckford.

Address

The Administrator
Lennoxlove House
Haddington
East Lothian EH41 4NX
Tel: 01620 823720
Fax: 01620 825112
e-mail: lennoxlove@compuserve.com
Website: www.lennoxlove.org

Opening Times

Open Easter weekend to end Oct on Wed, Thurs, Sun and most Sats, please check. Guided tours start at 2pm, last tour 4.30pm, other times by appointment.

Hall Admission

Adult £4.00
Child £2.00
Group Rate £3.50

Facilities

Gardens open all year round, Corporate entertainment, Family Chapel for weddings, Film and TV location. Free parking.
Clarissa Dicksen Wright's 'Garden Cafe' open Tue - Sun 11am - 5pm and by special appointment.

Hopetoun House

Hopetoun House, located 12 miles west of the City of Edinburgh, is set in 100 acres of magnificent parkland. The building of Hopetoun was started in 1699 by the well known Scottish architect, Sir William Bruce. Much of the original interior may still be seen in the central part of the House.

Considerable changes were made after 1721 by William Adam, another famous Scottish architect whose alterations included the building of the State Apartments and the realignment of the Colonnades and Pavilions, resulting in the magnificent frontage to the house considered by many to be his finest work. William Adam died in 1748. His son, John, superintended the completion of the building and the interior decoration which may be admired in the State Apartments to this day.

The House contains fine carving and elegant plaster ceilings, trompe l'oeil and other paintings by famous artists, wall hangings and furnishings designed for Hopetoun in the 18th century. From the Rooftop Platform visitors may enjoy panoramic views over the countryside and the River Forth with its famous Bridges.

Around the North Pavilion lie a Wildlife Centre, a 'Horse and Man' exhibition and an exhibition entitled 'The Building of Hopetoun'. To the west, encircling the vast lawn where once lay a formal parterre of arabesque and shell design, are woodland walks with Deer Parks extending to the shoreline. Nature Trails have been laid out and Countryside Rangers are on hand to provide extra information as required.

Hopetoun has been the home of the Earls of Hopetoun (later created Marquesses of Linlithgow) ever since it was built. The present head of the family, Adrian Hope, is the fourth Marquess. In 1974 the family established a charitable trust to own and preserve the house with its historic contents and surrounding landscape for the benefit of the public for all time. The family, therefore, are no longer the owners, but they still have a home in part of the house as tenants of the Trust.

Hopetoun House is open to visitors from Easter to the end of September and for functions and special events throughout the year.

Address
Hopetoun House
South Queensbury
West Lothian
EH30 9SL

Tel: 0131 331 2451

BALLATHIE HOUSE HOTEL
Kinclaven by Stanley, Perthshire PH1 4QN
Telephone: 01250 883268 Fax: 01250 883396
28 Rooms (all en suite), 1 Four Poster, plus 16 new Riverside Rooms & Suites. AA ☆☆☆, STB ☆☆☆☆
Macallan 'Taste of Scotland Country House Hotel of the Year' award, Michelin, Egon Ronay, AA ❀❀, Johansens. Situated on its own estate overlooking the River Tay near Perth, Ballathie House offers Scottish hospitality in a house of character and distinction. Elegant public rooms, antique furnishings and period bathrooms with all modern facilities. Award winning food of the highest standard in dining room overlooking the river.

 🅒🗄☕ P 🍴 V GF ⊘ 🥄 🌸 🎒 🎠 SPECIAL
1️⃣2️⃣3️⃣4️⃣ A

CROMLIX HOUSE (Nr. Stirling)
Kinbuck, By Dunblame, Perthshire, Scotland FK15 9JT
Telephone: 01786 822125. Fax: 01786 825450
www.cromlixhouse.com
E-mail: reservations@cromlixhouse.com
14 Rooms (all en suite), 8 suites. AA ☆☆☆ (Red) ❀❀, STB ☆☆☆☆☆. Good Hotel Guide. Egon Ronay 82%. Michelin etc. Cromlix is one of Scotlands Top Country House (Hotels). Within its own 2,000 acre Estate the calm and serenity of this "Time Capsule" is a different world, only 35 mins from Glasgow and 45 mins from Edinburgh. A Home which is immediately relaxing, welcoming and obviously well loved. Masses of thoughtful "extras". Award Winning Cuisine and friendly helpful staff add a special touch to a house where 'understatement' is the norm. Cromlix remains in a class of its own.

RS 🅒🗄☕ P 🍴 V ⊘ 🥄 🌸 🎒 🎠 SPECIAL
1️⃣2️⃣3️⃣4️⃣ A (B in low season)

Blair Castle

To the north of the Perth to Inverness road, where it turns westward at the Pass of Killiecrankie, in the wide Strath of Garry, near the village of Blair Atholl, a short detour along a great avenue of lime trees rewards the traveller with the sight of Blair Castle. Twice a day the sound of the resident piper may be heard, echoing around the gleaming white-harled walls of a stronghold which has been home to the Earls and Dukes of Atholl since 1269.

Just 250 years ago the last siege of a Castle in the British Isles took place here. In 1746, the year after 'Bonnie Prince Charlie' had stayed here on his way south, Lord George Murray, brother to the 2nd Duke led the 'Atholl Brigade' and lay siege to Blair Castle upon its occupation by Hanoverians.

More peaceful times followed and the 2nd Duke resumed his creation of a new park, restyling the Castle as a Georgian house. The fortified appearance was restored in 1869 when the 7th Duke engaged architect, David Bryce to recastellate the building, adding the present entrance and the ballroom to the North. The main tower now resembled the 13th century original whose foundations were begun, by John Cumming of Badenoch, after whom it is traditionally known as Cumming's (or Comyn's) Tower. Blair Castle became a Duke's home in 1703 when the 2nd Marquis of Atholl was created first Duke of Atholl by Queen Anne.

Queen Victoria visited Blair in 1844 when the 6th Duchess of Atholl, Lady Glenlyon was Her Majesty's Lady of the Bedchamber. The loyalty of the bodyguard so impressed Her Majesty and Prince Albert that she bestowed upon them, formally, the title of 'The Atholl Highlanders', which remains Britain's only Private Army.

Today Blair Castle is Scotland's most visited privately-owned historic house. Thirty two fully furnished rooms are open to view and each contains an aspect of the fine collections so skillfully and passionately tended, over the years, by the Murray family. There is great variety wherever the visitor looks, with Ancestral and Landscape Paintings, Arms and Armour, China, Lace, Embroidery and Tapestry all displayed to perfection. The Castle hosts many events during the year, from World Piping Championships and Highland Games to Horse Trials and Highland Balls, in and out of season.

Blair Castle is set in parkland which covers some 130,000 acres, includes a 70,000 acre deer forest, and is populated with giant larches, Scots firs, beeches and colourful rhododendrons. The natural beauty of picturesque rivers and romantic, forest-clad mountains beyond perfectly complement the grandeur of the castle's interior.

Address

Blair Castle
Blair, Atholl
Pitlochry
Perthshire PH18 5TL

Tel: 01796 481207
Fax: 01796 481487

Opening Times

Early April to late October,
10am-6pm daily.
Last entry 5pm
Mar 27th-Oct 31st
10am-6pm daily.
Last entry 5pm

Admission

Adults – £6.00
Senior Citizens – £5.00
Students/Children – £5/£4
Disabled – £2
Reductions for groups
over 12

Facilities

Gift shop, Restaurant, Toilet facilities, Parking, Nature trails, Deer Park, Picnic area, Pony trekking

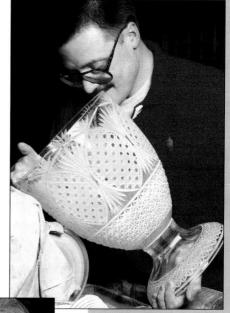

Drummond Castle Gardens

Estate Office, Muthill, Perthshire PH5 2AA
Tel: 01764 681433 Fax: 01764 681642
Email: thegardens@drummondcastle.sol.co.uk

These are Scotland's most important formal gardens and among the finest in Europe. The upper terraces offer stunning views and overlook a magnificent parterre celebrating the saltire, the three rivers of Perthshire and the famous multiplex sundial by John Milne, Master Mason to Charles I.

Featured in United Artists' *Rob Roy*.

Open Easter weekend, then daily 1st May to 31st Oct, 2pm to 6pm (last entry 5pm).

Entrance 2m south of Crieff off A822.

Scone Palace
Perth, Scotland R12 6BD
Tel: 01738 552300   Fax: 01738 552588
Email: visits@scone-palace.co.uk   www.scone-palace.co.uk

Close to the city of Perth lies Scone Palace, situated on one of the most historic sites in Scotland, and the one-time crowning palace of Scottish Kings on the Stone of Destiny. In spite of being only two miles from the centre of Perth, Scone Palace retains its rural charm and peace. Today it is the hereditary family home of the Earl of Mansfield, and is a place that any visitor – or native – to Scotland cannot miss. In the Palace are magnificent contents and priceless collections, whilst outside are gardens, wooded grounds and the famed pinetum (David Douglas of David Douglas Fir fame was born at Scone), peacocks and animals, maze, gift shop, produce shop, restaurants – and even a children's playground.

The Black Watch Museum

Two and a half centuries of treasures of Scotland's oldest Highland Regiment, The Black Watch. Open May-September, Monday-Saturday (inc. public holidays), 10.00am-4.30pm excluding last Sat of June. October-April, Monday-Friday 10.00am-3.30pm. Closed over Christmas and New Year. Admission free (donations welcome). Groups of 10+ please telephone in advance. Gift shop (mail order available), Parking.

Regimental Headquarters
THE BLACK WATCH
Balhousie Castle
Perth PH1 5HR
Tel: 0131 310 8530 Fax: 01738 643245
Email: bw.rhq@btclick.com

FARLEYER HOUSE HOTEL
Aberfeldy, Perthshire PH15 2JE
Telephone: 01887 820332 Fax: 01887 829430
15 Rooms (all en suite). STB ♛♛♛♛ Deluxe.
Situated in a beautiful mature parkland setting overlooking the Tay Valley, Farleyer offers fine food, deluxe accommodation and an ideal touring base for central Scotland. Golf, walking and salmon fishing all available.

Perthshire

Perthshire, renowned the world over for its beauty, history and culture, has been aptly described as "All of Scotland". These 2,000 square miles in the very heart of Scotland summon up images of magnificent scenery, ancient castles, pretty cottages and Highland Games, with the ever-present musical accompaniments of clinking whisky glass and lilting bagpipes.

For hundred of years, this area has been the crossroads of the nation, and today's modern road, rail and air links maintain that tradition. Fast roads converge on Perthshire from all directions, Perth is at the centre of the Scottish rail network, and Edinburgh and Glasgow Airports are just one hour away.

Once arrived, Perthshire's glories immediately become apparent. Everywhere, there is room to move, space to breath and time to unwind. Exploring Perthshire is an experience to be savoured. Soaring mountains and jewel-like lochs; a rich historical legacy; colourful and exciting events and entertainments; flower-bedecked towns and villages; the creative skills of local cratfspeople – all are waiting to be discovered.

Perthshire's sporting and leisure facilities are renowned. In an area of such natural beauty, it is not surprising that virtually every outdoor activity imaginable is catered for. Golfing (on 31 courses!), hillwalking, riding, sailing, salmon and trout angling, ski-ing – the opportunities are almost endless. A full range of packaged activity and special interest holidays for all ages and abilities is available – telephone Perthshire Activity Line on (01738) 444144 for all the details.

When it comes to finding somewhere to stay, Perthshire can offer a wider range of accommodation than any other part of Scotland. From five-star hotel to farmhouse B & B, from log cabin to luxury caravan – over 900 establishments are ready to provide a traditional welcome and fine hospitality. Eating out is a pleasure, with most restaurants making full use of superb-quality local produce; Perthshire's salmon, beef, game and soft fruits are particularly renowned.

Sir Walter Scott once wrote:

> "If an intelligent stranger were asked to describe the most varied and the most beautiful province in Scotland, it is probable that he would name the county of Perth."

Today's visitors simply say: "Perthshire is All of Scotland".

For Further Free Information, contact: Perthshire Tourist Board, Lower City Mills, West Mill Street, Perth PH1 5QP, Scotland. Tel (01738) 627958 Fax (01738) 630416

E-mail: perthtouristb@perthshire.co.uk info@ptb.ossien.net

Internet: www.perthshire.co.uk

In this issue we have split Wales into three - North, Mid and South. The counties contained within these regions are shown below:_

WALES

North Wales
Conwy
Denbighshire
Flintshire
Gwynedd
Isle of Anglesey
Wrexham

Mid Wales
Powys
Ceredigion

South Wales
Blaenau Gwent
Bridgend
Caerphilly
Cardiff
Carmarthenshire
Merthyr Tydfil
Monmouthshire
Neath Port Talbot
Newport
Pembrokeshire
Rhondda Cynon Taff
Swansea
Torfaen
Vale of Glamorgan

Wales Tourist Board
Brunel House
2 Fitzalan Road, Cardiff,
CF24 0UY
Tel: 02920 499909

London Office
The Britain Visitor Centre
1. Regent Street, London,
SW1Y 4XT
Tel: 0207 808 3838

TOURIST BOARD RATINGS

At the point of going to press many of our advertisers had not been advised of their new tourist board ratings which are now commended in stars rather than crowns.

Therefore, some of the establishments will be showing their new ratings in stars whilst others will be showing the old crown ratings.

All the hotels should now know their ratings and will be happy to let you know upon request.

The same applies to the various symbols for Bed and Breakfast, Guest House and Self Catering accommodation

For a detailed account of all ratings please contact :

British Tourist Authority
Thames Tower
Blacks Road
Hammersmith
London, W6 9EL
Tel: 020 8846 9000

WALES

Portmeirion, Gwynedd, North Wales

The National Botanic Garden of Wales

**Middleton Hall, Llanarthne,
Carmarthenshire SA32 8HG
Tel: 01558 667134 Fax: 01558 667138
Email: ian@gardenofwales.org.uk
www.gardenofwales.org.uk**

Deep in the beautiful Towy valley of South West Wales lies a world glass garden for the new millennium. The broadwalk and gardens take the visitor on a fascinating geological timewalk through the Welsh nation. There are interactive exhibitions and demonstrations, lakeside walks, the Millennium Square visitor centre, a Mediterranean Garden, the walled Wallace Garden, an Energy Zone and the Great Glasshouse. The spectacular focal point of the Garden of Wales is the largest single span glasshouse in the world. Inside you can experience the aftermath of an Australian bush fire, pause in a Spanish olive grove and delight in the fuschias of Chile – you'll find rock faces and ravines, streams, waterfalls and a small lake.
Group rates: adults £5.00, concessions £4.00, children £2.00.

Discover a different country within Britain – head for WALES, a land with its own history and heritage, its own culture and cuisine and its very own language and traditions.

Although an integral part of Britain, Wales is as different from England as Singapore is from Malaysia and it is this difference which makes a visit to Wales such a delightful experience which more and more travellers are discovering every year.

Wales is sometimes referred to as one of Britain's best kept secrets. An air of mystery surrounds the purple-headed mountains of Wales, the green round hills rolling away to infinity, and the beguiling Celtic character of this country on the Western shores of Britain.

On the eve of the new Millennium, Wales is experiencing the most exciting period in its recent history; Europe's oldest culture redefining itself in a dynamic combination of old and modern, past, present and future. Basking in the light of the successful hosting of the European Council meeting in June of last year and preparing this year for its first National Assembly in 600 years, Wales and its young and vibrant capital, Cardiff, now turns its attention to hosting the last major event of this Millennium, the 1999 Rugby World Cup.

Harlech Castle, North Wales

Preparations are long under way for this prestigious event; by the first kick off, Cardiff and Wales will be proud beneficiaries of the majestic new Millennium Stadium, two new five-star luxury hotels, the most exciting waterfront development in Europe at Cardiff Bay and a wealth of amenities and entertainment to suit all palates. Befitting for a major European capital city; a flagship of which this small nation should be justifiably proud.

When the world focuses its attention on Wales, its people will be waiting.

With a population just under three million, Wales is a compact country which has an endless variety of landscape and terrain. Its mountains and lakes, rivers and valleys, coast and country offer the visitor a break from the pressures of everyday living; Wales has all the benefits of a relaxing escape without any of the disadvantages attributed to travelling long distances. Add to this one of Europe's richest cultures, the explosion of young talent in the Arts on to the world scene in recent years and the resurgence of the lyrical native tongue in this latter half of the twentieth century and an image emerges of a nation whose stars are very much in the ascendant.

Cardiff, the capital of Wales, is one of Europe's youngest capital cities and is a delightful mix of ancient and modern – Victorian and Edwardian shopping arcades rub shoulders with modern shopping precincts.

The city's classically designed civic centre made from Portland stone is an

Chrik Castle, Clwyd, North Wales - Courtesy of The National Trust

architectural delight while Cardiff Castle in the very heart of the city is a three-in-one historic site – part Roman, part Norman and part Victorian. Not only is Cardiff the country's centre of commerce and business but it is also the cultural and sporting capital of Wales, home of the internationally acclaimed Welsh National Orchestra and the National Museum of Wales which houses a priceless collection of modern art including many notable impressionist paintings.

Cardiff, which developed rapidly as a sea port in the 19th century, has a cosmopolitan air, a colourful cafe quarter and an excellent year round programme of entertainment ranging from rock and pop concerts to opera and orchestral concerts, from ballet to modern dance and drama.

During the summer, Cardiff Festival offers a packed six week programme of free entertainment, making it one of the biggest and best summer festivals in Europe.

Wales has three National Parks within its boundaries; protected areas of exquisite beauty making up almost a quarter of the country's total area. They are home to close knit communities and an array of flora and fauna.

Covering 840 square miles, Snowdonia National Park in the north west of Wales, takes its name from the highest mountain range in England

495

and Wales and is the largest of Wales, three National Park. In Welsh, it is called, Eryri, which possibly come from land of eagles. The highest point is Mount Snowdon or, Yr Wyddfa, in Welsh which means the burial place, which is often associated with legends connected to King Arthur. The melting of glaciers in the last Ice Age were responsible for the formation of this dramatic landscape; Snowdonia's mountains were a training location for the first team to conquer Everest and the proving ground for trail-blazing British climbers such as Joe Brown. They harbour mystical valleys and lakes in their folds. It is also a region of great variety; Mount Snowdon itself is only 10 miles from the sea and the park also includes wooded valleys, moorland, rivers, forest lakes and waterfalls. It stretches south to Machynlleth and Barmouth on the coast and east to Bala.

The highest peaks in southern Britain are in the Brecon Beacons National Park in South Wales. There are four ranges within the park – the Black Mountains near the English/Welsh border, the Brecon Beacons themselves, Fforest Fawr and Black

Tredegar House, Newport, South Wales

Chrik Castle, Clwyd, North Wales - Courtesy of The National Trust

Mountain near Llandeilo on the western boundary of the park. With its wild terrain of bare hilltops and deep valleys, isolated lakes and invigorating waterfalls, is an outdoor enthusiast's Utopia; covering 519 square miles of mainly upland area, visitors get an amazing feeling of space and freedom. The park is made largely of soft red sandstone rock, which accounts for the wave-like effect of the boulder-shape hilltops. Apart from walking, activities vary from caving, potholing and canoeing to horseriding and canal cruising.

Britain's only coastal National Park lies in the extreme South West of Wales; the coastal path stretches for about 180 miles from St Dogmaels near Cardigan in the north, to Amroth, near Tenby, in the south and encompasses some of Europe's most spectacularly beautiful natural coastal scenery. It also includes the mystical moorland range of the Preseli Hills, rising to 536m and the location of many ancient Celtic remains. The park can in fact be separated into four distinct areas; the lonely, wild and rugged cliffs of the north, the huge sandy arc of St Bride's Bay, the sheltered, lush greenery of the twisting Daugleddau estuary and the towering limestone cliffs and sheltered sandy coves of the south. It is hailed as, gwlad hud a lledrith, (land of magic and enchantment). Its steep rugged cliffs are home to hundreds of seabirds and other wildlife, as are the off-shore islands of Skomer, Skokholm, Grassholm and Ramsey which are world-famous sea bird sanctuaries. The area is also a playground for all genre of watersports and outdoor activities and popular with people who want to relax and get away from it all in beautiful surroundings.

Wales also has five Areas of Outstanding Natural Beauty, namely the Gower Peninsula, The Wye Valley, The Llyn Peninsula, the Anglesey

Coast and the Clwydian Range – three in the North and three in the South.

The Gower Peninsula was Britain's first designated Area of Outstanding Natural Beauty in 1956. 15 miles long, it juts out into the Bristol Channel to the west of Swansea and is known for its sandy bays, steep cliffs and inland hills dotted with ancient relics.

The Wye valley, adjacent to the England border, is a painter's favourite. Its steep wooded valley and historic remains such as Chepstow castle and Tintern Abbey, have inspired the likes of Turner and Wordsworth. It is particularly charming in the Autumn, when its acres of woodland are ablaze with colour.

The Llyn Peninsula is on the extreme western tip of North Wales, some 25 miles long and varying from five to ten miles wide, it stretches out into the Irish sea. It is wild and desolate in parts and is popular with visitors for

Plas Newydd, Gwynedd, North Wales - Courtesy of The National Trust

precisely this reason. Its unspoilt natural beauty and the peacefulness of the area lure people back again and again.

The Anglesey coastline is popular for similar reasons; miles and miles of totally unspoilt coastline which seems to have everything. Excellent connections with the rest of Britain and Ireland, high cliffs alive with wildlife, sheltered bays perfect for watersports, picturesque coastal villages and a rich history.

Finally, the Clwydian Range run south-east from Rhyl to just north of Llangollen. Although not as high as their neighbouring ranges in Snowdonia, these mystical hills are very popular with walkers. The summit, Moel Fammau, rises to a modest 600m and is the only mountain surrounded by rounded hills. The area has many links with King Arthur, represented in some place names such as Moel Arthur, which means Hill of Arthur, who reputedly lived there plotting against the Saxons.

An outdoor enthusiast's dream as it evidently is, Wales offers much more to the visitor. There are many tourist attractions to keep even the most restless entertained, such as the Great Little Trains of Wales, the industrial heritage museums tracing Wales, mining and industrial past, theme and

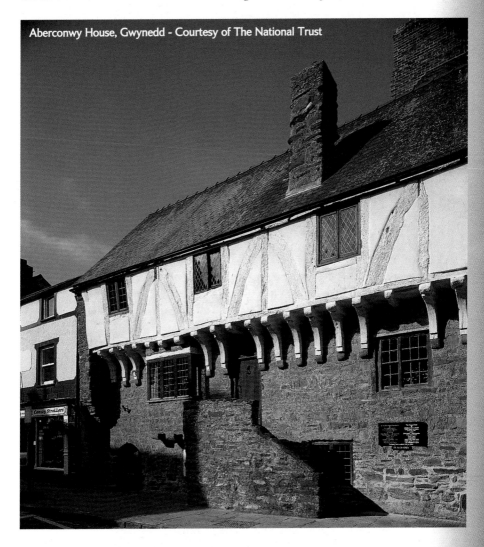

Aberconwy House, Gwynedd - Courtesy of The National Trust

Above: The Banqueting Hall at Cardiff Castle

wildlife parks like Oakwood Leisure Park and Welsh Mountain Zoo at Colwyn Bay, excellently preserved country houses and estates and of course more castles per square mile than any other country in Europe. There are also the slightly more unusual sites, such as Portmeirion, the Italianate village in North Wales, creation of architect Sir Clough Williams-Ellis and location for the filming of the 60s cult series The Prisoner. It's like stepping into another world.

Colby Woodland Garden, Dyfed - Courtesy of The National Trust

Above: Powis Castle, Powys, Mid Wales - Courtesy of the National Trust

Further south in Snowdonia National Park is the innovative Centre for Alternative Technology, a self-sufficient community living almost entirely by means of natural energy sources. Nearby, in the town of Machynlleth, stands Celtica, an interactive interpretation centre of the history of the Celtic nations.

There is also a host of other attractions ranging from the hands-on science discovery museum Techniquest in Cardiff Bay, to aquariums, caves, country parks and so on. The list is endless.

One of its greatest assets is its people. Whether they are entertaining you at one of the many festivals and concerts or chatting over a cappuccino in Cardiff's Continental-style Quarter, they are friendly, vivacious and ready to give a warm Welsh Welcome – Croeso I Gymru.

For further information please contact WALES TOURIST BOARD PRESS OFFICE ON 01222 475291.

Powis Castle, Powys, Mid Wales
Courtesy of The National Trust

Cardiff

GREAT VALUE FOR MONEY

Famous for its hospitality and good value, Cardiff has been best value-for-money for visitors for five years now in a survey of 16 major cities around the world including London, New York and Paris*. Ancient castles, majestic architecture, spacious parklands, Edwardian arcades and sparkling new shopping malls make Cardiff a city for all seasons. Fine and friendly hotels, excellent eating places, opera and music of all sorts, theatre, ballet and international sport delight our visitors. There's the new and impressive Cardiff International Arena, and the newly-restored waterfront is attracting thousands of visitors.

GREAT ENTERTAINMENT

The big stars are regularly in Cardiff, from Luciano Pavarotti and Tina Turner to the Royal Shakespeare Company and Anthony Hopkins. Welsh National Opera première all their new productions here. Cardiff is a city of world-class events: the International Animation Festival and the Cardiff Singer of the World Competition, the Cardiff Proms, International Festival of Street Entertainment, Roald Dahl Children's Festival, and the International Squash Championships. Our Ice Hockey team have been four times British Champions and Cardiff Arms Park hosts Five Nations Rugby and international soccer.

SO MUCH TO SEE AND DO

Shopping is a particular pleasure in the delightfully compact city centre, with speciality shops and all the famous High Street names within easy walking distance of the top hotels, Central Station, concert halls and theatres, Castle and Civic Centre. The National Museum and Gallery of Wales has some superb Impressionist art and exhibitions on the history of this rugged Principality. Living displays of Wales' past fill 100 acres at the Museum of Welsh Life. At the rapidly-developing Inner Harbour Techniquest offers hands-on science experience for all ages, and the Cardiff Bay Visitor Centre explains the enormous and exciting redevelopment of Cardiff's historic docklands through videos and a huge model.

SO EASY TO GET TO

Cardiff is on the M4 Motorway and London is just two hours away by InterCity, with daily flights to Cardiff-Wales Airport from Amsterdam, Paris and Brussels and cities throughout Britain.

For accommodation to suit all pockets, and for what's on, what to see and do and where to stay, call Cardiff Marketing on 01222 667773. * BTA Survey May 1995

Tourist Information Centre
Central Station
Central Square
Cardiff
United Kingdom
CF1 1QY
Tel: 01222 227281

Cardiff Accommodation Hotline
Tel: 01222 395173
(Mon-Fri 9.00-5.30)

The
Dylan Thomas
Centre

Superbly restored in 1995, The Dylan Thomas Centre – the historic (1825) Georgian colonnaded, formery City Guildhall – is an elegant building in a delightful setting with excellent facilities and friendly and helpful staff in the best of Welsh traditions.

As well as the impressive Dylan Thomas Exhibition, the centre also offers visitors a thriving Literary events programme, a book/coffee shop and one of the best culinary experiences in Swansea in its award winning Grade II listed restaurant overlooking the River Tawe and Swansea Marina Moorings.

**The Dylan Thomas Centre
Somerset Place, Maritime
Quarter
Swansea SA1 1RR
Tel: +44 (0)1792 463980
www.dylanthomas.org**

CITY & COUNTY OF SWANSEA • DINAS A SIR ABERTAWE

Swansea & Gower

Although Swansea is a small, friendly city, from earliest times it has been recognised as an important centre in Wales. The Vikings, attracted by the beautiful coastline, colonised the area and gave Swansea or 'Sweyn's Eye' as it was known, its name. The Norman Lords of Gower built castles to protect their lands. Their remains can be still seen today on the Gower Peninsula. This was the first area in the UK to be designated one of Outstanding Natural Beauty and is famous for its breathtaking views of rugged bays and sandy beaches.

Arthur's Stone, the cromlech atop Cefn Bryn — Gower's highest point, is said to be a stone thrown from the shoe of legendary King Arthur. Early man also left his mark in the limestone caves along our craggy coastline; whilst in later years, they were used by smugglers and wreckers to hide ill-gotten gains and contraband. Gower has many ancient sites which add a touch of mystery to the spectacular scenery and can be explored by car, on foot or on horseback.

Swansea's rich cultural traditional and strong industrial and maritime heritage are commemorated in the city's Museums and Art Gallery. Swansea Museum is the oldest in Wales and the Industrial and Maritime Museum is situated in the city's award winning Maritime Quarter.

The city celebrates its heritage whilst looking towards a literary future in The Dylan Thomas Centre, the National Literature Centre for Wales. This is the first purpose built literature centre in the UK. The Dylan Thomas Centre has a permanent exhibition on the life and works of Dylan Thomas and an annual Dylan Thomas Festival.

Swansea and the surrounding area has a wealth of history, tradition and culture to share with you — you can even take part in one of the Hwyrnos (translated — late night!) evenings and enjoy traditional Welsh fare, singing and dancing, accompanied by harp and fiddle.

For more information contact The Information Centre, Singleton Street, Swansea SA1 3QG or telephone +44 1792 468321, fax +44 1792 464602 or email swantrsm @ cableol.co.uk.

St. Davids Cathedral

St. Davids Cathedral rests at the bottom of a deep wooded valley cut through by the river Alun. Approaching from the town, the visitor enters the walls of the cathedral close through the gatehouse, the only remaining one of four original entry gates, and from the top of 39 steps is met by a stunning view of the Cathedral and neighbouring Bishop's Palace. The medieval close contains a collection of stone houses which, with their walled gardens and quiet air of history add to the remarkable peace of the valley.

The Cathedral, begun in 1181, is at least the fourth church to have been built on a site reputed to be that on which St. David himself founded a monastic settlement in the 6th century. The outstanding features of the building are the magnificent ceilings - oak in the Nave and painted in the Choir and Presbytery - and the sloping floor. The stalls of the Chapter of the Cathedral contain medieval miscricords and the Chapter is unique in having the reigning Sovereign as a member. The Cathedral has been an important place of pilgrimage for nearly fourteen centuries. In 1124, Pope Calixtus II declared that two pilgrimages to St. Davids were equal to one to Rome and that three were equal to one to Jerusalem itself.

On the north side of the Cathedral is St. Mary's Hall, connected by the remains of the fourteenth century cloisters. It is all that remains of St. Mary's College, built in 1365, and is used as the Cathedral hall, in the summer housing an exhibition of local Pembrokeshire crafts.

The Cathedral has a strong musical tradition. There are choral services throughout the week, with choral Mattins and Evensong each Sunday, and a programme of concerts through the year. St. Davids was the first cathedral to have a girls choir, which has twice toured in America, frequently performed for radio, and is featured on two CDs. The St. Davids Cathedral Festival has just enjoyed its twenty first annual week-long programme of music performed by musicians of note from around the country.

St. Davids Cathedral is a very special place.

St. Davids Cathedral
The Deanery,
The Close,
St. Davids,
Pembrokeshire, Wales

Telephone:
01437 720 199
Facsimile:
01437 721 885
(The Dean and Chapter).

Daily Services
Open 08:00a.m.
to 06.00p.m.
Disabled Access
Bookshops

Cathedral Music Festival
26 May - 3 June.

TREDEGAR HOUSE AND PARK
Newport, South Wales

Set in 90 acres of award-winning gardens and parkland, Tredegar House is one of the architectural wonders of Wales. For over five hundred years it was the ancestral home of the Morgans, later Lord Tredegar. Visitors can now discover what life was like 'above' and 'below' stairs in thirty restored rooms. The intriguing tours explore the lavish state rooms and the curious servant's quarters, uncovering the Morgan stories and mysteries.

Facilities on site: Tearoom, Gift Shop, Craft Shops, Picnic Areas, Toilets and Car Park. Disabled Facilities, access to ground floor only.

Opening times: Easter to end September, Wed to Sun. Special Christmas openings. First tour at 11.30 am and last tour at 4.00 pm.

Admission price (2000): £4.75 Adult, £3.65 Concessions, £2.25 Child, £12.95 Family.

Just off the M4 at Junction 28. Bus 15 or 30 (short walk).

WATERWYNCH BAY HOTEL
Waterwynch Bay, Tenby,
South Pembrokeshire SA70 8TJ
Telephone: 01834 842464 Fax: 01834 845076
Email: waterwynchhousehotel.co.uk
www.waterwynchhousehotel.co.uk

Situated on the National Parks Coastal path in 27 acres of secluded woodlands/gardens and its own private beach with glorious views over Carmarthen Bay. Waterwynch House, a class II building, built in 1820 by artist Charles Norris, is now a luxury Hotel with the Highest Cuisine reputation. Ideal base for South-west Wales. 17 Rooms (all en suite) plus 5 lounge suites with jacuzzi baths.
WTB 👑 👑 👑 Highly Commended.

Merthyr Tydfil
Gateway to the Brecon Beacons National Park

WHERE IN WALES WAS . . .

The first Ballot Box used? The first Steam Engine to run on rails? The Sinclair C5 made? The Mabinogion translated into English? Laura Ashley born? The first Labour MP elected? 'Myfanwy' composed? The Red Flag first flown?

Find out at Cyfarthfa Castle Museum & Gallery
Merthyr Tydfil – full of surprises!
Tel: 01685 379884 for a free information pack, or fill in and return the coupon.

Name: _____

Address: _____

_____

Post to: The Tourism Section, Merthyr Tydfil County Borough Council, Castle St., Merthyr Tydfil CF47 8AN.

DYFFRYN GARDENS

**St Nicholas
Vale of Glamorgan
CF5 6SU
Tel: (01222) 593328
Fax: (01222) 591966**

The gardens, which are some 3 miles from Cardiff, include some of Wales' finest landscaped grounds which overflow with rare and exotic plants and trees.

There are formal Round, Pompeiian and Theatre gardens and the informal West garden and Arboretum. The Rose garden contains a superb selection grown through the Centuries, the Cloisters has examples of plants grown in Shakespearean times and the Physic garden contains plants used for medicinal properties.

With sweeping lawns, archways, follies, paved courts, a vine walk, water lily canal and herbaceous borders over 100 metres long, Dyffryn Gardens offers a fabulous variety of colour and form all year round.

GERDDI
DYFFRYN
GARDENS

Vale of Usk and Wye Valley

The Vale of Usk and Wye Valley combines 300 square miles of outstanding natural beauty with more ancient castles than almost anywhere else in Britain. Centuries of border strife between the Welsh and English have left a rich legacy to the region, of time ravaged fortresses and magnificent castle ruins.

Discover the fascinating history of the Marches – plots and conquests, kings and revolutionaries. Some are blood thirsty tales, others a more peaceful insight into medieval life.

Mighty Chepstow Castle, on the cliffs above the Wye, was built by William the Conqueror's men as part of the conquest of south east Wales. Once a valiantly defended fortress and palatial Tudor residence, Raglan Castle still has signs of its former glory visible today. At Caldicot, the Great Hall still reverberates with the sound of lavish banquets, where guests can experience at first hand, the traditions of a by-gone age. While in the north, in peaceful settings, visitors can explore Skenfrith, Grosmont and White Castles which once formed a triangular defence system for the borderland. An eighteen mile circular route links the three castles enabling the keen walker to enjoy the quiet countryside.

Stepping back further in time the fortress, baths and amphitheatre at Caerleon are some of the most significant Roman finds in Britain. Not far away, at Caerwent, are the remains of an important Roman city.

Visitors have travelled to the Wye Valley since the late eighteenth century when poets, artists and gentlemen of leisure flocked to admire the river scenery and splendid Tintern Abbey. The 12th century Abbey was built by famous Cistercian monks and is still one of the most serene and faithfully preserved ruins in Britain.

With market towns of character, accommodation to suit all tastes and ample opportunities for outdoor activity this is a perfect touring region.

Wye Valley & Vale of Usk
Tourism Planning &
Economic Development
Monmouthshire C.C.
County Hall
Cambrian Way
NP44 2XH
Tel: 01633 644847
Fax: 01633 644800

THE LAKE COUNTRY HOUSE

Llangammarch Wells, Powys, Wales LD4 4BS
Tel: 01591 620202/620474 Fax: 01591 620457
E-mail: lakehotel@ndirect.co.uk
www.ndirect.co.uk/~lakehotel

A country house set in 50 acres with riverside walks and a large well-stocked trout lake. The grounds are a haven for wildlife. Guests can fish for trout or salmon on the lake and river Irfon that runs through the grounds. Other leisure facilities include a nine-hole par 3 golf course, tennis court, croquet lawn and billiards room. The rooms are very comfortably furnished with thoughtful attention to details; sumptuous sofas beside log fires, fine antiques and fresh flowers. Excellent food is served in our award-winning restaurant. Special breaks available throughout the year.

THE *M*ANOR HOTEL

Brecon Road, Crickhowell, Powys NP8 1SE
Tel: 01873 810212   Fax: 01873 811938

The Manor Hotel is situated in the Black Mountains, near the Brecon Beacons, and commands panoramic views over the Usk Valley. There are plenty of historic landmarks to be visited and activities that can be organised. We have 22 individually styled en-suite bedrooms with all the modern conveniences that the discerning traveller requires. All residents have complimentary use of our leisure suite – swimming pool, jacuzzi, steam room & gymnasium. With our restaurant offering the best in modern British cooking the Manor Hotel provides the ideal location for a 'get away from it all' break. AA ☆☆☆.

GLIFFAES COUNTRY HOUSE HOTEL
Crickhowell, Powys NP8 1RH
Telephone: 01874 730 371 Fax: 01874 730 463
www.gliffaeshotel.com
22 Rooms (all en suite).
AA ☆☆☆ ❀❀. RAC ☆☆☆. WTB ☆☆☆. Ashley Courtney, Johansen, Signpost, Which Hotel.
Spectacularly situated in the Usk valley in 33 acres of magnificent grounds and gardens with many rare and beautiful trees and shrubs, Gliffaes offers the welcome and comfort for which country houses were built. Enjoy the relaxed atmosphere and unwind in our spacious sitting rooms and attractive conservatory. Afternoon tea on the terrace overlooking the river is a must! Dinner, from imaginative menus, covers the best of National dishes, using local produce, as well as Mediterranean specialities. Our elegant and comfortable en-suite bedrooms all vary in size and views. $2^{1}/_{2}$ miles of wild Brown Trout and Salmon fishing. Log fires in winter.

THE CASTLE OF BRECON HOTEL
The Castle Square, Brecon, Powys
Telephone: 01874 624611 Fax: 01874 623737
Email: hotel@breconcastle.co.uk
www.breconcastle.co.uk
45 Rooms (all en suite), 1 Four Poster.
AA ☆☆, WTB ☆☆ Hotel.
A charming historic hotel that has grown out of the remains of Brecon Castle. It is renowned for its excellent views, good food and friendly service. Brecon is a very small, ancient town surrounded by outstanding scenery in an area packed with castles and historic monuments.

THE METROPOLE
Temple Street, Llandrindod Wells, Powys LD1 5DY
Telephone: 01597 823700 Fax: 01597 824828
http://www.metropole.co.uk
122 Rooms (all en suite).
AA ☆☆☆, RAC ☆☆☆, WTB ☆☆☆
Built in the late 19th century by the great grandmother of the current owners, the Metropole is a warm hospitable hotel. Comfortable en suite bedrooms with modern facilities. Excellent traditional cuisine using local produce and residents bar. Superb indoor leisure complex. Spa town centre nearby. Best Western Hotel.

CASTLE INN
Pengenffordd, Nr Talgarth, Powys LD3 0EP
Tel: 01874 711353
5 Rooms (2 en-suite)
WTB 2 Crown Commended, AA QQQ, CAMRA Listed B&B.
This country inn is overlooked by the ancient fortress of Castle Dinas (the highest castle site in Wales). The Inn has its own spring-water drinking supply. A home-cooked meal, a traditional ale and a warm bed awaits you.

MID WALES

Lakes & Mountains

Mid Wales Lakes and Mountains is a country lover's paradise 365 days of the year. Stretching through some of the most spectacular countryside in Wales, from the magnificent Brecon Beacons National Park in the south to the verdant Elan Valley in the "Heart of Wales" to the wild Berwyn Mountains in the North.

A refreshing region in which activities abound....you can savour the atmosphere of the traditional market towns, walk along ancient footpaths, tour the peaceful roads and byways by bike, cruise along canal ways, fish on three classic Welsh rivers, tee off at superb golf courses, and at the end of the day return to the comfort of a country house hotel, cosy inn, farmhouse or cottage.

For a full colour guide of the area, please telephone the 24hr Tourism Brochure Request line.

Tel 01874 611729,
quoting EO 2001

A day out in Wales

With 106,000 acres of countryside, 132 miles of coastline and some of the

most spectacular historic properties in Wales, the National Trust has something for everyone.

all shapes

From impressive stately homes, castles and gardens to modest country cottages, celebrated works of art to working industrial

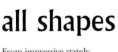

with the heritage sites, the National Trust cares for properties great and small. Each is different from the last. Each significant in its own right and with an extensive

National Trust

programme of events each offering visitors a vastly different experience and endless ways to spend their days.

comes in

For further details of National Trust properties and events in Wales call in to a Tourist –

and sizes.

Yr Ymddiriedolaeth Genedlaethol
The National Trust

THE SIGN OF A GREAT DAY OUT

Llandudno, Colwyn Bay and the Conwy Valley

So much to discover beside the sea

Llandudno is Wales' premier resort. With its carefully preserved Victorian architecture and superb natural setting, it offers the idyllic location to "get away from it all".

North Shore is a lively beach, spanning the two mile crescent bay for which Llandudno is famed. On the pier there are stalls and amusements with supervised activities for children. On the opposite end of the promenade, toddlers love splashing about in the paddling pool.

Dominating the town is the towering limestone headland of the Great Orme. Some 300 million years old, history, nature and exciting new attractions combine together to form a "must" on any sightseeing agenda. Travel to the summit on the Great Orme Tramway. Opened in 1902, it is the longest cable hauled tramway in Britain. Alternatively, take a thrilling ride on the cable car. The North Wales Theatre in Llandudno opened in July '94 and is gaining a reputation for being the premier entertainment venue in Wales and the North West.

Fine Golden Coastline

With three miles of golden sandy beaches the Bay of Colwyn is a holiday favourite. Relaxing on the sands can be combined with the many exciting amusements and attractions on offer. Eirias Park unites neatly laid out gardens and spacious parks with superb sporting facilities.

An attraction the children will love is Dinosaur World, with life-like prehistoric models. Set high above the town is the Welsh Mountain Zoo. There are hundreds of animals from all over the world.

Rhos-on-Sea is a pretty village with a relaxed atmosphere and select shops. A centre for fishermen, the little harbour is an ideal base for watersport enthusiasts.

East of Colwyn Bay is the busy market town of Abergele. Nearby, Pensarn, Towyn and Kinmel Bay offer fine sandy beaches and plenty of amusements to keep the children happy.

Gateway to Snowdonia

The County Borough of Conwy boasts some of the most spectacular countryside in Britain, incorporating 261 square miles of the Snowdonia National Park. There are snowcapped mountain ranges, verdant forests, cascading waterfalls and picturesque villages.

Just outside Llandudno is Conwy, acknowledged as a perfect example of a mediaeval walled town and classed as a World Heritage Site. Up the Conwy Valley is the market town of Llanrwst, set on the edge of Snowdonia National Park. Nearby Trefriw is a centre for the woollen industry and the working mill is a popular visitor attraction. Venture a little further south and you will encounter Betws y Coed, the most popular inland resort of North Wales. Beneath the distinctive peak of Moel Siabod is Capel Curig. To the west, lies Snowdon.

The Tourist Information Centres are packed with information on places of interest, special events, accommodation, entertainment and attractions.

Llandudno
1/2 Chapel Street
Tel: 01492 876413
Open all year

Colwyn Bay
Imperial Building's
Princess Drive
Tel: 01492 530478
Open all year

Betws-y-Coed
Snowdonia National Park,
Royal Oak Stables
Tel: 01690 710426
Open all year

Conwy
Cadw Visitor Centre,
Castle Entrance
Tel: 01492 592248
Open all year

Rhos-on-Sea
Promenade,
Tel: 01492 548778
Seasonal – Easter to September

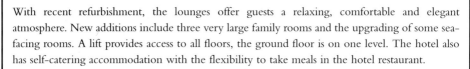

Portmeirion - Gwynedd

Portmeirion was built by Clough Williams-Ellis as an *"unashamedly romantic"* resort on Snowdonia's southern shore. His aim was *"to demonstrate how a naturally beautiful site could be developed without defiling it"*. Portmeirion became his most famous work and one of the most successful British architectural projects of the twentieth century.

The village stands on a rugged cliff top on its own private peninsula and is surrounded by 70 acres of sub-tropical woodlands. All the houses form part of the hotel with rooms and suites within comfortable walking distance of the main building on the quayside. The curvilinear dining room overlooking the estuary serves fresh local produce in elegant surroundings. During the Winter, from 1st November to 31st March, the hotel offers its popular Winter breaks of three nights for the price of two.

The village is also a popular year round venue for day visits with its shops, restaurants, gardens and beaches. It is one of Wale's premier attractions welcoming over 200,000 visitors per annum. Many know Portmeirion as the location for Patrick McGoohan's "The Prisoner" television series. It is also renowned for its Portmeirion Pottery, designed by Clough's daughter Susan Williams-Ellis.

A major development will be completed at Portmeirion in May 2001 with the opening of the Castell Deudraeth brasserie and bar where informal meals will be served all day and evening throughout the year in a family friendly atmosphere. This Victorian castle and its gardens have been carefully restored and facilities include meetings rooms and spacious accommodation on the first and second floors. Admission is free to Castell Deudraeth and its gardens.

Portmeirion is owned by a registered charity called the Portmeirion Foundation. The Foundation is dedicated to preserving Clough Williams-Ellis's work at Portmeirion and at the Brondanw Estate where he lived, five miles away. Clough's motto was *"Cherish the past, adorn the present, construct for the future"* and this philosophy is followed at Portmeirion to this day. He fought for beauty, *"that strange necessity."*

Portmeirion, Gwynedd
LL48 6ET Wales

Telephone: 01766 770000
Fax: 01766 771331

E-mail:
info@portmeirion-village.com
website:
www.portmeirion.com

Directions
Signposted off A487 between Penrhyndeudraeth and Porthmadog

Opening times
Open daily all year 09.30 - 17.30

Accommodation
51 rooms and suites and
17 self-catering cottages

The WEST ARMS Hotel

nestles in the Ceiriog Valley, surely one of the loveliest in Wales

Surrounded by sheep-studded hills and forest, there is little to disturb the tranquility of this setting – peace and relaxation for which The West Arms is widely renowned.

A charming Country Inn, it is over 400 years old and the visitor is immediately aware of the warmth and character of by-gone years that pervade – slate-flagged floors, vast inglenooks and timberwork abound, all set off by period furnishings.

This period quality extends into the bedrooms, spacious and comfortable and all with private bathrooms

There are two large suites with lounge and TV, ideal for family occupation.

Historic Chirk Castle, Powys Castle and Erddig Hall (all NT) are an easy drive away and, just a little further, the medieval border towns of Shrewsbury and Chester.

Llanarmon Dyffryn Ceiriog
Ceiriog Valley • North Wales • LL20 7LD
Tel: 01691 600665 Fax: 01691 600622
Email: gowestarms@aol.com
www.hotelwalesuk.com

Tir·y·Coed
Country House Hotel
Rowen, Conwy LL32 8TP
Tel/Fax: 01492 650219

Relax amidst magnificent scenery in the peaceful, rural setting of a delightful Snowdonia National Park village, four miles inland from the medieval walled town of Conwy, a World Heritage Site.

Eight tastefully decorated and furnished comfortable bedrooms (all ensuite), most with magnificent views. Imaginative high quality meals for all diets. No smoking dining room.

Within easy reach of mountains, coast, castles and stately homes and gardens. D.B.B. from £39.00 p.p.p.n. Licensed. WTB ☆☆☆ Country Hotel, AA ☆☆ RAC, Ashley Courtenay Highly Recommended.

Heritage Britain

**Hotels, Inns, Bed & Breakfast
Historic Houses, Castles & Gardens,
Antiques & Curios,
Arts & Crafts, Books & Tours**

Welcome to Heritage Britain, a brand new website with more than 2000 years of history and culture. Whatever your interest in Britain, we aim to help you find out more within these pages.

Visit the definitive heritage site and discover the history behind Britain and Ireland's long and colourful past.

Stay in a splendid country house hotel or a medieval inn and savour the delights of the British countryside or a historic British town.

Travel back in time by visiting the myriad of historic houses, castles and gardens or museums and galleries that adorn this Sceptred Isle

Scour the local shops or fairs for arts and crafts, antiques, collectables, curios or objets d'art.

You can even contact a genealogist to help you trace your family tree.

Heritage Britain - the essential website for domestic travellers and overseas visitors to Britain and Ireland.

www.heritagebritain.com
mail@heritagebritain.com

Bodelwyddan Castle Trust

Bodelwyddan Castle, through a unique collaboration between the National Portrait Gallery and Clwyd County Council, was opened to the public in July 1988, and was winner of the Museum of the Year Award in 1989.

Set in rolling parkland and landscaped gardens, Williams Hall, the part of Bodelwyddan Castle which houses the National Portrait Gallery's 19th century portraits, has been restored to its former glory as a Victorian country house. Striking furnishings and painting techniques of the period have been lavishly used by Roderick Gradidge, the expert on Victorian and Edwardian architecture appointed by the Gallery to re-create the interiors. In this sumptuous setting approximately two hundred of the Gallery's most important 19th century portraits are hung.

The portraits are displayed thematically: in the Dining Room there are political figures such as Joseph Chamberlain by John Singer Sargent, and Henry and Millicent Fawcett by Ford Madox Brown; the Ladies' Drawing Room is dedicated to famous women including Florence Nightingale, Elizabeth Browning and Frances Trollope, and also includes the charming portrait of the Novello family, grouped around a piano; while in the Billiard Room there is a display of famous sporting figures and 'Vanity Fair' cartoons. The main drawing room has been transformed into a Sculpture Gallery where, in addition to works from the National Portrait Gallery, there are several statues by the North Wales sculptor John Gibson, on loan from the Royal Academy, and the magnificent Star of Brunswick Table (1851) from the Victoria and Albert Museum.

The Victoria and Albert Museum has lent a number of other important pieces of furniture to complete the country house setting. These include a beautiful piano designed by Alfred Waterhouse and an 1815 mahogany sideboard. On the first floor there is a display covering several rooms in which the Victorian Art World is explored in more detail, including numerous portraits of artists as well as a small display of important early photographs from the National Portrait Gallery collection. Further galleries house the fascinating inter-active Victorian Amusements and Inventions Exhibitions. A programme of temporary exhibitions and events takes place throughout the year.

The Castle is managed by the Bodelwyddan Castle Trust, which is a registered charity.

Address
Bodelwyddan Castle
Tel: 01745 584060
Fax: 01745 584563

Opening Times
Open throughout the year

Admission
Adult £4.30

Location
Bodelwyddan Castle located on the A55, the North Wales Expressway. Just 30 minutes from Chester and the M56/M53 Motorways.

Facilities
Audio guide to the collections, Gift Shop, Refreshments, Car Park, Gardens, Parkland and Woodland Walk, Facilities for the disabled.

How to use the Bed & Breakfast Section

BARTON GRANGE
Westcott, Dorking, Surrey, RH4 1PG
Tel: 01306 777444 Fax: 01306 777444
4 Rooms (2 ensuite), 1 Four Poster
A delightful Victorian family house standing in an acre of landscaped garden. Within easy travelling distance of London and the south coast. Rooms exquisitely appointed. Excellent evening meals prepared, if required, using fresh local produce. **£18.00.**

KEY TO SYMBOLS

♟	=	Pubs/Restaurants nearby
🚭	=	No Smoking Rooms
📺	=	TV in all rooms
☕	=	Tea/Coffee Making
ⅲ	=	Evening Meals available
⤴	=	Golf Courses nearby
🐟	=	Fishing nearby
❀	=	Garden over half-acre
⌂	=	Buiding of Historic interest
⌂	=	Historic Attraction nearby
CW	=	Children welcome
CC	=	Credit Cards accepted
🚭	=	No Smoking Establishment
●	=	Open All Year
P	=	Parking
V	=	Special Diets catered for
TB	=	Tourist Board inspected

If there is a price at the end of an entry this is quoted as a minimum figure per person per night for bed and breakfast. Obviously we would advise that you determine the price of the room when booking.

Some have been awarded ratings and gradings from various bodies (eg Tourist Board Crowns, AA QQQ's, Egon Ronay, Which? etc) and some have not. Small establishments like these pride themselves on their own levels of personal service and these are often unrewarded by a Tourist Board only interested in facilities.

We would not hesitate in recommending any of the B&B's or inns in this publication particularly for price, for personal service and above all for the 'experience'!

BRITISH BED AND BREAKFAST

ENGLAND

BERKSHIRE

ASCOT

LYNDRICK GUEST HOUSE
The Avenue, Ascot, Berkshire
Tel: 01344 883520 Fax: 01344 891243
5 Rooms (2 en suite, 1 private facilities).
A 5-bedroom Victorian House located in a quiet tree-lined avenue. Breakfast is served in a pleasant conservatory. Windsor Castle and Savill Gardens are nearby. London is 50 mins by train, Heathrow airport is 25 mins away. **From £35**

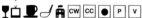

KINTBURY

THE DUNDAS ARMS
53 Station Road, Kintbury,
Berkshire RG17 9UT
Tel: 01488 658263 Fax: 01488 658568
www.dundasarms.co.uk
5 Rooms (all en suite) from £60.00 per night inc. breakfast
A River and Canalside pub with 5 en suite bedrooms overlooking the river. We have an excellent restaurant and a fine bar restaurant with an excellent wine list. **From £60**

BUCKINGHAMSHIRE

AYLESBURY

POLETREES FARM
Ludgershall Road, Brill, Nr Aylesbury, Bucks.
Tel: 01844 238276 Fax: 01844 238276
3 Rooms (1 en-suite).
The farm sits in a quiet wood valley, below a remote windswept hilltop village where red-brick houses cluster around a variety of spacious greens. We provide spacious and comfortable accommodation in a 15th century family home.

CHESHIRE

CHESTER

MITCHELL'S OF CHESTER
Helen and Colin Mitchell
Green Gable House, 28 Hough Green,
Chester CH4 8JQ
Tel: ++44 (0)1244 679004 Fax: ++44 (0)1244 659567
6 Rooms (all en-suite)
ETB ♛♛ Highly Commended ♦♦♦♦, Which? Travel Guide Recommended, plus other prestigious guides.
Tastefully restored Victorian residence. Well appointed corniced rooms, complemented by a sweeping staircase and antique furniture. All en-suite rooms equipped with full facilities. Off-street parking, walking distance to city centre. No smoking in bedrooms, dining room and hallways. £22

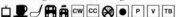

MOORHAYES HOUSE HOTEL
27 Manchester Road, Tytherington, Macclesfield,
Cheshire SK10 2JJ
Tel: 01625 433228 Fax: 01625 429878
9 Rooms (7 en suite). ETB ♦♦♦ Commended, RAC ♦♦♦.
Thoughtfully appointed 1930s style house surrounded by pleasant garden with ample parking. Situated ½ mile north of town centre at Tytherington, on A538. 5 minutes from Peak District National Park, 25 minutes to Manchester and airport.
From £20-£38 per night

CORNWALL

PENZANCE

WELLINGTON HOTEL
Market Square, St Just, Penzance, Cornwall
Tel: 01736 787319 Fax: 01736 787906
11 Rooms (all en-suite), 1 Four Poster
AA ☆☆☆, ETB ♛♛♛
Imposing granite building, overlooking market square. Good value menu, local fish and crab, steaks, daily specials. Ideal centre for walking, climbing, bird watching, water sports, beaches, golf and fishing.

ST. AUSTEL

ANCHORAGE HOUSE GUEST LODGE
Nettles Corner, Tregrehan Mills, St. Austell, Cornwall
Telephone: 01726 814071
Email: enquiry@anchoragehouse.co.uk
www.anchoragehouse.co.uk
3 Rooms (all en suite). AA ♦♦♦♦♦, Nominated for Landlady of the Year (AA) 1999 & 2000. Nominated for Best British Breakfast Award 1999 & 2000.
Every attention has been paid to the smallest detail in this impressive antique-filled house featured in a national magazine. Guests are treated to heated pool, satellite TV, large beds, conservatory and luxurious en suite rooms with everything to make you very comfortable. Breakfast is worth getting up for. Dine by arrangement. Steven (American) and Jane (English) combine wonderful hospitality and pleasing informality for a special stay.

POLPERRO

TRENDERWAY FARM
Pelynut, Polperro, Cornwall
Telephone: 01503 272214 Fax: 01503 272991
Email: trenderwayfarm@hotmail.com
www.trenderwayfarm.co.uk
4 Rooms (all en suite), 1 Four Poster, 2 Suites.
AA ☆☆☆☆☆, ETB ♦♦♦♦ Highly Commended, Silver Award for 2000 ETB.
Built in the late 16th century, the farm is set in peaceful, beautiful countryside at the head of the Polperro Valley. Bedrooms here are truly superb and are decorated with the flair of a professional interior designer. A hearty farmhouse breakfast is served in the sunny conservatory, using local produce. Totally no smoking.

CUMBRIA

AMBLESIDE

CAMBRIDGE VILLA
Mr and Mrs A F Wilson
2 Cambridge Villa, Church Street
Ambleside, Cumbria LA22 9DL
Tel: 015394 32142
AA QQQ Recommended

Cambridge Villa is a small family run guest house, close to the centre of Ambleside. It is convenient for shopping and restaurants and there is miniature golf, tennis courts and a bowling green within 50 yards. Ambleside is now a popular holiday resort with facilities for fell walking, boating, fishing, coach tours etc., and can be easily reached by car or public transport. All our rooms have colour televisions and tea and coffee making facilities. Overnight car parking is available on the public car park at the rear of the villa. **£15.50 to £17.50.**

COCKERMOUTH

RIGGS COTTAGE
Routenbeck, Cockermouth, Cumbria, CA13 9YN
Tel: 017687 76580 Fax: 017687 76580
3 Rooms (1 en-suite).
16th century cottage off the beaten track in very quiet location between the historic towns, Keswick and Cockermouth. Inglenook log fire, authentic oak beams. We serve excellent country food including our homemade jams and breads. £19.

GRANGE OVER SANDS

GREENACRES COUNTRY GUEST HOUSE
Lindale, Grange Over Sands, Cumbria LA11 6LP
Tel/Fax: 015395 34578
4 Rooms (all en suite)
ETB ♛♛♛ Highly Commended.
Greenacres is a charming 19th century cottage, ideally placed for exploring the Lakes and Yorkshire Dales – lovely in all seasons. A warm welcome, all comforts and good home cooking are assured. You will not be disappointed. **From £25**

GRASMERE

OAK BANK HOTEL
Broadgate, Grasmere, Cumbria LA22 9TA
Telephone: 015394 35217 Fax: 015394 35685
Email: grasmereoakbank@btinternet.com
15 Rooms (all en suite), 1 Four Poster.
AA ☆☆ ❀, RAC ☆, ETB ♛♛♛ Highly commended,
Enjoy being looked after by professional hoteliers. Award winning cordon bleu cuisine and fine wines. We offer log fires, delightful dining room/conservatory overlooking the garden and River Rothay. Hospitality at its best. £30-£42 **B&B + £10 DB&B**

DERBYSHIRE

BUXTON

BUXTON WHEELHOUSE HOTEL
19 College Road, Buxton, Derbyshire
Tel: 01298 24869 Fax: 01298 24869
9 Rooms (all en suite). AA QQQQ Selected, ETB ♛♛♛ Commended, Welcome Host.
Elegant Victorian Hotel superbly situated in quiet, yet central location. Spacious comfortably furnished bedrooms, en suite bathrooms, dining room, TV lounge, bar lounge, sun porch, private parking. Friendly personal service, excellent home cooking. Non-smoking. **From £21.**

GROSVENOR HOUSE HOTEL
1 Broad Walk, Buxton, Derbyshire SK17 6JE
Tel: 01298 72439 Fax: 01298 72439
8 Rooms (all en-suite)
ETB ♛♛♛ Commended, AA QQQQ Selected, Which? Good B&B Recommended 1996/97/98/99/2000.
Privately-run Victorian residence on quiet promenade in centre of historic spa town of Buxton. Commanding position overlooking 23 acres landscaped gardens and theatre. Excellent home-cooked cuisine. Scenic countryside. Many Heritage locations and ideal touring centre. Children welcome (min 8 yrs). **From £25 pp pn (sharing)**

EYAM

MINERS ARMS INN
Water Lane, Eyam, Hope Valley S32 5RG
Tel: 01433 630853
7 Rooms (all en suite)
Which Guide and Egon Ronay Recommended.
Quiet village inn offering comfortable accommodation and excellent food. Situated in the historic plague village of Eyam. Ideal for relaxing and walking weekends. £27.50

HOPE VALLEY

UNDERLEIGH HOUSE

off Edale Road, Hope Valley, Derbyshire S33 6RF
Telephone: 01433 621372 Fax: 01433 621324
Email: underleigh.house@btinternet.com
www.underleighhouse.co.uk
6 Bedrooms (all en suite). ETB ♦♦♦♦, Silver Award, AA
Premier Collection.
Secluded cottage and barn conversion near the village of
Hope, with magnificent countryside views. Ideal for
walking and exploring the Peak District. Delicious
breakfasts, featuring local and home-made specialities,
served in flagstoned dining hall. Welcoming and relaxed
atmosphere with a log fire on chilly evenings in the
charming beamed lounge.

DEVON

EXETER

RAFFLES

11 Blackall Road, Exeter, Devon
Tel: 01392 270200 Fax: 01392 270200
Email: raffleshtl@btinternet.com
7 Rooms (all en-suite). ETB ♕ ♕ ♕ Comm.
Centrally located small hotel, beautifully furnished with
antiques, home cooked dinners with a fine selection of
wines. Raffles offers a high standard of comfort and care.

KINGSBRIDGE

HELLIERS FARM, ASHFORD

Aveton Gifford, Kingsbridge, South Devon TQ7 4ND
Tel: 01548 550689 Fax: 01548 550689
4 Rooms (3 en suite).
ETB ♦♦♦♦ Highly Commended.
Helliers Farm is a small sheep farm set on a hill overlooking
a lovely valley in the South Hams. An ideal centre for
touring the coasts, moors, golf courses, National Trust
houses and walks, and the city of Plymouth. Tastefully
appointed rooms with a comfortable lounge and dining
room where excellent farmhouse breakfasts are served.
Closed Christmas and New Year. 1 Family room, double,
twin & single. Double and twin en suite, and 1 double
family with own private bathroom. From £20-£25

TIVERTON

MANOR MILL HOUSE

Brampton, Tiverton, Devon Ex16 9LP
Telephone: 01398 332211 Fax: 01398 332009
Email: stay@manormill.demon.co.uk
www.manormill.demon.co.uk
3 Rooms (all en suite), 2 Four Posters.
ETC ♦♦♦ Silver Award.
Relax in our welcoming 17th century miller's home with its
beams, log fires and delicious breakfasts using local produce.
Enjoy the gardens overlooking watermeadows or wander
round historic Bampton, winner of 'Britain in Bloom'
awards. Ideally situated for exploring Exmoor, National
Trust properties and walking.

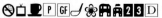

TOTNES

THE RED SLIPPER

Stoke Gabriel, Totnes, Devon TQ9 6RU
Tel: 01803 782315 Fax: 01803 782315
e-mail: red.slipper@virgin.net
5 Rooms (all en-suite).
AA ♦♦♦♦, Which? Good Bed & Breakfast.
Set in the heart of this tranquil Devon village, The Red
Slipper offers comfortable en-suite accommodation and food
of a high standard. Ideally situated for touring South Devon
and Dartmoor or simply to relax. £22.50

DORSET

SHERBORNE

THE THREE ELMS

North Wootton, Sherborne, Dorset DT9 5JW
Tel: 01935 812881
3 Rooms, 1 Four Poster.
This rural pub offers both a wide-ranging traditional menu
and an imaginative home-cooked specials board. Our
exclusive large vegetarian selection is always popular as are
our wide range of traditional beers and cider. £25

MANOR FARMHOUSE

High Street, Yetminster, Sherborne, Dorset DT9 6LF
Telephone: 01935 872247 Fax: 01935 872247
4 Rooms (all en suite)
Modernised to a high standard, a 17th century farmhouse
with many original features, in the centre of an historic
village, described as the best stone-built village in the South
of England. Ann offers intimate knowledge of the county,
both historically and geographically. Fresh produce cooked
to traditional recipes. Marvellous centre for exploring Hardy
Country and Wessex. As featured on BBC2 *House and Home*
and recommended in *The Sunday Times* and *Which? Dorset
Holidays*. From April 2001: single £35, double £70, Dinner
from £15.

ESSEX

BURNHAM-ON-CROUCH

YE OLDE WHITE HARTE HOTEL

The Quay, Burnham-on-Crouch, Essex CM0 8AS

Tel: 01621 782106 Fax: 01621 782106

19 Rooms (11 en-suite).

RAC ♦♦

17th century building overlooking River Crouch. Exposed beams and fireplaces in bedrooms and public areas. **From £19.80**

HAMPSHIRE & THE ISLE OF WIGHT

BARTON ON SEA

CLEEVE HOUSE

58 Barton Court Avenue, Barton-on-Sea,

New Milton, Hants BH25 7HG

Tel/Fax: 01425 615211

4 Rooms (2 en suite).

AA ♦♦♦♦ Selected, ETC ♦♦♦♦

Large comfortable character family home with spacious gardens, near New Forest, beaches, sea, cliffs, golf and sailing. Ideal touring base. Self-catering annexe available. Ample parking, non-smoking house, brochure on request.

ISLE OF WIGHT

BROOKSIDE FORGE HOTEL

Brookside Road, Freshwater, Isle of Wight PO40 9ER

Tel: 01983 754644

7 Rooms (All en-suite).

ETC ⚜ ⚜ Commended, Which? magazine nominated. Ideally located for countryside, West Wight Bays and swimming pool. Large gardens for privacy and relaxation, plentiful home-cooked food, 7 bedrooms en-suite with C/TVs, licensed bar. Ferry arranged. **£20.00 B&B**

WEST MEON

HOME PADDOCKS

West Meon, Hampshire GU32 1NA

Tel: 01730 829241 Fax: 01730 829577

E-mail: homepaddocks@compuserve.com

2 Bedrooms (1 en-suite, 1 with own bathroom).

This family home has attractive living rooms for guests' use. It is surrounded by a large garden with croquet lawn and tennis court. You will be warmly welcomed by the Ward family. **£25**

WINCHESTER

CHURCH FARM

Barton Stacey, Winchester, Hampshire SO21 3RR

Tel: 01962 760268 Fax: 01962 761825

7 Rooms

15th century tithe barn with Georgian additions, attractive furnished living rooms leading out of Tudor Hall, with its original flagstone floor, onto the croquet lawn. There is a recently converted coach house, centrally heated like the main house, and candlelit dining room. **£22-£35**.

HEREFORDSHIRE

HEREFORD

CHARADE'S GUEST HOUSE

34 Southbank Road/Bodenham Road, Hereford, Herefordshire HR1 2TJ

Tel: 01432 269444

6 Rooms (4 en-suite)

ETB ⚜ ⚜, Which? Hidden Places of the Welsh Borders. A large Victorian house in pleasant grounds with ample parking. Spacious en-suite bedrooms with tea-making facilities and TV in all rooms. Comfortable TV lounge, good English breakfast within 10 minutes' walk of city centre, rail and bus stations. **£20**

KENT

CANTERBURY

CLARE ELLEN GUEST HOUSE

9 Victoria Road, Canterbury, Kent CT1 3SG

Telephone: 01227 760205 Fax: 01277 784482

Email: loraine.williams@clareellenguesthouse.co.uk

www.clareellenguesthouse.co.uk

6 Rooms (all en suite).

ETC ♦♦♦♦ Silver Award, AA ♦♦♦♦ 2 Eggcups.

A warm welcome and bed and breakfast in style. Large elegant en suite rooms all with colour TV, hair dryer, clock/radio and tea/coffee facilities. Full English breakfast. Vegetarians and special diets on request. Six minutes walk to city centre, four to Canterbury East railway station. Private car park/garage available.

BED & BREAKFAST

LINCOLNSHIRE

WOODHALL SPA

CLAREMONT GUEST HOUSE
9/11 Witham Road, Woodhall Spa, Lincs. LN10 6RW.
Tel: 01526 352000.
9 Rooms (3 en-suite). ETB ♦♦, AA ♦♦
Homely B&B in an unspoilt Victorian house in the centre of Woodhall Spa, Lincolnshire's unique spa resort. An ideal peaceful location for exploring Lincolnshire's heritage or relaxing in Woodhall with its many unusual attractions. **From £15.**

LONDON

ALISON HOUSE HOTEL
82 Ebury Street, Belgravia, London SW1 9QD
Tel: 020 7730 9529 Fax: 020 7730 5494
12 Rooms (2 en-suite).
A friendly and clean Bed & Breakfast Hotel in the heart of the exclusive Belgravia district of London. Close to Victoria train and coach terminals and walking distance to Buckingham Palace, Westminster Abbey and Knightsbridge.

NORTHUMBERLAND

SLALEY

RYE HILL FARM
Slaley, Nr. Hexham, Northumberland NE47 0AH
Tel: 01434 673259 Fax: 01434 673259
Website: www.ryehillfarm.co.uk
6 Rooms (all en suite).
ETB ♦♦♦♦
300 years old, small working farm set in a beautiful rural setting high above Hexham. We have recently converted the barns adjoining the house into modern accommodation. We are noted for good food and a relaxed and friendly atmosphere. **From £20**

OXFORDSHIRE

BUCKLAND

THE LAMB AT BUCKLAND
Lamb Lane, Buckland Nr Faringdon, Oxon SN7
Tel: 01367 870484 Fax: 01387 810478
4 Rooms (all en suite)
Michelin, Egon Ronay, Good Food Guide.
The 18th century Lamb is situated at the heart of the historic village of Buckland, where the descendants of the Duke of Wellington still live today and is midway between Oxford and Swindon. **From £36-£57**

OXFORD

OXFORD

COURTFIELD PRIVATE HOTEL
367 Iffley Road, Oxford OX4 4DP
Tel: 01865 242991 Fax: 01865 242991
6 Rooms (4 en-suite).
RAC Acclaimed, AA QQQ.
Individually designed house situated in tree-lined road with modern spacious bedrooms, majority are en-suite. Close to picturesque Iffley village and River Thames, yet easily accessible to Oxford's historic city centre and colleges. Private car park. **£22**

SOMERSET

NORTON ST. PHILIP, BATH

MONMOUTH LODGE
Norton St Philip, Bath, Avon BA3 6LH
Tel: 01373 834367
3 Rooms (all en-suite).
AA QQQQQ Premier Selected, Winner of the West Country "AA Best Newcomer" Award, RAC Highly Acclaimed, ETB Highly Commended.
Monmouth Lodge is a delightful house, carefully remodelled with ground floor bedrooms en-suite, own patio doors, king-size beds and quality furnishings. A sumptuously furnished lounge and secluded garden for our guests. A short drive from Bath. **£27.**

SURREY

HORLEY

THE LAWN GUEST HOUSE
30 Massetts Road, Horley, Surrey RH6 7DE
Tel: 01293 775751 Fax: 01293 821803
e-mail: info@lawnguesthouse.co.uk
http://www.lawnguesthouse.co.uk
12 Rooms (all en suite).
ETC/AA/RAC: ♦♦♦♦ Silver award.
Attractive Victorian house, 1½ miles from Gatwick and 2 minutes walk from Horley with its pubs, restaurants, shops and railway to London and the south coast. All rooms en suite with CTB, telephones, tea/coffee tray, hairdryers. **From £25.00 per person in a twin/Double.**

SPRINGWOOD GUEST HOUSE
58 Massetts Road, Horley, Surrey RH6 7DS
Tel: 01293 775998 Fax: 01293 823103
Email: ernest@springwood58.u-net.com
11 Rooms. All en-suite inc. 2 with wheelchair access.
An attractive Victorian house situated close to restaurants, pubs, town centre and airport. Offering a friendly welcome.

SUSSEX

LEWES

THE RAM INN
Firle, Nr. Lewes, East Sussex BN8 6NS
Tel: 01273 858222
Open all day
Simple 17th century Inn in quiet, unspoilt Firle village at foot of Southdowns. Close to Firle Place, Glyndebourne Opera House and Charleston Farmhouse once the home of Vanessa Bell and Duncan Grant. Food available all day. Children very welcome. Firle is 1/2 mile off A27 – 3 miles east of Lewes.

WILTSHIRE

BRADFORD-ON-AVON

PRIORY STEPS
Newtown, Bradford-on-Avon, Wilts BA15 1NQ
Tel: 01225 862230 Fax: 01225 866248
e-mail: priorysteps@clara.co.uk
5 Rooms (all en-suite).
Which? Hotel guide, County Hotel of Year 1992.
Extremely comfortable spacious rooms 17th century Weavers house. All bedrooms have superb views over the beautiful small town of Bradford-on-Avon towards Salisbury Plain. Many houses and gardens open to public within 10 miles as well as Bath. Phone for brochure, or see us at www.priorysteps.co.uk   £35–£40.

SALISBURY

HAYBURN WYKE GUEST HOUSE
72 Castle Road, Salisbury, Wiltshire SP1 3RL
Tel/Fax: 01722 412627
Email: hayburn.wyke@tinyonline.co.uk
Website: www.hotels.uk.com/hayburnwyke.htm
7 Rooms (4 en-suite). AA, RAC ◆◆◆
The owners, Dawn and Alan, make you very welcome at this Victorian house which has all modern facilities. Situated in Victoria Park, a short walk by the River Avon from the city centre and cathedral. Stonehenge 9 miles. **B&B from £19.50 pp**

MANOR FARM BED & BREAKFAST
Manor Farm, Burcombe, Salisbury, Wilts, SP2 0EJ
Tel: 01722 742177 Fax: 01722 744600
2 Rooms (2 en-suite).
ETB ◆◆◆◆
This comfortable farmhouse is centrally heated with a warm welcome for guests. An attractive sitting room leads into a walled garden. An ideal spot for walking or visiting many interesting place, historical houses and cities. £20

WORCESTERSHIRE

BROADWAY

THE OLIVE BRANCH GUEST HOUSE
78 High Street, Broadway, Worcs. WR12 7AJ
Tel: 01386 853440 Fax: 01386 859070
Email: clive@theolivebranch.u-net.com
www.olivebranch.u-net.com
7 Rooms (all en suite). **From £25**
ETB ♛♛♛ Commended, AA QQQ, RAC Acclaimed. Stay in our friendly family run 16th century guest house with antique furnished en suite bedrooms, in the delightful village of Broadway. Ground floor and single room available. Vegetarian breakfasts, car park and walled garden.

YORKSHIRE

MASHAM

PASTURE HOUSE
Healey, Masham, N. Yorks
Tel: 01765 689149
ETB ♛ Commended.
Pasture House is a large house providing comfortable accommodation in the quiet of the beautiful Yorkshire Dales. A perfect centre for visiting many places of historic interest. Delicious home-cooked food and a warm welcome.

The Old Manse
GUEST HOUSE
Middleton Road, Pickering
North Yorkshire YO18 8AL
Tel: 01751 476484 Fax: 01751 477124
◆◆◆◆ E.T.C.

The guest house, a former home of Methodist ministers, is a fine Edwardian house in its own grounds in the picturesque market town of Pickering. The guest house has a large secluded garden, orchard and private carpark. Pickering – gateway to the North Yorkshire Moors and "Heartbeat" country, is the start of 18 miles of the scenic N.Y.M. Steam Railway and an ideal location for touring and walking. **From £19 pp**

THIRSK

SPITAL HILL
Thirsk, Yorkshire YO7 3AE
Telephone: 01845 522273 Fax: 01845 524970
Ten minutes from the A1, this quiet, peaceful house, set in
1/2 acre of garden surrounded by parkland, is convenient for
a stopover and for exploring the Dales and Moors. A warm
welcome awaits you together with superb food
complimented by a sensible wine list. A no-smoking house.

EASINGWOLD

THE OLD RECTORY
Thormanby, Easingwold, York YO6 3NN
Tel: 01845 501417
3 Rooms (2 en-suite), 1 Four Poster.
The Old Rectory was built in 1737. Furnished with many
antiques, 3 spacious bedrooms (2 en-suite), easy access to
York, Yorkshire Dales and Moors. There are many country
houses, abbeys and castles in the area. Also self catering
cottages sleeping 4/6. £16-£18

SCOTLAND

ABERDEENSHIRE

ABERDEEN

KILDONAN GUEST HOUSE
410 Great Western Road, Aberdeen AB10 6NR
Tel: 01224 316115
Email: dey@kildonan.fsbusiness.co.uk
8 Rooms (7 en-suite)
AA ◆◆◆ STB ☆☆
Personally run, comfortable guest house. On main city bus
route and very conveniently situated for touring Royal
Deeside and Donside. Ground floor rooms available. All
rooms are non-smoking. From £18.

ARGYLL & MULL

ISLE OF MULL

RED BAY COTTAGE
Deargphort, Fionnphort, Isle of Mull,
Argyll PA66 6BP
Tel: 01681 700396
3 Rooms.
Red Bay Cottage is a modern house overlooking the Sound
of Iona. An ideal base for touring Mull, Iona, Staffa and the
Treshnish Isles. Also well known locally for the quality of its
food. £16.50

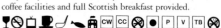

EDINBURGH

CRAIGELACHIE HOTEL
21 Murrayfield Avenue, Edinburgh EH12 6AU
Tel: 0131 337 4076 Fax: 0131 313 3305
e-mail: info@craig01.globalnet.co.uk
website: www.users.globalnet.co.uk/craig01
9 Rooms (All en-suite)
STB ☆☆☆.
Victorian terraced hotel situated close to the city centre. High
standards of comfort and accommodation complemented by a
unique style of warm friendly service. Colour TV, tea and
coffee facilities and full Scottish breakfast provided.

THE TOWN HOUSE GUEST HOUSE
65 Gilmore Place, Edinburgh
Tel: 0131 229 1985
Email: susan@thetownhouse.com
Website: www.thetownhouse.com
5 Rooms (all en-suite)
STB ☆☆☆☆ Guest House,
Attractive, privately owned Victorian Town House situated
in the city centre. The Town House offers a high standard of
accommodation in a non-smoking environment. The
bedrooms are all tastefully decorated. Pubs and fine
restaurants are all nearby. Ample private car parking.
£28-£36 pp

MORAY

KEITH

THE HAUGHS
Keith, Moray
Tel: 01542 882238
4 Rooms (3 en-suite, 1 with private facilities)
STB ☆☆☆, AA QQQQ.Selected.
This traditional farmhouse is ideally placed for touring. Bedrooms are bright and cheery with all modern comforts. There is an attractive sitting room and a south-facing dining room where good home-cooked meals are served. £18

PERTHSHIRE

ABERFELDY

FERNBANK GUEST HOUSE
Kenmore Street, Aberfeldy, Perthshire PH15 2BL
Tel: 01887 820345
7 Rooms (all en suite)
AA ♦♦♦♦ Premier Selected, STB ☆☆☆☆ Guest House
An elegant Victorian house where a warm welcome awaits all who appreciate quality, comfort and a non-smoking environment. Fernbank is an ideal base for exploring highland Perthshire and beyond. **From £24**

PITLOCHRY

BENDARROCH HOUSE
Strathtay, Pitlochry, Perthshire PH9 0PG
Scotland
Tel: 01887 840420 Fax: 01887 840438
Email: bendarroch-house@de
Website: www.bendarroch-house.de
5 Rooms (4 en suite), 1 Family Room,
2 Kingsized brass beds.
Scottish Tourist Board ☆☆☆, AA QQQQ Selected.
Bendarroch House, a refurbished stately Victorian house, set in 6 acres of landscaped grounds overlooking panoramic views of mountains and forests with the River Tay running past the boundary of the estate. Languages spoken. £25

SOUTH WALES

CARMARTHEN

CAPEL DEWI UCHAF FARM/COUNTRY HOUSE
Capel Dewi, Carmarthen, Carmarthenshire SA32 8AY
Tel: 01267 290799 Fax: 01267 290003
Email: uchaffarm@aol.com
3 Rooms (all en-suite). 1 Family Suite.
AA QQQQ Selected, WTB 🌸 🌸 🌸 Highly Commended, RAC Highly Acclaimed, Which? Top 20 '95.
Beautifully restored 500-year-old farmhouse furnished in country style with modern conveniences. Renowned breakfast and evening meals, served in our baronial style dining room. Set in 34 acres of the Towy Valley with salmon and sewin fishing rights. £25.

SAUNDERSFOOT

PPRIMROSE COTTAGE
Stammers Road, Saundersfoot,
Pembrokeshire SA69 9HH
Tel: 01834 811080
2 Rooms (1 en-suite)
Primrose Cottage is a lovingly restored, small Victorian home with a pretty, secluded garden. Guests have their own dining room and lounge with TV and hi-fi. Saundersfoot's beautiful beaches and harbour are within a short distance (50 yds). **From £18.50**

LLANDRINDOD WELLS

LLANERCH 16th CENTURY INN
Llanerch Lane, Llandrindrod Wells, Powys
Tel: 01597 822086 Fax: 01597 824618
Email: llanerchinn@ic24.net
13 Rooms (12 en-suite).
WTB ☆☆ Inn.
Relax in this historic inn, retaining original character, excellent selection of meals and snacks, 3 traditional ales (Camra & Good Pub Guides). Terrace and beer garden with childrens' play area. A welcome for all the family.

LLANGORSE

THE RED LION HOTEL
Llangorse, Brecon, Powys LD3 7TY
Tel: 01874 658238 Fax: 01874 658595
10 Rooms (5 en-suite).
WTB ☆☆ Inn.
Friendly 18th century inn with comfortable bedrooms. Real ales and good home-cooked food served in our bars and restaurant. Near Llangorse lake, in the Brecon Beacons National Park. Ideal base for exploring the area. £20-£27

ADVERTISERS INDEX

WALES

BED & BREAKFAST ACCOMMODATION INDEX

THE BED &
BREAKFAST
SECTION CAN BE
FOUND BETWEEN
PAGES 524 & 533

Back　Forward　Stop　Refresh　Home　Favorites　History　Search　AutoFill　Larger　Smaller　Print　Mail　Preferences

Address: http://www.heritagebritain.com　Go

Heritage Britain

**HOTELS
INNS &
B & B**

**PLACES
TO
VISIT**

**MUSEUM
&
GALLERIES**

**ANCESTRY
& FAMILY
TREES**

**ANTIQUES
&
CURIOS**

**ARTS
CRAFTS
& FAIRS**

**MILLEN-
NIUM
BRITAIN**

**BOOKS
&
TOURS**

Welcome to Heritage Britain, a brand new website with more than 2000 years of history and culture. Whatever your interest in Britain, we aim to help you find out more within these pages.

Visit the definitive heritage site and discover the history behind Britain and Ireland's long and colourful past.

Stay in a splendid country house hotel or a medieval inn and savour the delights of the British countryside or a historic British town.

Travel back in time by visiting the myriad of historic houses, castles and gardens or museums and galleries that adorn this Sceptred Isle

Scour the local shops or fairs for arts and crafts, antiques, collectables, curios or objets d'art.

You can even contact a genealogist to help you trace your family tree.

Heritage Britain - the essential website for domestic travellers and overseas visitors to Britain and Ireland.

**www.heritagebritain.com
mail@heritagebritain.com**

NEXT

heritagebritain.com
Compass House
30-36 East Street
Bromley, Kent
BR1 1QU
Tel: 020 8290 6633
Fax: 020 8290 6622
mail@heritagebritain.com

BROCHURE REQUEST

THE ESSENCE OF ENGLAND, SCOTLAND, WALES & IRELAND - 2001

We offer a free service to all of our readers enabling you to pursue and peruse hotel, historic house or area information at your leisure without the considerable inconvenience of writing dozens of letters. You may wish to consider several hotels for example before making your final decisions. If there is any further information you require on anything at all featured within these pages then simply jot down the page number and the name in the box below and send it to us in London. We will ensure that whatever you require is dispatched forthwith. It may also help if you gave us an idea of when you are thinking of travelling.

If there is not enough room you can always put them on a blank piece of paper. Do not forget to give us your full name, address and zip code. We guarantee absolutely not to pass you details on to any other company.

ADVERTISER	PAGE

NAME...

....

.ADDRESS.................................

....

....

....

....

....

....

....

....

Tel No:.......................................

....

The Heritage Handbook Co
Compass House, 30-36 East Street,
Bromley, Kent
BR1 1QU

SUBSCRIPTIONS

We hope that you have both enjoyed this publication and have found it useful. Although print runs will almost certainly increase for the next issue, we anticipate that demand will be such that securing the next issue may well be difficult. Should you wish to guarantee that you receive it, you can subscribe by filling in the form below and take advantage of the lowest possible price. The publication(s) will then be sent from England directly to your home. You can also order more copies if you wish for friends or family.

- -

I WOULD LIKE TO ORDER THE FOLLOWING TITLES:-

THE ESSENCE OF ENGLAND, SCOTLAND,
WALES & IRELAND 2001 THIS EDITION_____@ £12.00 per copy inclusive*

THE ESSENCE OF ENGLAND, SCOTLAND,
WALES & IRELAND 2002_____@ £12.00 per copy inclusive*

BOTH PUBLICATIONS_____@ £20.00 per copy inclusive

*** Please send the equivalent in dollars, guiders, francs or marks if you are
ordering from overseas**

Please write and tell us what you think of the handbook and
if there are any ways in which we might improve on our last issue.
Finally, don't forget to use our brochure request service on page 543

Name_____

Address_____

_____

_____

_____

_____Code_____

Please make sure that you enclose
your cheque and make it payable to:
**The Heritage Handbook Co. .Ltd,
Compass House
30-36 East Street
Bromley, Kent
BR1 1QU**